PETER EISENMAN

THE FORMAL BASIS OF MODERN ARCHITECTURE

PETER EISENMAN

THE FORMAL BASIS OF MODERN ARCHITECTURE

ORIGINAL SUBMITTED IN AUGUST 1963
FIRST PUBLISHED IN 2006 BY LARS MÜLLER PUBLISHERS
WITH AN AFTERWORD BY PETER EISENMAN

THE FORMAL BASIS OF MODERN ARCHITECTURE

This dissertation is submitted for the degree of Doctor of Philosophy.

Peter D. Eisenman

Trinity College

University of Cambridge

August 1963

PREFACE

ALL WORK IN THIS DISSERTATION EXCEPT THOSE PORTIONS COVERED BY FOOTNOTES ARE THE ORIGINAL WORK OF THE AUTHOR. HOWEVER, I SHOULD LIKE TO ACKNOWLEDGE THE HELP OF SEVERAL PEOPLE WHO HAVE ASSISSTED ME IN THE DEVELOPMENT OF THE FINAL FORM OF THIS WORK. FIRST MY SUPERVISOR, PROFESSOR SIR LESLIE MARTIN, WHO HAS PATIENTLY DIRECTED AND CHANNELED MY THOUGHTS FROM THE BEGINNING. SECOND, SOME OF MY COLLEAGUES ESPECIALLY COLIN ROWE, COLIN ST.J. WILSON, PETER BICKNELL, CHRISTOPHER CORNFORD AND PATRICK HODGKINSON WHO HAVE STIMULATED MUCH OF THE THINKING IN THIS DISSERTATION, AND WHO HAVE HELPED ME IN CORRECTING AND EDITING THE WRITTEN TEXT. THIRD, TO SOME OF MY STUDENTS ESPECIALLY ANTHONY VIDLER, BARRY MAITLAND, AND CAILEY HUTTON WHO ASSISTED ME WITH THE DRAWINGS AND THE COMPILATION OF THE FOOTNOTES. AND FINALLY TO MY THREE TYPISTS: MRS. FAITH BROADBENT, MISS MAUREEN FRANCIS, AND MRS. ELIZABETH DONALD WHO IS NOW MY WIFE, WHOSE HELP IN TYPING THE MANY DRAUGHTS OF THIS PAPER WAS INVALUABLE.

PETER D. EISENMAN

TRINITY COLLEGE, CAMBRIDGE

AUGUST 1963

THE FORMAL BASIS OF MODERN ARCHITECTURE.

PETER D. EISENMAN. 1963.

IN THE 'HEAVENLY CITY OFTTHE EIGHTEENTH CENTURY PHILOSOPHERS', KARL BECKER EXAMINED THE PROBLEM OF EPISTEMOLOGY, OF THE BASES OF KNOWLEDGE, WHICH IN THE INTERVENING YEARS SINCE THE PUBLICATION OF THE BOOK, HAS BECOME PROGRESSIVELY MORE ACUTE. HE IMAGINES THAT IF DANTE OR ST THOMAS AQUINAS WERE CALLED TO APPEAR BEFORE US, THEY WOULD PROVIDE DEFINITIONS WHICH WOULD NOT BE PRODUCED BY CONTEMPORARY THOUGHT. BECKER DESCRIBES THE MODERN CLIMATE OF OPINION AS FACTUAL RATHER THAN RATIONAL: THE ATMOSPHERE BEING SO SATURATED WITH THE ACTUAL, THAT THE THEORETICAL IS EASILY PASSED OVER. FOR BECKER, HISTORY, THE QUESTION OF FACTS AND HOW THEY ARE RELATED, HAS REPLACED REASON AND LOGIC, THE QUESTION OF 'WHY?'. HE SEES THE WORLD AS AN EVER CHANGING TIME SEQUENCE, WHERE MAN IS NO LONGER ABLE TO DEFINE, BUT RATHER IS ONLY ABLE TO PROVIDE AN ACCOUNT OF WHAT THINGS WERE BEFORE THEY REACHED THEIR PRESENT STATE; THIS STATE BEING CONSIDERED AS ONLY TRANSITORY. HERE THE TRUTH FO THINGS IS UNDERSTOOD TENTATIVELY AS IT HAS NO TERMINATION. IN FACT IT IS THIS CONDITION THAT CAN BE CONSIDERED THE REASON, OR THE EXCUSE FOR PUTTING FORWARD THIS THESIS.

THESE OBSERVATIONS ARE USEFUL IN THAT THEY CAN READILY BE TRANSFERRED FROM THE GENERAL SENSE TO THE SPECIFIC CASE OF ARCHITECTURE. THE MODERN MOVEMENT HAS TENDED TO IDENTIFY ITSELF WITH CHANGE AND IDEAS OF CHANGE, BECAUSE IT TOO HAS CONCEIVED ITSELF TO BE A 'PERMANENT REVOLUTION' AND CONSEQUENTLY ITS PARTICULAR MODE OF SPECULATION HAS BEEN HISTORICAL RATHER THAN LOGICAL. THERE IS AN INHERENT DANGER IN THIS ABSENCE OF LOGICAL THOUGHT. WITHOUT THEORY, HISTORY BECOMES THE DOMINANT DISCIPLINE, AND AS HAS BEEN INFERRED ABOVE, IT EVEN CEASES TO BE POSSIBLE TO EVALUATE THE SIGNIFICANCE OF HISTORICAL MANIFESTATIONS.

Contemporary architectural thinking has tended, often without recognising it, to an emphasis upon history, except when issues of technics and technology are involved. The meaning of such theoretical concepts as 'rationalism' and 'functionalism' has become obscured by the use of these terms in a historical context. This has caused a misinterpretation of the theoretical basis of architecture and more specifically of the modern movement. Two contemporary British architectural critics have raised the whole issue of theory and history in these terms. Reyner Banham in his book 'Theory and Design in the First Machine Age' is preoccupied with the ideas of change, and therefore he is obliged to embrace, although perhaps unconsciously, an entirely historicist point of view.

John Summerson in a lecture to the R.I.B.A. of 21 May 1957 puts forward several ideas again towards the development of a theory of architecture. He says: 'It is simply a question of two rather prolonged exercises in analysis and synthesis'. One of these is to assemble ideas, 'examining their common trends of meaning and reaching a series of general concepts'. Summerson later concludes his argument by saying that a basic principle of modern architecture is the unity deriving from the programme. He states '....that although the rationalist writers of the 18th and 19th centuries tended to exclude antiquity as the ultimate authority, antiquity remained insistently there as <u>the source of unity</u> the focus at which the architectural design was realised .... the source of unity in modern architecture is in the social sphere, in other words in the architects programme.' But the situation is more complicated than Summerson allows for, and if seeing a work of architecture in terms of its programme is the only alternative to seeing it in terms of history, it must be admitted that criticism is not very far advanced.

ERWIN PANOFSKY, IN HIS BOOK 'MEANING IN THE VISUAL ARTS' HAS STATED THE PROBLEM IN A MORE EXEMPLARY FASHION. HE SAYS: 'IT HAS RIGHTLY BEEN SAID THAT THEORY, IF NOT RECEIVED AT THE DOOR OF AN EMPIRICAL DISCIPLINE, COMES IN THROUGH THE CHIMNEY LIKE A GHOST AND UPSETS THE FURNITURE, BUT IT IS NO LESS TRUE THAT HISTORY, IF NOT RECEIVED AT THE DOOR OF A THEORETICAL DISCIPLINE CREEPS INTO THE CELLAR LIKE A HORDE OF MICE AND UNDERMINES THE GROUNDWORK'.

THE FOLLOWING DISSERTATION CAN BE CONSIDERED ESSENTIALLY CRITICAL RATHER THAN HISTORICAL, IN THAT IT WILL EXAMINE CERTAIN PROPOSITIONS CONCERNING FORM IN RELATION TO ARCHITECTURE IN A THEORETICAL AND NOT A HISTORICAL SENSE. THE SOPHISTICATION OF ART HISTORY AND THE ADVANCES MADE IN PERCEPTUAL PSYCHOLOGY HAVE RENDERED THE LAST PHASE OF ECLECTIC THEORY AS REPRESENTED BY TALBOT HAMLIN'S 'FORMS AND FUNCTIONS OF TWENTIETH CENTURY ARCHITECTURE' A LITTLE NAIVE. IN GENERAL CRITICAL ATTITUDES TOWARDS ARCHITECTURE TEND TO PLACE EMPHASIS ON THE ICONOGRAPHICAL, THE PERCEPTUAL AND THE CONCEPTUAL. IN ART HISTORY, FOR INSTANCE AND PARTICULARLY IN THE WORK OF THE WARBURG INSTITUTE, THERE HAS BEEN AN INCREASING AWARENESS OF ICONOGRAPHICAL ISSUES, AND THE GREAT PART THAT THEY PLAY IN THE CREATION OF ARCHITECTURAL STYLE IN ANY SPECIFIC HISTORICAL SITUATION. SIMILARLY, THE EXPONENTS OF GESTALT PSYCHOLOGY HAVE PRODUCED A CLIMATE OF SENSITIVITY IN WHICH EVERYTHING THAT CONCERNS A WORK OF ART, AS SOMETHING EXPERIENCED BY THE EYE, MUST BE ANALYSED. HOWEVER, THIS THESIS INTENDS A MORE RESTRICTIVE DEFINITION OF FORMAL CONSIDERATIONS. IT IS THEREFORE PROPOSED AT THE RISK OF DISTORTING THE TRUTH, TO EXCISE AS FAR AS POSSIBLE ICONOGRAPHICAL AND PERCEPTUAL REFERENCES. ALTHOUGH AN ANALYSIS OF THE SYMBOLIC CONTENT OF A BUILDING AND ITS MEANING MAY BE CONSIDERED CRUCIAL, BY THEIR EXCLUSION IT WILL NOT BE NECESSARY TO DISCUSS ANY VALUE-JUDGEMENTS IN RELATION TO FORMAL CONTENT. EQUALLY

IN SUPRESSING PERCEPTUAL CONSIDERATIONS, OPTICAL REFINEMENTS, AND THOSE ILLUSIONS WHICH ARE SOMETIMES THOUGHT OF AS LARGELY CONTRIBUTING TO THE VITALITY OF A BUILDING, THEIR INHERENT PSYCHOLOGICAL PROBLEMS CAN BE AVOIDED. HOWEVER, IN ORDER TO CONSIDER PRIMARY CONFIGURATIONS, IT WILL STILL BE NECESSARY TO QUALIFY THE ARGUMENT IN TERMS OF GESTALT PSYCHOLOGY; THESE TERMS BEING INVOKED ONLY TO PROVIDE A BASIS FOR THE RECOGNITION OF FORM, RATHER THAN TO VALIDATE ANY PARTICULAR SUBJECTIVE INTERPRETATION OF IT. IT IS THE DESIRE HERE TO CONSIDER BUILDINGS AS A STRUCTURE OF LOGICAL DISCOURSE, AND TO FOCUS ATTENTION ON CONSISTENCY OF ARGUMENT, ON THE MANNER IN WHICH SPATIAL AND VOLUMETRIC PROPOSITIONS MAY INTERACT, CONTRADICT, AND QUALIFY EACH OTHER.

THIS DISSERTATION THEREFORE IS CONCERNED WITH CONCEPTUAL ISSUES, IN THE SENSE THAT FORM IS CONSIDERED AS A PROBLEM OF LOGICAL CONSISTENCY, IN OTHER WORDS, AS THE LOGICAL INTER-ACTION OF FORMAL CONCEPTS. THE ARGUMENT WILL TRY TO ESTABLISH THAT CONSIDERATIONS OF A LOGICAL AND OBJECTIVE NATURE CAN PROVIDE A CONCEPTUAL, FORMAL BASIS FOR ANY ARCHITECTURE. HOWEVER,SINCE IT IS NECESSARY TO PLACE ANY ARGUMENT IN A FRAMEWORK OF PREVIOUS DISCUSSION AND CRITICISM THIS DISSERTATION CAN BE CONSIDERED AGAIN IN THE CONTEXT OF THE PROPOSITIONS PUT FORWARD BY SUMMERSON AND BANHAM. SUMMERSON, IN THE SAME LECTURE, QUESTIONS THE VALIDITY, 'OF ABSTRACTING FORMAL CHARACTERISTICS FROM A SELECT REPERTORY OF MODERN BUILDINGS, ELIMINATING MERELY MODISH ELEMENTS AND PROVIDING A GRAMMAR OF FORM'. HE DISMISSES THIS APPROACH BY ADDING: 'IT IS HOPELESSLY GIMCRACK. ONLY IMAGINE FOR A MOMENT THE TASK OF ISOLATING CHARACTERISTICALLY MODERN FORMS FROM WHOLE BUILDING'. RATHER HE PROPOSES TWO MEANS FOR RESOLVING THE CONTEMPORARY PROBLEM ONE OF WHICH CONCERNS THE NOTION OF FUNDAMENTAL SOLIDS AS A BASIS FOR ARCHITECTURAL FORM: 'ON THIS PRONCIPLE OF GEOMETRICAL ABSOLUTES IT IS POSSIBLE TO

ERECT SYSTEMS OR DISCIPLINES TO GUIDE THE ARCHITECT TOWARDS THE FINAL ORDERING OF FORM WHICH HE MUST ACHIEVE.' FOR SUMMERSON, HOWEVER, SYSTEMS MEAN: 'THE ERECTION OF PROPORTIONAL DISCIPLINES.' REYNER BANHAM, IN HIS BOOK 'THEORY AND DESIGN IN THE FIRST MACHINE AGE', WOULD SEEM TO DENY THE POSSIBILITY OF ESTABLISHING ANY PRINCIPLES BASED ON CONSIDERATIONS OF FORM. HE QUESTIONS THE VALIDITY OF LE CORBUSIER'S EQUATION OF THE RULES OF PHILEBAN SOLIDS WITH THE PRINCIPLES WHICH GOVERN OUR UNIVERSE. FOR BANHAM ANY SYSTEM REFERRING TO REGULAR SOLIDS OR SYMBOLIC FORMS WOULD BE MERELY A RESURRECTION OF A DEAD LANGUAGE.

NO ATTEMPT WILL BE MADE IN THIS DISSERTATION TO ISOLATE 'MODERN' FORMS OR TO PROPOSE A COMPREHENSIVE SYSTEM FOR DESIGN AND CRITICISM ORDERED BY THE USE OF GEOMETRIC SOLIDS. RATHER A LANGUAGE WILL BE DISTINGUISHED AND A SYSTEMIC ORDER FOR THIS LANGUAGE, WHICH USES GEOMETRIC SOLIDS ONLY AS ABSOLUTE POINTS OF REFERENCE. BY MEANS OF THIS REFERENCE, IT WILL SEEK TO CLARIFY THE RELATIONSHIP OF FORM TO ANY ARCHITECTURE. THE QUALIFICATION 'MODERN' IN THIS THESIS IS GIVEN ONLY TO PROVIDE A REFERENCE FOR THE EXAMPLES CONSIDERED; THE PRINCIPLES IN THIS DISCUSSION ARE RATHER TO BE THOUGHT OF AS BEING UNIVERSALLY VALID. MOREOVER, THE CONTENTION WILL BE THAT FORMAL CONSIDERATIONS ARE BASIC TO ALL ARCHITECTURE REGARDLESS OF STYLE, AND THAT THESE CONSIDERATIONS DERIVE FROM THE FORMAL ESSENCE OF ANY ARCHITECTURAL SITUATION. IT WILL PROVIDE A MEANS OF COMMUNICATION EVOLVED FROM THIS ABSOLUTE BASIS; A LANGUAGE THAT WILL COMMUNICATE THE NATURE OF THE FORMAL ESSENCE OF ANY ARCHITECTURE. ANY SUCH LANGUAGE MUST OBVIOUSLY BE QUALIFIED BY, AND EVOLVED FROM, THIS ESSENCE: IT IS THEREFORE A FORMAL LANGUAGE.

THE PREMISES OF THIS ARGUMENT DERIVE SPECIFICALLY FROM LE CORBUSIER'S DISCUSSION OF FORM. INDEED THIS THESIS CAN BE THOUGHT OF AS AN INVESTIGATION AND INTERPRETATION OF THE CONCEPTUAL BASIS OF LE CORBUSIER'S 'FOUR COMPOSITIONS', ILLUSTRATED IN THE 'OEUVRE COMPLETE'. IMPLICIT IN LE CORBUSIER'S DIAGRAMS ARE THE VOCABUALRY, GRAMMAR AND SYNTAX OF A FORMAL LANGUAGE: THE INTENTION HERE IS TO MAKE THEM EXPLICIT.

IT IS NOT ENOUGH MERELY TO RESTATE THE POLEMIC OF LE CORBUSIER, THIS HAVING BECOME PART OF THE HISTORY OF THE MODERN MOVEMENT; ITS APPLICATION TODAY COULD BE INTERPRETED AS LITTLE MORE THAN 'MODERN ECLECTICISM'.

HOWEVER, THE PUTTING FORWARD OF A FORMAL LANGUAGE IS NOT ENOUGH IN ITSELF, SINCE ANY MEANS OF COMMUNICATION MUST HAVE A RECOGNISABLE ORDER, EITHER INHERENT OR IMPOSED. IT WILL BE DEMONSTRATED THAT THE INHERENT ORDER DERIVES FROM A GEOMETRIC REFERENCE, FROM THE PROPERTIES OF THE FORM ITSELF. THE IMPOSED ORDER WILL EVOLVE FROM A SYSTEM WHICH QUALIFIES AND ORDERS THE VOCABULARY OF FORM WITHIN THE DESIGN PROCESS. IT WILL BE SEEN THAT SYSTEMS PROVIDE A DISCIPLINE RATHER THAN A LIMIT TO THIS PROCESS. THEY ARE NOT RIGID BUT ALLOW FOR GROWTH; THEY ACCOMMODATE THE 'SCHERZO'; THEY CAN BE ELABORATED TO ENCOMPASS INFINITE VARIATIONS AND COMPLEXITIES. SYSTEMS DENY ONLY THE ARBITRARY, THE PICTURESQUE AND THE ROMANTIC: THE SUBJECTIVE AND PERSONAL INTERPRETATIONS OF ORDER.

THIS DEVELOPMENT OF SYSTEMS AND ITS USE IN THE DESIGN PROCESS CAN BE BEST ILLUSTRATED BY DETAILED ANALYSES OF CONTRASTING ARCHITECTURAL EXPRESSION AS SEEN IN THE WORK OF FOUR COMTEMPORARY ARCHITECTS: LE CORBUSIER, AALTO, WRIGHT AND TERRAGNI. THEIR WORK WILL BE ANALYSED IN TERMS OF GENERIC PLAN TYPES AND THESE

ANALYSES WILL BE CONFINED TO THE CONSIDERATIONS OF THEIR FORMAL CONCEPTUAL BASIS. IT IS ONLY THROUGH THIS KIND OF ANALYSIS THAT A FORMAL SYSTEMIC ORDER, FUNDAMENTAL TO THE MODERN MOVEMENT CAN BE UNDERSTOOD. IT WILL BE SEEN THAT THE CONTEMPORARY INTERPRETATION OF THESE PLANS BOTH ICONOGRAPHICAL AND PERCEPTUAL ARE IRRELEVANT TO THIS ENQUIRY AND WILL THEREFORE BE DISREGARDED.

THIS WORK CAN BE LITTLE MORE THAN AN INDICATION OF A WAY OF THOUGHT OWING TO THE NECESSARY LIMITATION OF ITS LENGTH. IT CANNOT FILL THE VOID NOTICEABLE IN CONTEMPORARY ARCHITECTURAL THINKING, BUT IT WILL AT LEAST SERVE TO DENOTE THE EXISTENCE OF THIS VOID, AND THUS MAKE SOME CONTRIBUTION TO THE DEVELOPMENT OF A THEORY OF ARCHITECTURAL FORM.

The essence of any creative act is the communication of an original idea from its author, through a means of expression, to a receiver. The means of expression must be such as to transmit the original intention as clearly and fully as possible to the receiving mind. This need for clarity and comprehensibility, so much stressed by the Gestalt psychologists, is critical to the development of any means of communication.[1] Such factors as scale, harmony and pattern should therefore be thought of primarily as aids towards comprehensibility of expression.[2] Formal order, therefore, cannot be considered as an end in ttself but only as subservient to clarity. Architecture, as a means of expression, can call upon several elements to contribute to the architectural equation, which can be thought of as: concept or intent; function; structure; technics; form.[3] It will become obvious as these elements are investigated that they do not have equal magniture or importance.

In the past there have been theorists who have claimed that architecture if in general to be equated with one or tther of these elements, but these theorists have differed as to which one should receive priority. It would seem from certain passages in Choisy that architecture should be thought of as predicated by technics.[4] Other late noneteenth century theorists, among them Louis Sullivan, would have said that architecture is primarily a manifestation of function.[5] Early modern theorisrs have characteristically inclined towards a sociological of historicist position, as when they speak of archi-

1: See Kurt Koffka : 'Principles of Gestalt Psychology'. New York 1935. Page 642.

2: These are for Bruno Zevi, the 'Laws, Qualities, Rules and Principles' of the 'Formalist Interpretation' c.f. Bruno Zevi: 'Architecture as Space'. p.p.193

3: Most contemporary writers have tended to obscure their initial statement of 'the architectural equation' by introducing specific perceptual qualities. Thus: 'Les elements ...: Lumier, fonction, materiaux, volume, temps, espace, couleur.' Theo Van Doesburg, Conference at Madrid 1930.

4: See for example his discussion on the shape of doric pediments; Choisy, A: 'Histoire de L'Architecture.' Paris, 1899. Vol.1

5: c.f. Louis Sullivan : 'Kindergarten Chats' N.Y. 1947.

TECTURE AS EXPRESSING THE 'SPIRIT OF THE AGE' OR THE 'WILL OF THE EPOCH' THEREBY IMPLICITLY GIVING PREFERENCE TO THE ELEMENT OF CONCEPT OR INTENT.[6] BUT NONE OF THESE THEORISTS HAVE ATTEMPTED TO DEFINE THE PRECISE MEANING OF THE TERMS THEY USE, NOR THE EXTENT TO WHICH FORM IS EITHER SUBSERVIENT OR PREDOMINANT AMONG THE ELEMENTS NAMED: THOUGH, TO BE SURE, THE RELATIVE IMPORTANCE OF THESE ELEMENTS AND THEIR RELATIONSHIP TO ONE ANOTHER CANNOT BE ESTABLISHED BY DEFINITION ALONE, SINCE THIS WOULD CONSTITUTE ONLY AN INITIAL CATEGORISATION OF THE PROBLEM. SUCH A PARTIAL ORDERING CANNOT BY ITSELF FURNISH A RATIONAL DISCIPLINE FOR ARCHITECTURE, AND BECOMES DANGEROUS WHEN USED IN A WILFUL OR CAPRICIOUS MANNER IN THE DESIGN PROCESS.

6: c.f. Mies van der Rohe : 'Baukunst Und Zeitwille'. Der Querschnitt. 4:31-2. 1924. ('Architecture is the will of the epoch translated into space.') and again in G. No.2 1923

THE ROOT CAUSE OF THE ARCHITECTURAL CONFUSION THAT ALL TOO OFTEN CONFRONTS US IS THE UNCO-ORDINATED OR NON-RATIONAL INVOKING OF THIS OR THAT ELEMENT. NOR IS THE PROBLEM EASILY RESOLVED: FOR EXAMPLE, THE DICTATES OF FORM ARE NOT ALWAYS WHOLLY RECONCILABLE WITH THE REQUIREMENTS OF FUNCTION; AND AGAIN, A FUNCTION THAT APPEARS AS SYMBOLIC TO ONE PARTICULAR CULTURE MAY APPEAR AS UTILITARIAN TO ANOTHER.[7] THIS IS NOT TO IMPLY THAT THE ELEMENTS NAMED ARE BY NATURE MUTUALLY ANTAGONISTIC, BUT RATHER THAT WHEN THEY ARE WEIGHTED EQUALLY THEIR SIGNIFICANT IDENTITIES ARE LOST IN A WAY WHICH INEVITABLY VITIATES THE EFFECT OF THE RESULT. IT FOLLOWS FROM THIS THAT A RATIONALLY CONCEIVED HIERARCHY OF THE ELEMENTS IS A NECESSARY PRECONDITION FOR THE SOLVING, AND INDEED FOR THE CLEAR FORMULATION, OF AN ARCHITECTURAL PROBLEM. SUCH A HIERARCHY COULD BE DERIVED FROM BOTH THE PARTICULAR AND THE GENERAL DEMANDS WHICH THE PROBLEM IMPOSES. TO STATE THIS POINT ANOTHER WAY: A BASIC PRIORITY MUST BE ESTABLISHED IN ARCHITECTURE WHICH IS EVOLVED FROM THE DIALECTIC BETWEEN RELATIVE AND ABSOLUTE ENDS.

7: Hence, as Rudolf Wittkower has poined out, the misrepresentation of Renaissance symbolic values in the nineteenth century: 'The ethical fallacy' of Ruskin. Rudolf Wittkower: 'Architectural Principles in the Age of Humanism' (originally vol.19, studies of the Warburg Institute) London 1952. Chapter 1

The proposing of this priority is of critical importance today since our social economic and technological environment has become so overwhelmingly distended that no significant order can be perceived by the individual. Moreover the proliferation of new technological means has evolved beyond the architect's ability to utilize rationally its full potential. In these circumstances architecture seems to have taken refuge in mannerism and the cult of self expression in a compulsive emphasis on the isolated creation without regard to a total order.[8] This need for individual expression is a legitimate one, but if it is to be satisfied without prejudice to the comprehensibility of the environment as a whole, a general system of priorities must be proposed; and it will be argued here that such a system mustsnecessarily give preference to absolute over temporal ends. The need for such a hierarchy may be seen in the opposition that may arise between the internal and the external (or environmental) requirements of a particular building. Different weighting of these two factors could produce opposite priorities. Thus the building might be conceived initially in response to the demands of internal function. If this were to be exclusively the case, in the sense that the existence of external factors was denied, the priority implied would be absolute even though the internal considerations relate only to the building in question. Such a building might be said to predicate an ideal future situation by virtue of its rejection of existing patterns. If on the other hand the design were in fact to acknowledge the existence of external conditions and were to be modified by them, then its internal resolution would be subordinated to an external state of affairs, and this would initially establish a priority of relative ends.

8: c.f. Colin Rowe 'Mannerism and Modern Architecture'. Architectural Review. Vol.107.1950. ('Abstraction in Contemporary Art' makes reference to a world of personal sensation, and typifies the private workings of the artist's mind')

However, if we postulate the general situation, the total external order, as

OUR ABSOLUTE, THEN IT FOLLOWS THAT A SPECIFIC SITUATION BY ITS VERY NATURE LIMITS US TO RELATIVE ENDS: THAT IS TO SAY THE INDIVIDUAL BUILDING IS NOW SEEN AS A RELATIVE END WITH REGARD TO ITS ENVIRONMENT. THE INDIVIDUAL BUILDING CAN NOT NOW BE REGARDED AS AN ISOLATED ENTITY, AS AN END IN ITSELF, BUT MERELY AS A TRANSITIONAL ELEMENT IN THE ESTABLISHMENT OF THE WHOLE. IT MAY STILL ASSUME AN INTEGRAL CONDITION, AN 'IDEAL' STATE IN ITSELF, BUT ONLY WITHIN THE LIMITATIONS IMPOSED BY AN ENVISAGED FUTURE ORDER. IN PRAGMATIC TERMS IT IS CLEARLY IMPOSSIBLE TO CREATE A SPECIFIC BUILDING WITH A FIXED ABSOLUTE END IN VIEW, BECAUSE EACH NEW UNIT WILL NOT ONLY CHANGE THE EXISTING PATTERN BUT WILL ALSO MODIFY BY ITS PRESENCE ANY FUTURE UNITS. FOR EXAMPLE, IN CONSIDERING A BUILDING, ENTRANCES CANNOT BE LOCATED WHERE NO MEANS OF ACCESS EXISTS AT THE MATERIAL TIME. TO THIS EXTENT ANY BUILDING MUST ACKNOWLEDGE GIVEN EXTERNAL PATTERNS, ALTHOUGH THESE MIGHT ADMITTEDLY BE CONSIDERED AS PARTS OF A FUTURE ABSOLUTE ORDER. TO COMPLICATE THE ISSUE STILL FURTHER, ANY PLANNING MUST TAKE INTO ACCOUNT THAT ANY FUTURE ORDER BY ITS NATURE, CANNOT BE A CONSTANT OR STATIC ENTITY. IT MUST RATHER BE THOUGHT OF AS CONTINUOUS, AND CAPABLE OF ACCEPTING GROWTH AND CHANGE.[9] ANY NOTION OF A FUTURE ORDER IN ABSOLUTE TERMS WOULD BE OPEN TO THE CRITICISM THAT IT IS ROMANTIC-UTOPIAN.[10] SANT'ELIA'S DESIGNS FOR A 'CITTA NUOVA' ARE NOTABLE EXAMPLES OF THIS KIND OF VISIONARY APPROACH.[11] FOR SANT'ELIA, THE FUTURIST NOTIONS OF ENERGY AND SPEED WERE ABSOLUTES FOR WHICH HE SOUGHT ARCHITECTONIC EXPRESSION.[12] BUT IN DOING SO HE INVOLVED HIMSELF IN AN ESSENTIAL CONTRADICTION, SINCE THE BUILDINGS HE DESIGNED, BEING NECESSARILY SPECIFIC, COULD ONLY PRESUPPOSE A RELATIVE, I.E. A FIXED, FUTURE STATE. UPON THESE SPECIFIC DESIGNS HE IMPOSED AN AESTHETIC OF AERODYNAMIC STREAMLINING SYMBOLIC OF THE FUTURIST UTOPIA. NO MATTER HOW STIMULATING MAY BE THE EFFECT

9: Hence the preoccupation of contemporary planners with 'biological' ways of growth and change; 'Continuity' together with 'Renewal' (c.f. Robert Jeffery: Arch. Design. May 1963)

10: Colin Rowe in 'Granta' January 1959 questions whether 'The revolutionary instrument utopia' is 'in any way compatible with all those ideas of motion, change, growth and history which in the last 150 years have gradually pervaded all thought.'

11: See Giulio Carlo Argan: 'IL pensiero critico di Antonio Sant'Elia'. 'L'Arte', September 1930 and Bruno Zevi: 'Poetica di Sant'Elia e Ideologica Futurista', in 'L'Architettura' November 1956.
'I sudi progetti non inquadrano una effecttiva problematic dell'architettura moderna; ...e pathos di una modernita sentita come nuova giovinezza del mondo...danno un'immagine di vivo nitore ideale.' M. Calvesi: 'IL Futurista Sant'Elia. La Casa 6

12: c.f initial manifesto of Futurism: "Le Figaro", Paris 1909. ('We declare that the worlds' Splenfour has been enriched by a new beauty; the beauty of speed..' pt.4)

OF THESE IMAGES, THEY REMAIN UNHELPFUL TO ANY REALISTIC THINKING ABOUT THE PROBLEM OF A CONTINUOUS FUTURE PATTERN.[13] A RATIONAL APPROACH TO THIS MUST PREDICATE A TOTAL ORDER – OR, IN THE TERMS OF THIS THESIS, AN ABSOLUTE WHICH IS CAPABLE OF ENCOMPASSING CHANGE AND GROWTH WHILE STILL RETAINING ITS CHARACTER AS AN ABSOLUTE. IT IS THE CONCEPT OF THE PRIORITY OF AN ABSOLUTE OF THIS NATURE WHICH IS CRITICAL HERE, SINCE IT ALONE CAN PROVIDE US WITH THE BASIS FOR A HIERARCHICAL ORDERING OF THE FIVE ELEMENTS. THIS MAJOR TASK MUST NOW BE ATTEMPTED. THE CONTENTION WILL BE THAT ARCHITECTURE IS IN ESSENCE THE GIVING OF FORM (ITSELF AN ELEMENT) TO INTENT, FUNCTION, STRUCTURE AND TECHNICS. THUS FORM IS RAISED TO A POSITION OF PRIMACY IN THE HIERACHY OF ELEMENTS. TO CLAIM SUPREMECY FOR FORM IN THIS WAY IS TO ADOPT AN ORIGINAL STANDPOINT DESPITE THE FACT THAT ALL ACADEMIC AND RATIONALIST THINKING WELL INTO THIS CENTURY WOULD HAVE PLACED FORMAL CONSIDERATIONS ABOVE ALL OTHERS.[14] BUT THESE WERE FORMAL CONSIDERATIONS OF A DIFFERENT KIND: PREOCCUPATIONS WITH 'FORM FOR FORMS SAKE', WITH MULTI-AXIAL COMPOSTIONS, WITH ARTIFICIALLY SYMMETRICAL AESTHETIC, THE BLATANTLY NON-FUNCTIONAL NATURE OF WHICH DROVE MODERN ARCHITECTS INITIALLY TNTO THE SEARCH FOR A NEW MEANS OF EXPRESSION.[15] BUT IF IT IS DEMANDED OF FORM THAT IT SHOULD PROVIDE THE MEANS FOR GIVING COMPREHENSIBILITY TO A TOTAL ENVIRONMENT, IT FOLLOWS THAT A CLEAR PRIORITY ACCRUES TO THE FORM-GIVING PROCESS. ON THIS RECKINING THE FORM OF AN INDIVIDUAL BUILDING NEED NOT NECESSARILY LY BE EXPRESSIVE OF ITS INTENT OR FUNCTION, AS LONG AS IT CONTRIBUTES TO THE ORDER, SCALE, HARMONY AND PATTERN OF THE TOTAL ENVIRONMENT.

IF THIS POSITION IS TO BE SUSTAINED, A VITALLY IMPORTANT SUBDIVISION MUST BE MADE OF THE GENERAL CATEGORY 'FORM', INTO TWO TYPES: 'GENERIC' AND 'SPECIFIC'. THE TERM GENERIC FORM IS HERE UNDERSTOOD TO MEAN FORM THOUGHT OF IN A PLATONIC SENSE, AS A DEFINABLE ENTITY WITH ITS OWN INHERENT LAWS. THE TERM 'SPECIFIC FORM', ON

13: c.f. Colin Rowe: op. cit., note 10: 'Utopia cannot become the society which it changes; and it cannot therefore change itself.'

14: see for example, Howard Robertson: 'The principles of Architectural Composition ' London 1924. p.p.38 et seq.: 'The presence of such apparently illogical forms, (pediment and cornice) if these are necessary from the point of view of composition, is therefore not to be hastily condemned.'

15: 'IV. La fonction. La Nouvelle architecture est fonctionelle, c.a. d. qu'elle est fondee sur la synthese des exigences pratiques.' "L'Esprit Fondamental De L'Architecture contemporaine" . Barcelona 1930

THE OTHER HAND, CAN BE THOUGHT OF AS THE ACTUAL PHYSICAL CONFIGURATION REALIZED IN RESPONSE TO A SPECIFIC INTENT AND FUNCTION. GENERIC FORM, BECAUSE OF ITS TRANSCENDENT OR UNIVERSAL NATURE, MUST TAKE PRECEDENCE OVER THE OTHER FOUR ELEMENTS. BUT EVEN WHEN FORM IS CONSIDERED IN ITS SPECIFIC SENSE, IT WILL BE SEEN THAT IT STILL REFERS TO, OR IS DERIVED FROM, THE GENERIC - AND THIS ASSOCIATION OR REFERENCE IS AN ESSENTIAL FACTOR IN ITS COMPREHENSION. GENERIC FORM IN ITS ARCHITECTURAL CONTEXT CAN BE CONSIDERED UNDER TWO CATEGORIES: THE LINEAR AND THE CENTROIDAL. A CUBE AND A SPHERE ARE CENTROIDAL. A DOUBLE CUBE AND A CYLINDER ARE LINEAR. EACH OF THESE BASIC SOLIDS HAS BY ITS NATURE CERTAIN INHERENT DYNAMICS, AND THESE MUST BE UNDERSTOOD AND RESPECTED IF ANY GRAMMATICAL USAGE OR INTERPRETATION OF A GIVEN SOLID IS TO BE ATTEMPTED.[16] THE CUBE AS A CENTROIDAL FORM EVOLVES EQUALLY IN A VERTICAL AND A HORIZONTAL DIRECTION FROM A DEFINED CENTRUM. THIS QUALITY IS PRIMARY TO THE UNDERSTANDING OF IT. OF SECONDARY IMPORTANCE IS THE EQUALITY OF VERTICAL AND HORIZONTAL AXES, THE EQUALITY OF ALL SURFACES, THE DIAGONAL AXES, AND THE LOCATION OF ALL THE CORNERS. BUT THE ESSENTIAL POINT TO NOTE HERE IS THAT THESE PROPERTIES OF THE CUBE, AS OF ANY GENERIC FORM, STAND ABOVE ANY AESTHETIC PREFERENCE. THEY ARE, QUITE SIMPLY, INHERENT CHARACTERISTICS WHICH CAN ONLY BE CONSIDERED IN AN OBJECTIVE SENSE; THEY ESTABLISH THE ABSOLUTE NATURE OF GENERIC FORM, AND BY DEFINITION ITS TRANSCENDENCY OVER SPECIFIC FORM.

16: See Paul Klee, 'The Thinking Eye' edited by Jurg Spiller, London 1961. 'The basic forms, their tensions and inner relations ... the universal cause (of which) is a reciprocal tension, a pull in two directions at once', and also Gyorgy Kepes. 'The language of Vision ' p.32: 'To maintain the same constant structure, every organism must achieve a dynamic unity...the dynamic tendency towards balance.'

THE SAME CONCLUSION IS REACHED WHEN THE MUCH-CANVASSED FORM-FUNCTION INTERRELATIONSHIP IS CONSIDERED.[17] SINCE NO ONE FUNCTION CAN DO MORE THAN SUGGEST A SPECIFIC FORM, (I.E. CANNOT DETERMINE IT) IN OTHER WORDS THERE IS NO ONE FORM FOR ANY FUNCTION, SPECIFIC FORM CAN BE CONSIDERED TO BE OF A RELATIVE NATURE

17: c.f. Horatio Greenough 'Form and Function : Remarks on Art ' Los Angeles 1947.

(RELATIVE, THAT IS, TO A PARTICULAR INTERPRETATION OF A PROGRAMME) AND THEREFORE OF A LESSER DEGREE OF IMPORTANCE IN THE HIERARCHY THAN GENERIC FORM. SPECIFIC FORM DEMANDS PERCEPTUAL RESPONSES OF AN AESTHETIC OR SUBJECTIVE NATURE, I.E. TO SUCH FACTORS AS ITS PROPORTION, QUALITY OF SURFACE, STRUCTURE, SYMBOLISM ETC. GENERIC FORM DOES NOT ASK TO BE CONSIDERED IN THESE TERMS. IT IS NOT A QUESTION OF OUR LIKING OR DISLIKING A CUBE: IT IS A QUESTION OF OUR ACCEPTING ITS EXISTENCE AND RECOGNISING ITS INHERENT PROPERTIES. BUT SPECIFIC FORM, SINCE IT EXISTS IN A CLOSE SYMBIOTIC RELATIONSHIP WITH THE OTHER ELEMENTS OF THE ARCHITECTURAL EQUATION MUST BE ANALYSED IN RELATION TO THEM. THERE IS, HOWEVER, THE APPARENT CONTRADICTION BETWEEN, ON THE ONE HAND, THE CONCEPT OF A FUTURE PATTERN WHICH IS CAPABLE OF CONTINUAL GROWTH, AND ON THE OTHER HAND THE CONCEPT OF GENERIC FORM, WHICH, CONSIDERED IN ITSELF, IS A STATIC ENTITY, AND NOT CAPABLE OF CHANGE.[18] RECONCILIATION IS POSSIBLE IN VIEW OF THE FACT THAT ANY GENERIC FORM HAS AN ADDITIVE OR REPRODUCTIVE QUALITY WHICH ALLOWS IT TO GENERATE AND MULTIPLY, SO THAT EVEN THOUGH THE PROPERTIES OF A SINGLE CUBE HAVE BEEN STATED AND ANALYSED ANOTHER CUBE OR A SERIES OF CUBES CAN ALWAYS BE ADDED TO IT: THE ONLY STIPULATION BEING THAT THESE ADDITIONS BE UNDERSTOOD AS CAUSING PERCEPTIBLE CHANGE IN THE STATE OF THE ORIGINAL CUBE.[19]

IN AN ARCHITECTURAL SITUATION THE EMERGENCE OF GENERIC FORM ALWAYS FOLLOWS FROM A CONSIDERATION OF THE STATED CONDITIONS. A BUILDING DOES NOT DEVELOP INITIALLY FROM A PLATONIC NOTION OF FORM, BUT RATHER FROM CONSIDERATIONS OF INTENT AND FUNCTION. THIS LEADS TO THE ASSEMBLAGE OF A SPECIFIC FORM, WHICH MAY THEN BE CRITICISED AND MODIFIED WITH REFERENCE TO ITS COGNATE GENERIC FORM. THUS, FOR EXAMPLE, WHEN THE SPECIFIC FORM OF A CUBE WITH A CENTRAL

18: see Herman Weyl, 'Symmetry' Princeton 1952.

19: Thus Focillon when talking of 'forms in the realm of matter': 'all different kinds of matter ...are form....Their form in its raw state evokes, suggests, and propagates other forms, .. this is because this form liberates other forms according to its own laws.

But ..all these varieties of matter which demand so much from form and which exert so powerful an attraction upon the forms of art, are in theirown turn, profoundly modified .' 'The Life of Forms in Art' 1942

COURT IS EVOLVED FROM A PARTICULAR INTENT AND FUNCTION, IT MUST BE SUBJECTED TO AN ANALYSIS IN GENERIC TERMS BEFORE ITS ORIGINAL SELECTION CAN BE JUSTIFIED AND DEVELOPED APPROPRIATELY.

ALL SPECIFIC FORM IN ARCHITECTURE IS CONCEIVED INITIALLY FROM A CRITIQUE OF TWO OF THE ELEMENTS, INTENT AND FUNCTION - A FACT WHICH CLEARLY INDICATES THAT A PRIORITY MUST BE GIVEN TO CONSIDERATIONS OF INTENT AND FUNCTION OVER THOSE OF STRUCTURE AND TECHNICS. A FURTHER DEFINITION OF INTENT WILL PERHAPS SUBSTANTIATE THIS POINT: THE WORD IS HERE USED TO MEAN THE PRIMARY CONCEPTION OF A THING.[20] FOR EXAMPLE, BEFORE WE CAN BUILD A 'TEMPLE' WE MUST HAVE HAD AN IDEA OR CONCEPT 'TEMPLE'.[21] OWING TO OUR EXPERENTIAL AND HISTORICAL ASSOCIATIONS IT IS DIFFICULT FOR US TO ISOLATE THE CONCEPT 'TEMPLE' FROM THE FUNCTION 'TEMPLE' OR FROM WHATEVER SPECIFIC FORM WE ASSOCIATE 'TEMPLE'. HENCE THE CLOSE ASSOCIATION BETWEEN INTENT AND FUNCTION: WE MUST ALWAYS HAVE THE CONCEPT OF SOMETHING BEFORE WE CAN ATTRIBUTE A FUNCTION TO IT. BY WAY OF ILLUSTRATION: IT IS EVIDENT THAT THE SAME CONCEPT 'TEMPLE' DID NOT PRODUCE THE SAME SPECIFIC FORM FOR THE GREEKS AS IT DID FOR THE ROMANS OR FOR THE PEOPLE OF THE MIDDLE AGES. INDEED IT NOW BECOMES CLEAR THAT FUNCTION IS A TERM WITH AN INCONVIENTLY WIDE RANGE OF MEANINGS AND APPLICATIONS: A DISTINCTION MUST BE MADE AT THIS STAGE BETWEEN THE PHYSICAL OR UTILITARIAN AND THE METAPHYSICAL OR SYMBOLIC SENSES OF THE WORD. AT ITS MOST OBVIOUS LEVEL 'FUNCTION' CAN BE THOUGHT OF AS AN ACTIVITY OR USAGE PROPER TO ANYTHING. IF THE FUNCTION STATED IS VERTICAL MOVEMENT, THEN WE CAN PRODUCE THE RESPONSES STAIR, RAMP, OR LIFT, EACH OF WHICH WOULD GENERATE A MORE OR LESS CONSTANT RESULT IN TERMS OF SPECIFIC FORM. IT IS NECESSARY TO NOTE THAT THIS PRODUCTION OF A FORM IS A RESPONSE TO FUNCTION PLUS INTENT, AND NOT TO INTENT ALONE. IT IS ALSO NECESSARY TO NOTE

20: See Erwin Panofsky, 'Meaning in the Visual Arts'. N.Y. 1955 p.11 for a discussion of 'invention'.

21: Erwin Panofsky, 'to perceive the relation of signification is to separate the idea of the concept to be expressed from the means of expressing it'. Similarly 'to perceive the relation of construction' it is necessary to separate the idea of function from the means of fulfilling it. 'Meaning and the Visual Arts' N.Y. 1955 p9.

THAT THE RESPONSE TO A STATED UTILITARIAN FUNCTION CAN PRODUCE A SPECIFIC FORM WHEREAS THE RESPONSE TO A SYMBOLIC FUNCTION IN GENERAL CANNOT. BUT THERE IS A POINT AT WHICH VERTICAL MOVEMENT MAY BE THOUGHT OF IN A SENSE OTHER THAN THE PURELY UTILITARIAN. THIS COMES ABOUT AS SOON AS 'RAMP', 'STAIR' AND 'LIFT' ARE THOUGHT OF AS A TRANSITION, AS MINOR SPACES CONNECTING TWO MAJOR SPACES. THENCEFORWARD THE FUNCTION OF THIS SPACE IS NO LONGER CONCEIVED OF AS ENTIRELY UTILITARIAN, BUT SHIFTS INTO THE REALM OF THE 'SYMBOLIC'. IT IS THEN NO LONGER ADEQUATE MERELY TO INSERT A STAIR OR A LIFT BETWEEN THE FLOORS OF A BUILDING: THE EXPERIENCE OF THE STAIR OR LIFT MUST RATHER BE CONSIDERED IN ITS BROADER IMPLICATIONS,[22] IN ITS ROLE AS THE 'SYMBOLIC' TRANSITION BETWEEN ONE SPACE AND THE NEXT.

SYMBOLIC FUNCTION MUST NOT BE CONFUSED WITH INTENT, SINCE THE FORMER IS THE REPRESENTATION OF A TRANSCENDENTAL IDEA. IN ARCHITECTURE THE INHERENT DIFFICULTY THAT ARISES IS THAT THE TYPES OF SPECIFIC FORM IN COMMON USE CHANGE WITH EACH SUCCEEDING AGE, AND THEREFORE THEIR MEANING AS SYMBOLS TENDS TO BE DIFFERENT FOR EACH GENERATION.[23] THE SYMBOLIC FUNCTION, IN THE SENSE OF IMPACT ON THE BEHOLDER, OF A GOTHIC CATHEDRAL TODAY IS OBVIOUSLY NOT THE SAME AS IT WAS TO THE PEOPLE OF THE MIDDLE AGES.[24] THIS SUBJECTIVE AND TEMPORAL CHARACTER OF SPECIFIC ARCHITECTURAL SYMBOLS PREVENTS THEIR USE AS ABBASIS FOR RATIONAL ARGUMENT. MOREOVER, NOT ALL ARCHITECTURE NECESSARILY[25] INVOLVES A SYMBOLIC FUNCTION, OR THE NEED TO SATISFY THIS REQUIREMENT. THE NOTION 'VERTICAL MOVEMENT'- STAIR' DOES NOT DEMAND SYMBOLIC REPRESENTATION, WHEREAS THE EMBODIMENT OF SPIRITUAL, MORAL OR INTELLECTUAL ASPIRATION IN THE DESIGN OF A TEMPLE DOES. FURTHERMORE, AS HAS ALREADY BEEN SUGGESTED, THE RESPONSE TO UTILITARIAN FUNCTION TENDS TO PRODUCE SPECIFIC

22: 'This is the humanism of architecture: the tendency to project the image of our functions into concrete forms is the basis for architecture of creative design. The tendency to recognise, in concrete forms, the image of those functions is the true basis in its turn of critical appreciation.' Geoffrey Scott, 'The Architecture of Humanism.' p.213.

23: Thus E. Baldwin Smith: 'The problem of presenting a convincing exposition of symbolic intent... is made difficult by the modern conviction that architecture ... has always been created for utilitarian and aethetic reasons.' 'The Architectural Symbolism of Imperial Rome and the Middle Ages'. Princeton 1956. Similarly E. Gombrich 'First the symbolic function was denied a place in art, then the representational function as such was placed outsède the pale; we have become used to the identification of all art with the function of expression'. 'The visual image in Neo-Platonic Thought'. Journal of the Warburg and Courtauld institutes. Vol. XI 1948.

24: c.f. Otto von Simson 'The Gothic Cathedral' N.Y. 1956. Introduction p.XIX.

25: See Nikolaus Pevsner 'An Outline of European Architecture' Introduction.

FORM, WHEREAS THE RESPONSE TO SYMBOLIC FUNCTION TENDS TO PRODUCE GENERIC FORM - THE PLATONIC SOLID AND THE PLATONIC IDEA ARE CLOSELY RELATED. THE SITUATION IS COMPLICATED BY THE USES IN CERTAIN CASES OF SPECIFIC FORMS, DERIVED INITIALLY FROM UTILITARIAN FUNCTION, TO GIVE SYMBOLIC MEANING. THUS FORMS ARE FOUND IN MODERN ARCHITECTURE THAT ORIGINALLY SERVED A UTILITARIAN PURPOSE APPEARING AS SYMBOLIC REFERENCES TO THE IDEA OF A MODERN SOCIETY.[26] THIS INVESTITURE WITH QUASI-TRANSCENDENTAL VALUES OF CERTAIN SPECIFIC FORMS SEEMS PECULIAR TO MODERN ARCHITECTURE. IN PANOFSKY'S TERMS IT IS THIS TRANSFERENCE THAT LEADS TO A DEVALUATION OF THE ORIGINAL MEANING OF THE FORM IN QUESTION. AN EXAMPLE WOULD BE STREAMLINING, WHICH WAS ORIGINALLY A UTILITARIAN RESPONSE TO THE EFFECT OF EXTREME WIND STRESSES.[27] THIS KIND OF FORM HAS SINCE, AS MANY CRITICS HAVE POINTED OUT, BEEN ARBITRARILY APPLIED IN A WIDE RANGE OF DESIGN SITUATIONS ASAA[28] SYMBOLIC EVOCATION OF TWENTIETH CENTURY ATTITUDES AND SENSIBILITY.

26: Hence the arguments put forward by the member of Team X to explain the limitations of the 'Four Routes' of C.I.A.M.

27: 'Meaning in the Visual Arts', p.13 footnote. 'Streamlining was, originally a genuine functional principle etc.'

28: for example the work of the German Expressionist School - notably the Einstein Tower, Potsdam, 1919-21. by Eric Mendelsohn.

AS ANOTHER ILLUSTRATION OF THIS POINT, THE EXAMPLE OF THE TEMPLE CAN BE USED AGAIN. CLEARLY IN ANY GIVEN INSTANCE BOTH KINDS OF FUNCTION (THE UTILITARIAN AND THE SYMBOLIC) MUST DERIVE FROM THE ORIGINAL CONCEPT 'TEMPLE'.[29] IN THE PURELY UTILITARIAN SENSE THE FUNCTION 'TEMPLE' COULD BE EQUATED WITH 'GATHERING-PLACE-FOR-LARGE-GROUPS-OF-PEOPLE'. FROM THIS THE IMAGE OF A LARGE SPACE WITH A ROOF OVER IT COULD BE EVOKED. BUT FURTHER IF THIS 'TEMPLE' IS GOING TO SERVE AS 'FOCAL-POINT-OF-THE-WORSHIP-OF-THE-COMMUNITY' A SYMBOLIC FUNCTION IS IMPUTED TO IT. THE RESPONSE IN TERMS OF A SPECIFIC FORM CAN NO LONGER BE 'A-SPACE-WITH-A-ROOF-OVER-IT'. THIS ROOF IS NOW SEEN AS DIFFERENT FROM ALL OTHER ROOFS IN PROXIMITY TO IT. IT MAY TAKE A DIFFERENT FORM, HAVE A DIFFERENT STRUCTURE, BE CONSTRUCTED OF DIFFERENT MATERIALS, ALL OFMWHICH WOULD TEND TO ISOLATE THE

29: The Symbolic functions of Ciboria and city gates are examined exhaustively by E. Baldwin Smith, op. cit. note 23.

THE BUILDING FROM ITS SURROUNDINGS, THUS CAUSING IT TO BE SEEN AS A FOCAL POINT. THIS CLEARLY CAN BE CONSIDERED AS A RESPONSE TO THE DEMANDS OF SYMBOLIC FUNCTION. INITIALLY THE RESPONSE TO UTILITARIAN FUNCTION CAN PRODUCE FROM THE NOTION 'ROOF'[30] THE SPECIFIC FORM 'DOME' RATHER THAN ANY OTHER SPECIFIC FORM OF ROOF. THE TEMPORAL AND SUBJECTIVE NATURE OF SPECIFIC FORMS IS SEEN IN THE FACT THAT THE PERCEPTION OF A DOME PRODUCES DIFFERENT RESPONSES IN DIFFERENT PEOPLE. AN ENGINEER MIGHT SEE IT ONLY IN TERMS OF HOW IT IS SUPPORTED AND THE PROBLEMS INHERENT IN ITS CONSTRUCTION, SUCH AS EDGE STRESSES, CONTINUOUS SURFACES ETC. A RELIGIOUS LEADER MIGHT THINK OF THIS SAME STRUCTURE IN ITS MYSTICAL CONNOTATIONS AND ITS RELATION TO CHURCH LITURGY. A PSYCHOLOGIST MIGHT THINK OF ITS SEXUAL ASSOCIATIONS, AND SO ON. THESE ARE ALL TYPES OF RESPONSES TO THE <u>PERCEPT</u> 'DOME' AS A SPECIFIC FORM. BUT THERE IS ALSO A RANGE OF RESPONSES TO THE <u>CONCEPT</u> 'DOME' WHICH ARE OF A GENERIC NATURE. A DOME IS CENTROIDAL. IT IS EQUALLY EXPANSIVE IN ALL DIRECTIONS. IT SUGGESTS CENTRIFUGAL MOTION. THESE ARE FORMAL ABSOLUTES, ALTHOUGH OF COURSE THEY MUST BE REALISED IN TERMS OF THE PARTICULAR PROBLEM BEFORE IT CAN BE SAID THAT THE PROPER SPECIFIC FORM, THE ACTUAL SHAPE OF DOME, IS APPROPRIATE TO THE SPECIFIC CIRCUMSTANCES. FOR EXAMPLE, IF THERE IS NOT EQUAL ACCESS TO A SITE IT IS HARD TO JUSTIFY THE CHOICE OF A CENTROIDAL FORM IN PREFERENCE TO A LINEAR ONE. IT WOULD BE EQUALLY DIFFICULT TOTRATIONALISE THE PLACEMENT OF A CRUCIFORM OR PINWHEEL BUILDING ON A CORNER SITE, SINCE THIS USE OF THIS GENERIC FORM WOULD PRESUPPOSE A SITE WITH ACCESS FROM ALL FOUR SIDES.

IT IS ONLY WHEN A SPECIFIC FORM IS ESTABLISHED FROM A CONSIDERATION OF UTILITARIAN FUNCTION THAT THE PROPERTIES INHERENT IN THE GENERIC FORM CAN BE

30: See Louis Hautecoeur 'Mystéque et Architecture ' Symbolisme du cercle et de la coupole. Paris 1954, and Jacques Maritain, 'Sign and Symbol. Journal of the Warburg Institute Vol. I. 1937.

ANALYSED TO TEST THEIR RELEVANCE TO THE SPECIFIC CONDITIONS. THIS IS BY NO MEANS AS RESTRICTIVE AS IT MAY SOUND. A GREAT VARIETY OF COMPLEX SYSTEMS CAN BE DERIVED FROM GENERIC FORM UNDER ANY GIVEN CONDITIONS, AND THE DETAILED DEMONSTRATION OF THIS WILL BE ATTEMPTED IN CHAPTER THREE.

FORM MUST NOW BE EXAMINED IN ITS RELATION TO STRUCTURE AND TECHNICS.[31] STRUCTURE MAY BE THOUGHT OF AS THE BONES, VEINS AND ARTERIES OF ANY BUILDING. IT IS THE FRAMEWORK FOR THE TRANSLATION OF INTENT AND FUNCTION INTO PHYSICAL REALITY. IT INCLUDES NOT ONLY THE COLUMNS AND THE SLABS OF THE STRUCTURE, BUT THE PIPES DUCTS AND CONDUITS OF THE MECHANICAL SERVICES. IF STRUCTURE IS CONSIDERED IN THIS SENSE, THEN TECHNICS ARE THE LIGAMENTS OF ANY BUILDING: THE METHODS USED TO LINK, ARTICULATE AND CONSOLIDATE THE STRUCTURE; WHICH CLEARLY ESTABLISHES A SUBORDINATE RELATIONSHIP OF TECHNICS TO STRUCTURE IN THE HIERARCHY OF ELEMENTS. STRUCTURE MUST NOW BE CONSIDERED IN RELATION TO THE OTHER ELEMENTS. AN ORTHOGONAL ARRANGEMENT OF COLUMNS AND SLABS IN ITS ABSTRACT AND ABSOLUTE STATE CAN BE ANY SIZE, ITS ONLY LIMITATION, ONCE IT BECOMES SPECIFIC, BEING THAT IMPOSED BY THE PHYSICAL PROPERTIES OF THE MATERIALS EMPLOYED. THE SIMPLICITY, REGULARITY AND SCALE OF THE COLUMNS ARE AS YET NOT AFFECTED BY ANY OTHER CONSIDERATIONS. AS THESE COLUMNS STAND UNMODIFIED BY INTENT, FUNCTION OR FORM, THEY ARE OBEYING ONLY THE ABSOLUTE CONDITIONS NECESSARY TO THEIR OWN ORGANISATION. THIS FURTHER TESTIFIES TO THE TRANSCENDENCE OF GENERIC CONDITIONS OVER SPECIFIC CONDITIONS, SINCE STRUCTURE IN THIS SENSE CAN BE CONSIDERED TO BE GENERIC IN CHARACTER.

31: Rather as Michelangelo thought of the 'orders' c.f. J Ackerman 'The Architecture of Michelangelo. Chapter I: Michelangelo's 'theory' of Architecture.'

IT IS ONLY WHEN CONSIDERATIONS OF INTENT AND FUNCTION BECOME OPERATIVE THAT

The unit-size may be determined, not only in terms of structural economy but also in terms of a scale suited to accommodate the maximum number of specific functions. These two exigencies may well be in mutual conflict, and it is here that the whole mechanism of priorities or hierarchy of elements must be called into play. If at the outset a preference has been stated for internal function, then the columnar arrangement is distorted to suit the function and the selection of material for it is then based on the requisite bay size. This distortion resulting from internal functional considerations would be an example of a priority being accorded to temporal over absolute ends. But to correct this initial distortion, while still acknowledging internal functional considerations would be an attempt to re-establish the priority of absolute ends.

Decisions as to specific structural form are thus seen to be derived ultimately from generic form. There is no limitation arguable from the other elements which can dictate whether a column is to be round, square, cruciform, or rectilinear etc.. This is a decision that can only evolve from the exigencies, either of a total order or of the particular generic form in question.

Technics are the details and methods of architecture: its means of fabrication and production, and its methods of joining, sealing, and fixing. Because of its utilitarian nature, technics relate almost entirely to the specific rather than the generic, and consequently receives the lowest priority in the hierarchy of elements. This would seem to be a contradiction in terms in the light of contemporary thinking about standardization and prefabrication.[32] How-

32: c.f. Walter Gropius 'In all great epochs of history the existance of standards - that is the conscious adaption of type forms - has been the criterion of a polite and well ordered society - the main task of contemporary design is therefore the achievement of these norms in terms of an industrial technique.' and earlier, Hermann Muthesius; 'It is only by standardisation that they (architecture and the activity of the Werkbund) can recover that universal importance which they possessed in ages of harmonious civilisation.' etc.. Annual Meeting ing of the Werkbund, Cologne 1914.

-EVER, THIS LOW PRIORITY DOES NOT DENY THE IMPORTANCE OF TECHNOLOGY, BUT RATHER ATTEMPTS TO PLACE IT IN RELATION TO AN ABSOLUTE SCALE OF VALUES. IT IS OBVIOUS THAT A MORE COMPLEX SOCIETY DEMANDS FUNCTIONS OF A MORE COMPLEX NATURE, WHICH IN TURN GIVE RISE TO A NEED FOR A MORE ELABORATE TECHNOLOGY. IN ANY PROCESS THERE IS OFTEN A 'FEED-BACK' IN THE RELATIONSHIP OF PARTS TO EACH OTHER. THEREFORE AS THE MEANS EXPAND SO DO THEIR SCOPE OF APPLICATION WHICH THEN SUGGESTS NEW FORMS AND FUNCTIONS. FOR EXAMPLE, IF A NEW PRODUCT IS DEVELOPED, THERE IS A CORRESPONDING COMPULSION TO USE IT. THE DANGER HERE DOES NOT LIE IN THE FACT THAT A TECHNICAL AGE WILL PRODUCE ITS OWN FORMS, BUT RATHER THAT THESE FORMS, EVOLVED FROM PURELY UTILITARIAN, TECHNICAL PROCESSES WILL BECOME INVESTED WITH SYMBOLIC MEANING. IN THE FIRST INSTANCE, HOWEVER, TECHNICS DO HAVE AN EFFECT ON SYSTEMIC DEVELOPMENT AS WILL BE NOTED IN THE FOLLOWING CHAPTERS. A CUBE CONCEIVED OF IN CONCRETE CANNOT EVOKE THE SAME SYSTEMIC RESPONSE AS A CUBE CONCEIVED OF IN STEEL. WHEREAS A CONCRETE CUBE COULD BE TREATED AS EITHER 'MASS' OR 'SURFACE', IT WOULD BE DIFFICULT TO CONCEIVE OF A STEEL CUBE TREATED AS A 'MASS' SINCE IT IMPLIES A COLUMNAR ORDER. BUT CONVERSELY, IT COULD BE ARGUED FROM THE HIERARCHY OF ELEMENTS THAT A GENERIC CUBE SHOULD NOT INITIALLY RECEIVE THE SPECIFIC LIMITATIONS IMPOSED BY THE TECHNICS OF STEEL AND CONCRETE.

THERE ARE, HOWEVER, SITUATIONS WHERE TECHNICS WILL OBVIOUSLY RECEIVE A STRONGER WEIGHTING, DEPENDING UPON PROGRAMMATIC REQUIREMENTS. IT IS OBVIOUS THAT 'PRESTIGE' BUILDINGS, AS LONG AS THEY EXIST AS FOCAL POINTS IN THE FRAMEWORK OF A TOTAL ENVIRONMENT, WILL NOT REQUIRE THE SAME DEGREE OF STANDARDIZATION OR PREFABRICATION OF PARTS AS WILL LARGE SCALE HOUSING AND INDUSTRIAL PROJECTS. HOWEVER, THE NOTION OF 'TECHNIQUE' THOUGHT OF AS THE PRESISE IMPLEMENTATION OF

TECHNICS, WOULD PROBABLY RECEIVE MORE IMPORTANCE IN THE INDIVIDUAL BUILDING THAN IN THE LARGE SCALE DEVELOPMENT. IT MUST BE REMEMBERED THAT 'TECHNIQUE' AND 'TECHNICS' CANNOT BE MERELY AN APPLIQUE TO ARCHITECTURAL SITUATIONS. THE SPECIFIC FORMS THAT ARE GIVEN TO 'TECHNICS' AND THE FORM THAT EVOLVES AS A RESULT OF THE BINDING TOGETHER OF PARTS THROUGH TECHNICS MUST BE SUBSERVIENT TO A TOTAL ORDER; TECHNOLOGY SHOULD NOT BE IMPOSED ON CONCEPT, FUNCTION, STRUCTURE, OR FORM. ONLY AN ARCHITECTURAL LOGIC BASED ON GENERIC FORM CAN ACHIEVE THIS ORDER; NEVERTHELESS, IT CANNOT BE TOO STRONGLY EMPHASISED THAT THE END-PRODUCT CAN ONLY BE A SYNTHESIS OF FORM WITH THE OTHER ELEMENTS OF THE ARCHITECTURAL EQUATION.

THIS SYNTHESIS CAN BE SEEN IF A POINT BLOCK WHICH IS GENERICALLY CENTROIDAL IS COMPARED WITH A SLAB BLOCK WHICH IS GENERICALLY LINEAR. BOTH EVOLVE FROM THE INTENT AND FUNCTION OF A VERTICAL PLACEMENT OF UNITS. EACH BLOCK MUST CLEARLY EXPRESS ITS GENERIC DERIVATION AS A CENTROIDAL OR A LINEAR CONFIGURATION. THE RESOLUTION OF THE PROBLEM OF VERTICAL CIRCULATION, COMMON TO BOTH, WOULD SEEM A LOGICAL BASIS FOR BOTH THEIR EVOLUTION AND THEIR CORRELATION WITH GENERIC FORM. A MERE GRAFTING OF A LIFT TOWER TO EITHER (AS IS SOMETIMES DONE WITH THE IDEA THAT THE EXPRESSION OF VERTICAL ORIENTATION IS THEREBY CLARIFIED) ONLY AMOUNTS TO A PICTURESQUE MANIFESTATION OF ITS UTILITARIAN FUNCTION. IF INSTEAD A SPECIFIC FORM WAS EVOLVED FOR THIS VERTICAL MOVEMENT THAT SATISFIED NOT ONLY ITS UTILITARIAN FUNCTION BUT ALSO ITS 'SYMBOLIC' FUNCTION AS A TRANSITION FROM GROUND LEVEL TO ANY RAISED LEVEL, AND WAS FURTHERMORE EXPRESSIVE OF THE GENERIC QUALITY OF LINEAR FORM, THEN IT WOULD BE PRESENTING THE REQUIRED SYNTHESIS. THUS A CORKSCREW MOVEMENT FROM LEVEL TO LEVEL COULD DEFINE THE CENTROIDAL ASPECTS

OF A POINT BLOCK WHILE A CASCADING, CONTINUOUS MOVEMENT COULD DEFINE THE LINEAR ASPECTS OF A SLAB BLOCK, AND IN EITHER CASE WITHOUT NECESSARILY CREATING A DIVORCE BETWEEN THE SUCCESSIVE LEVELS AND THE MEANS OF MOVEMENT BETWEEN THEM.

THIS CLEARLY DEMONSTRATES THAT THE GIVING OF FORM IS FAR MORE THAN THE MAKING OF SHAPES, OR THE CREATION OF BEAUTIFUL AND AESTHETICALLY PLEASING OBJECTS IN THEMSELVES, FOR THESE ONLY SATISFY THE PERCEPTUAL AND NOT THE CONCEPTUAL ASPECTS OF THE PROBLEM. THE PRESENTATION OF AN ORDER MUST BE INHERENT IN THE GIVING OF FORM, WHETHER IT BE DIRECTED TOWARDS THE CLARITY OF INTENT AND FUNCTION OF A SPECIFIC BUILDING, OR TOWARDS THE CLARITY OF THE RELATIONSHIP BETWEEN THE INDIVIDUAL BUILDING AND THE TOTAL ENVIRONMENT. FORM, IS THEREFORE SPECIFIC, YET AT THE SAME TIME GENERAL. IT PROVIDES FOR ARCHITECTURE, THE PARTICULAR MEANS OF EXPRESSING INTENT AND ACCOMMODATING FUNCTION, AND THE GENERAL MEANS FOR CREATING AN ORDERED ENVIRONMENT.

The argument so far has postulated a hierarchy of architectural elements with 'form' at its apex. Some sort of definition of the word 'form' as relevant to architecture has tended to emerge but no attempt has been made to determine its precise meaning. The dictionary is not much help, since it is obliged to define words in terms of other words which are nearly, but not quite, synonymous. Thus, in the case of 'form' we shall find, among other definitions, 'shape', and under 'shape this is only reversed. Such descriptions as 'configuration' or 'relation of parts to a whole' however, do provide a valuable indication by evoking the standard definition of a 'gestalt' as proposed by the theorists of that school of psychological thought, namely 'that which at any given moment is seen as a separate whole in the total perceptual field', and that whole being derived from a process of organization which is 'diametrically opposed to mere juxtaposition or random distribution'. This however would be inadequate by itself to describe what is meant by form in architecture, since it is somewhat visual or pictorial in its suggested emphasis - and it is precisely the visual or pictorial concept of form which in the context of this thesis will be argued against. To understand the conceptual basis of architectural form, it is necessary to isolate those properties which relate to generic form in its architectural context. These would be volume, mass, surface, and movement: movement being considered as a property of generic form, essential to the experience and therefore the comprehension of any architectural situation. These properties will provide the basic vocabulary for a formal language, that will clarify the conceptual, as well as the pictorial aspects of a specific situation. Terms

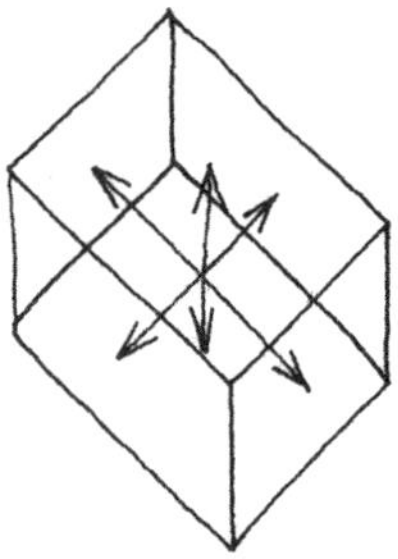

1.

VOLUME IS DEFINED AND CONTAINED SPACE.

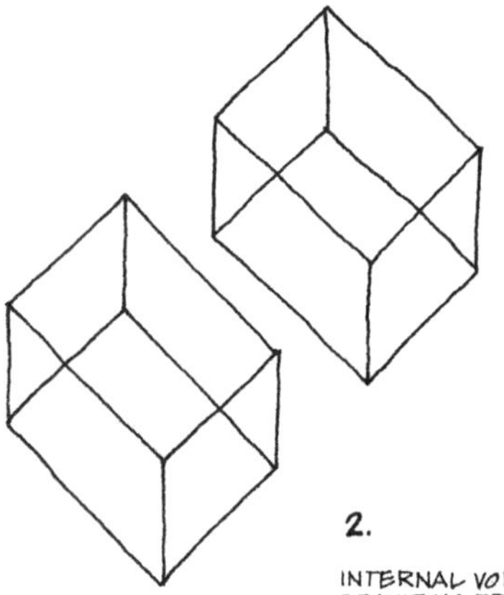

2.

INTERNAL VOLUME IS POSITIVE RESULTING FROM A PURPOSE STATEMENT OF ENCLOSURE

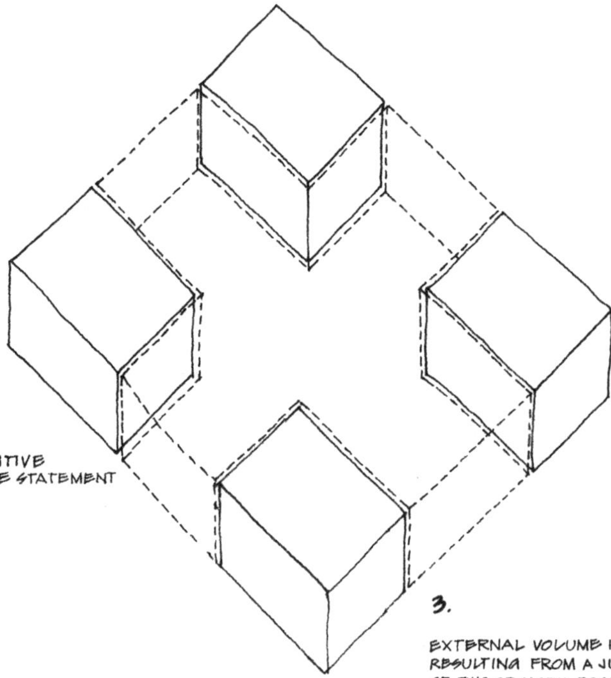

3.

EXTERNAL VOLUME IS NEGATIVE RESULTING FROM A JUXTAPOSITION OF TWO OR MORE POSITIVE VOLUMES.

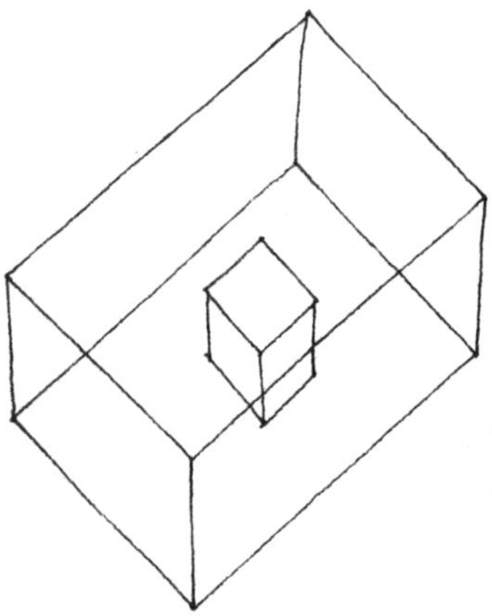

4.

ANOTHER INTERPRETATION POSITS ALL VOLUME AS NEGATIVE RELATIVE TO ANY OBJECT PLACED WITHIN IT.

SUCH AS LIGHT, BALANCE, PROPORTION. SCALE, AND SHAPE WILL BE DISCUSSED LATER BUT ONLY AS CONSIDERED IN RELATION TO A SPECIFIC FORM IN A SPECIFIC CONTEXT.[4.] THE GENERATING PROPERTY OF ALL ARCHITECTURAL FORM IS VOLUME, SINCE ARCHITECTURE ALONE AMONG THE PLASTIC MEANS OF EXPRESSION DEMANDS COMPREHENSION BOTH INTERNALLY AND EXTERNALLY.[5.] IT IS NECESSARY TO THE DEVELOPMENT OF THIS THESES TO CONSIDER ARCHITECTURE IN TERMS OF VOLUME RATHER THAN SPACE - A DISTINCTION WHICH IS NOT MERELY ACADEMIC AND PHILOLOGICAL.[6.] IN MODERN CRITICISM THE TERMS VOLUME AND SPACE HAVE OFTEN BEEN USED LOOSELY AND INTERCHANGEABLY SO THAT NEITHER IS ANY LONGER A USEFUL INSTRUMENT OF RATIONAL DISCOURSE. THE ESSENTIAL DIFFERNCE BETWEEN THE TERMS IS THAT VOLUME CAN BE THOUGHT OF IN A DYNAMIC SENSE: IT IS PARTICULARIZED, DEFINED AND CONTAINED SPACE. IT CAN BE THOUGHT OF AS BOTH EXERTING A PRESSURE AND CAPABLE OF RESISTING PRESSURES EXERTED UPON IT. THUS, 'SPACE', CONSIDERED AS A CONTINUOUS, UNBOUND CONDITION BECOMES A REDUNDANT TERM, EVEN THOUGH IT MUST BE CONCEDED THAT ALL FORMS EXIST IN THIS STATE. SPACE[7.] CANNOT ACT, FLOW, OR INTERPENETRATE IN ITS OWN RIGHT. ARCHITECTURAL FORM CAN BE THOUGHT OF AS 'VOLUME' THAT EXISTS IN 'SPACE'. VOLUME IS THE DYNAMIC CONDITION OF SPACE, BROUGHT ABOUT BY ITS LIMITATION AND CONTAINMENT: IT[8.] CANNOT BE THOUGHT OF IN AN UNSTRESSED CONDITION SINCE BY DEFINITION IT IS ACTIVATED SPACE. IT IS FURTHER NECESSARY TO DIFFERENTIATE BETWEEN INTERNAL AND EXTERNAL VOLUME.[9.] IT WILL BE ASSUMED THAT ALL INTERNAL VOLUME IS POSITIVE; RESULTING FROM A PURPOSEFUL STATEMENT OF ENCLOSURE AND CONTAINMENT, AND THAT ALL EXTERNAL VOLUME IS NEGATIVE; THE RESULTANT OF A JUXTAPOSITION OF TWO OR MORE POSITIVE VOLUMES WHICH CREATE AN ACTIVATED SPACE BETWEEN THEM. THIS ASSUMPTION PARTIALLY DENIES TWO POSSIBLE INTERPRETATIONS WHICH DO NOT SEEM RELEVANT OR PRECISE ENOUGH FOR THIS ARGUMENT. THE ONE POSITS ALL VOLUME AS NEGATIVE RELATIVE TO THE INDIVIDUAL PERSON TO ANY POSITIVE OBJECT PLACE WITHIN IT. THIS

4: c.f. Bruno Zevi - 'Architecture as space' see footnote above Chapter1 note.

5: see Luigi Moretti. 'Strutture e sequenze di spazi ' Spazio 7. Dec. 1952. He posits architecture as being read through chiaroscuro, plastic values, inside space and quality of material used; the most represent tive term of these being 'space'.

6: In 'The Earth, the Temple and the Gods' Yale 1962, Vincent Scully talks loosely of positive and negative space implying that negative space has no inherent forces: here the term 'volume' implies an initial conditioning of neutral space.

7: The word 'space' is here used as defined by Newton 'Absolute space in its own nature, without relation to anything external, remains always similar and immovable. Relative space is some movable dimension or measure of the absolute spaces'. 'Principia Mathematica'

8: Thus Panofsky, 'Meaning in the Visual Arts', p.21. - the 'one basic anti-thesis, differentiation versus continuity - volumetric limits versus illimited expanse (space) '.

9: see above note 6.

10: For the first see Arnheim 'Art and Visual Perception' London. 1955. The second interpretation is put forward by Erno Goldfinger, 'The Sensation of Space' Architectural Reviw. VXC. 1941. And also by

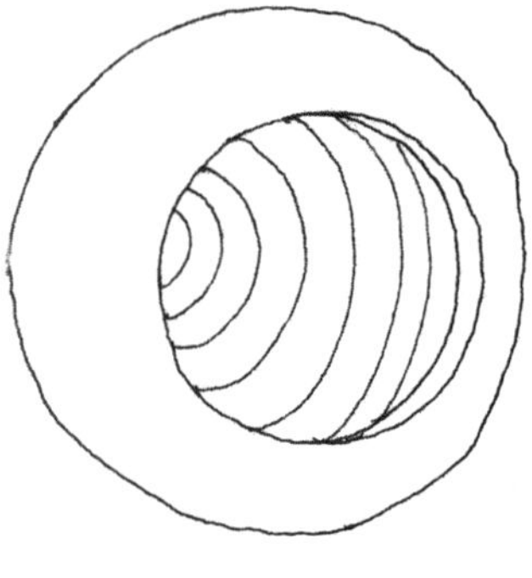

5.

A SECOND INTERPRETATION SAYS INTERNAL VOLUME IS CONCAVE –

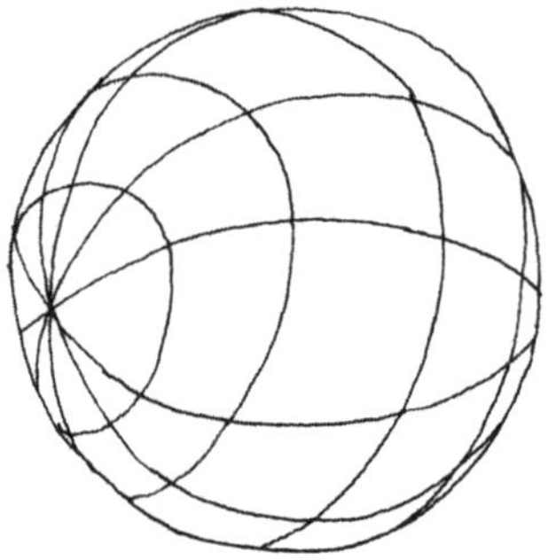

6.

– AND EXTERNAL VOLUME IS CONVEX.

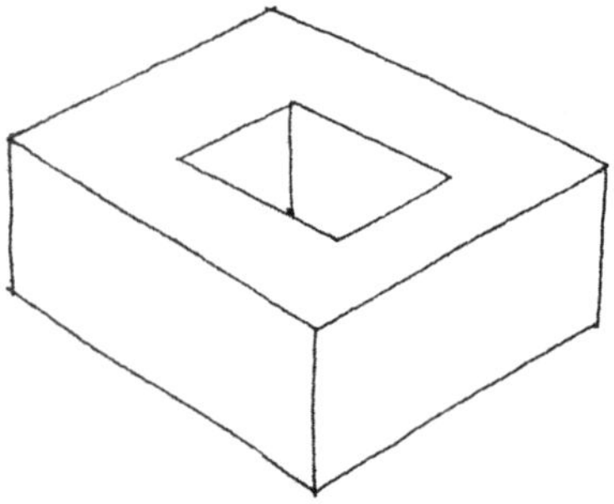

7.

CONVEX QUALITIES OF EXTERNAL VOLUME ARE HERE REGARDED AS 'MASS'

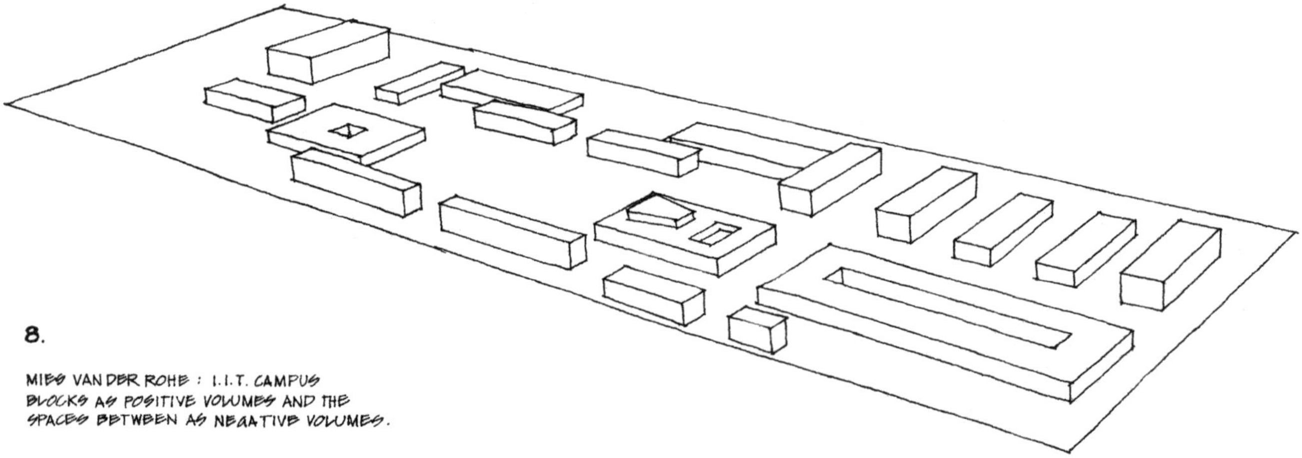

8.

MIES VAN DER ROHE : I.I.T. CAMPUS BLOCKS AS POSITIVE VOLUMES AND THE SPACES BETWEEN AS NEGATIVE VOLUMES.

ESTABLISHES THE INDIVIDUAL AS A UNITY BUT FAILS TO DISTINGUISH BETWEEN ENCLOSURE AND INTERVAL BOTH OF WHICH ARE TREATED AS NEGATIVE IN RELATION TO A HUMAN POSITIVE. THE SECOND INTERPRETATION WOULD ATTRIBUTE TO INTERNAL VOLUME THE QUALITIES OF CONCAVITY AND TO EXTERNAL VOLUME THE QUALITIES OF CONVEXITY WHICH ARE HERE CONSIDERED TO BE THOSE OF 'MASS', OR POSITIVE VOLUME;[10.] NEITHER OF THESE ASSUMPTIONS ASSIST IN ESTABLISHING THE CONCEPT OF TOTAL ENVIRONMENT PRODUCED FROM THE CONTROL OF BOTH POSITIVE AND NEGATIVE VOLUME. IT IS RATHER THE NOTION OF VOLUME AS THE BASIC UNITY THAT ALLOWS ALL CONDITIONS OF ENCLOSURE TO BE CONSIDERED AS POSITIVE AND ALL CONDITIONS OF INTERVAL AS NEGATIVE. THUS AT THE I.I.T. CAMPUS OF MIES VAN DER ROHE THE INDIVIDUAL BLOCKS BECOME THE POSITIVE VOLUMES, AND THE SPACES BETWEEN THEM THE NEGATIVE ONES. BOTH POSITIVE AND NEGATIVE ARE OF THE SAME SCALE AND CONFIGURATION AND BEGIN TO PRODUCE AN INTERWEAVING OR, IN GESTALT PSYCHOLOGICAL TERMS, A FIGURE-GROUND RELATIONSHIP, WHICH GIVES AN INITIAL ORDER TO THE TOTAL COMPOSITION.[11.]

INITIALLY, THE DYNAMIC STATE OF VOLUME RESULTS FROM THE NECESSITY TO RESIST THE CONTAINING FORCES ACTING UPON IT: THESE FORCES RESULTING FROM ANY DISTURBANCE, PHYSICAL OR ABSTRACT, THAT AFFECT THE NEUTRAL CONDITION OF SPACE. THE INTERNAL PRESSURE MAY BE THOUGHT OF AS A RESISTENCE TO THE LIMITING CONDITIONS: CONTAINING SURFACES, MOVEMENT OR CIRCULATION, AND OBJECTS (THOUGHT OF AS MASS) PLACED WITHIN THE VOLUME. FURTHERMORE ANY VOLUME CAN BE THOUGHT OF AS BOTH GIVING OR RECEIVING FORM, AGAIN ACCORDING TO THE SPECIFIC CONDITION OF BOTH INTERNAL AND EXTERNAL FORCES.[12.]

IT WILL BE NECESSARY TO DISCUSS IN DETAIL THE TWO BASIC CATEGORIES OF LIMITING

10: contin.

Steen Eiler Rasmussen. 'Experiencing Architecture' London. Goldfinger defines sculpture as 'Convex' and Architecture as 'Concave'.

11: c.f. Vincent Scully. Perspecta 4. 'Modern Architecture: toward a redefinition of style.' 'mass and void are defined by a single module'. Also G. Kepes op.cit. 'No fundamental exists in an optical sense between figure and back - ground, between positive and negative space'.

12: Moretti (op.cit. note 5 above) lists the properties of internal space as: geometric form: quantity of volume; density of light: pressure or energetic charge in relation to its limits (wall masses) and the energies these release. and again Kepes 'The vitality of any equilibrium depends upon the strength of the opposing forces which are in balance.' (p.121 op. cit.) See also Geoffrey Scott 'The Architecture of Humanism'. page 210: 'these masses are capable like ourselves of pressure and resistance.'

CONDITIONS: THE ONE, THE REMAINING PROPERTIES OF GENERIC FORM (MASS, SURFACE, AND MOVEMENT); THE OTHER, AN IMPLIED OR ACTUAL CARTESIAN GRID. IT IS THIS LATTER CONCEPT THAT PROVIDES THE MATRIX FOR ORDERING ANY VOLUMETRIC ENTITY. THIS GRID IS OF SUCH PERTINENCE TO THE CONTROL OF GENERIC FORM THAT IT MUST BE CONSIDERED IN A SEPARATE CONTEXT.

THE CONCEPT OF A SPATIAL, THREE-DIMENSIONAL, OR 'CARTESIAN' GRID THOUGHT OF AS A CONTINUUM PROVIDES THE ABSOLUTE REFERENCE FOR ARCHITECTURAL FORM, WHETHER GENERIC OR SPECIFIC.[13]

IN RELATION TO ANY FORM THIS GRID MUST BE THOUGHT OF AS AN ABSTRACT ENTITY. IT IS THE FRAME OF REFERENCE FOR ALL PERCEPTION: DERIVING, PRIMARILY FROM OUR PHYSICAL SENSE OF THE FORCES OF GRAVITY. WHEN SOMETHING DROPS IT DOES SO IN A STRAIGHT LINE THROUGH A VERTICAL PLANE (THE PLUMB-BOB IS THE MOST OBVIOUS EXAMPLE OF THIS). AGAIN WHEN A RECTILINEAR OBJECT IS PLACED ON END IT MUST STAND VERTICALLY OR IT TOPPLES OVER. IT IS SEEN TO STAND VERTICALLY IN RELATION TO ITS ANGLE OF INTERSECTION WITH THE HORIZONTAL PLANE, THE OTHER ASPECT OF THE GRID. THESE TWO COORDINATES CROSS REFER BECAUSE OF THEIR CRITICAL ANGLE OF INTERSECTION, THE RIGHT ANGLE.[14] IT IS EVIDENT THAT THESE COMPONENTS ULTIMATELY REFER TO THE FORCES OF GRAVITY, FOR IF THE HORIZONTAL PLANE IS CANTED THE VERTICAL ELEMENT WILL TOPPLE. THE HORIZONTAL PLANE MOREOVER RELATES VISUALLY TO THE HORIZON OR TO ANY WATER LEVEL, NEITHER OF WHICH THOUGH IS STRICTLY PLANAR: YET THEY BOTH MUST BE CONSIDERED AS PERCEPTUAL ABSOLUTES IN THIS CONTEXT. THE HORIZONTAL PLANE MAY BE CONCEIVED OF AS A PROJECTION OF ANY TANGENT TO THE EARTH'S SURFACE. IN ITS ARCHITECTURAL REFERENCE THE HORI-

13: See Max Jammer 'Concepts of Space' N.Y. 1960 . 'The use of a Three-dimensional co-ordinate system, and in particular of a rectangular spacial co-ordinate system was not thought reasonable until the 17th century (Descartes, Frano van Schooren etc.) '

14: See Le Corbusier 'City of Tomorrow' 'The right angle is the essential and sufficient implement of action because it enables us to determine space with an absolute exactness..' 'There is only one right angle '. He also relates this to a condition of culture (rather as the later proponents of standardisation- Prof. Ciribini etc.) 'Culture is an orthogonal state of mind'.

-ZONTAL SHOULD BE THOUGHT OF AS NON-DIRECTIONAL SINCE CRITICAL POINTS OF INTERSECTION COULD ARISE FROM A DIRECTIONA QUALITY BEING ATTRIBUTED TO THIS PLANE.

EVERYTHING IS SEEN IN SOME RELATION TO THIS GRID WHETHER IT BE MAN MADE OR NATURAL. WHEN WE SEE A TREE, WE DESCRIBE IT AS BEING DEFORMED FROM A GENERIC ANTECEDENT – ITS VERTICAL AXIS. WHEN WE PERCEIVE A LANDSCAPE, WE NOTICE ITS DEFORMATIONS – ITS ROLLING QUALITIES, ITS HARSH OR GENTLE NATURE ALWAYS RELATIVE TO A HORIZONTAL ABSOLUTE.[15] IN THE SAME WAY ALL MAN-MADE OBJECTS ARE PERCEPTUALLY REFERED TO A GENERIC ABSOLUTE, THE PLATONIC SOLIDS: CONES, SPHERES, CUBES, ETC., EACH HAVING AN AXIAL REFERENCE AS THEIR BASIS. THEREFORE ANY LINEAR OR CENTROIDAL FORM CAN BE COMPREHENDED WITH REFERENCE TO THE SPATIAL GRID. A LINEAR FORM IS PERCEIVED THROUGH A WEIGHTING OF ONE AXIS, EITHER THE HORIZONTAL OR THE VERTICAL. THUS A CYLINDER REFERS TO EITHER A VERTICAL OR A HORIZONTAL AXIS, WHILE A CENTROIDAL FORM SUCH AS A CUBE HAS NO DOMINANT REFERENCE EVEN THOUGH THE GENERATION OF THE FORM IS IMPLIED FROM THE EQUALITY OF ALL THREE AXES.

15: See for example George Santayana 'The Sense of Beauty' New York, 1955. 'organised nature the source of apperceptive forms..by a constant repetition of certain sequences and a recurring exactitude of mathematical relations.'

IN ITS SPECIFIC SENSE THE SPATIAL GRID HAS PARTICULAR SIGNIFICANCE TO MODERN ARCHITECTURE. THE DEVELOPMENT OF THE POINT-SUPPORT AND THE NON-LOADBEARING WALL HAS ALLOWED CERTAIN SPECIFIC QUALITIES TO ACCRUE TO THE GRID.

IT CAN BE POSTULATED THAT THE GRID PROVIDES THREE COODINATES: ONE HORIZONTAL AND TWO VERTICAL, AND THAT THESE MAY BE GIVEN DIFFERENT VALUES DEPENDING ON THE SPECIFIC SITUATION; BECAUSE OF ITS ASSOCIATIONS WITH THE FORCES OF GRAVITY THE HORIZONTAL REFERENCE OFTEN PREDOMINATES. THIS REFERENCE CAN BE SEEN IN MOST OF MIES' PLANNING.

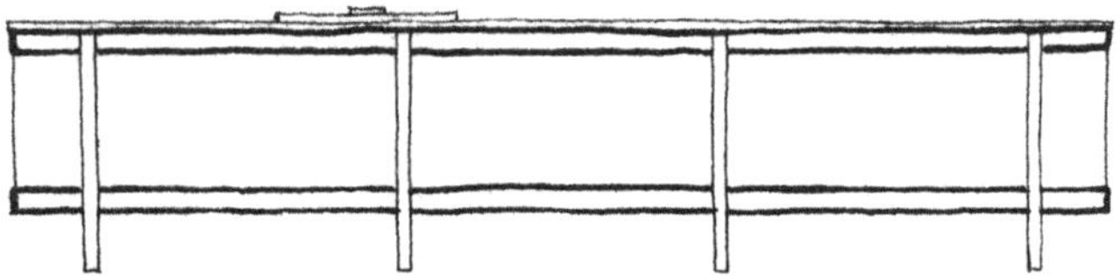

9.

MIES VAN DER ROHE: FARNSWORTH HOUSE
ABSOLUTE QUALITY OF THE HORIZONTALS.

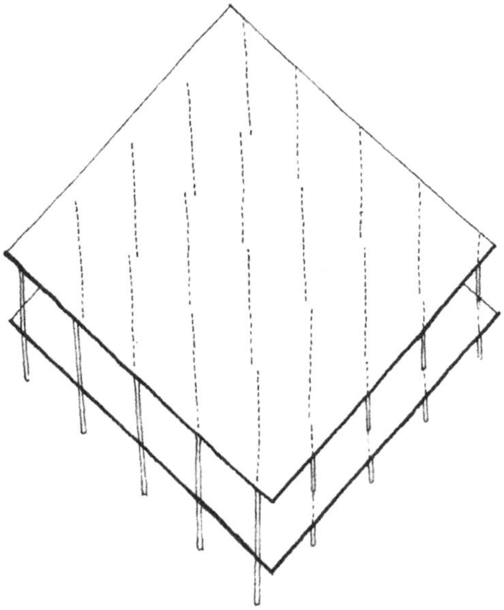

10.

LE CORBUSIER : POISSY
A HORIZONTAL CONTINUUM.

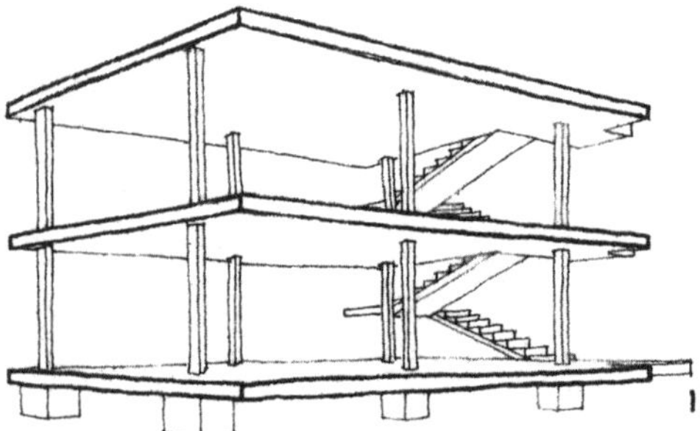

11.

LE CORBUSIER : MAISON DOMINO :
HORIZONTAL ABSOLUTE RELATIVE
TO A VERTICAL GRID.

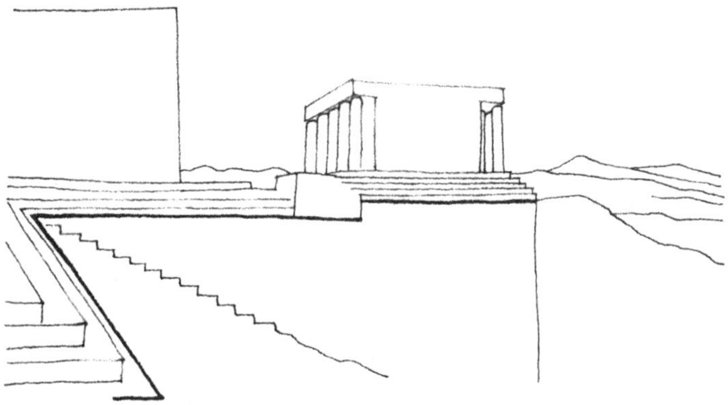

12.

THE VERTICAL AND HORIZONTAL PLANES OF
THE ACROPOLIS ACT AS THE ABSOLUTE
REFERENCES FOR THE MOUNTAINS BEYOND.

Mies van der Rohe uses the horizontal in specific situations to state clearly its absolute quality.[16.9] In doing so he is merely presenting a fragment of an infinite grid: a similar condition is implied by Mondrian in his painting. For Mies the column only provides a volumetric definition, and not a reference to a vertical absolute. In this context an interesting study could be made of the changing column section in Mies' architecture and its implications both to the particular and absolute situations. It will suffice to note here that he uses different column sections to imply directional movement as well as static and continuous volumetric order. This emphasis on the horizontal is clearly shown in Le Corbusier's house at Poissy, where he also proposes a horizontal continuum.[17.10] Le Corbusier's early diagram for the 'Maison Domino' also postulates a horizontal absolute using horizontal volumetric slices relative to a vertical grid.[18.11] In each case the plan becomes free to take any specific form in relation to this absolute. Indeed, in all of Le Corbusier's work the concept of the grid as an absolute reference can be noted. This reference has its basis in Le Corbusier's analysis of the acroposis in 'Vers Une Architecture'.[19.12] Here the Acropolis can be considered as the horizontal plane and the columnar grid of the Parthenon as the vertical plane. These then act as the absolute references and provide the perceptual tension to the mountains beyond which may be thought of as 'mass' as the specific conditon, This juxtaposition of the specific form – mountains, and the generic form – the columnar grid creates a dialectic situation.[20.] This implication is inherent in all of Le Corbusier's architecture, and it is from this dialectic basis that the systemic development of his work can be traced and analysed. It is evident that the columnar order necessary to the volumetric definition and to the organis-

16: Thus the Barcelona Pavilion: 'its horisontal planes... and its scattered vertical surfaces ... mark out one of Moholy's (Nagy) "pieces of space" in such a way that a 'full penetration with outer space' is effectively achieved. 'if there is a building in which the horizontal slabs are absolute, it is Mies's Barcelona Pavilion'. Reyner Banham. 'Theory and Design in the First Machine Age'. London 1960.

17: Le Corbusier 'Oevre Complete' Vol. I.

18: 'Oevre Complete' Vol. I.

19: 'Vers une Architecture' (English Edition pp. 43, 50 and chapter III

20: This relationship is also hinted at by Vincent Scully in 'The Earth, the Temple, and the Gods'. The value of the horizontal absolute in unifying the Greek temenos is also pointed out by Dr. Martienssen, 'The Idea of Space in Greek Architecture'; he also stresses the columnar order providing volumetric cohesion relating exterior and interior space.

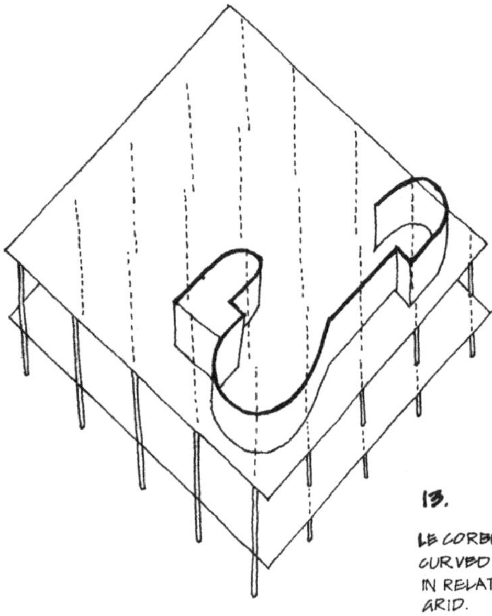

13.

LE CORBUSIER : POISSY:
CURVED SURFACES TENSIONED
IN RELATION TO AN ABSOLUTE
GRID.

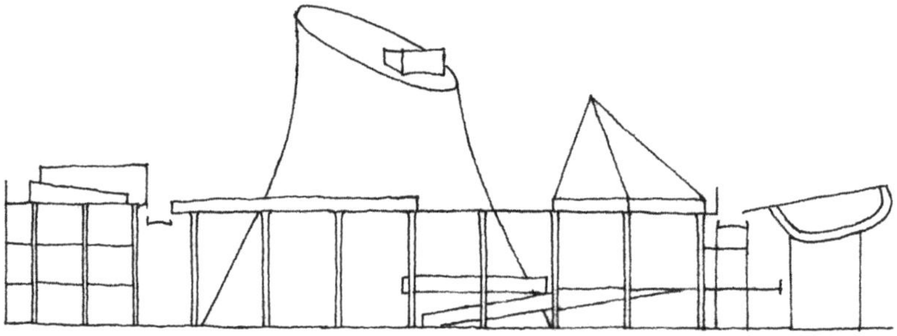

14.

LE CORBUSIER : ASSEMBLY PALACE, CHANDIGARH
MATURE STATEMENT OF MASS-GRID RELATIONSHIP.

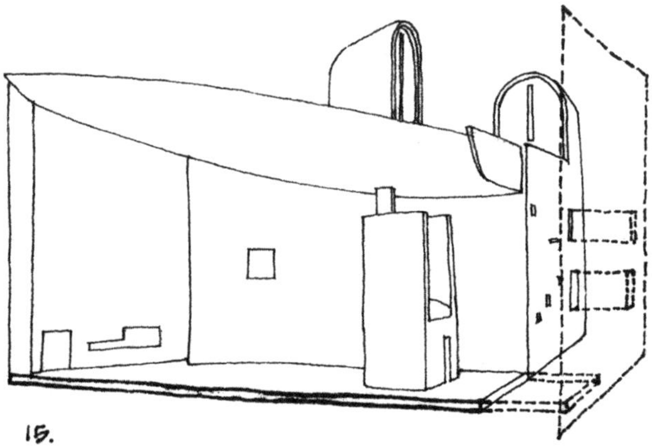

15.

LE CORBUSIER : RONCHAMP, STRESSING OF CURVED 'SURFACES' SEEN AS 'MASS'
IN RELATION TO A PICTURE PLANE OR ABSOLUTE GRID

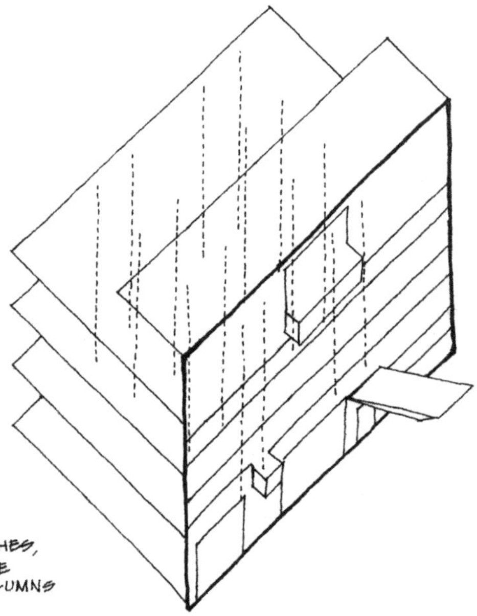

16.

LE CORBUSIER : GARCHES,
FRONTALS AS SURFACE
ORTHOGONALS AS COLUMNS

-ation of the specific curved surfaces[13] at Garches[21.] and Poissy[22.] is derived from this reference to geometric absolutes. The curved surfaces, as can be seen in later projects, are merely incipient 'mass' which receive their precise location in some reference to the grid. The 'mass-grid' relationship reaches maturity in the Assembly Palace at Chandigarh[23.] and at La Tourette[24.] where the curved surfaces are replaced by fully stated 'mass'.[14] Moreover at La Tourette the implications of the systemic development can only be comprehended in relation to the spatial grid. Perhaps the most mature statement of the 'mass - grid' relationship appears at Ronchamp.[25.][15] The essence of the building is a complex 'mass-surface' dialectic which becomes fully stressed only in relation to the orthogonal grid. Here the grid is an implied, conceptual reference. The only physical acknowledgement to it can be seen in the rectilinear cuts in the warped surfaces andin the altars on the external podium. The openings and the altars seem to have been pulled from the wall by an external force: from the spatial grid which acts to hold the total complex in a rigid, tensioned state. The exterior podium, which bears no actual relation to the internal floor level, provides a further reference, by stating a horizontal absolute, to the orthogonal grid. It is also possible in certain situations to discriminate between the two vertical coordinates: the frontal and the othogonal. Le Corbusier makes this distinction at Garches where the frontal is read as a surface while the orthogonals are expressed by a columnar organisation[16] Thus the horizontal and frontals which are both treated as 'planes ' are given the same relative quality and thereby an inverse or anti-gravitational reading is inferred from them. In most cases when the horizontal is not discriminated the vertical columnar order must provide the absolute grid ref-

21: Oevre Complete Vol. II. 1929-34

22: Oevre Complete Vol. II.

23: Oevre Complete Vol VI. 1952-7

24: Oevre Complete Vol VI. See also Colin Rowe, Arch. Review June 1961

25: Oevre Complete Vol. VI.

-ERENCE AND THIS CONSEQUENTLY RESTRICTS THE DEVELOPMENT OF THE PLAN WITHIN IT. NO CONDITION OF TOTAL ORDER IS POSSIBLE IF NEITHER THE HORIZONTAL NOR THE VERTICAL IS TREATED AS AN ABSOLUTE SINCE ANY RESULTANT FORM WILL HAVE NO FRAMEWORK OF REFERENCE.

TO UNDERSTAND VOLUME WE MUST INTRODUCE THE NOTION OF MOVEMENT, AND POSTULATE THAT AN EXPERIENCE OF ARCHITECTURE IS THE SUM OF A LARGE NUMBER OF EXPERIENCES - EACH ONE OF THEM APPREHENDED VISUALLY, IT IS TRUE AS WELL AS THROUGH OTHER SENSES; BUT ACCUMULATED OVER A MUCH LONGER TIME SPAN THAN IS REQUIRED FOR THE INITIAL APPRECIATION OF A PICTORIAL WORK; AND BUILDING UP INTO A CONCEPTUAL, NOT A PERCEPTUAL, WHOLE.[26] AND SINCE THIS WHOLE IS CONCEPTUAL IT MUST HAVE A CLARITY OF CONCEPT: ITS ARGUMENT MUST BE INTELLECTUALLY AS WELL AS VISUALLY COMPREHENSIBLE. THE GESTALT PSYCHOLOGISTS HAVE CONCLUSIVELY DEMONSTRATED THAT COMPREHENSIBILITY DEPENDS ON ESSENTIALLY SIMPLE CONFIGURATIONS, OF WHICH THE SQUARE, THE RECTANGLE, AND THE CIRCLE ARE EXAMPLES. WHEN THESE ARE PROJECTED INTO THE THIRD DIMENSIONS THEY BECOME THE CUBE, THE RECTANGULAR BLOCK, AND THE SPHERE, IN SHORT, THE GENERIC FORMS AND BASIC SOLIDS THAT HAVE BEEN DISCUSSED ABOVE. EQUALLY, ONCE THEY TAKE THE FORM OF AN ARCHITECTURAL ENTITY WHICH MUST BE EXPERIENCED FROM WITHIN AND WITHOUT, AND IN MOST CASES FROM A VARIETY OF LEVELS, THE TOTAL OF APPERCEPTION IS BUILT UP THROUGH THE PROCESS OF MOVEMENT OR CIRCULATION. IN THIS SENSE MOVEMENT IS CONSIDERED TO BE A FACTOR THAT IS EXTERNAL TO THE FABRIC OF THE BUILDING: IT IS NOT A QUALITY OF THE WORK ITSELF BUT RATHER A PATTERN OF BEHAVIOUR WHICH THE BUILDING ENFORCES ON THE INDIVIDUAL.[27] MOVEMENT CAN THEN BE DEFINED AS THE CIRCULATION OF PEOPLE IN ANY ARCHITECTURAL ENVIRONMENT. MOVEMENT CAN BE THOUGHT OF AS EITHER A GEOMETRIC VECTOR OR AN EX-

26: c.f. Geoffrey Scott : p. 227. 'Space in fact is liberty of movement. That is its value to us and as such it enters our physical consciousness....the space has suggested a movement (the nave of a church) A symmetrical space, on the other hand, duly proportioned to the body invites no movement in any one direction more than another'. Also see G. Kepes p.59 op.cit.

27: H. Woelfflin and others tended to regard movement as a quality of the specific work of art itself. James Adam praised Vanbrugh for his 'quality of movement as picturesque'

-TERNAL FORCE AND EVEN AS A NEGATIVE VOLUME, WHICH CAN THEN BE GIVEN AN APPROXIMATE VALUE FROM ITS SIZE, INTENSITY AND DIRECTION. THUS A SINGLE DOOR WITH AN INFREQUENT PASSAGE OF PEOPLE THROUGH IT WOULD NOT PRODUCE A VECTOR OF EQUAL MAGNITUDE TO A SERIES OF DOORS SERVING CONSTANT TRAFFIC. THE NEED FOR FORMAL CLARITY AND UNMISTAKEABLE REFERENCE TO SOME WELL-UNDERSTOOD ARCHETYPAL SOLID THEREBY BECOMES STILL MORE URGENT, SINCE THE PERSON EXPERIENCING ANY ORGANISATION MUST BE ABLE TO HOLD IN HIS VISUAL AND SOMATIC MEMORY AT THE END OF THE PROCESS EVERYTHING WHICH HAS IMPINGED UPON IT SINCE THE BEGINNING. MOREOVER IT IS NOT ONLY THIS CLARITY OF EXPRESSION WHICH GIVES MEANING TO OUR MOVEMENT, BUT IT IS THE MOVEMENT ITSELF WHICH GIVES MEANING AND COMPREHENSIBILITY TO THE TOTAL ORGANISATION.[28.] THUS THE TERM MOVEMENT IS USED HERE IN THE SENSE THAT MANY CRITICS HAVE USED THE WORD TIME. HOWEVER 'MOVEMENT' SEEMS TO BE A MORE PRECISE DEFINITION OF THE ARCHITECTURAL EXPERIENCE THAN 'TIME', SINCE 'TIME' COULD IMPLY A STATIC INTERPRETATION WHEREAS 'MOVEMENT' ENCOMPASSES 'TIME', 'INTERVAL', AND 'CIRCULATION'. IT IS IN THIS CONTEXT THAT THE TERM 'MOVEMENT' MUST BE THOUGHT OF AS A PROPERTY OF GENERIC FORM. VOLUME CANNOT BE THOUGHT OF WITHOUT MOVEMENT INTO IT, SINCE BY ITS NATURE IT EXISTS TO ACCOMMODATE MOVEMENT. THEREFORE THE NEUTRAL STATE OF VOLUME CAN ONLY BE CONSIDERED IN THE ABSTRACT, SINCE ALL PHYSICAL MANIFESTATIONS OF VOLUME ARE AFFECTED BY MOVEMENT. THIS MOVEMENT AFFECTS AND MODIFIES THE EQUILIBRIUM OF GENERIC FORM, AND THEREBY PLAYS AN INTEGRAL PART IN THE GIVING OF FORM AND THE RESULTING MANIFESTATION OF THIS PROCESS. IT WILL BE SEEN THAT THIS PROPERTY OF MOVEMENT IS ONE OF THE GENERATING ELEMENTS IN THE DEVELOPMENT OF ANY ARCHITECTURAL SYSTEM.

IT IS NOT POSSIBLE TO CONSIDER THE NOTIONS OF 'MASS' AND 'SURFACE' IN ISOLATION

27: contin.

(both Sir Joshua Reynolds in 13th Discourse and Woelfflin link the 'Principle of movement' with a 'picturesque' quality). Robert Adam (1st Vol. of 'works') defines architectural movement as 'that rising and falling, advancing and receding, with the convexity and the concavity' . James Adam wrote from Rome in 1762 'of the elevation and its movement ': 'nothing contributing half so much to the beauty of buildings viewed from a distance as movement', and he talks of 'movement in the section' contributed by the 'vaults and the domes'.

28: See for example Martienssen's analysis of Greek temene, and the inherent movement patterns. Scully also talks of the 'informing principle of movement'.

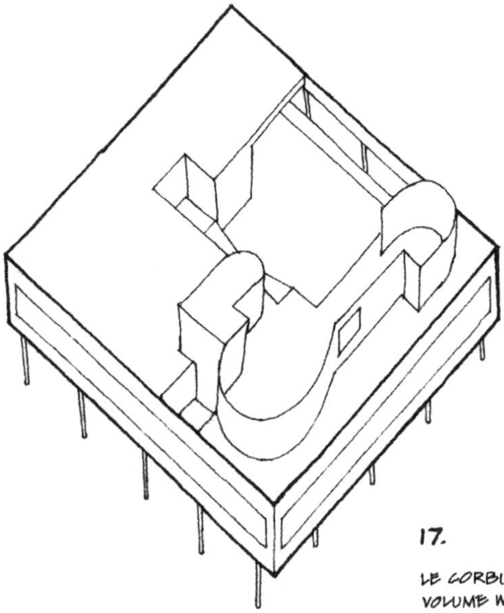

17.

LE CORBUSIER : POISSY
VOLUME WITH A SURFACE MEMBRANE
STRETCHED AROUND IT.

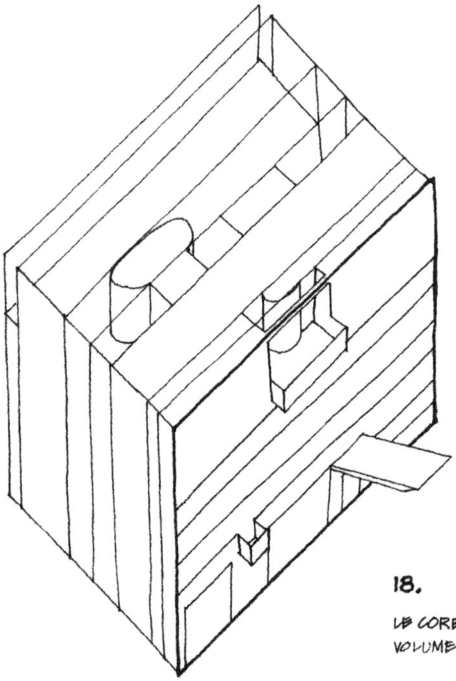

18.

LE CORBUSIER : GARCHES
VOLUME AS A SERIES OF VERTICAL PLANES

SINCE THEY EXIST IN RELATION TO EACH OTHER, AND INDEED TO MOST ARCHITECTURAL EXPRESSION THEY ARE PLACED IN A DIALECTICAL SITUATION TO CLARIFY THEIR EXISTENCE MORE FORCEFULLY.[29] AS BOTH OF THESE CONCEPTS ARE MEANS OF CONTAINING SPACE THEY MUST BY DEFINITION BE PROPERTIES OF GENERIC FORM, SINCE THEY ARE INHERENT TO THE CONTROL OF ANY VOLUME. PURELY IN TERMS OF LOGIC IT WOULD BE POSSIBLE TO SAY THAT 'MASS' COULD ONLY BE CONSIDERED AS AN ABSTRACT IDEA, SINCE ONLY THE EXTERNAL LAYER OF 'MASS', THE SURFACE, IS SEEN, FROM WHICH 'MASS' IS INFERRED. AGAIN, IN ABSOLUTE TERMS, THE VALIDITY OF DISCUSSING SURFACE AS A SEPARATE ENTITY COULD BE QUESTIONED, IN THAT SURFACE COULD BE CONSIDERED AS EITHER THE LAST LAYER OF A VOLUME, ITS 'SKIN', OR CONVERSLY THAT VOLUME COULD BE THOUGHT OF AS MADE UP OF AN INFINITE NUMBER OF SURFACES,OR PLANES.[30] EXAMPLES OF BOTHE THESE INTERPRETATIONS OF SURFACE CAN BE SEEN IN LE CORBUSIER'S HOUSES AT POISSY AND GARCHES. THE FORMER CAN BE CITED AS AN EXAMPLE OF A VOLUME WITH A SURFACE MEMBRANE STRETCHED TIGHTLY ABOUT IT, WHILE THE LATTER IS A VOLUME EXPRESSED BY A SERIES OF VERTICAL SURFACES;[17,18] THE VOLUME ITSELF BEING CONSIDERED AS A SERIES OF VOLUMETRIC SLICES OR THICKENED PLANES MUCH AS AN IMAGINARY SOLID THAT COULD BE FORMED FROM A PACK OF CARDS. HOWEVER THESE DEFINITIONS DO NOT HEOP IN ESTABLISHING THESE TWO PROPERTIES IN RELATION TO EACH OTHER. IT IS NECESSARY TO MAKE A DISTINCTION BETWEEN THE TWO IN ORDER TO RELATE THEM AS PROPERTIES OF GENERIC FORM.

MASS IN SCIENTIFIC TERMS IS THE QUANTITY OF MATTER THAT A BODY CONTAINS, A DENSE AGGREGATION, — IN OTHER WORDS, A SOLID. IT IS THIS CONCEPT OF MASS THOUGHT OF AS A SOLID THAT CAN BE USED IN A METAPHORICAL SENSE, TO PROVIDE A DEFINITION THAT IS ANTI-THETICAL TO SURFACE. IT CAN NOW BE SAID THAT MASS IS

29: See Giulio Carlo Argan. Vol. IX. 'Journal of the Warburg and Courtauld Institutes'. 1946. 'The Architecture of Brunelleschi and the Origins of Perspective Theory.' 'The plane, as a complete representation of space; and the surface.. is..still matter ..The outer skin of things, although it is the extreme limit of matter, its suture with space. The plane is.. a geometric entity, the 'intersection'- a pure mental abstraction'.

30: Argan, (op.cit. above note 29) 'But the principle of the homogeneity of space destroys that of the homogeneity of matter: for in order to think of space as homogenous, that is, as uninterrupted by the presence of bodies, it is necessary to think of those bodies as composed of space, that is as broken up into a succession of planes.'

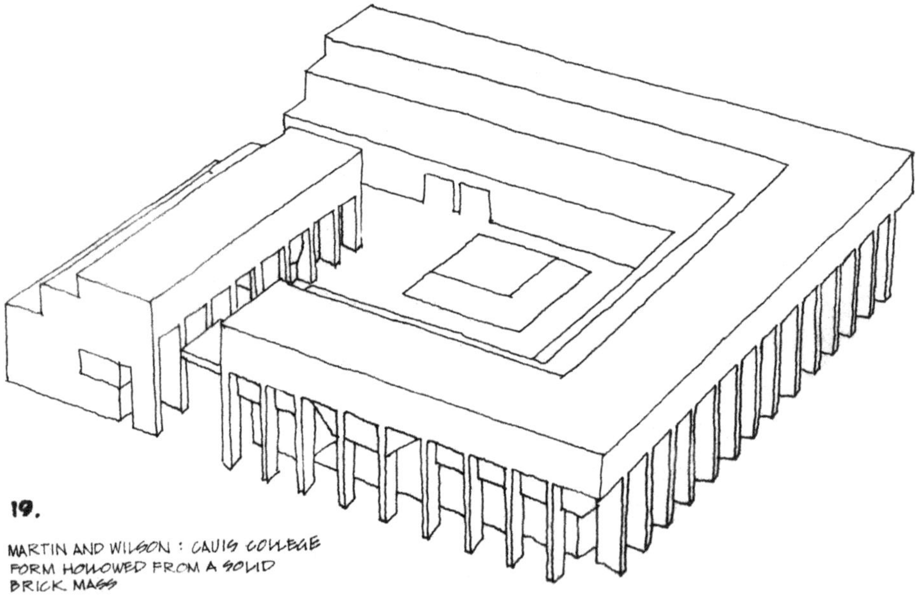

19.

MARTIN AND WILSON : CAUIS COLLEGE
FORM HOLLOWED FROM A SOLID
BRICK MASS

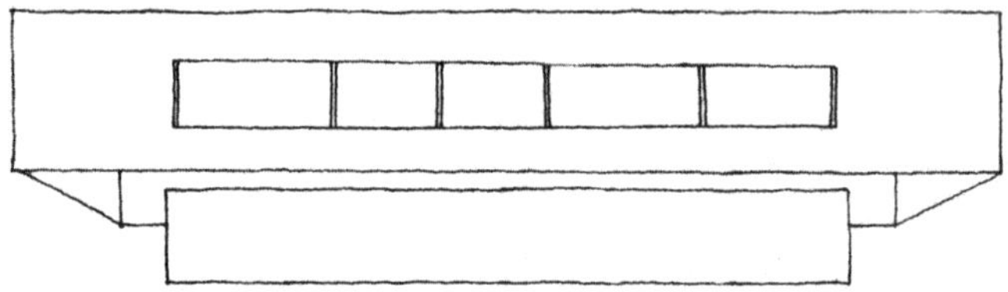

20.

MARCEL BREUER : CANTILEVERED HOUSE
MITRING OF WOOD AT CORNERS TO EXPRESS
SURFACE SKIN.

LUIGI MORETTI : CASA ASTREA

21.

LUIGI MORETTI : CASA GIRASOLE
EVIDENT INTENTION TO EXPRESS SURFACE PLANES

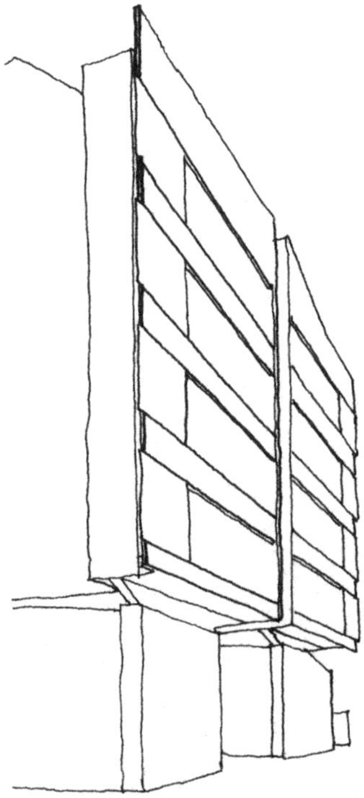

LUIGI MORETTI : CASA GIRASOLE

THAT STATE OF AN ARCHITECTURAL COMPOSITION, THAT APPEARS TO HAVE BEEN A SOLID IN ITS ORIGINAL STATE, BUT WHICH HAS BEEN CORRODED AND EATEN AWAY TO PRODUCE ITS RESULTANT FORM. MICHELANGELO'S REFERENCE TO A SCULPTURE AS 'THE SORT THAT IS EXECUTED BY CUTTING AWAY FROM THE BLOCK' SERVES AS AN ADEQUATE DEFINITION OF 'MASS' IN TERMS OF GENERIC FORM.[31] THE NEW CAIUS COLLEGE HOSTEL BY SIR LESLIE MARTIN AND COLIN ST. J. WILSON IS AN EXAMPLE OF A 'MASS' BUILDING.[32.19] HERE THE COURTYARD AND THE PERIMETER ARCADES SEEM AS IF THEY HAVE BEEN HOLLOWED OUT FROM A SOLID BRICK 'MASS'. AS 'MASS' IN MICHAELANGELO'S TERMS REFERS TO SCULPTURE, SO 'SURFACE' REFERS TO HIS DEFINITION OF PAINTING: 'THE SORT THAT IS EXECUTED BY BUILDING UP RESEMBLES A PAINTING'.[33] IN THIS CONTEXT SURFACE STANDS IN OPPOSITION TO MASS; IT CAN NOT MERELY BE THOUGHT OF AS THE EXTERNAL LAYER OF VOLUME. IT MUST NOW BE CONSIDERED SURFACE WHEN THERE IS A CLEAR INTENT TO PRESENT THE EXTERNAL APPEARANCE OF A BUILDING AS BEING BUILT-UP, AS FROM A PACK OF CARDS, IN AN ADDITIVE PROCESS. SURFACE THOUGHT OF IN THIS CONTEXT IS BY NATURE PLANAR AND THEREFORE CAN BE EASILY READ IN ANTITHESIS TO MASS. HOWEVER, THER IS ANOTHER INTERPRETATION OF SURFACE, THAT OF A MEMBRANE OR SKIN, WHICH IS NOT AS EASILY DISTINGUISHED FROM 'MASS'. THE DIFFERENTIATION BETWEEN SURFACE 'SKIN' OR SURFACE 'PLANE' AND 'MASS'. DEPENDS LARGELY ON THE PLACEMENT AND SIZE OF OPENINGS, THE TREATMENT OF CORNER CONDITIONS, AND THE MATERIAL USED. THUS IN MARCEL BREUER'S CANTILEVER HOUSE THE MITRING OF THE WOOD AND THE BUTTING OF THE GLAZING AT THE CORNERS WOULD IMPLY A SURFACE SKIN OR MEMBRANE STRETCHED TIGHTLY AROUND THE BUILDING.[20] MORETTI'S INTENTION TO EXPRESS A SERIES OF SURFACE PLANES AT THE CASA GIRASOLE IS EVIDENT IN THEIR ARTICULATION FROM THE BODY OF THE BUILDING.[34. 21,22]

31: See Anthony Blunt, 'Artistic Theory in Italy'.

32: c.f. Casabella.

33: For an equation between mass: sculpture; painting: surface see Erno Goldfinger op. cit. above.

34: c.f. Moretti, Spazio 7, 'Space has as a Rind the Surface that conditions it and which at the same time the space itself has generated.'

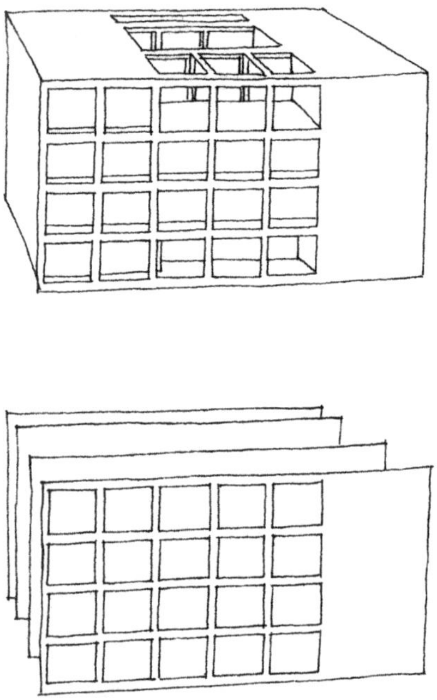

22.

GIUSEPPE TERRAGNI : CASA DEL FASCIO
SOLID-CUT-AWAY OR ADDITIVE PLANES

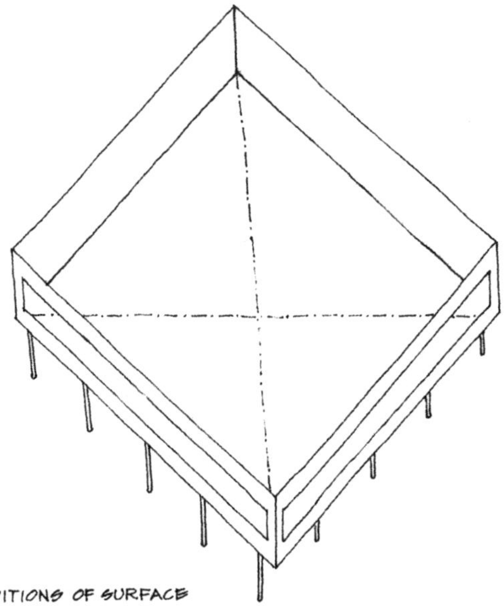

23.

ALL CONDITIONS OF SURFACE
SKIN SEEN AS CENTROIDAL.

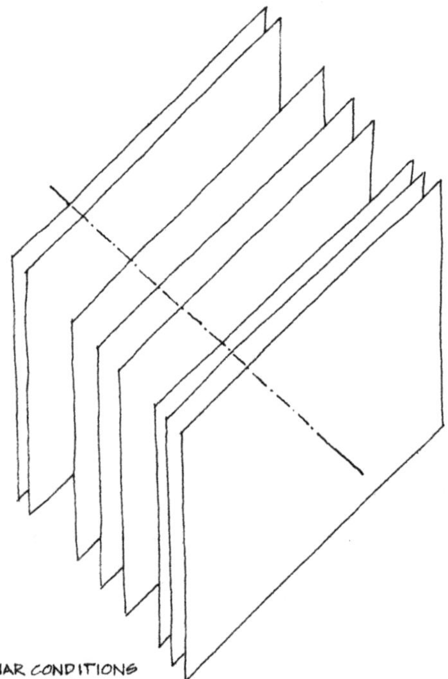

24.

ALL PLANAR CONDITIONS
SEEN AS LINEAR

The concept of an additive as opposed to a cutaway building can be used in a dialectical situation to produce a purposeful ambiguity and a resultant tension in the external form. This ambiguity may perceptually denote a conceptual opposition inherent in the internal and external requirements. A good example of this is Terragni's Casa del Fascio where a subtle placing of voids with respect to solids can be read in one instance as solid-cut-away and another as additive planes.[22] Initially it would seem that all conditions of surface 'skin' could be categorized as centroidal, since the wrapping quality of a skin presupposes some central element which is to be contained.[23] On the other hand all conditions requiring a 'planar' expression could be thought of a linear since they usually evolve from a directional vector.[24] In this sense, Garches, even though it is cubic in volume might be considered as 'linear' because of the directional planar development from the front facade, whereas Poissy which is enclosed by a surface 'skin' can be thought of as 'centroidal'. It is the intent to produce a building as either 'mass', 'surface', or a dialectic involving both that must be clearly stated; and that this statement must provide a perceptual clarification and order for the conceptual basis of any system. The importance of the distinction between mass and surface to the expression and clarity of a complex volumetric system relative to its generic origin, will be amplified in the analyses of formal systems.

It has been demonstrated that all specific architectural form can be related to a generic antecedent and that the properties of this generic root cannot be considered subjectively. The comprehensibility of the generic antecedent is the necessary precondition for the clarity of the intent and function of the specific form. From the fundamental state of generic form, its formal con-

-DITION, WHICH SUGGESTS ITS OWN INHERENT ORDER A FORMAL LANGUAGE CAN BE DEVELOPED THAT ORDERS THE EVOLUTION OF SPECIFIC FORMS IN A PARTICULAR ARCHITECTURAL SITUATION. MOREOVER IT IS THE ABSOLUTE AND THEREBY DEFINITIVE NATURE OF THESE GENERIC PROPERTIES THAT ALONE CAN PROVIDE THE RATIONAL BASIS FOR THIS FORMAL LANGUAGE.

35: Thus Luigi Moretti in 'Eclettismo e Unita di Linguaggio', Spazio I. July 1950. 'Ogni desidevio e spinta esspressivi travano percio in un linguaggio raggiunto, lo schema, la matrice (la forma?) per distendervi i loro andamenti - esigenze - essenziali; i residue espressivi - i minori rapporti - sono lasciati alla piena liberta di resoluzione contingente che non scalfisce l' ordine generale'. And Bruno Zevi in 'Poetica dell'Architettura Neoplastica'. p.9. - 'Della sintassi e della grammatica tuttavia, e piie facile dire male che farne a meno'.

IN THE FIRST PART OF THIS THESIS THE IDEA WAS INTRODUCED THAT AN ESSENTIAL REQUIREMENT OF ANY MEANS OF COMMUNICATION IS THAT THERE SHOULD BE CLARITY AND COMPREHENSIBILITY IN THE TRANSMISSION OF AN IDEA FROM ITS AUTHOR TO ITS RECEIVER: HENCE THE NEED FOR A FORMAL ORDERING CAPABLE OF MAKING PERCEPTUALLY MANIFEST THE CONCEPTUAL ESSENCE OF A BUILDING. IT IS THIS ORDERING OF FORM THAT MUST BE CONSIDERED AS A NECESSARY PRECONDITION FOR ANY VALID OR RATIONAL ARCHITECTURE.

1: c.f. Bruno Zevi, 'Architecture as Space'.

THIS ORDER CAN BE REGARDED AS A COMPLEX DIALECTIC RESULTING FROM THE RESPECTIVE DEMANDS OF GENERIC AND SPECIFIC FORM WITHIN THE DESIGN PROCESS. FORM IN ITS GENERIC STATE WILL PROVIDE THE CONCEPTUAL REFERENCE FOR ALL PHYSICAL MANIFESTATIONS OF SPECIFIC FORM, AS WELL AS GIVE THE BASIS FOR THE SPECIFIC ORDERING OF THIS FORM. FORM THOUGHT OF IN ITS CONCEPTUAL STATE MUST ACKNOWLEDGE THE REQUIREMENTS OF THE GENERIC CONDITIONS THE UNDERSTANDING OF THIS STATE IS REALISED THROUGH AN ANALYSIS OF ITS INHERENT PROPERTIES, VOLUME, SURFACE, MASS, AND MOVEMENT.

FORM IN ITS SPECIFIC STATE PROVIDES THE PERCEPTUAL MEANS FOR THE COMPREHENSION OF THE SYSTEMIC ORDER. THIS ORDER IS CLARIFIED BY SUCH PROPERTIES OF SPECIFIC FORM AS SHAPE, COLOUR, TEXTURE, SIZE, SCALE AND PROPORTION.

A BUILDING WHICH IS REALISED AS A SPECIFIC FORM MUST HAVE A GENERIC ANTECEDENT.

This antecedent relates to the formal aspects of that building: the elementary state of that building and the essence of that state. This essence, of any form must be abstracted, understood, and ordered before any valid specific condition can be obtained. The ordering of the specific state develops from the generic form which in itself has an inherent or implied order.[2] For example, in Gestalt terms, if we see a square with one of its corners cut away we read it first as a square, the generic antecedent, before we read the resultant figure, since the generic form of a square is a simpler more absolute configuration for the eye to perceive and comprehend. Moreover, it is these basic configurations that must be used as a point of reference for any more complex forms. Thus in architectural situations where a multiplicity of programmatic requirements leads to a need for a more complex order, it is even more essential for there to be some reference to a geometric absolute.

2: Geoffrey Scott: 'Forms impose their own aesthetic character .. The suggestions of these forms is they are genuinely felt will not be modified by anything we may intellectually discover about the complex mechanical conditions, which in a given situation may actually contradict the apparent message of the forms. The message remains the same'. See also Focillon 'The life of Forms in Art'. p.4. 'The fundamental content of form is a formal one'.

Any ordering or organization of architectural form within the design process can be called a system: more explicitly a formal system.[3] A rational architecture has always had a systemic basis; irrespective of style and period, architects, consciously, inadvertently, and perhaps intuitively have invoked some system in the development of their work, and these systems have ordered and determined the resultant specific form of their buildings. It is not contended that the architects to be discussed below necessarily analysed their own work in exactly these terms: the object is rather to develop in the course of such analysis, a terminology for architectural form which might serve as a basis for communication, whether between teacher and pupil, architect and client, or critic and public.

3: c.f. Geoffrey Scott p.118. op.cit. 'Architecture is a grouping of material bodies subject to certain elementary laws.' And Argan op.cit. note 29. chapt 11. talking of Brunelleschi he says: 'the building is the instrument which, through the rationality of its process of construction, transfroms a confused and unlimited reality into a clear and ordered nature.'

SYSTEMS ARE AN ORDER TO THE VOCABULARY OF FORM[4]. THEY PROVIDE THE FRAMEWORK WITHIN WHICH THE SYNTAX AND THE GRAMMAR OF THIS VOCABULARY ARE DEPLOYED. AS SYSTEMS ARE PRIMARILY INVOKED TO ORDER AND CLARIFY THE INTENT AND FUNCTION OF ANY BUILDING THERE MUST BE INHERENT IN THEIR DEVELOPMENT THE SYNTAX AND GRAMMAR NECESSARY TO ALL FORMS OF COMMUNICATION. THE SYNTAX OR BASIC SET OF RULES THAT CONTROLS THE GRAMMATICAL ARRANGEMENT MUST THEREFORE BE DERIVED FROM THE GENERIC ANTECEDENT. THE GRAMMAR OF ANY SYSTEM IS ESSENTIALLY CONCERNED WITH THE IMPLEMENTATION OF THE FORMAL VOCABULARY IN THE SPECIFIC SITUATION. THEREFORE THE DISTORTIONS FROM THE GENERIC FORM CAN BE THOUGHT OF AS THE GRAMMAR, THE SPECIFIC USAGE OF THE VOCABULARY, AND THE RULES GOVERNING THE DISTORTIONS CAN BE THOUGHT OF AS A SYSTEM. THESE SYSTEMS EACH HAVE THEIR OWN ESSENTIAL GENERIC CHARACTER AND THEIR OWN SELF-GENERATED LAWS WHICH MUST BE COMPREHENDED AND FOLLOWED.

THE FOLLOWING DISCUSSION WILL BE LIMITED TO ESTABLISHING THE BASIS FOR DEVELOPING ANY SYSTEM RATHER THAN PROVIDING A DICTIONARY OR COMPENDIUM OF FORMAL SYSTEMS. THIS DISCUSSION WILL BE IN THE FORM OF BASIC NOTATIONS; IT WILL PROVIDE A FRAMEWORK THROUGH WHICH THE SUBJECTIVE PROCESSES OF THE ARCHITECT CAN BE RATIONALISED YET NOT CONFINED: IT WILL DEMONSTRATE THAT THERE IS A NEED FOR ORDER AND SUGGEST A POSSIBLE WAY OF PRODUCING THAT ORDER; THIS WILL IN TURN PROVIDE A BASIS FOR A MORE RATIONAL ARCHITECTURE.

THE IMAGINATION AND INTUITION OF THE ARCHITECT COME INTO PLAY IN THE SUBTLE INTERWEAVING OF SYSTEM WITH FUNCTION. THERE ARE NO ARBITARY DECISIONS. NO FORMAL ELEMENT IS GOOD OR BAD IN ITSELF: IT IS ONLY SO WHEN CONSIDERED AS A PART OF A NEXUS OF RELATIONSHIPS. A SYSTEM OR ORDERING PROCESS CAN BE FOUND

4: 'Meaning is conveyed by the fo
and order of words, not by the
themselves, and no precision o
meaning can be reached without
cision of style'. George Sant
op.cit. above. Italian archi
tural critics (for example Ren
Bonelli, Carlo Argan, Maria Ca
have long used linguistic term
such as 'philological', 'gramm
'syntax' etc., relating them t
buildings they analyse. The t
however, are used very loosely
only Argan has recognised any
ed systemic development. And
Bruno Zevi - 'Style is the lan
or rather the linguistics of d
p.200 'Architecture as Space.'

FOR ANY COMPLEX FUNCTION: THE ARGUMENT THAT A BUILDING MUST HAVE THIS OR THAT FORM BECAUSE OF A SPECIFIC FUNCTION CANNOT BE SUSTAINED, SINCE ALTHOUGH ALL SYSTEMS ORIGINATE FROM GIVEN PROGRAMMATIC CONDITIONS, THERE IS NORMALLY MORE THAN ONE SYSTEM CAPABLE OF SATISFYING THEM. IF A BUILDING DOES NOT RELATE IN ITS ENTIRETY TO THE SYSTEM, THEN THE SYSTEM WAS POORLY CONCEIVED. AN ATTEMPT MUST BE MADE TO ESTABLISH THE RELATIONSHIP OF SYSTEMIC CONTROL TO THE SPECIFIC REQUIREMENTS OF A GIVEN PROGRAMME AND SITE, AS WELL AS TO UNDERSTAND THE APPLICATION OF FORMAL SYSTEMS IN THE DESIGN PROCESS.

IN THIS PROCESS THERE IS A COMPLEX INTERRELATIONSHIP BETWEEN ON THE ONE HAND THE ARCHITECT, THE INTERPRETER AND ON THE OTHER HAND THE BUILDING - THAT WHICH IS INTERPRETED. IN THIS SENSE, THE ARCHITECT ONLY INTERPRETS THE INTENT OR FORMAL ESSENCE OF THE BUILDING, AND CREATES IN THE SENSE THAT HE GIVES PHYSICAL FORM TO THE GENERIC REQUIREMENT OF THAT BUILDING. FORMAL SYSTEMS ORDER THIS DEVELOPMENT AND PRESENT IT CLEARLY FROM ITS INCEPTION THROUGH THE ARCHITECT TO THE RECEIVER. IT IS NECESSARY THEREFORE TO DERIVE AND THEN IMPOSE THIS INTELLECTUAL, ABSTRACT AND ABSOLUTE PROCESS FOR THE ORDERING OF FORM. THE SPECIFIC FORM PRODUCED CANNOT BE JUDGED AS GOOD OR BAD IN ITSELF FOR IT SHOULD NOT COMPLY WITH ANY SUBJECTIVE INTERPRETATION OF BEAUTY, STYLE, OR TASTE, BUT SHOULD RATHER BE EXPRESSIVE OF THE ESSENCE OF THE BUILDING: THE REALISATION OF ITS REQUIREMENTS, BOTH FORMAL AND FUNCTIONAL. THERE IS A FUNDAMENTAL DIFFERENCE BETWEEN THE MEANING AND APPLICATION OF THE WORD 'FORMAL' AS DEFINED HERE AND THE SAME WORD AS USED BY MANY OF THE 'BEAUX ARTS' SCHOOL OF THOUGHT. FOR THESE ACADEMICS AND THEIR INTERPRETERS, FORMALISM WAS ONLY CONSIDERED IN ONE ASPECT; ITS RELATION TO CERTAIN CONCEPTS OF BEAUTY AND STYLE. AXIAL AND SYM-

5: 'Without formality architecture lacks the syntax of its speech .. formality furnishes its own theme and makes lucid its own argument. Formal' architecture is to the 'picturesque' as the whole body of musical art to the lazy hum and vaguely occupying murmur of the Summer fields'. 'Formality is the basis of design.' Geoffrey Scott. (op.cit. above.)

6: Thus for Paul Klee (The Thinking Eye' p. 60) 'formalism is form without Function'. See also Bruno Zevi. (op cit above) p193 'Formalist interpretation'.

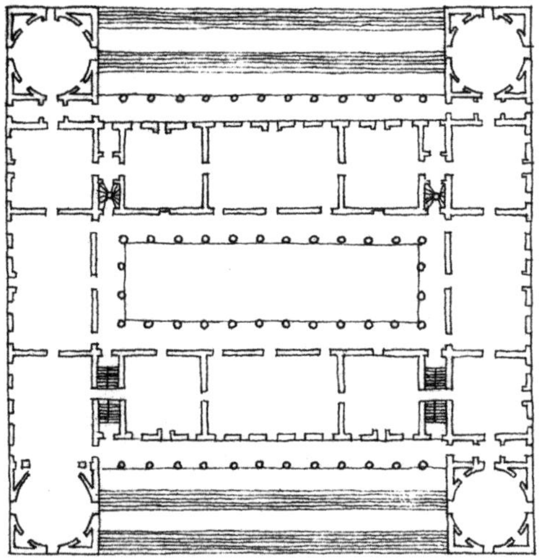

THEATER

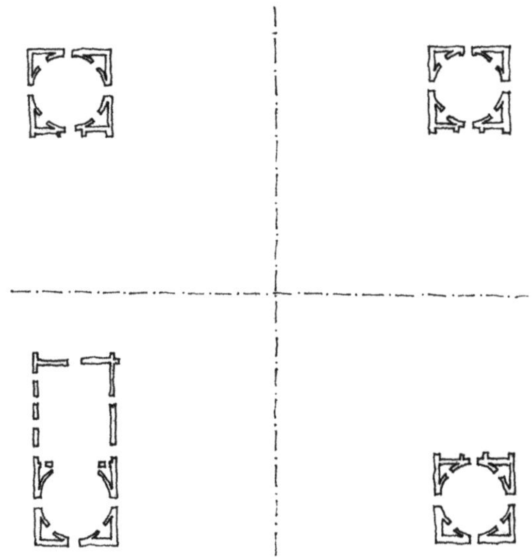

THEATER

1.

J.N.L. DURAND - MAISON DE CAMPAGNE
TWO PART FUNCTIONAL ORGANIZATION OF THEATER
ARTICULATED IN A SIMILAR FASHION TO THE
FOUR OTHER CORNERS

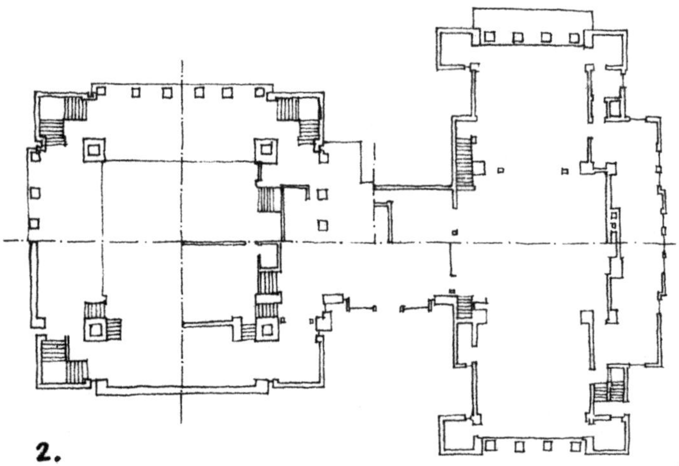

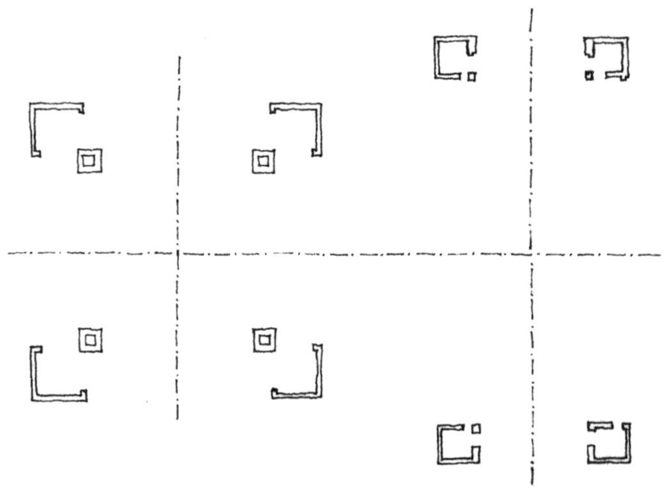

2.

F.L. WRIGHT : UNITY TEMPLE
CORNERS ARTICULATED TO EXPRESS
DIFFERENT FUNCTIONS.

-METRICAL COMPOSITIONS WERE CONCEIVED OF ONLY IN A FORMALISTIC SENSE: FOR THE BEAUTY OF THE THING IN ITSELF AND NOT AS A RESPONSE TO THE NATURE OF THE SPECIFIC ORGANISM. THESE ARTICULATIONS EXPRESSED IN SPECIFIC SITUATIONS THESE METHODS OF COMPOSITION REGARDLESS OF THEIR MEANING. FOR EXAMPLE IN HIS 'PRECIS DES LECONS' DURAND ILLUSTRATES MANY PLAN TYPES SEVERAL OF WHICH COULD BE USED TO EXEMPLIFY THE FORMALISTIC SENSE AS DEVELOPED IN ACADEMIC COMPOSITIONS.[7.1] IN HIS MAISON DE CAMPAGNE, THE PLAN IS ARTICULATED AT THE FOUR CORNERS AS THE ACKNOWLEDGEMENT OF A CENTROIDAL PLAN; CONCEPTUALLY, A CENTROIDAL REFERENCE REQUIRES A CORNER DEFINITION TO DISTINGUISH BETWEEN CORNER AND SIDE. HOWEVER ON CLOSER EXAMINATION THOSE CORNERS ARE FOUND TO BE CONCEIVED ALMOST TOTALLY ON <u>FORMALISTIC</u> GROUNDS. THE CYLINDER WITHIN A CUBE DERIVING SPECIFICALLY FROM THE REQUIREMENTS OF THE CHAPEL IS THEN REPEATED ON THE OTHER THREE CORNERS, IN THE LIBRARY, THEATRE AND BOUDOIR. IT IS IN THE THEATRE THAT THE NON-FUNCTIONAL NATURE OF THIS REPITITION BECOMES APPARENT. THE THEATRE FUNCTIONALLY REQUIRES A TWO-BAY ORGANISATION BUT IT IS ARTICULATED IN THE SAME WAY AS THE OTHER CORNERS WHICH REQUIRE ONLY A SINGLE BAY. IT HAS BEEN PROPOSED EARLIER THAT THE MEANING OF THE WORD'FORMAL' IMPLIES THAT ANY BUILDING SHOULD EVOLVE FROM PROGRAMMATIC REQUIREMENTS AND ANY ARTICULATIONS OF THIS BUILDING WOULD DERIVE FROM ITS SPECIFIC NEEDS. THIS CAN BE ILLUSTRATED BY WRIGHT'S 'FORMAL' COMPOSITION FOR UNITY TEMPLE.[8.2] HERE THE CORNER ARTICULATIONS INITIALLY EXPRESS THE G GENERIC CENTROIDAL ASPECT OF THE PLAN. THEY ARE NOT DERIVED HOWEVER FROM ARBITRARY, SUBJECTIVE, 'FORMALISTIC' REASONS, BUT RATHER FROM A FORMAL WAY OF THOUGHT PREDICATED BY A TOTAL FUNCTIONING ORGANISM. THUS THE ARTICULATED CORNERS EXPRESS THE DISPARATE FUNCTIONS OF VERTICAL CIRCULATION, SERVICING AND CHAIR STORAGE; ALL OF THESE ARTICULATIONS INTERLOCK AND ARE THEN RESOLVED INTO

7: Durand, J.N.L. 'Precis des Lecons'. Paris 1802. Vol. II.

8: Hitchcock, H. Ressel. 'In the Nature of materials'. 1942 N. Y.

A SYSTEM IS THEN THE ORGANISATION AND CONTROL, BOTH PERCEPTUAL AND CONCEPTUAL, OF THESE ARTICULATIONS AND DISTORTIONS. IT IS DERIVED INITIALLY FROM A GENERIC FORM WHICH WAS SUGGESTED BY THE PROGRAMMATIC REQUIREMENTS. IT USES A VOCABULARY DERIVED FROM THE INHERENT QUALITIES OF THIS GENERIC FORM. IT ORDERS THIS VOCABULARY BY A GRAMMAR AND SYNTAX TO PRODUCE A FINAL STATE WHERE ALL PARTS ARE FULLY STRESSED AND UTILISED, AND EXIST IN A DELICATE BALANCE AND EQUILIBRIUM.

THE TWO MAIN CATEGORIES OF FORMAL SYSTEMS, LINEAR AND CENTROIDAL FOLLOW FROM THE CLASSIFICATION OF GENERIC FORM. FROM THESE TWO CATEGORIES ALL SYSTEMS RECEIVE THEIR BASIC ORDERING: THAT IS FTOM THE INHERENT DYNAMICS OF BOTH LINEAR AND CENTROIDAL GENERIC FORM. THIS INTRINSIC NATURE IS AN ABSOLUTE REFERENCE FROM WHICH ALL SPECIFIC DISTORTIONS IN ANY SYSTEM DERIVE. ALL SYSTEMS ARE THEREFORE BASED ON THE PROPERTIES OF GENERIC FORM: VOLUME, MOVEMENT, MASS AND SURFACE. ALTHOUGH THESE PROPERTIES PROVIDE THE PERCEPTUAL AND PHYSICAL DEFINITION FOR ANY SYSTEM THEY MUST REFER BACK TO A GENERIC ANTECEDENT FOR THEIR SYNTAX AND GRAMMAR. FOR EXAMPLE THE CUBE CONSIDERED AS A GENERIC ANTECEDENT, HAS ITS OWN FORMAL ESSENCE: EQUAL AXES, EQUAL SIDES, ETC.. THIS PROVIDES THE INITIAL CONCEPTUAL ORDERING, FROM WHICH THE SYNTAX OR RULES, OF A FORMAL SYSTEM IS EVOLVED. THIS CUBE ALSO HAS GENERIC PROPERTIES, (VOLUME, MASS, AND SURFACE) WHICH PROVIDE THE PERCEPTUAL BASIS FOR THE DEVELOPMENT OF THIS VOCABULARY.
THE VOCABULARY AND THE GRAMMAR, ITS DIFFERENT USES IN SPECIFIC SITUATIONS, ARE BOTH ORDERED BY THE SYNTAX, THEIR SPECIFIC ORDER DERIVING FROM THE COMBINATION OF BOTH PERCEPTUAL AND CONCEPTUAL REQUIREMENTS.

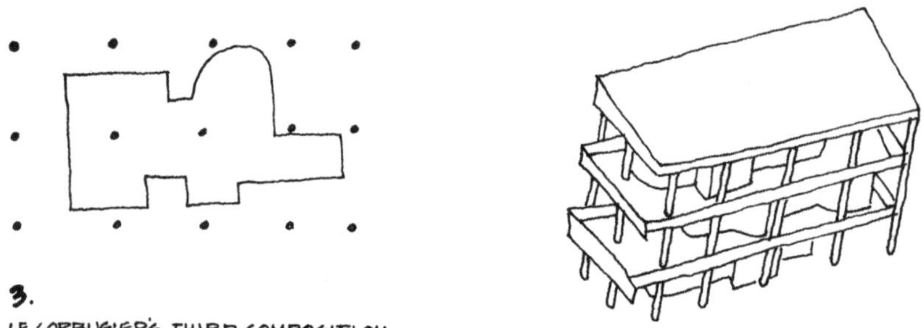

3.

LE CORBUSIER'S THIRD COMPOSITION
SPECIFIC VOLUMETRIC ORGANIZATION
WITHIN AN ABSOLUTE GRID.

VOLUMETRIC CONTINUITY DEFINED BY A GRID.

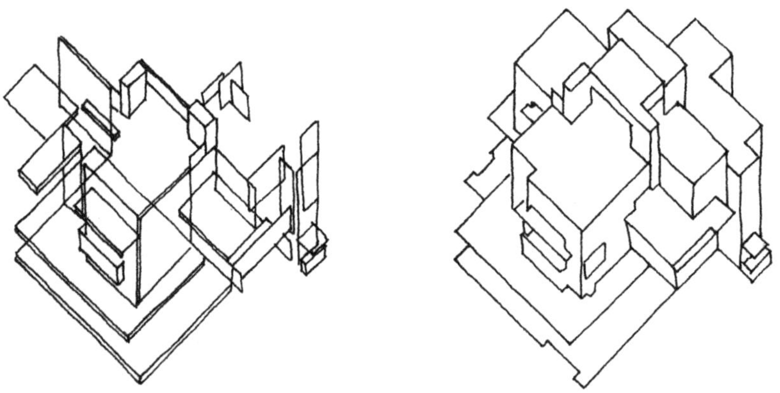

4.

VAN DOESBURG · VAN EESTEREN · RIETVELD · HOUSE 1922
VOLUMETRIC CONTINUITY DEFINED BY PLANES.

Since volume is that property of generic form put forward as being fundamental to any architectural expression, quite naturally, some form of volumetric ordering will occur in any system, without necessarily providing the basis for that system. Moreover, in situations where a volumetric order is dominant, this order can either be continuous or static: both applicable to either a centroidal or a linear situation. There is a third type of volumetric order that is not comparable with either the continuous or the static: that order which is conceived of as a series of volumetric planes. This type can best be considered in its relationship to a mass-surface system development.

In a continuous system the movement or circulation is interconnected with, yet subservient to, the volumetric ordering. This created an organism where each volume relates to every other volume, or to the whole, by a sequence of interpenetrations, its absolute reference being to an implied or actual structural grid, in which the walls and surfaces have been relieved of their load bearing function. The free plan is a natural result of this, it can be seen in the third of Le Corbusier's 'Four Compositions', illustrating a specific volumetric organisation within an absolute grid.[3] But as this system depends on the structural grid for its reference there is a certain ambiguity, since the specific order seeks to deny the volumetric definition provided by the grid. Compartmentation is denied, in the sense that the volumes are not articulated by the grid. They do not stand as separate entities but rather as a continuous whole,[9.] each volume only existing in relation to the total organism. The continuous system was associated with modern architecture in the first quarter of this century by virtue of its dependence on, and derivation from the new technology

9: c.f. Laszlo Moholy-Nagy 'Von Material zu Architecture'. Munich 1929. (The New Vision, Documents of Modern Art: vol. 3', N.York 1949) 'Out of cosmic space, 'a piece of space is cut by means of a, sometimes complicated-seeming, network of limiting and interpenetrating stips.....as if space were a divisible compact substance. Thus modern architecture is founded on a full interpenetration with outer space.'

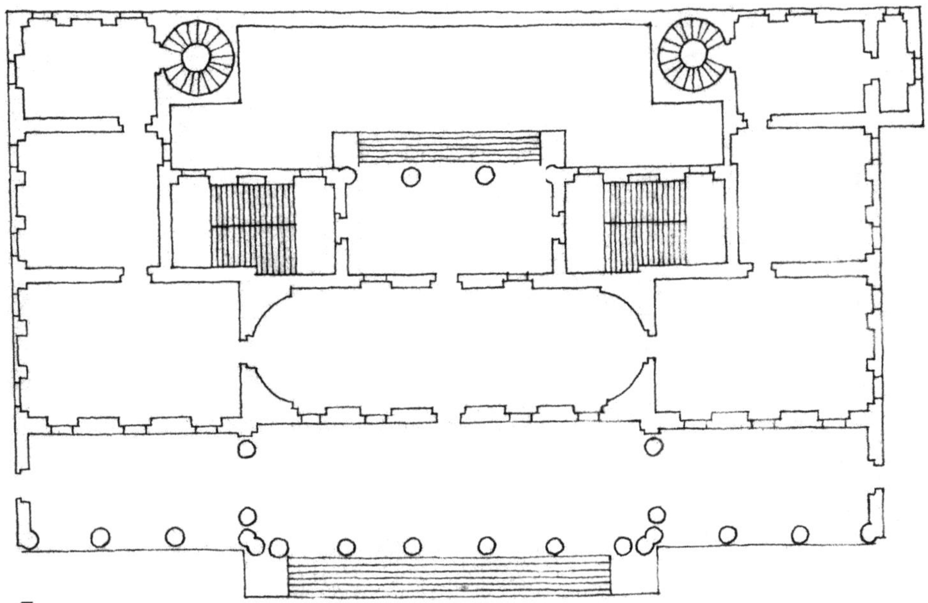

5.

ANDREA PALLADIO : PALAZZO CHIERICATI

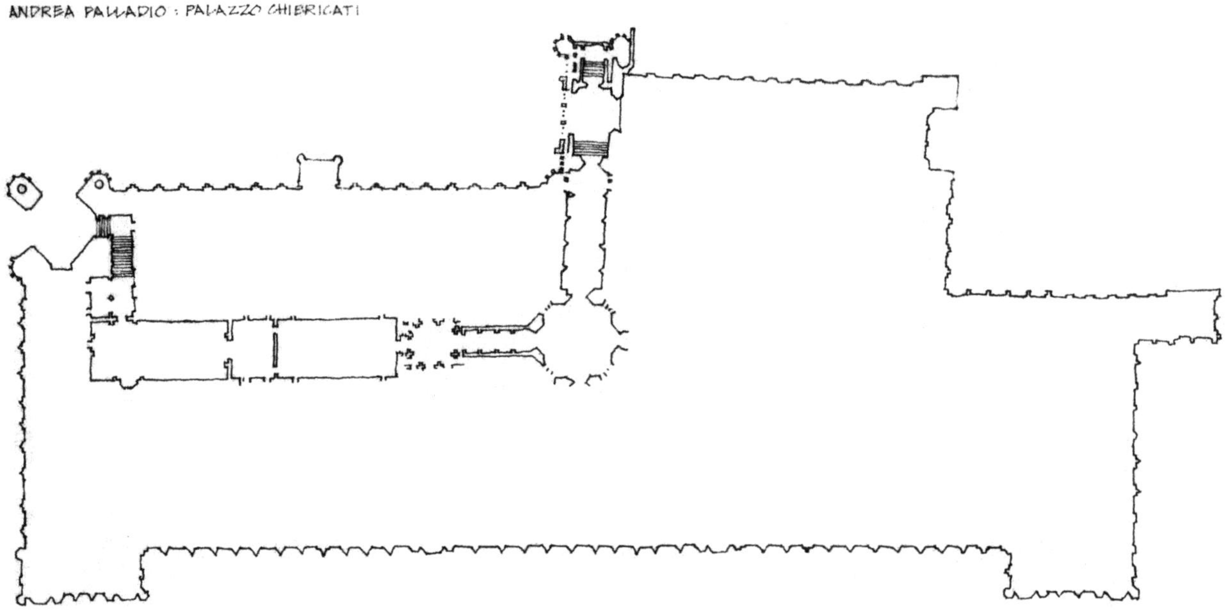

CHARLES BARRY : HOUSES OF PARLIAMENT

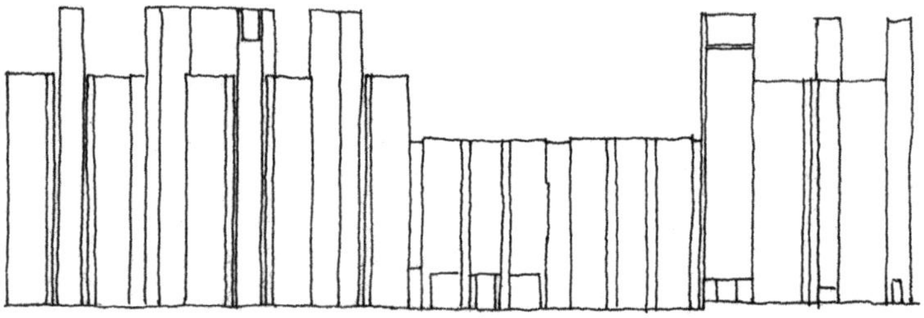

6.

LOUIS KAHN : RICHARDS LABORATORY

LINEAR STATIC SYSTEM

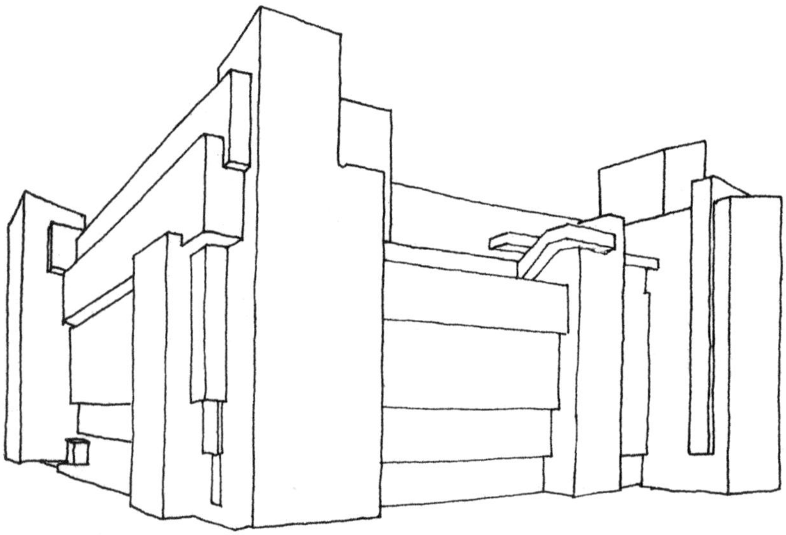

PAUL RUDOLPH : YALE ARCHITECTURE BUILDING

CENTROIDAL STATIC SYSTEM

of point supports; the general acceptance of the time-space interrelationship provided an additional conceptual basis for this system. Thus we find examples of continuous volumetric ordering in the De Stijl house projects of van Doesburg, van Eesteren, and Rietveld, and the early cubist and purist exercises of Le Corbusier. In the De Stijl houses the volumetric system is combined with a surface of planer system[10] while in Le Corbusier's work the volumetric ordering is related to a system of movement.[11.4]

In a static system, each volume is expressed or articulated as an individual entitiy. A sense of the total organism is only achieved by means of a sequential progression: volumes are linked together as beads on a string. The impetus to make this progression in experiencing a building is provided by the dynamic qualityes in each successive volume, which by expansion or contraction, force or ease one through the total complex. The static system is not a development from any particular style or idiom in the way that the continuous system relates specifically to the modern movement. Palladio's Pallazo Chiericati[12.5] and Barry's Houses of Parliament[13.6] can both be thought of as examples of static systems. This type of order might better be described as volumetrically articulated but for the fact that this phrase does not stand in clear antithesis to the term 'continuous system'.

Initially it would seem that these volumetrically articulated systems because of their sequential nature could be classified as linear organisations. However, where Louis Kahn's Richards Medical building in Philadelphia could be thought of as a linear static system, Paul Rudolph's proposed architecture building at Yale conversly could be termed a centroidal static system.[6] In the

10: c.f Bruno Zevi: 'Poetica dell' Architettura Neoplastica'. Milan 1953.

11: Le Corbusier et Pierre Jeanneret: 'Oeuvre Complete'. vol. I. 1910-1929.

12: See Rudolph Wittkower, 'Architectural Principles in the Age of Humanism'.

13: c.f. H.R. Hitchcock, 'Architecture: Nineteenth and Twentieth centuries', and 'Early Victorian Architecture in Britain'. 2Vols. - London 1954.

7.

BOTH A SPIRAL AND A PINWHEEL ACKNOWLEDGE
A CENTRUM

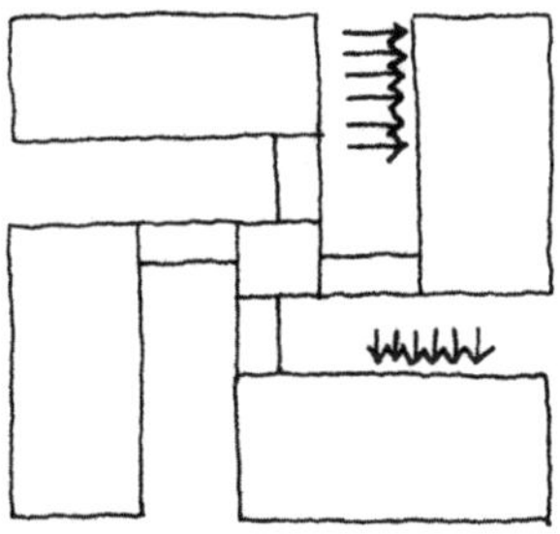

8.

PINWHEEL MOVEMENT
LIKE A WINDMILL MOVING
WITH AIR CURRENTS -

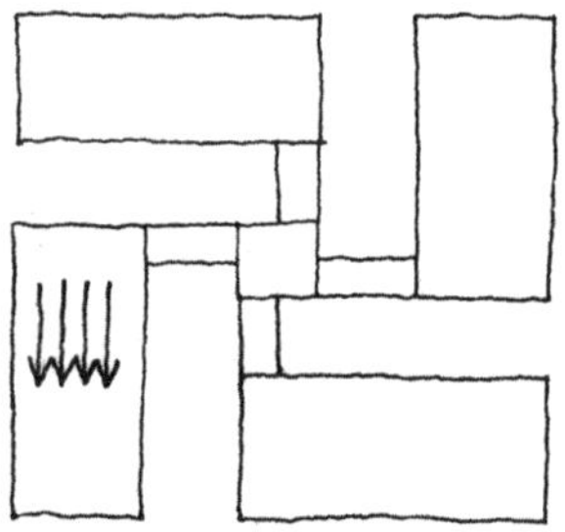

9.

-OR THOUGHT OF AS MOVING BY
THE FORCE OF GRAVITY ON THE
VANES THOUGHT OF AS WEIGHTS

CASE OF ALVAR AALTO'S TALLINN MUSEUM THE VOLUMETRIC SYSTEM IS STATIC AND CENTROIDAL THOUGH INITIALLY DEVELOPED FROM A LINEAR MOVEMENT.

ALTHOUGH BOTH OF THESE VOLUMETRIC SYSTEMS STRESS AN INTERNAL ORGANISATION, IT WILL BE SEEN IN A LATER DISCUSSION OF MASS-SURFACE SYSTEMS THAT THEY MAY HAVE A VOLUMETRIC ORDERING THAT IS EVOLVED FROM EXTERNAL CONSIDERATIONS. CONTINUOUS AND STATIC SYSTEMS ARE ESSENTIALLY BASIC CATEGORIES, APPLICABLE REGARDLESS OF THE NATURE OF THE SPECIFIC SYSTEM CHOSEN AND ARE THEREFORE IMPLIED REFERENCES IN ANY PARTICULAR SITUATION. THEIR DIRECT REFERENCE IS TO A TOTAL ORDERED ENVIRONMENT SINCE IT IS THE VOLUMETRIC ORDERING THAT MUST PROVIDE THE BASIS FOR THIS CONDITION.

THERE ARE THREE EASILY RECOGNISABLE TYPES OF MOVEMENT SYSTEMS: THE PINWHEEL, SPIRAL AND ECHELON; THE FIRST TWO DEVELOP ESSENTIALLY FROM AN INTERNAL CENTROIDAL REQUIREMENT. IN THE SENSE THAT ALL MOVEMENT IS A FORM OF LINEAR EXPRESSION THE POSSIBILITY OF ANY CENTROIDAL REFERENCE MIGHT BE QUESTIONED, BUT IN FACT BOTH THE SPIRAL AND THE PINWHEEL ACKNOWLEDGE A CENTRUM.[7]

THE PINWHEEL CAN BE CLASSIFIED AS A MOVEMENT SYSTEM IN THE SENSE THAT THE TOTAL ORGANISATION IS CONCEPTUALLY THOUGHT OF AS BEING IN MOTION. IT IS NOT GENERATED BY PATTERNS OF MOVEMENT BUT RATHER BY A THREE OR FOUR PART VOLUMETRIC ORDERING FROM A DEFINED CENTRE. IT IS THE VOLUMETRIC ORDERING AND NOT THE INTERNAL MOVEMENT THAT IS NECESSARY FOR THE PERCEPTION OF THIS SYSTEM. THERE ARE TWO WAYS IN WHICH THE SYSTEM CAN BE THOUGHT OF AS BEING IN MOTION. FIRSTLY THE PINWHEEL CAN REFER IN A METAPHORICAL SENCE TO A WINDMILL; THE

10.

LE CORBUIER : MUSEUM PROJECT 1939
CENTRIFUGAL MOVEMENT.

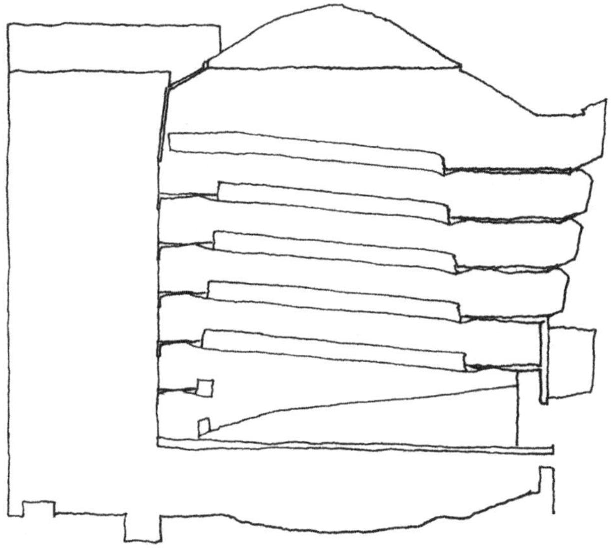

11.

FRANK L. WRIGHT : GUGGENHEIM MUSEUM
CENTRIPETAL MOVEMENT.

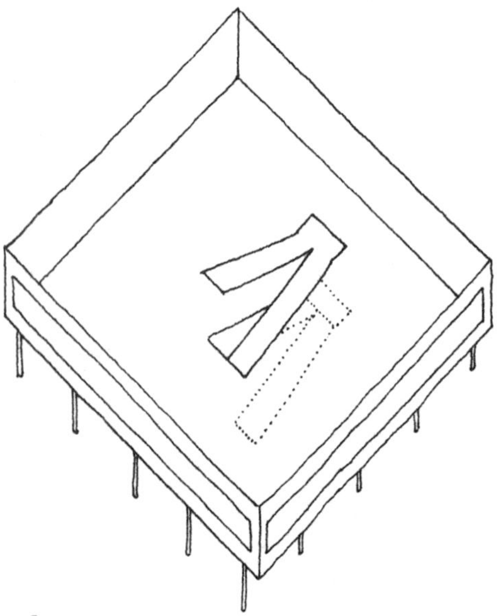

12.

LE CORBUSIER : POISSY
SPIRAL NEITHER ON PERIPHERY
OR IN CENTER

DIRECTION OF MOVEMENT CAN BE THOUGHT OF AS FOLLOWING THE MOVEMENT OF THE ARMS AND VANES AS DIRECTED BY CURRENTS OF AIR.[8] SECONDLY, THE PINWHEEL COULD BE ONE IN WHICH THE VANES ARE THOUGHT OF AS WEIGHTS AND THE RESULTANT MOVEMENT CAUSED BY THE GRAVITATIONAL PULL OF THOSE WEIGHTS ON THE ARMS.[9]

THE SPIRAL, WHICH IS BASICALLY A MOVEMENT SYSTEM, DEPENDS UPON A PROGRESSION ABOUT A FIXED CENTRUM FOR ITS DEFINITION WHETHER THE MOVEMENT BEGINS EITHER FROM THE CENTRE OR FROM THE PERIPHERY: THE ESSENTIAL CHARACTERISTIC BEING THE ACKNOWLEDGEMENT OF THE CENTRAL POINT AND THE PROGRESSION ABOUT THAT POINT. THERE ARE THREE POSSIBLE SPIRAL SYSTEMS: THE FIRST WHERE THE ENTRY IS IN A CENTRAL LOCATION AND THE TERMINATION OF THE SPIRAL IS EFFECTED ON THE EXTERIOR; THE SECOND IS THE OPPOSITE CONDITION, THE BEGINNING OF THE SPIRAL BEING ON THE PERIPHERY; AND THE THIRD WHERE THE BEGINNING AND THE END ARE NEITHER ON THE EXTERIOR NOR IN THE CENTRE. IN THE FIRST EXAMPLE THE MOVEMENT IS CENTRIPETAL AS IN LE CORBUSIER'S MUSEUM PROJECT OF 1939;[10] IN THE SECOND, THE MOVEMENT IS CENTRIFUGAL AS IN WRIGHT'S GUGGENHEIM MUSEUM;[11] WHILE IN THE THIRD THE DIRECTION OF THE MOVEMENT IS NOT A CRITICAL FACTOR IN THE ORDERING OF THE SYSTEM. LE CORBUSIER'S HOUSE AT POISSY CAN BE CITED AS AN EXAMPLE OF THIS LATTER TYPE.[12] IN ALL THREE CONDITIONS THE SPIRAL GROWTH CAN BE CONSTANT AS IN LE CORBUSIER'S MUSEUM OR PROGRESSIVE, LIKE THE GROWTH OF A SNAIL-SHELL, AS EXEMPLIFIED IN WRIGHT'S GUGGENHEIM MUSEUM.

THE ECHELON IS ESSENTIALLY A LINEAR ORGANISATION WHICH IN CERTAIN SITUATIONS CAN BE DERIVED AS CENTROIDAL. IT CAN BE A COMBINATION OF BOTH VOLUMETRIC AND MOVEMENT ORGANISATIONS BUT INITIALLY IT DEPENDS ON A PROGRESSION OF MOVEMENT

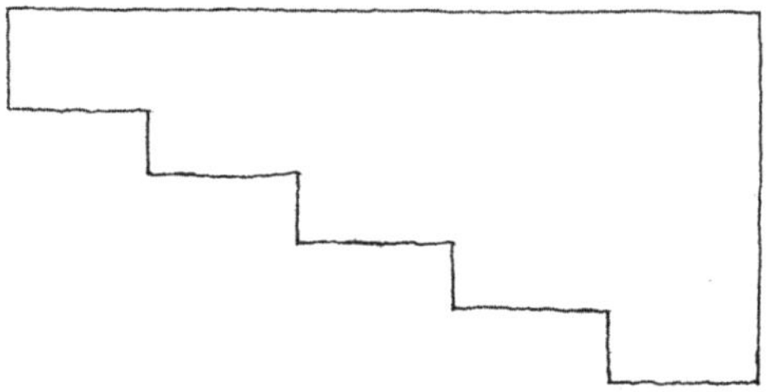

13.

THE ECHELON : CONTINUOUS REGULAR ORDERING FROM A LINEAR STEM

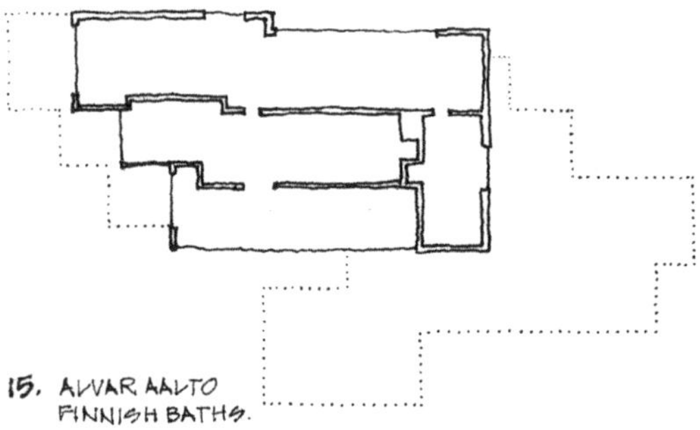

15. ALVAR AALTO FINNISH BATHS.

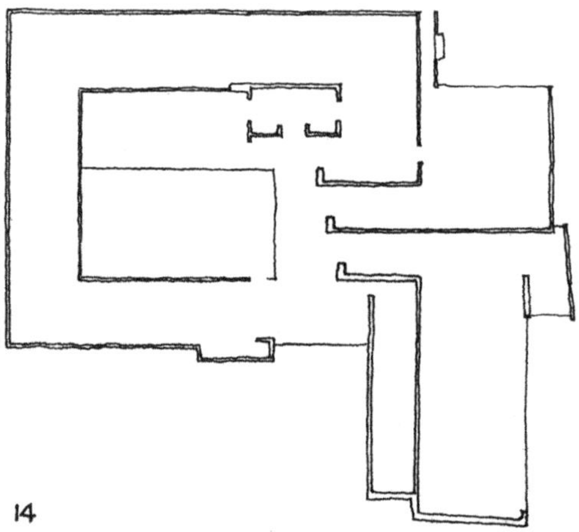

14

ALVAR AALTO : TALLINN MUSEUM SECONDARY ECHELON WITHIN A DOMINANT SPIRAL.

LE CORBUSIERS FOUR COMPOSITIONS

1

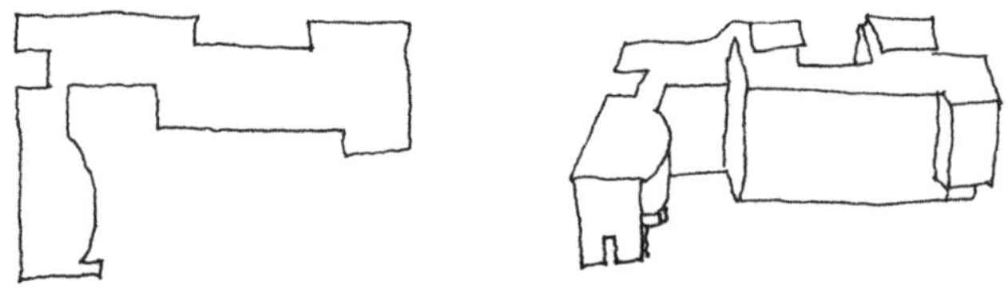

16. 'MASS'

2

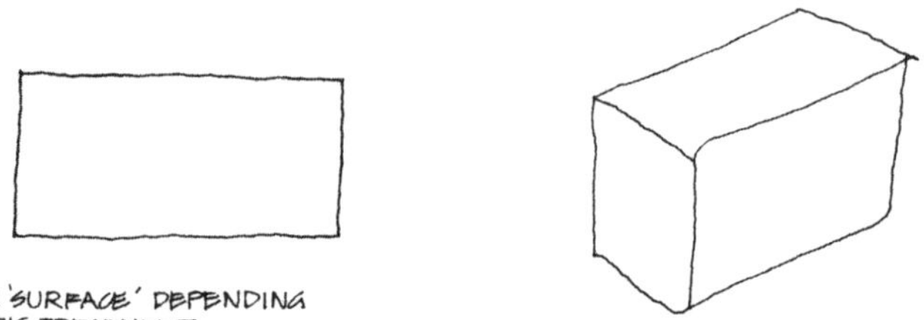

17. 'MASS' OR 'SURFACE' DEPENDING ON SPECIFIC TREATMENT.

3

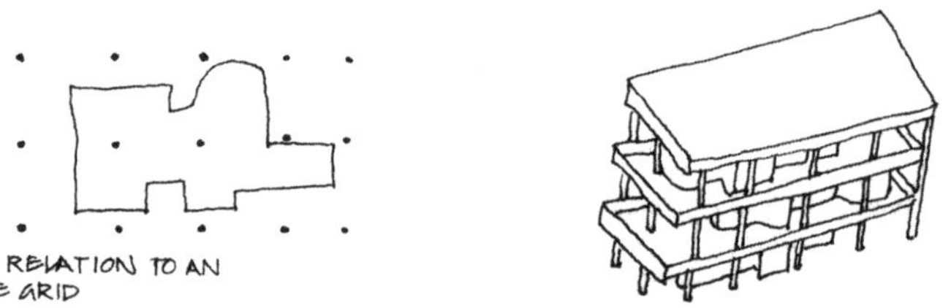

18. 'MASS' IN RELATION TO AN ABSOLUTE GRID

4

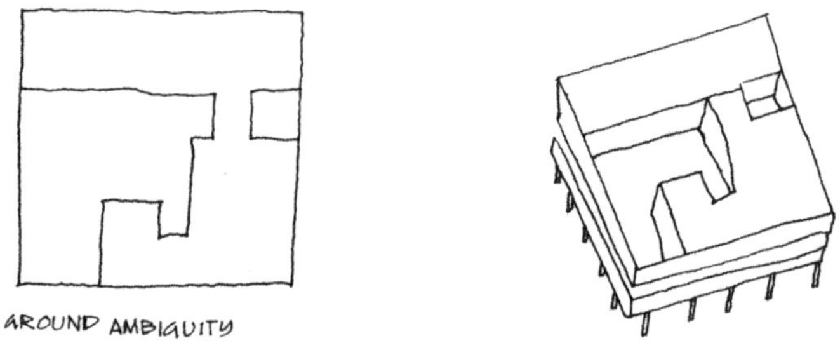

19. FIGURE - AROUND AMBIGUITY

FOR ITS CONCEPTUAL DEFINITION. THIS PROGRESSION USUALLY RELATES TO A LINEAR STEM LIKE RIBS FROM A BACKBONE; THE DIFFERENCE BEING THAT THE ECHELON RELIES ON A CONTINUOUS, REGULAR AND DIRECTIONAL ORDERING FOR ITS PERCEPTUAL DEFINITION.[13] IT CAN EXIST ALONE, OR IN COMBINATION WITH OTHER SYSTEMIC DEVELOPMENTS. IN AALTO'S TALLINN MUSEUM PROJECT THE ECHELON IS A SECONDARY SYSTEM WITHIN A DOMINANT CENTRAL SPIRAL.[14] IN HIS FINNISH BATHS PROJECT FOR 1946 THE ECHELON BECOMES PART OF A LINEAR SYSTEM OF VOLUMETRIC PLANES:[15] IN BOTH CASES THE SPECIFIC FORM OF THE ECHELON RESULTS FROM SPECIFIC DISTORTIONS OF A GENERIC REFERENCE, AND ARE RECOGNISABLE THROUGH THE ORDERING OF THESE DISTORTIONS.

MOST SYSTEMS OF MOVEMENT ARE IN FACT MUTATIONS OF THESE BASIC TYPES. THEY ARE COMPLEX ORGANISMS AND DEPEND ON THE SPECIFIC GRAMMAR EMPLOYED BY THE ARCHITECT FOR THEIR COMPREHENSION.

IT MUST AGAIN BE EMPHASISED THAT IN THE CASE OF SPIRALS, PINWHEELS, AND ECHELONS THE SPECIFIC SYSTEMIC DEVELOPMENT RESULTS FROM AN ORDERING OF DISTORTIONS FROM A GENERIC ABSOLUTE. THE SPECIFIC GRAMMATICAL IMPLEMENTATION IN EACH CASE EVOLVES FROM THE PARTICULAR PROGRAMMATIC REQUIREMENTS. THEREFORE IT WOULD BE IMPOSSIBLE AND IN FACT IRRELEVANT TO CATALOGUE EVERY POSSIBLE APPLICATION OF THESE SYSTEMS: THEY ARE LISTED HERE ONLY TO INDICATE THE MANNER OF THEIR USE IN THE DESIGN PROCESS.

THE MASS-SURFACE DIALECTIC RECEIVED ITS INITIAL DEFINITION IN LE CORBUSIER'S 'FOUR COMPOSITIONS': THE FIRST CAN BE INTERPRETED AS 'MASS';[16] THE SECOND COULD BE EITHER 'MASS' OR 'SURFACE' DEPENDING ON THE SPECIFIC TREATMENT;[17] THE THIRD STATES A SPECIFIC 'MASS' IN RELATION TO THE ABSOLUTE GRID;[18] THE FOURTH IS A PURE

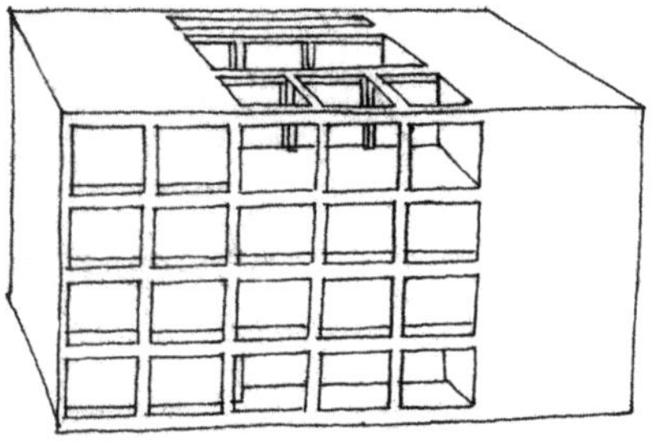

20.
GIUSEPPE TERRAGNI · CASA DEL FASCIO · MASS-SURFACE DIALECTIC
'MASS' - THE GENERIC INTERNAL STATE.

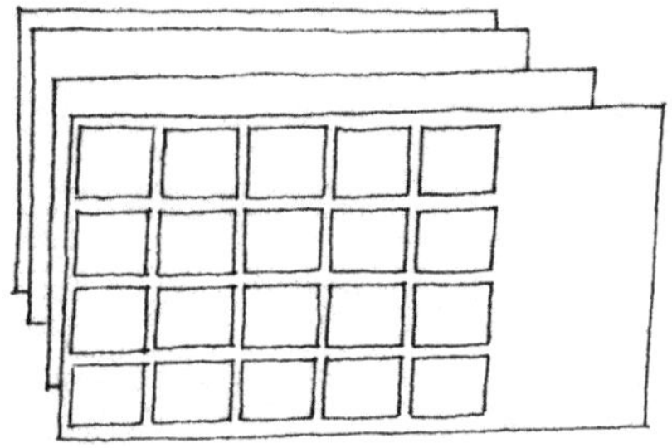

'SURFACE' - DISTORTION OF INTERNAL STATE BY EXTERNAL FORCES

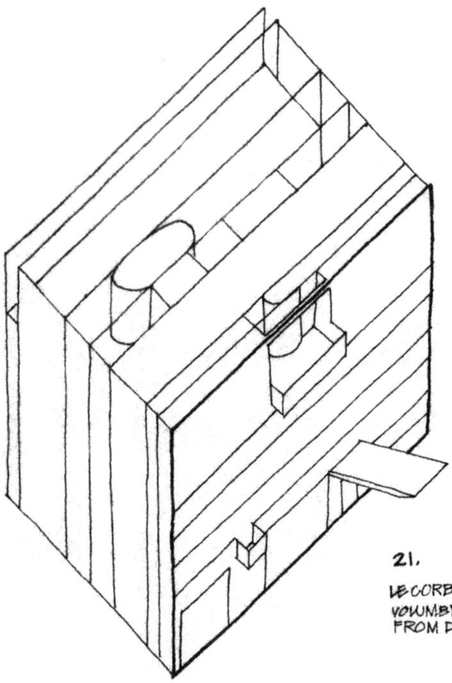

21.
LE CORBUSIER : GARCHES : VERTICAL VOLUMETRIC PLANES TENSIONED FROM DOMINANT FACADE.

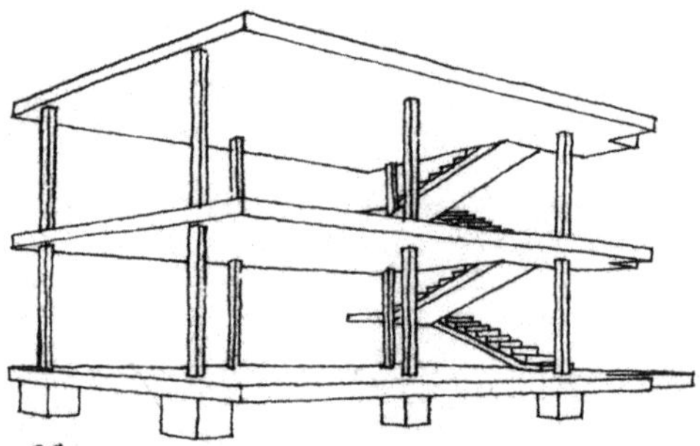

22.
LE CORBUSIER 'MAISON DOMINO'
HORIZONTAL VOLUMETRIC PLANES.

EXAMPLE OF THE DIALECTIC CONDITION, IN THAT IT PRESENTS THE CLASSICAL FIGURE-GROUND AMBIGUITY.[19] THIS CAN BE READ AS EITHER 'MASS', OR SOLID THAT HAS BEEN CUT AWAY, OR 'SURFACE', A BUILDING THAT HAS BEEN BUILT UP BY AN ADDITION OF A NUMBER OF LAYERS OR 'PLANES'.

SYSTEMS INVOLVING A MASS-SURFACE DIALECTIC ARE USUALLY INVOKED WHERE EXTERNAL AND INTERNAL REQUIREMENTS ARE IN OPPOSITION. IN THESE SITUATIONS THEY ARE USUALLY THE DOMINANT MEANS OF CONTROL. IN THE CASA DEL FASCIO THIS DIALECTIC EXPRESSION TAKES ITS FORM FROM THE RESOLUTION OF AN INTERNAL-EXTERNAL CONFLICT; 'MASS' REPRESENTING THE GENERIC INTERNAL STATE, AND 'SURFACE' REPRESENTING THE DISTORTION OF THAT STATE BY EXTERNAL FORCES.[20] HOWEVER THE MERE RECOGNITION OF A BUILDING AS ESSENTIALLY 'MASS' OR 'SURFACE' DOES NOT NECESSARILY IMPLY THAT THE OPERATIVE SYSTEM WAS EVOLVED FROM THIS VOCABULARY. MOREOVER 'MASS-SURFACE' SYSTEMS DO NOT ALWAYS OCCUR IN A DIALECTICAL CONTEXT. WHERE THEY ARE USED INDIVIDUALLY, AS IN SAY, A SURFACE SYSTEM THEY GENERALLY DEFINE OR ORDER A VOLUMETRIC ORGANISATION. THERE ARE THREE RECOGNISABLE TYPES OF VOLUMETRIC SYSTEM WHICH DEPEND UPON A SURFACE ORDERING FOR THEIR DEFINITION; THE ESSENTIAL CHARACTERISTIC OF THESE IS THAT THE VOLUMETRIC ORDERING RELATES TO A SURFACE OR JUXTAPOSITION OF SURFACES FOR ITS REFERENCE. THE FIRST TYPE IS A SERIES OF VOLUMETRIC PLANES TENSIONED FROM A VERTICAL REFERENCE, ILLUSTRATED BY LE CORBUSIER'S HOUSE AT GARCHES.[21] THE COMPOSITION IS ORDERED BY A SERIES OF VOLUMETRIC PLANES DEFINED INITIALLY BY THE FRONT FACADE. THE SECOND TYPE, A SERIES OF HORIZONTAL VOLUMETRIC PLANES, IS DEFINED BY A SEQUENCE OF HORIZONTAL SURFACES, TENSIONED USUALLY FROM AN ARTICULATED FLOOR OR ROOF PLANE: THE PROTOTYPE OF THIS BEING THE 'MAISON DOMINO'.[22] THE THIRD TYPE OF MASS-SURFACE SYSTEM

23.
LE CORBUSIER : VILLA SHODHAN
VOLUMETRIC PLAID

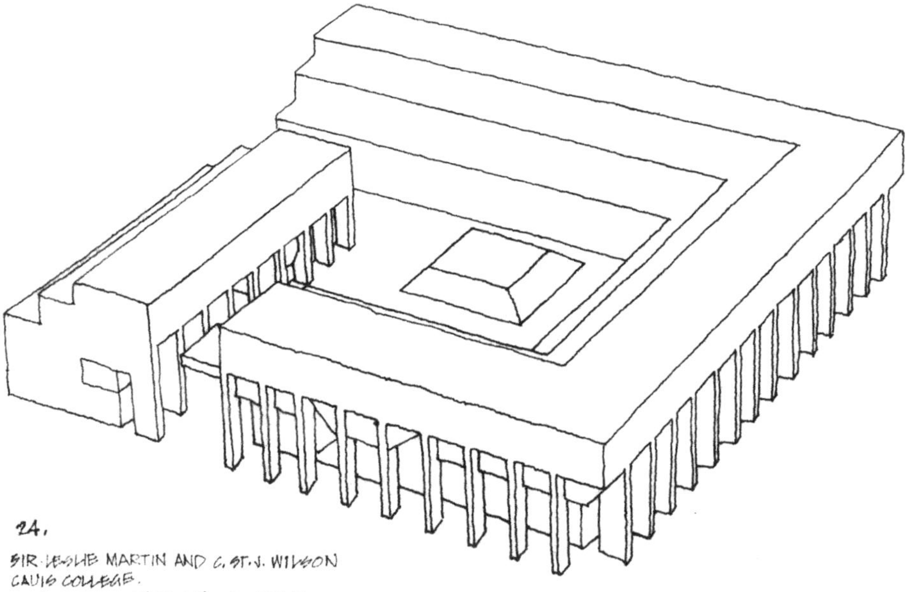

24.
SIR LESLIE MARTIN AND C. ST. J. WILSON
CAIUS COLLEGE.
GENERIC SOLID 'MASS' CUT-AWAY.

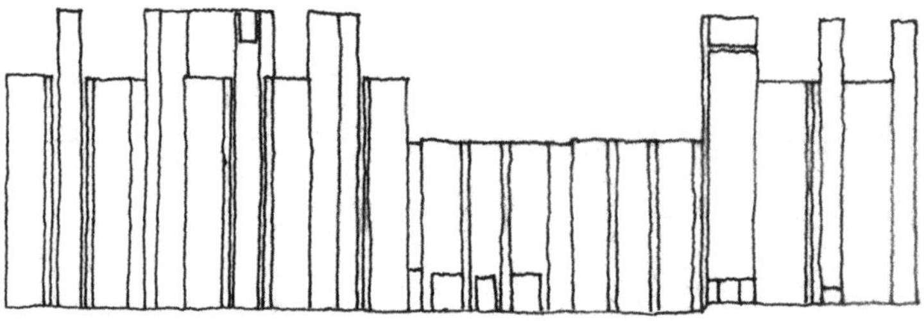

25. LOUIS KAHN : RICHARDS LABORATORY
JUXTAPOSED 'MASS'

IS THE VOLUMETRIC PLAID WHICH DERIVES ITS ORDER FROM TWO ADJACENT SURFACES: ONE HORIZONTAL AND ONE VERTICAL PLANE IN JUXTAPOSITION. THE VILLA SHODHAN BY LE CORBUSIER COMBINES THE PRINCIPLES OF THE MAISON DOMINO WITH THOSE OF GARCHES TO PRODUCE THE RESULTANT PLAIDING.[23] THE NORTH EAST ENTRY FACADE IS ARTICULATED FROM THE BODY OF THE HOUSE, INITIATING THE VERTICAL ORDERING, AND THE WEST FACADE CLEARLY PRESENTS THE HORIZONTAL READING BY AN ORDERING OF HORIZONTAL SLABS TENSIONED FROM THE ARTICULATED 'FLOATING' ROOF SURFACE.

MASS SYSTEMS BY DEFINITION MUST BE EXTERNAL REPRESENTATIONS OF AN INTERNAL VOLUMETRIC ORDER, AND ARE GENERALLY FOUND WHERE BRICK AND CONCRETE ARE EMPLOY-ED IN LOAD BEARING SITUATIONS. THESE OFTEN CONVEY THE CONCEPTION OF A GENERIC SOLID THAT HAS BEEN ERODED OR CUT AWAY; AS IN THE NEW CAIUS HOSTEL BY SIR LESLIE MARTIN AND COLIN ST. J. WILSON.[24] HOWEVER MASS SYSTEMS CAN ALSO BE USED TO EXPRESS A SEQUENCE OF PAVILIONS OR GEOMETRIC SOLIDS SUCH AS PYRAMIDS OR ZIGGURATS. HERE THE MASS IS NOT THOUGHT OF AS HAVING BEEN ERODED BUT RATHER AS JUXTAPOSTIONED IN ITS 'GEOMETRIC' CONDITION TO ORDER THE EXTERNAL SYSTEM; AN EXAMPLE OF THIS WOULD BE THE RICHARD'S LABORATORY BY LOUIS KAHN.[25]

THESE SYSTEMS HAVE ONLY BEEN PRESENTED IN OUTLINE. NO ATTEMPT HAS BEEN MADE TO ANALYSE THEM IN DETAIL WITH REFERENCE TO THEIR SPECIFIC SYNTAX AND GRAMMAR AS THIS CAN BEST BE ATTEMPTED IN THE PARTICULAR CONTEXT OF THE ACTUAL BUILD-INGS TO BE STUDIED IN THE FOLLOWING CHAPTER. BUT BEFORE THIS CAN BE DONE, THE MAJOR PROBLEMS OF SYNTAX WHICH AFFECT ANY SYSTEM MUST ALSO BE OUTLINED.

THIS SYNTAX IS THE SET OF RULES WHICH DERIVES FROM THE GENERIC CONDITION OF

both the building and its environment. It is applied to the conditions of specific form which require its use for their resolution and clarification. To achieve any systemic organisation the vocabulary (volume, mass, surface and movement) must be ordered and therefore clarified by the syntax.

Linear and centroidal generic conditions will produce major syntactical requirements some of which can be applied to both situations. Included among the latter would be, for example, the acknowledgement of a system as a complete entity having a beginning a middle and an end. Thus a linear block cannot be just stopped when functionally it has no need to continue, but rather this ending must be expressed in formal terms as having been purposefully terminated as part of a total system. Similarly, the entry to a building should not merely acknowledge the transition from inside to outside but should also provide a beginning to a system of movement throughout the entire building. Another major syntactical requirement is the modification of the generic internal state produced by the external forces acting upon it. Thus an internal centroidal organisation, which initially suggests four equal sides in its generic state, when placed at right angles to an external axis of movement, must show the effect of this external axis in the resultant specific form. The distortions of the generic state resulting from the pressure of an axis at right angles to the building will therefore be of a different nature to distortions produced by an axis parallel to the building.[26] The resultant system must then acknowledge and order these deformations of the generic condition. Certain syntactical requirements apply only to centroidal generic form. These would include: an acknowledgement of the centre and its nature; the recognition of a

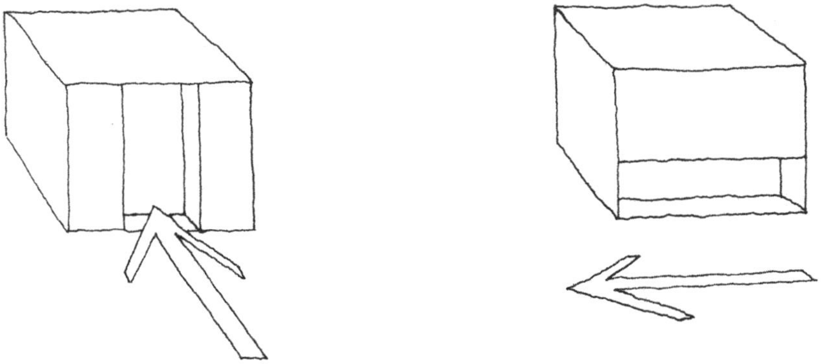

26.

DISTORTION OF GENERIC STATE DIFFERENT FOR AXES PERPENDICULAR OR PARALLEL

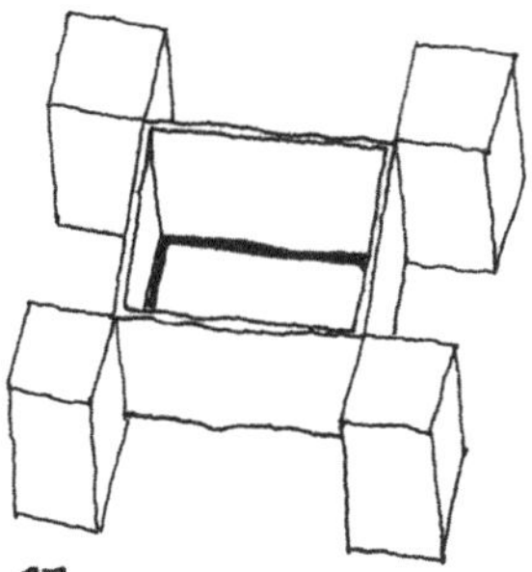

27.

CENTROIDAL SYNTAX:
ACKNOWLEDGEMENT OF CENTER
RECOGNITION OF ABSOLUTE HORIZONTAL
ARTICULATION IN SOME WAY OF CORNERS

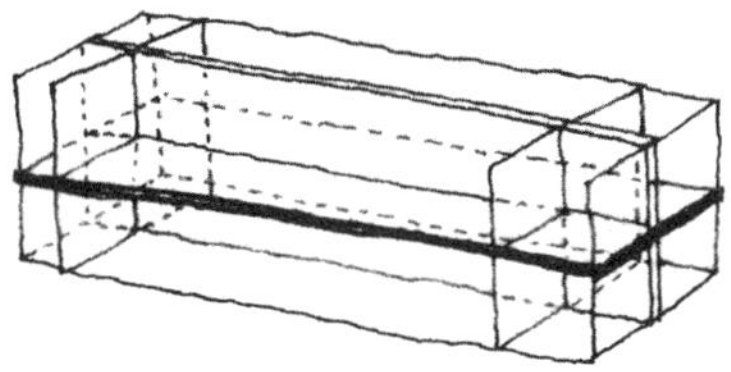

28.

LINEAR SYNTAX:
LINEAR NATURE OF FORM
EXPRESSION OF DOMINANT AXIS
AND DOMINANT PLANE OF REFERENCE
ARTICULATION OF ENDS.

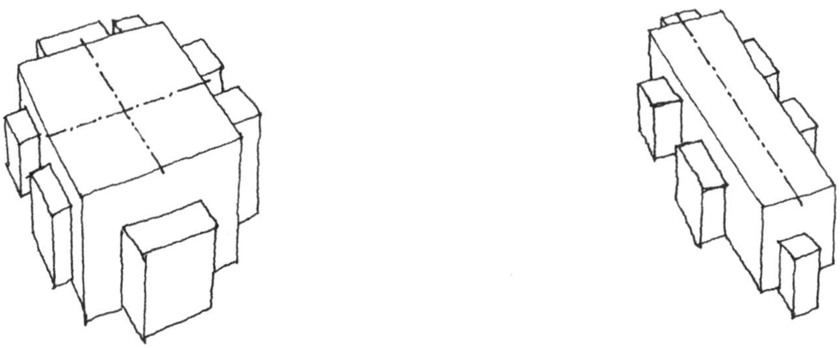

29.

INTERNAL CONFLICT PRODUCES DISTORTIONS:
CENTROIDAL THEATRE IN GENERIC STATE MAY
BE DISTORTED BY SPECIFIC CONDITIONS TO PRODUCE
A LINEAR FORM

HORIZONTAL QUALITY IF THE CENTRE IS A NEGATIVE VOLUME SUCH AS A COURT; AND THE ARTICULATIONS OF THE FOUR CORNERS.[27] IN RELATION TO A LINEAR GENERIC FORM THE SYNTAX WOULD RECOGNISE THE LINEAR NATURE OF THIS FORM: THE EXPRESSION OF THE DOMINANT AXIS: THE NATURE OF THE PROGRESSION ALONG THIS AXIS: THE ACKNOWLEDGE-MENT OF A LONGITUDINAL PLANE OF REFERENCE WHETHER VERTICAL OR HORIZONTAL : AND THE ARTICULATION OF THE ENDS.[28]

WITHIN BOTH THE ABOVE CATEGORIES OF GENERIC FORM THERE IS A POSSIBILITY OF AN INTERNAL CONFLICT WHICH WILL PRODUCE DISTORTIONS OF A SIMILAR NATURE TO THOSE DESCRIBED ABOVE. THUS A THEATRE, WHICH INITIALLY SUGGESTS A CENTROIDAL ORG-ANISATION, MAY BE DISTORTED TO PRODUCE A DOMINANT LINEAR VECTOR BY THE SPECIFIC DEMANDS OF THE SIZE AND SHAPE OF THE CENTRAL HALL WITH RESPECT TO THE STAGE HOUSE AND OTHER ANCILLIARY FUNCTIONS.[29]

THE ABOVE ONLY ESTABLISHES A BASIC OUTLINE OF THE SYNTACTICAL REQUIREMENTS. HOWEVER IT IS NECESSARY TO EXAMINE THE DISTORTIONS PRODUCED BY DIFFERENT COM-BINATIONS OF INTERNAL AND EXTERNAL VECTORS OR 'LINES OF FORCE' IN ORDER TO CLARIFY THE USE OF SYNTAX IN A SPECIFIC SITUATION. INITIALLY THE MEANING OF THESE INTERNAL CONDITIONS MUST BE DEFINED AND AMPLIFIED.

ALL INTERNAL GENERIC CONDITIONS DEVELOP INITIALLY FROM FUNCTIONAL ARRANGEMENTS: FROM THE DYNAMIC VECTORS INHERENT IN VOLUMETRIC OR MOVEMENT ORGANISATIONS. CENTROIDAL INTERNAL VECTORS DEVELOP FROM CENTRAL VERTICAL MOVEMENT OR SUCH CIR-CULATION PATTERNS AS SPIRALS AND PINWHEELS. IN VOLUMETRIC TERMS THESE VECTORS DEVELOP EITHER FROM A DOMINANT CENTRAL ORGANISATION, OF WHICH A CENTRAL COURT

OR HALL IS THE MOST COMMON, OR BY THE INTERRELATIONSHIP OF VOLUME AND MOVEMENT, SUCH AS IN LE CORBUSIER'S MUSEUM PROJECT WHICH TOGETHER CREATE A CENTROIDAL REFERENCE.

INTERNAL LINEAR CONDITIONS ARE THOSE WHICH DEVELOP INITIALLY FROM A PROGRAMMATIC ORGANISATION THAT DOES NOT DEMAND THE RELATIONSHIP OF MINOR FUNCTIONS TO A SINGLE MAJOR FUNCTION, BUT RATHER WEIGHTS ALL FUNCTIONS AS APPROXIMATELY EQUAL AND THESE FUNCTIONS THEMSELVES DO NOT REQUIRE ANY SPECIAL INTERCONNECTION AS IN AN OFFICE BUILDING OR BLOCK OF FLATS. THE ECHELON CAN BE CITED AS AN EXAMPLE OF EITHER A LINEAR VOLUMETRIC OR MOVEMENT SYSTEM. THE FINNISH BATHS PROJECT OF 1946 BY ALVAR AALTO PRESENTS A LINEAR VOLUMETRIC ECHELON AS THE DOMINANT MEANS OF CONTROL WITH A SECONDARY SPIRAL MOVEMENT SYSTEM. IN THE TALLINN MUSEUM PROJECT OF 1934 BY AALTO A LINEAR MOVEMENT ECHELON PROVIDES A SECONDARY ORDER TO THE TOTAL SYSTEM. HOWEVER, SOME BUILDINGS DO NOT HAVE A STRONG GENERIC PREFERENCE FOR EITHER A CENTROIDAL OR LINEAR ORGANISATION. IN THIS SITUATION THE INTERNAL ORGANISATION IS EASILY DISTORTED BY THE EXTERNAL CONDITION; THE INTERNAL ORGANISATION, IT MUST BE STRESSED, IS IN ANY SITUATION SUBSERVIENT TO THE EXTERNAL FORCES.

EXTERNAL CENTROIDAL VECTORS ARE DEVELOPED BY MOVEMENT IN RELATION TO A PARTICULAR SITE. IF ACCESS TO THIS SITE IS EQUAL ON ALL FOUR SIDES, THE SITE MAY BE CONSIDERED AS CENTROIDAL. THIS SITUATION WOULD IMMEDIATELY SUGGEST SOME TYPE OF INTERNAL BI-AXIAL SYMMETRY, INVOLVING THE EQUAL WEIGHTING OF THE ORTHOGANAL AXES; AND BECAUSE OF THE RATHER OBVIOUS NATURE OF THIS CONDITION, IT WILL NOT BE DISCUSSED IN DETAIL HERE. IT IS ENOUGH TO NOTE THAT WHEN THE INTERNAL CONDITIONS ALSO DEMAND A CENTROIDAL FORM THE MAJOR SYNTACTICAL REQUIREMENT MIGHT

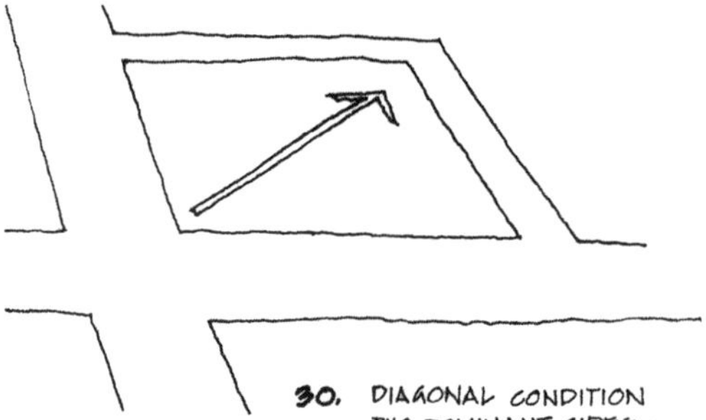

30. DIAGONAL CONDITION
TWO DOMINANT SIDES -

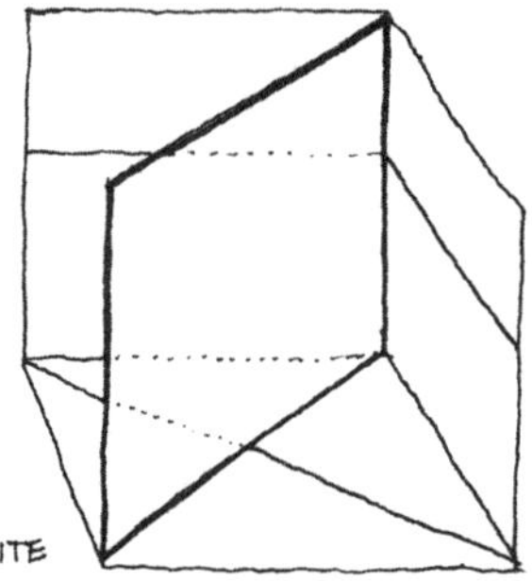

- OR A CORNER SITE

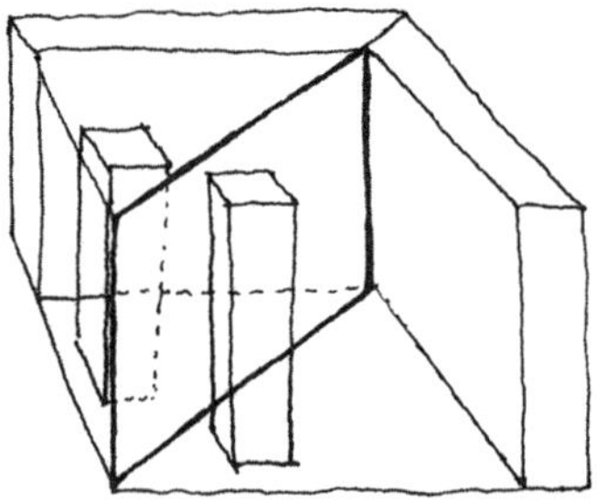

31. IF DIAGONAL IS ACKNOWLEDGED
SYMMETRY DEVELOPS -

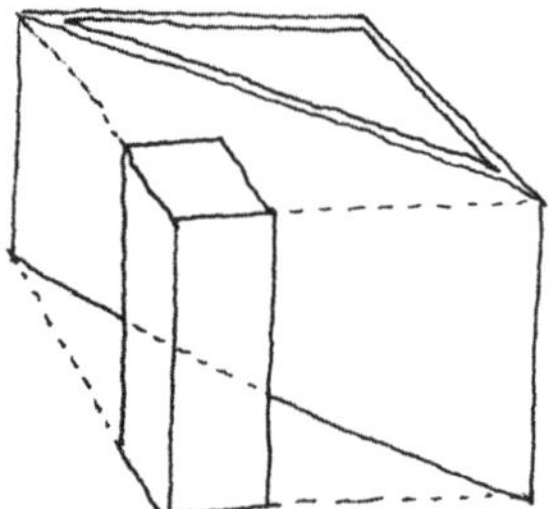

32.
- AND THERE MUST BE A COUNTERPOISE
ABOUT THE WEAK DIAGONAL.

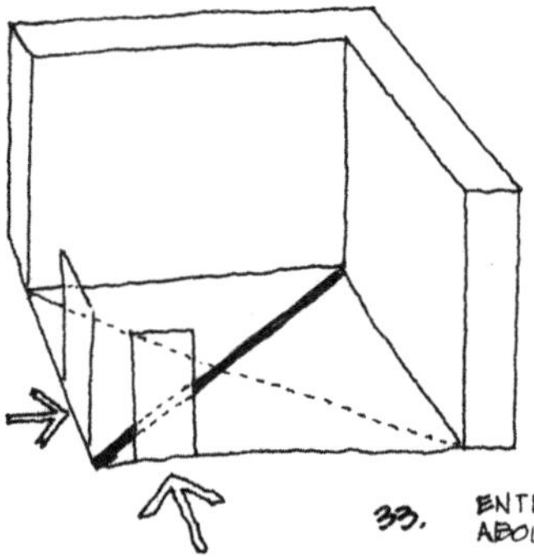

33. ENTRANCE SYMMETRICAL
ABOUT STRONG DIAGONAL

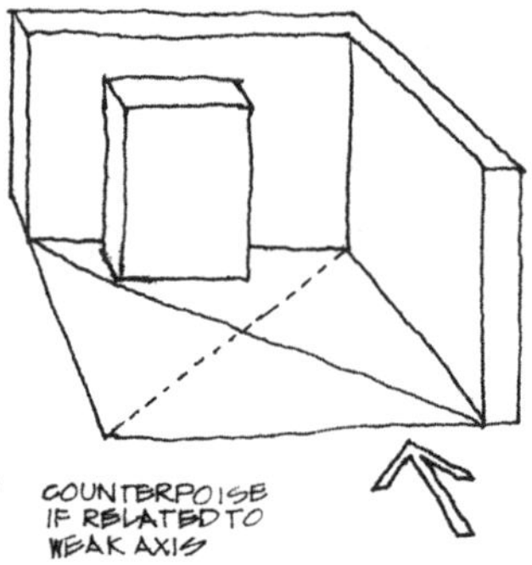

34. COUNTERPOISE
IF RELATED TO
WEAK AXIS

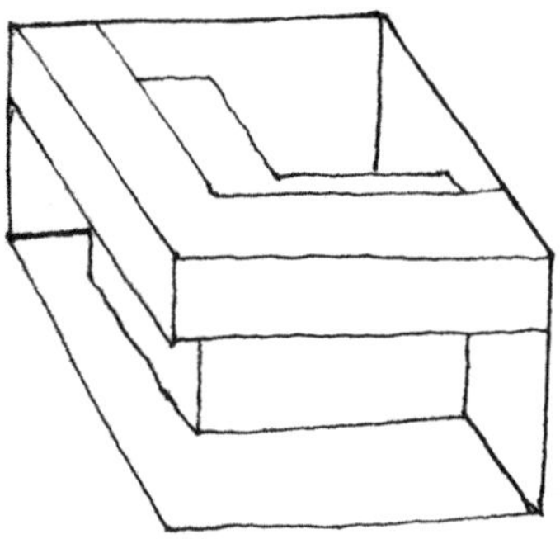

35.
RESULTANT
L-SHAPE INTERNAL ORGANIZATION
MAY BE A DISTORTION OF FUNCTION.

BE THE RESOLUTION OF FOUR SIDED ACCESS INTO A SINGLE ENTRANCE.

IF MOVEMENT TO A CENTROIDAL SITE IS DOMINANT ON TWO ADJACENT SIDES (A CORNER SITUATION) OR IF A SITE IS BOUNDED BY FOUR STREETS OF WHICH TWO ADJACENT SIDES ARE OF A DIFFERNET CHARACTER AND IMPORTANCE, THE SITE REMAINS CENTROIDAL BUT THE EXTERNAL VECTORS EMPHASISE ON OF THE DIAGONALS.[30] A SYSTEM CAN DEVELOP IN TWO WAYS FROM THESE GIVEN CONDITIONS: IT CAN EITHER ACKNOWLEDGE OR SEEK TO NEUTRALISE THE DIAGONAL AXIS. IF THE DIAGONAL AXIS IS TO BE AKNOWLEDGED A SYMMETRICAL CONDITION DEVELOPS ABOUT THIS AXIS;[31] A COUNTERPOISE OF ELEMENTS MUST BE ESTABLISHED ABOUT THE WEAK DIAGONAL TO RESTORE THE BALANCE, AND TO COMPENSATE FOR THE DISTURBANCE CAUSED BY THE STRESSING OF TWO ADJACENT SIDES.[32] MOREOVER THIS DIFFICULTY BECOMES ACUTE IN THE RESOLUTION OF THE ENTRY. IF THE ENTRANCE IS INFLUENCED BY THE STRONG DIAGONAL AXIS, IT IS AGAIN INVOLVED IN A SYMMETRICAL ARRANGEMENT WHICH WOULD REQUIRE A DUAL ENTRY.[33] CONVERSELY IF IT IS RELATED IN SOME WAY TO THE WEAK DIAGONAL IT IS THEREBY INVOLVED IN A COUNTERPOISE SITUATION REQUIRING A BALANCE FOR THE ENTRY VECTOR ON THE OPPOSITE SIDE.[34] THE INHERENT WEAKNESS IN BOTH OF THESE SOLUTIONS LIES IN A POSSILLE CONTRADICTION OF INTERNAL REQUIREMENTS. IF ONLY A SINGLE ENTRY IS REQUIRED THEN THE DUAL ENTRY BECOMES REDUNDANT, AND IF THE SINGLE ENTRY CANNOT BE RELATED TO THE WEAK DIAGONAL IT MAY ALSO BECOME A FUNCTIONAL DISTORTION. FURTHERMORE THE RESULTANT L-SHAPE INTERNAL ORGANISATION SUGGESTED BY THE DIAGONAL AXIS MIGHT BE AN INHERENT DENIAL OF THE INTERNAL REQUIREMENT.[35]

THERE IS ALSO THE POSSIBILITY OF DEVELOPING SYSTEMS WHICH DENY THE DIAGONAL, YET CONTAIN AN IMPLIED AKNOWLEDGEMENT OF ITS EXISTENCE.

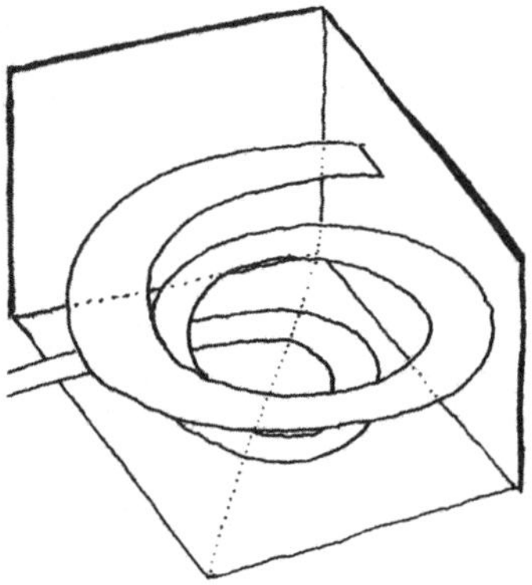

36.

SPIRAL SYSTEM COULD BE USED ON A DIAGONAL CONDITION SINCE IT DOES ACKNOWLEDGE THE DIAGONAL IN ITS ORGANIZATION.

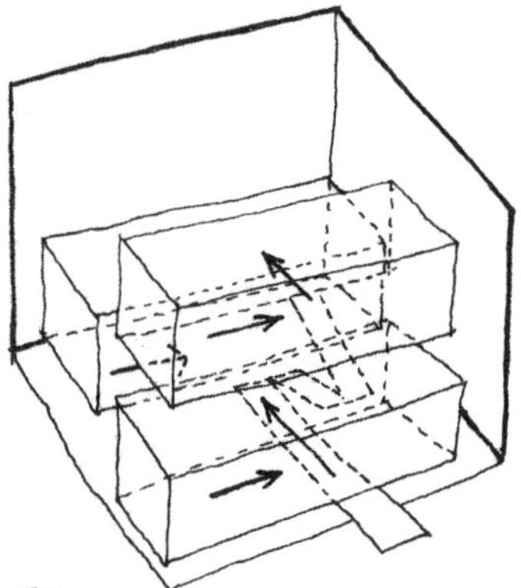

37.

A COUNTERPOISE OF VOLUME AND MOVEMENT EACH RELATING TO A DIFFERENT SIDE

UNDER THESE CONDITIONS THERE ARE TWO BASIC SOLUTIONS WHICH COULD BE SUGGESTED: THE ONE A SYSTEM OF MOVEMENT AND THE OTHER A VOLUMETRIC SYSTEM. THE FORMER MIGHT BE A SPIRAL WHICH BY VIRTUE OF ITS PARTICULAR MOTION DOES NOT REQUIRE EITHER THE EXPRESSION OR THE SUPPRESSION OF THE DIAGONAL AXIS.[36] HOWEVER, THERE MUST BE AN ACKNOWLEDGEMENT IN THE SYSTEM THAT THE SITE IS ARTICULATED: THAT THE DIAGONAL CONDITIONS EXIST. THIS WOULD REQUIRE THE INCORPORATION IN THE SYSTEM OF TWO DISTORTIONS: ONE THE RESOLUTION OF A DUAL ENTRY INTO A SINGLE ENTRY AND THE OTHER A PRESSURE ON ONE SIDE OF THE SPIRAL RESULTING FROM THE DOMINANT SIDES.

THE GUGGENHEIM MUSEUM IS AN EXAMPLE OF A CENTRIPETAL SPIRAL ON A CORNER SITE, WHICH CREATES A DIAGONAL CONDITION EVEN THOUGH THE ADJACENT STRESSED SIDES ARE NOT OF EQUAL MAGNITUDE. HERE THE MOVEMENT OF THE SPIRAL BEGINS EXTERNALLY AND MOVES FROM TOP TO BOTTOM TOWARDS A DOMINANT CENTRUM. THE DIFFICULTY OF ENTRY INTO THIS TYPE OF SYSTEM IS APPARENT HERE WHERE THE RESOLUTION AND LOCATION OF A SINGLE PERIPHERAL ENTRY SEEMS ARBITRARY, MAKING ANY TOTAL SYSTEM OF MOVEMENT FROM STREET TO VERTICAL CIRCULATION RATHER FORCED. IT IS THIS PROBLEM OF ENTRY INTO A CENTRIPETAL SYSTEM THAT IS ALWAYS CRUCIAL; AS THE INHERENT NATURE OF SUCH A SYSTEM SEEMS TO DENY CENTROIDAL EXTERNAL CONDITIONS, AND REQUIRES THAT THIS MULTI-ACCESS SITUATION BE RESOLVED INTO A SINGLE ENTRY: THE BEGINNING OF THE SPIRAL.

THE OTHER POSSIBLE SOLUTION IS ONE THAT IS BASED ON A VOLUMETRIC ORDERING; THIS WOULD INVOLVE THE TENSIONING AND RELATING OF A SERIES OF VOLUMETRIC PLANES TO THE STRESSED SIDES OF THE CENTROIDAL SITE. UNLESS THIS TENSIONING IS FULLY EXPRESSED THIS SYSTEM COULD DEVELOP INTO A CRUCIFORM OR A PLAIDING OF VOLUMES,

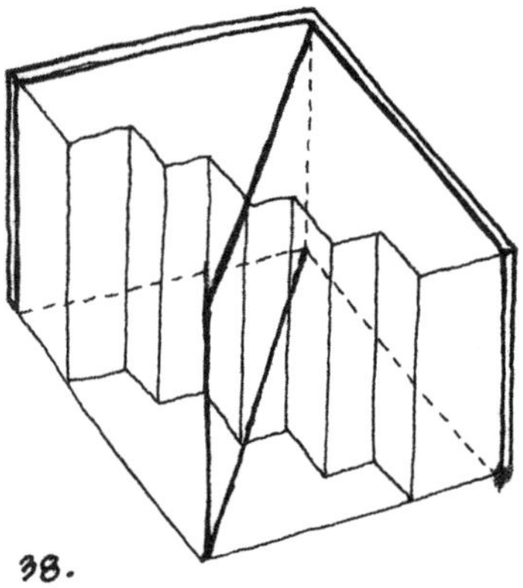

38.

ECHELON SYSTEM WOULD BE BROKEN BY THE DIAGONAL

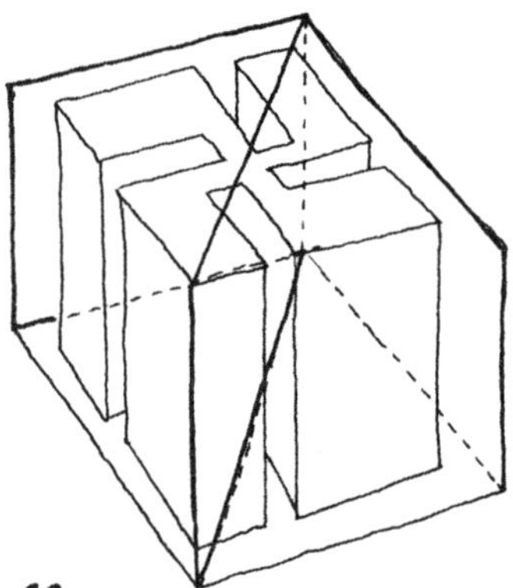

39.

PINWHEEL WOULD SUGGEST FOUR EQUAL SIDES

AND THIS WOULD FAIL TO ACKNOWLEDGE THE WEIGHTING OF THE TWO SIDES TO OVERCOME THIS DIFFICULTY, A COUNTERPOISE SITUATION COULD BE CONSIDERED WHEREBY CERTAIN VOLUMES WOULD RELATE TO ONE SIDE, AND ANOTHER ORDER OF VOLUMES, OR A SECONDARY SYSTEM OF MOVEMENT WOULD RELATE TO THE ADJACENT SIDE.[37] MOREOVER THIS COUNTER-POISE BETWEEN MOVEMENT AND VOLUMETRIC ORGANISATION MIGHT RESOLVE A PROBLEM OF SINGLE ENTRY THEREBY PRESENTING A HYBRID SYSTEM EXPRESSIVE OF THIS DUALITY. AN IMPORTANT SYNTACTICAL REQUIREMENT IN SUCH A SYSTEM WOULD BE THE ACKNOWLEDGE-MENT OF THE JUNCTIONS BETWEEN THESE SYSTEMS AND THE PRESSURES CREATED BY THESE INTERSECTION.

IT IS INTERESTING TO NOTE THAT THE OTHER TWO MAJOR MOVEMENT SYSTEMS: THE ECHELON AND THE PINWHEEL, ARE NOT APPLICABLE IN THIS SITUATION. THE ECHELON WHICH, IS ESSENTIALLY A LINEAR DEVELOPMENT DEPENDS ON A RHYTHMIC CONTINUITY FOR ITS RECOGNITION, WHICH WOULD OBVIOUSLY BE DENIED BY A DIAGONAL VECTOR CUT-TING THROUGH ITS CENTRE.[38] A PINWHEEL IN ESSENCE IMPLIES THREE OR FOUR EQUAL SIDES, IF NOT THREE OR FOUR MEANS OF ACCESS WHICH AGAIN WOULD CATEGORICALLY DENY THE DIAGONAL CONDITION.[39] THIS DOES NOT IRREVOCABLY RESTRICT THE USE OF THESE TWO SYSTEMS IN THESE CONDITIONS, ESPECIALLY IF THE INTERNAL ORGANISATION SUGGESTED NO OTHER POSSIBLE RESOLUTION. ANY SUCH DEVELOPMENT WOULD HOWEVER BE IN A SENSE PERVERSE AND MANNERED; AND THE SYSTEM WOULD THEN HAVE TO ACKNOWLEDGE THIS 'INVERSE' DISTORTION.

IF MOVEMENT IS DENIED FROM TWO OPPOSITE SIDES, THE AXIS OF ENTRY WOULD BE IM-MEDIATELY EMPHASISED, THUS CREATING A LINEAR EXTERNAL CONDITION, EVEN THOUGH THE SHAPE OF THE SITE MIGHT BE SQUARE WHICH PERCEPTUALLY MIGHT SUGGEST A CEN-TROIDAL SITUATION. ANY DOMINANT ORTHOGONAL AXIS IMPOSED ON A SITE PRODUCES AN

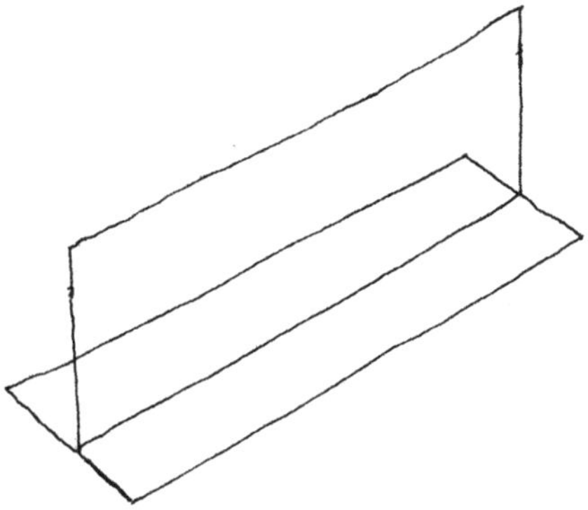

NEUTRAL STATE OF PLANE OF SYMMETRY IN A LINEAR VOLUME

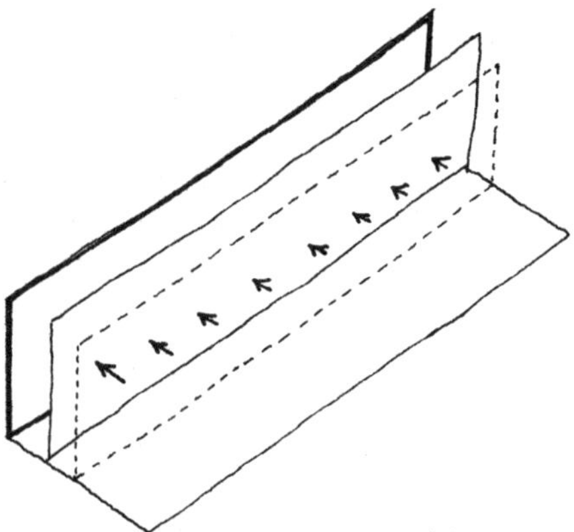

40.

IN CORNER SITE, WITH ONE SIDE DOMINANT · SURFACE OF SYMETRY IS DISLOCATED TOWARDS THE DOMINANT SURFACE TO RESTORE BALANCE

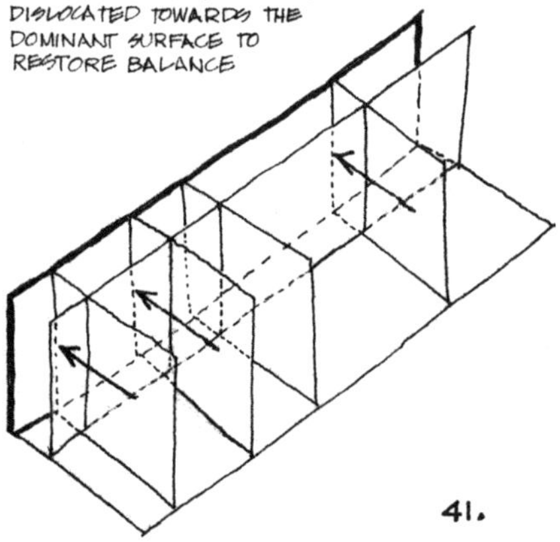

41.

ALL VERTICAL AND ORTHOGONAL PLANES ARE AFFECTED BY THIS DOMINANT SURFACE.

EXTERNAL LINEAR CONDITION REGARDLESS OF THE SPECIFIC SHAPE OF THE SITE. THESE CONDITIONS CAN RESULT FROM SEVERAL DIFFERENT FACTORS. ONE, MIGHT BE THE GROUPING OF ADJACENT POSITIVE VOLUMES IN SUCH A WAY AS TO SUGGEST A STRONG LINEAR AXIS. ANOTHER DOMINANT AXIS MAY BE DEVELOPED BY A MAJOR CIRCULATION ROUTE RUNNING PARALLEL TO, OR TERMINATING IN, THE SPECIFIC SITE; THIS MAY BE THOUGHT OF AS A NEGATIVE VOLUME IN JUXTAPOSITION TO THE GIVEN SITE. IT IS TO BE REMEMBERED THAT ONE AXIS IS DOMINANT IN ANY LINEAR EXTERNAL CONDITION, WHETHER IN JUXTAPOSITION TO, OR INCORPORATED IN, THE SITE ITSELF. IT MUST BE NOTED THAT ON A LINEAR SITE THE DIAGONAL RARELY DOMINATES, OWING TO THE STRENGTH OF THE ORTHOGONAL AXIS. AN EXCEPTION TO THIS CAN BE NOTED IN AALTO'S SAYNATSALO SCHEME, WHERE THE JUXTAPOSITION OF POSITIVE ELEMENTS ON A LINEAR SITE CREATED A STRONG DIAGONAL AXIS WHEN SEEN IN RELATION TO A CENTRAL COURT.

AS IN THE CASE OF CENTROIDAL SITUATIONS ONE OR MORE SIDES OF A LINEAR EXTERNAL VOLUME MAY BECOME STRESSED OR DOMINANT; AN EXAMPLE OF THIS WOULD BE A CORNER SITE WITH THREE SIDED ACCESS WHICH GIVES THE REMAINING SITE A DOMINANT QUALITY. IN SUCH SITUATIONS THE PLANE OF SYMMETRY MAY BE DISPLACED FROM ITS NEUTRAL CENTRAL POSITION TO ONE WHERE A DYNAMIC EQUILIBRIUM OF FORCES IS RESTORED.[40] THIS DISLOCATION IS CAUSED BY AN ATTRACTION, A TENSIONING FROM THE DOMINANT PLANE. THIS TENSIONING RESTORES THE STATE OF BALANCE ABOUT THE NEW AXIS OF SYMMETRY, BY CREATING ON THE ONE HAND A LARGE VOLUME WHICH IS IN EQUILIBRIUM ON THE OTHER HAND WITH THE DOMINANT SURFACE, AND SMALL VOLUME RESULTING FROM THE SHIFTING OF THIS AXIS. IT CAN ALSO BE ASSUMED THAT ALL SUCH VERTICAL PLANES, EITHER LONGITUDINAL OR TRANSVERSE, ARE AFFECTED IN A LIKE MANNER BY THIS DOMINANT REFERENCE,[41] AND CAN BE THOUGHT OF AS IN A STATE OF TENSION RESULTING FROM THE

ATTRACTION OF THIS PLANE. ANY SYSTEMIC DEVELOPMENT MUST ACKNOWLEDGE INTERNALLY THE EXTERNAL GENERIC STATE (THE NEUTRAL AXIS) AND THE DISTORTION OF THIS STATE (THE DISLOCATION OF THE NEUTRAL AXIS) CAUSED BY THE SPECIFIC VECTORS. UNDER THESE CONDITIONS A VOLUMETRIC SYSTEM, A SERIES OF VERTICAL PLANES, EITHER PARALLEL OR PERPENDICULAR TO THE LONG AXIS BUT TENSIONED FROM THE STRESSED SURFACE MIGHT BE DEVELOPED.

IN MANY SITUATIONS THE INTERNAL AND EXTERNAL CONDITIONS MAY BE IN CONFLICT; THESE CONFLICTS MUST THEN BE RESOLVED AND ACKNOWLEDGED IN THE PARTICULAR SYSTEMIC DEVELOPMENT. IT IS OBVIOUS THAT WHEN THIS CONFLICT OCCURS ANY DISTORTION WILL TAKE PLACE IN THE INTERNAL CONDITION. A SYNTAX IS STILL REQUIRED TO CLARIFY THE INTERRELATIONSHIP OF CENTROIDAL AND LINEAR CONDITIONS INVOLVED IN ANY SPECIFIC SITUATION EVEN THOUGH THEY ARE NOT IN CONFLICT.

THIS SYNTAX CAN INITIALLY BE ILLUSTRATED BY A SERIES OF ABSTRACTED SITUATIONS INVOLVING LINEAR AND CENTROIDAL FORMS. SUCH CONDITIONS ARE ENVISAGED WITHOUT REGARD TO FUNCTION OR CONTENT, WHICH IN AN ACTUAL SITUATION WOULD BE INITIAL FACTORS IN THE DEVELOPMENT OF THE SYSTEM.

IF WE TAKE A SINGLE CUBE (WHICH IS A CENTROIDAL FORM) AND IF WE WERE TO THINK OF A GROUND FOR THIS FIGURE IN THE MOST SIMPLE, ECONOMIC TERMS, THIS GROUND WOULD BE ANOTHER CUBE THAT WOULD JUST CONTAIN THE FIRST.[42] THEIR EXACT PROPORTIONAL RELATIONSHIP WOULD DEPEN ON THE SPECIFIC SITUATION. IF THE GROUND VOLUME IS DISTORTED TO PRODUCE A LINEAR EXTERNAL CONDITION, THEN THE ORIGINAL CUBE MUST BE PLACED TO ACKNOWLEDGE BOTH THE DISTORTION AND THE RECTILINEAR QUALITY O

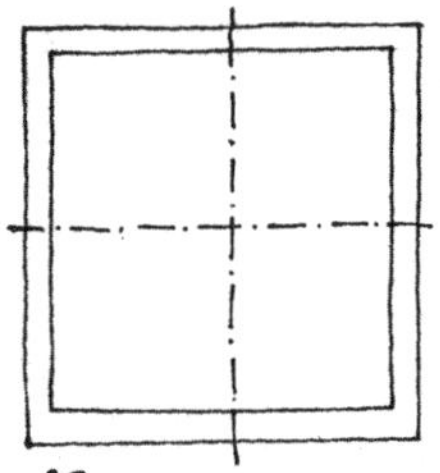

42.
CUBE WITHIN A CUBE

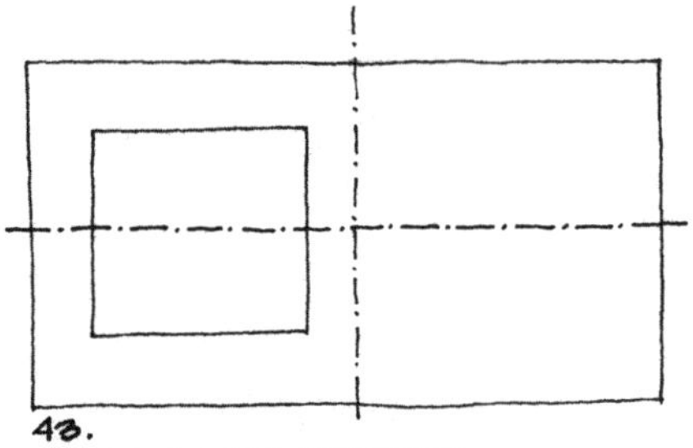

43.
AROUND VOLUME DISTORTED
CUBE PLACED TO ACKNOWLEDGE
DISTORTION

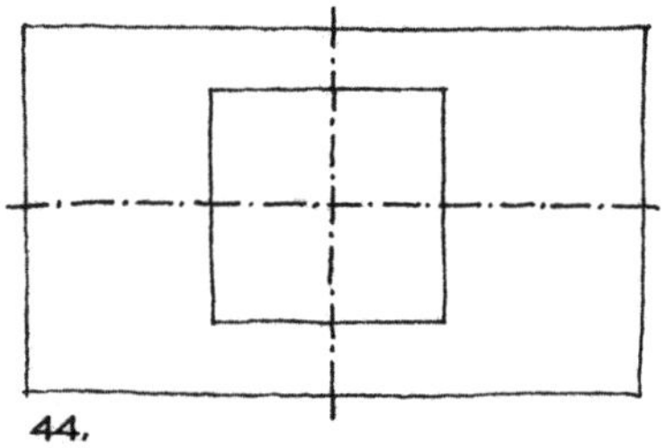

44.
A FURTHER DISTORTION RESTORES
CUBE TO CENTRAL POSITION STRESSING
MINOR AXIS

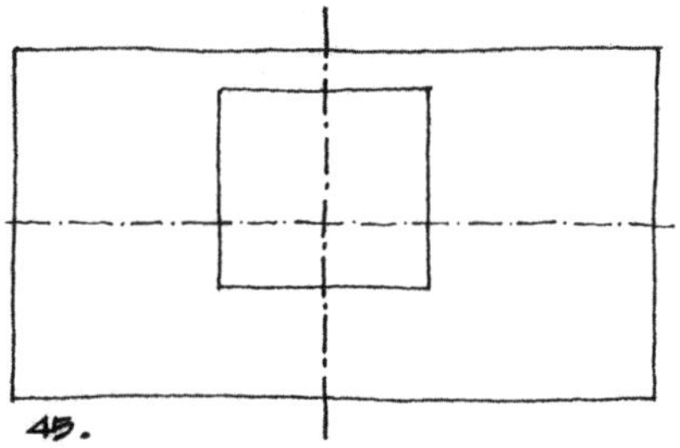

45.
MINOR AXIS BECOMES STRONGER BY
SHIFTING CUBE OFF THE MAJOR AXIS

THE GROUND VOLUME.[43] THIS WOULD MEAN PLACING THE CUBE AT ONE END OF THE RECTILINEAR GROUND VOLUME TO ACKNOWLEDGE THE FORCE OF THE LINEAR VECTOR. ALTERNATIVELY, THE RECTILENEAR GROUND CAN BE ACKNOWLEDGED BY A FURTHER DISTORTION WHICH DOES NOT RECOGNISE THE LINEAR QUALITY, BUT RESTORES THE ORIGINAL FIGURE TO A POSITION OF NEUTRALITY ABOUT BOTH AXES.[44] THIS TENDS TO RESTATE THE MINOR TRANSVERSE AXIS IN A POSITION OF PROMINENCE IN RELATION TO THE MAJOR LINEAR AXIS.[45] THIS EREATES A DISTORTED OR INVERSE READING WITH REGARD TO THE FORMAL ESSENCE OF THE LINEAR GROUND FIGURE WHICH IS NOW SEEN AS A <u>LINEAR</u> FIGURE WITH <u>TWO</u> DOMINANT AXES. THE SITUATION WOULD BECOME EVEN MORE PERVERSE IF THE CUBIC VOLUME WAS DEFLECTED FROM THE LINEAR AXIS ONLY RETAINING ITS POSITION ON THE TRANSVERSE AXIS THEREBY GIVING THIS AXIS A DOMINANT QUALITY IN RELATION TO THE ORIGINAL LINEAR AXIS. THESE DISTORTIONS ONLY BECOME A VALID ACKNOWLEGEMENT OF THE INITIAL GENERIC CONDITION IF THEY ARE INCORPORATED INTO A SYSTEM WHERE LIKE CONDITIONS ARE TREATED IN A SIMILAR MANNER. AN EXAMPLE OF THE SAME KIND WOULD BE THE PLACING OF A LINEAR FIGURE ON A CENTROIDAL GROUND RESULTING IN ANOTHER SERIES OF 'INVERSE' DISTORTIONS. THIS KIND OF 'MANNERED' SYSTEM CAN IN FACT FREQUENTLY DEVELOP AS HAS BEEN NOTED PREVIOUSLY.

THE MAJOR CATEGORY OF ANY DISTORTIONS DERIVES FROM THE RESOLUTION OF EXTERNAL LINEAR VECTORS IN CONFLICT WITH INTERNAL REQUIREMENTS. IN THESE SITUATIONS THE TRANSITION OR POINT OF ENTRY FROM EXTERNAL TO INTERNAL CONDITIONS TAKES ON AN ADDITIONAL IMPORTANCE. THIS ENTRY REQUIRES A DIFFERENT SYNTAX DEPENDING ON THE SPECIFIC SITUATION AND IT IS THE NATURE OF THIS SYNTAX, CRITICAL TO THE INITIAL DEVELOPMENT OF ANY SYSTEM, WHICH MUST BE AMPLIFIED. IN THE CASE OF A LINEAR AXIS RUNNING PARALLEL TO THE SITE EITHER A CENTROIDAL OR A LINEAR REQU-

irement internally can effect the specific means for deflecting or stopping the external axis to provide entry into the building; both of these internal requirements having their own specific syntax. In the former case the syntax governs the necessary cutting and deflecting of the external axis and the distorting of the internal condition to recognise single entry into a centroidal generic form. In the latter case both linear axes must be stopped or deflected and the resultant connection must be ordered as part of a total system of movement.

Le Corbusier's Museum project of 1939 and Terragni's Asilo Infantile can be cited as two examples of centroidal, internal conditions occuring parallel to a linear external vector. In each case the linear axis is cut in such a way as to resolve the problem of a single entry into a centroidal building. In the first example Le Corbusier develops a linear axis on the site which cuts the external axis at right angles. He then terminates this axis at the same time providing entry into the building by employing a spiral movement system as an end to the external vector. Here the movement is centrifugal which creates two inherent difficulties: the movement outwards must somehow be controlled to provide a termination to the system, and the spiral itself must be raised to allow for a central entry. This type of solution would seem valid regardless of the external conditions since both linear and centroidal external vectors could be compensated for in the raising of the spiral. In the specific grammatical resolution Corbusier raises the museum on pilotis to allow the linear axis to penetrate to the centre. The outward movement which is a continuous equal spiral is then terminated by an auxiliary stair.

Terragni in the Asilo Infantile, uses a system based on a series of volumetric planes relating vertically to a stressed entry surface which is parallel to the linear axis. The volumetric slices are tied together by an entry plug which implies a cutting of the external vector. In this case the stressed surface acknowledges the distortion in the centroidal generic form, and acts as the major reference for the systemic development. The Salvation Army Hostel by Le Corbusier is an example of a linear building parallel to a linear axis. The syntactical problem of entry is resolved by an elaborate en-suite pavillion development which provided the cutting of the parallel axes that is required. Where a single external axis terminates in the site the syntax controls the required blunting of the external vector at the same time as resolving the problem of a single entry into either a centroidal or linear internal condition. This problem of single entry will initiate and restrict the number of systems that could be employed.

The Casa Del Fascio in Como is an example of this condition. Here a centroidal internal requirement acts as the termination of the external linear axis. The distortions which prodice the specific form acknowledge two syntactical requirements: the termination of the linear axis and the control of a single entry in to a generic centroidal form. In the Pavillon Suisse the building itself is linear which provides the intitial blunting of the external vector. This deflecting of the external axis is then linked to the internal movement to produce a total spiral system which also resolves the problem of single entry into a linear building. In some cases where internal conditions deflect the external axis the system must somehow be fised and thus distorted to allow for a single entry. La Tourette is an example of this fixing. Here Le Corbusier

USES THE PINWHEEL AS A SECONDARY SYSTEM TO ACKNOWLEDGE THE CONTROL OF CORNER CONDITIONS. HE ARRESTS THE PINWHEEL BY DETATCHING THE FOURTH SIDE, THE CHAPEL, TO PROVIDE A CHECK TO THE SPINNING MOTION. FURTHER, IT CAN BE NOTED THAT IN THE FAÇADE THEREBY HEIGHTENING THE TENSION OF THE ARRESTED MOTION. IN CASES WHERE THE SYSTEM IS NOT ARRESTED SINGLE ENTRY BECOMES DIFFICULT, AS IN THE GRADUATE HOUSING FOR CHURCHILL COLLEGE. MOVEMENT HERE TENDS TO BE FORCED OUTWARD AND AWAY FROM THE CENTRE BY THE SPINNING MOVEMENT THUS MAKING ANY ENTRY INTO THE COMPLEX VIRTUALLY IMPOSSIBLE.

THIS CHAPTER HAS TRIED TO INDICATE THE RELATIONSHIP OF SYNTAX TO THE DEVELOPMENT OF A SYSTEM IT HAS NOT SOUGHT TO PRESENT EITHER A COMPLEX COMPILATION OF SYNTACTICAL REQUIREMENTS OR AN EXHAUSTIVE LIST OF SYSTEMIC RESPONSES WHICH DEVELOP FROM THIS SYNTAX, IT IS RATHER INTENDED TO DEMONSTRATE THAT SYSTEMS MUST DEVELOPE FROM BOTH THE EXTERNAL SITUATION AND THE INTERNAL FUNCTIONAL REQUIREMENTS; AND THAT THE GENERIC CONDITION SUGGESTED BY THESE REQUIREMENTS HAS ITS OWN SYNTAX. IT IS THIS SYNTAX WHICH GOVERNS THE TOTAL SPECIFIC ORGANISATION. THE EXAMPLES SELECTED ONLY SHOW THE POSSIBLE INITIAL DEVELOPMENTS OF ANY SYSTEM AND AS SUCH THEY CAN BE REGARDED AS AN INTRODUCTION TO THE DETAILED ANALYSES WHICH FOLLOW.

IN PROPOUNDING ANY THEORY IT IS NECESSARY TO PROVIDE SOME EMPIRICAL PROOF OF THE ASSUMPTIONS CONTAINED IN THE ARGUMENT. THEREFORE THIS CHAPTER EXAMINES EIGHT BUILDINGS, TWO BY EACH OF THE FOUR ARCHITECTS MENTIONED PREVIOUSLY, IN ORDER TO TEST THSE ASSUMPTIONS. IT IS NOT THE DESIRE HERE TO ANALYSE THE PARTICULAR METHOD OR STYLE OF EACH ARCHITECT NOR TO PROVE THE VALIDITY OF THEIR METHOD, BUT IT IS RATHER TO VERIFY THE METHOD PUT FORWARD IN THE PRECEDING CHAPTERS.

THESE PARTICULAR BUILDINGS HAVE BEEN CHOSEN FOR BOTH GENERAL AND SPECIFIC REASONS. IN GENERAL THEY CAN BE THOUGHT OF AS THE WORKS OF ACCEPTED 'MASTERS' WHICH REPRESENT OPPOSED AND DIVERGENT STYLES WITHIN THE MODERN TRADITION. IT WILL BE SEEN THAT REGARDLESS OF STYLE AND SPECIFIC FORM, THE VALIDITY OF THESE BUILDINGS ACCRUES FROM A CONCEPTUAL BASIS; IN EACH CASE THIS BASIS BEING ORDERED BY A SYSTEM WHICH MUST BE EXTRACTED AND ANALYSED. FURTHERMORE, THESE BUILDINGS HAVE BEEN SELECTED BECAUSE THEY SATISFY A PARTICULAR CONDITION DEMANDING A SYNTACTICAL RESOLUTION. THEREFORE BOTH BUILDINGS BY EACH ARCHITECT ARE OF A SIMILAR GENERIC TYPE: EITHER LINEAR OR CENTROIDAL. IN EACH CASE THE EXTERNAL CONDITIONS PRESENT AXES EITHER PARALLEL OR PERPENDICULAR TO THE INTERNAL DEVELOPMENT, THEREBY PROVIDING AN OPPORTUNITY TO ANALYSE THE EVOLUTION OF A SPECIFIC FORM IN SOMEWHAT SIMILAR OR CONTROLLED CONDITIONS; THE NOTION BEING THAT SIMILAR PROGRAMMATIC REQUIREMENTS SEEN IN TERMS OF GENERIC FORM, WHEN SUBJECTED TO THE SPECIFIC GRAMMAR OF EACH ARCHITECT WILL PROVIDE AN OPPORTUNITY TO

ANALYSE THE PARTICULAR SYSTEMIC RESPONSE. THESE ANALYSES WILL NOT BE CONCERNED WITH PROBLEMS OF A PERCEPTUAL NATURE: COLOUR, PROPORTION, TEXTURE ETC., BUT WILL ONLY ATTEMPT TO CONSIDER THE CONCEPTUAL BASIS OF THE FORMAL MANIFESTATIONS IN EACH EXAMPLE.

SINCE IT HAS ALREADY BEEN ACKNOWLEDGED THAT THE CONCEPTUAL BASIS OF THE FORMAL LANGUAGE, DEVELOPED IN THE PRECEDING CHAPTERS, IS ADUMBRATED BY MUCH OF LE CORBUSIER'S WORK, IT WOULD SEEM REASONABLE TO BEGIN THE DOCUMENTATION OF THIS LANGUAGE WITH THE CONSIDERATION OF TWO OF HIS BUILDINGS. THESE ANALYSES WILL NOT ATTEMPT TO VALIDATE THE WRITINGS OF LE CORBUSIER THROUGH HIS WORK. THEY ARE RATHER TO BE THOUGHT OF AS THE EMPIRICAL VERIFICATION OF THE USE OF THE LANGUAGE IN AN ARCHITECTURAL CONTEXT. THESE ANALYSES WILL CONSIDER THE CONCEPTUAL BASIS OF THE SPECIFIC FORMS INVOKED, THE GRAMMATICAL IMPLEMENTATION OF THE VOCABULARY, THE ACKNOWLEDGEMENT OF SYNTACTICAL REQUIREMENTS AND THE COMBINATION OF THESE INTO A SYSTEMIC ORDER.

THESE BUILDINGS HAVE BEEN SELECTED TO ELUCIDATE THE ORDER THAT LE CORBUSIER IMPOSES ON HIS GRAMMAR. THE DIFFERENCES IN THE PARTICULAR SITUATIONS FURTHER CLARIFY THE SYSTEMIC DEVELOPMENT. IN BOTH CASES IT WILL BE SEEN THAT LE CORBUSIER EVOLVES A TWO-PART SYSTEM EXPRESSING THE INDIVIDUAL ORDERING OF MOVEMENT AND VOLUME. THESE ORGANIZATIONS ARE DEVELOPED IN SYNTHESIS; THEY DO NOT PRESENT A DIALECTIC CONDITION AS THEY ARE NOT INTENDED TO REPRESENT AN EXTERNAL-INTERNAL CONFLICT. BOTH OF THE SELECTED BUILDINGS ARE LINEAR DEVELOPMENTS DERIVED FROM AN INTERNAL VOLUMETRIC ORGANIZATION. IN EACH CASE, THE MOVEMENT SYSTEM IS OF THE SAME IMPORTANCE AS THE VOLUMETRIC ORDER, DEVELOPING BOTH FROM THE GENERAL SYNTACTICAL REQUIREMENT OF THE EXTERNAL-INTERNAL TRANSITION, AND THE SPECIFIC SYNTAX OF THE PROBLEM OF SINGLE ENTRY INTO A LINEAR ORGANIZATION.

THE INTERNAL CONDITION IN EACH EXAMPLE IS LINEAR; AT THE PAVILLON SUISSE THE EXTERNAL AXIS IS AT RIGHT ANGLES TO THE INTERNAL AXIS, WHILE AT THE CITE DE

REFUGE IT IS PARALLEL. THIS DIFFERENCE GIVES RISE TO THE PARTICULAR GRAMMAR AND SYNTAX OF BOTH THE MOVEMENT AND THE VOLUMETRIC ORGANISATION, WHICH MESH TO BECOME A COMPOSITE TWO-PART SYSTEM ORDERING THE SPECIFIC FORM OF EACH BUILDING. INDEED, THESE FORMS ARE THE PRECISE INTERPRETATION AND MANIFESTATION OF THE CONCEPTUAL BASIS OF THE SYSTEM: ITS GENERIC CONDITION. FURTHERMORE THESE FORMS ARE SPECIFIC YET NOT ARBITARY AND PICTORIAL AS THEY ARE RIDGIDLY CONTROLLED WITHIN THE TOTAL ORDER; THEY ARE THE PERCEPTUAL EVIDENCE FOR THE CLARITY OF THE CONCEPTUAL BASIS. THE SYSTEMIC CONTROL IS BASED ON TWO FUNDAMENTAL ASSUMPTIONS. FIRSTLY THERE IS THE DEFINITION OF THE COORDINATES OF THE SPATIAL GRID WHICH CAUSES ALL PARTS OF THE BUILDING TO BE IN TENSION FROM A DOMINANT SURFACE OF REFERENCE AS WELL AS DIFFERENTIATING THE FRONTALS AND THE ORTHOGANALS. SECONDLY THERE IS THE RELATING AND CONTROLLING OF THE SPECIFIC VOLUMES TO THE AXES OF THE GENERIC CONDITION.

PAVILLON SUISSE

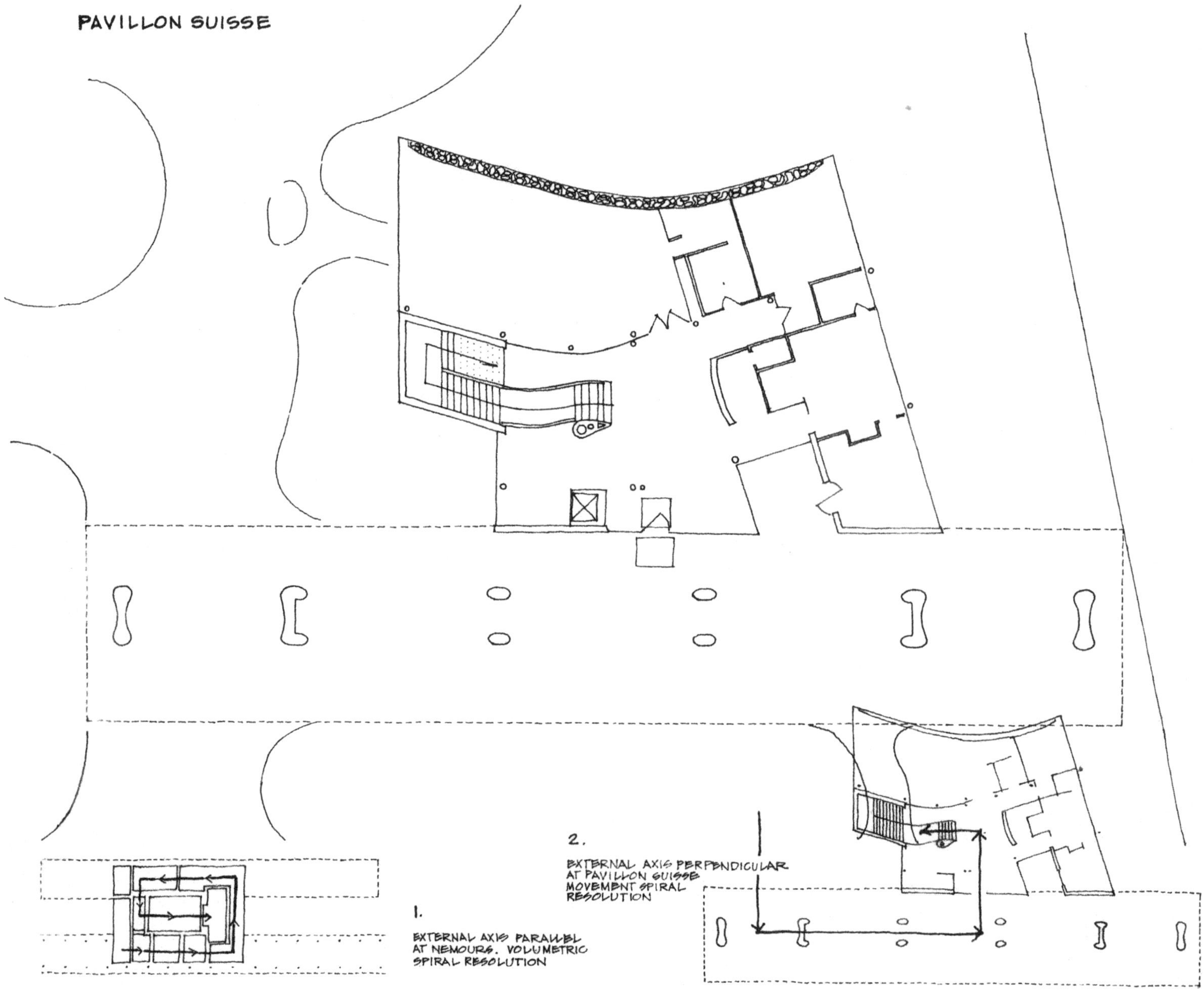

1. EXTERNAL AXIS PARALLEL AT NEMOURS. VOLUMETRIC SPIRAL RESOLUTION

2. EXTERNAL AXIS PERPENDICULAR AT PAVILLON SUISSE MOVEMENT SPIRAL RESOLUTION

THE INITIAL DISTORTIONS OF THE GENERIC STATE (WHICH CAN BE READ AS A RECTILINEAR BLOCK) ARE EVOLVED FROM THE SYNTACTICAL CONTROL OF A SINGLE ENTRANCE INTO A RECTILINEAR VOLUME. THE RESULTANT SEQUENCE OF DISTORTIONS IS PART OF THE SYSTEMIC ORDERING OF MOVEMENT AND VOLUME. MOREOVER THE COMPREHENSION OF THIS TWO-PART SYSTEM DEPENDS ON THE ESTABLISHMENT OF A SURFACE OF REFERENCE AND A RECOGNITION OF THE DISLOCATION OF PARTS FROM A GENERIC STATE. THE SYSTEM OF MOVEMENT ORDERS BOTH THE EXTERNAL AXIS OF APPROACH AND THE ACTUAL ENTRY INTO THE BUILDING. IN THIS CASE THE VOLUMETRIC SYSTEM CONTROLS THE DISTORTIONS FROM THE GENERIC STATE AND IS EXPRESSED BY A MASS-SURFACE DIALECTIC WHICH ESTABLISHES THE DOMINANT SURFACE.

CONCEPTUALLY THE BUILDING MAY BE THOUGHT OF AS A CROSS BETWEEN THE SPIRAL, CENTROIDAL SYSTEM OF POISSY AND THE LINEAR SURFACE DEVELOPMENT OF GARCHES. IN THE PAVILLON SUISSE IT IS THE LINEAR VOLUME THAT PROVIDES THE DOMINANT PERCEPTUAL REFERENCE BUT IT IS THE SPIRAL OR PARTIAL PINWHEEL THAT PROVIDES THE DOMINANT CONCEPTUAL REFERENCE. IN FACT, AN INTERESTING COMPARISON MIGHT BE MADE BETWEEN THE PAVILLON SUISSE AND THE IMMEUBLE DE COLONISATION A NEMOURS.[1] AT NEMOURS THE EXTERNAL AXIS IS PARALLEL AND NOT PERPENDICULAR TO THE INTERNAL AXIS. THIS GIVES AN ENTIRELY DIFFERENT CONCEPTUAL READING. WHERE AT THE PAVILLON SUISSE THE MOVEMENT SYSTEM IS A LOGICAL EXTENSION OF THE EXTERNAL AXIS, AND CAN BE THOUGHT OF AS SPINNING THROUGH THE LINEAR AXIS AND PINNING IT, THE OPPOSITE MUST BE INFERRED AT NEMOURS, SINCE THE PARALLEL EXTERNAL AXIS CANNOT CONCEPTUALLY GENERATE A SPIRALLING MOVEMENT INTO THE PARALLEL BLOCK.[2]

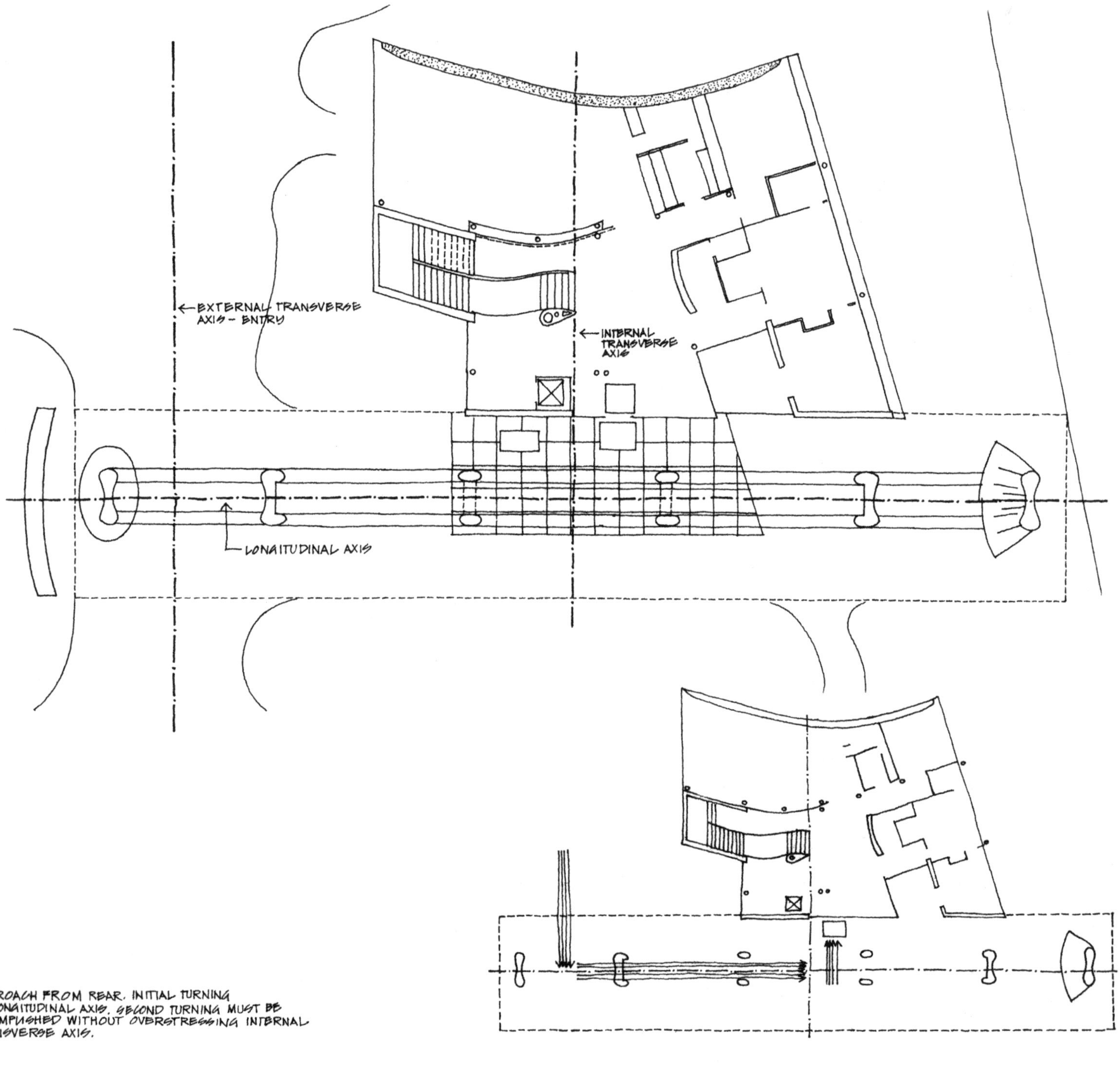

3.

APPROACH FROM REAR. INITIAL TURNING BY LONGITUDINAL AXIS. SECOND TURNING MUST BE ACCOMPLISHED WITHOUT OVERSTRESSING INTERNAL TRANSVERSE AXIS.

Therefore the spiral or pinwheel volumetric system at Nemours must be thought of as secondary and pinned between the parallel axes; the development of this system of movement resolves the problem of single entry into a linear element.[1] At the Pavillon Suisse the spiral system is a continuation of the external vector which is at right angles to the main internal axis; therefore the external axis must be blunted and turned to effect some kind of entry.[2] This turning begins the spinning movement which in successive turns becomes progressively restricted and flattened in a centripital fashion until access to the upper floors has been gained.

The approach to the building is from the rear which necessitates a double turning of this vector to effect an entry.[3] This is partially accomplished by placing the longitudinal aspect of the building across this axis providing the necessary blunting and turning. However there must be a second turning to gain access into the building itself. To effect this, Le Corbusier invokes a similar elaborate grammar to that used at the Cite de Refuge. There the grammar is imposed on a volumetric order while at the Pavillon Suisse it becomes part of a movement system. The second turning of this system acknowledges the minor transverse axis without overstressing it; if this axis were to be emphasised it would be brought into conflict with the dominant longitudinal axis, which is the major generic reference. Moreover this emphasis of the minor axis would tend to divide the linear block into a programmatically undesirable bi-nuclear organisation.

Initially, the base of the generic volume may be read as extruded or forced

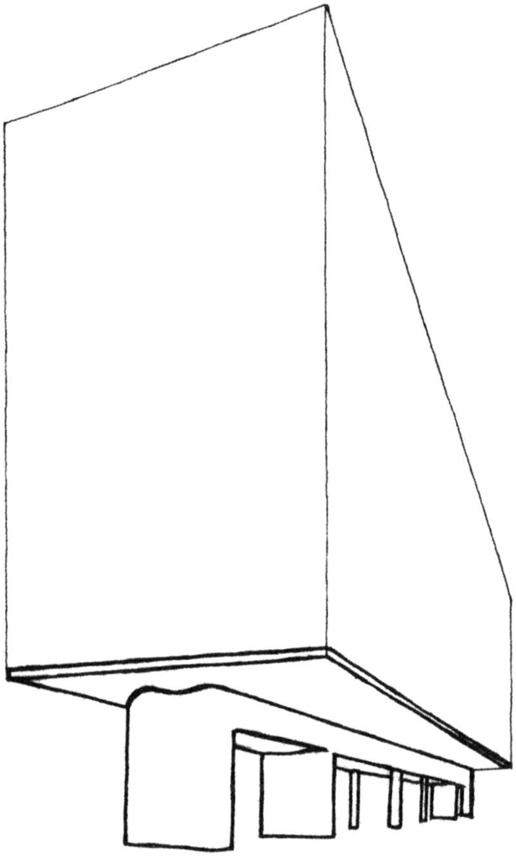

4. 'TABLE' STATED AS HORIZONTAL ABSOLUTE CANNOT BE ARBITRARILY BROKEN

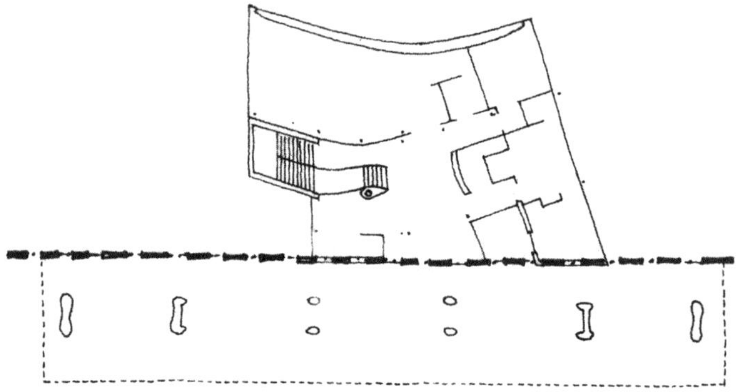

5.

ALL DISTORTIONS ORDERED WITH REFERENCE TO A VERTICAL ABSOLUTE OR 'BACKBONE' PLANE

FROM ITS GENERIC STATE BY THE PRESSURE OF THE SPIRALLING MOVEMENT. THIS DISLOCATION ALSO PROVIDES AN ACKNOWLEDGEMENT OF THE TRANSVERSE ENTRY VECTOR; THIS AXIS THEN ACTS AS A MINOR PLANE OF REFERENCE FOR A SERIES OF CRITICAL JUNCTIONS WHICH ARE COUNTERPOISED ABOUT IT. THE INTEGRITY OF THE DUAL FUNCTIONAL ORGANISATION OF THE BUILDING IS RECOGNISED BY THE STATEMENT OF A STRONG HORIZONTAL SLAB OR 'TABLE', WHICH ONCE ASSERTED AS AN ABSOLUTE CANNOT BE PUNCTURED BY AN ARBITRARY JUNCTION WITH THE CENTROIDAL MOVEMENT SYSTEM.[4] THE SPIRAL, SYSTEM OF MOVEMENT IS THEREFORE PULLED THROUGH THE LINEAR BLOCK THUS FIXING THE POSITION OF THE LINEAR VOLUME AND PROVIDING A PERCEPTUAL DISSOCIATION OF FUNCTION IN THE VOLUMETRIC ORGANISATION. THIS PINNING OF ELEMENTS IS A TENDENCY THAT IS APPARENT IN MANY CENTROIDAL SCHEMES. WHEN A CENTROIDAL MOVEMENT SYSTEM IS BROUGHT INTO A LINEAR CONTEXT ANY GYRATING MOTION TENDS TO BE ARRESTED AND STABILISED. AN EXAMINATION OF THE EXTRUDED ELEMENTS CLEARLY DEMONSTRATES NOT ONLY THE SPECIFIC GRAMMAR EMPLOYED, BUT ALSO THE EXTENT TO WHICH THIS GRAMMAR PRESENTS A PERCEPTUAL ORDER FOR THE CLARITY OF THE CONCEPTUAL BASIS.

ALL DISTORTIONS RECEIVE SOME ORDERING FROM THE GENERIC CONDITION. THE REFERENCE IS PROVIDED IN THE PAVILLON SUISSE BY AN ORTHOGONAL 'BACK BONE' PLANE, WHICH IS THE REAR FACADE OF THE MAIN VOLUME.[5] A COMPARISON CAN BE MADE WITH A SIMILAR USE OF THIS DIVICE BY LE CORBUSIER AT GARCHES AND THE CITE DE REFUGE. THE POSITION OF THE DOMINANT SURFACE REFLECTS THE PRESSURE UPON THE GENERIC VOLUME CAUSING THE CENTRAL LONGITUDINAL AXIS TO BE DISLOCATED TO THE REAR OF THE VOLUME. THE EXTRUDED VOLUMES MAY BE READ AS TENSIONED FROM THIS PLANE, AND THEREFORE PREVENTED FROM EXTENDING AND OOZING WITHOUT END FROM THE MAIN VOLUME.

THE INITIAL DISTORTION OF THESE EXTRUDED VOLUMES IS THE CURVATURE OF THE REAR,

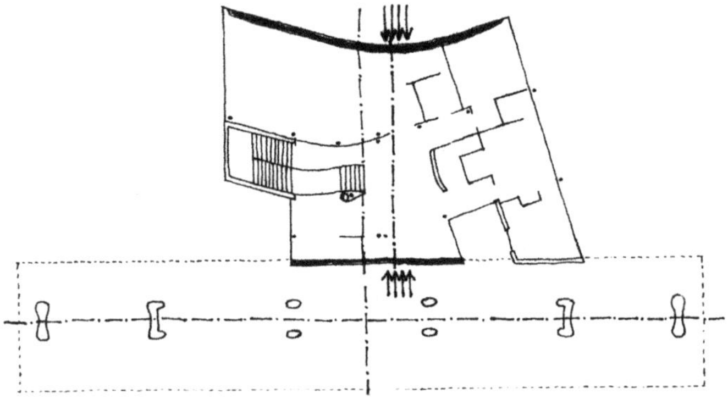

INITIAL DISTORTION OF EXTRUDED VOLUMES IS THE CURVATURE OF THE REAR WALL. ACKNOWLEDGES ON APPROACH FROM REAR THE ENTRY VECTOR.

6.

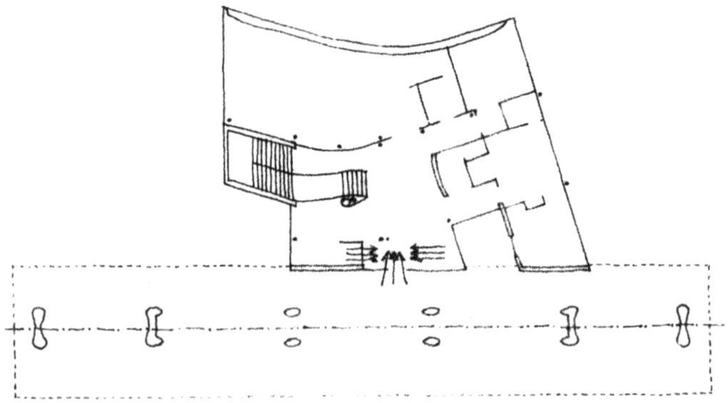

ENTRY PRESSURE HEIGHTENED BY RESTRICTION AT ENTRY

10.

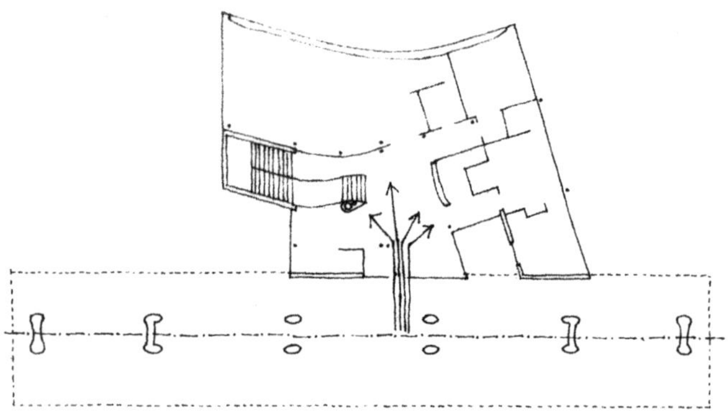

PRESSURE RELIEVED IN ENTRY HALL

11.

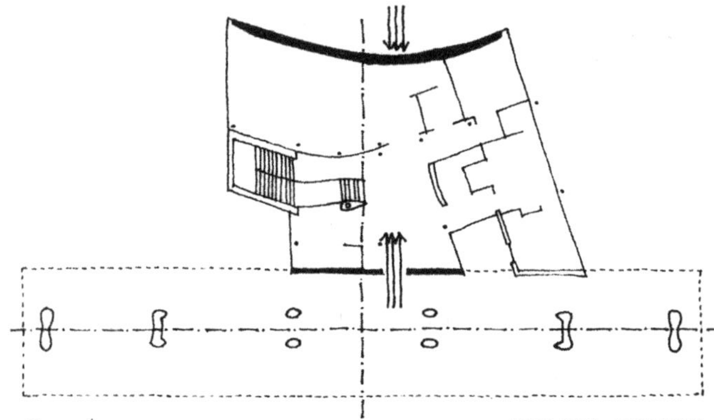

7.

ENTRY WALL REMAINS UNDEFORMED AS PRESSUR IS RELIEVED BY ACTUAL ENTRY

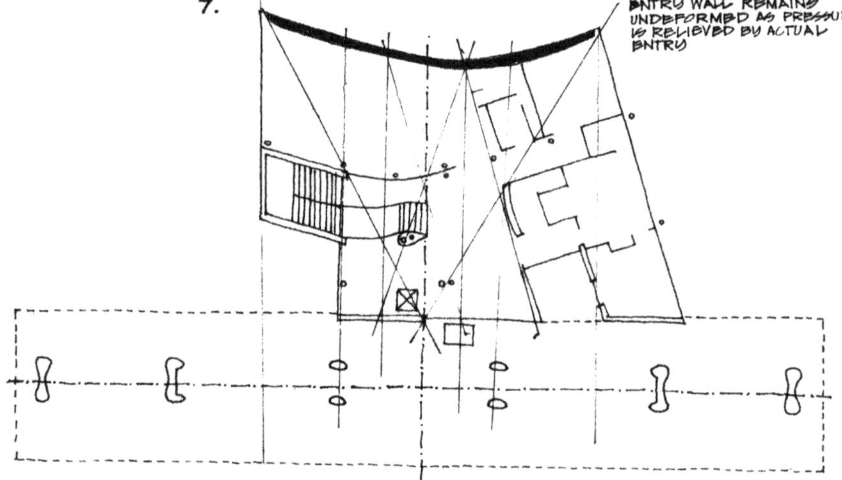

8. CURVE OF REAR WALL THE RESULT OF AN ELABORATE GRIDDING WHICH LOCATES MOST CRITICAL JUNCTIONS

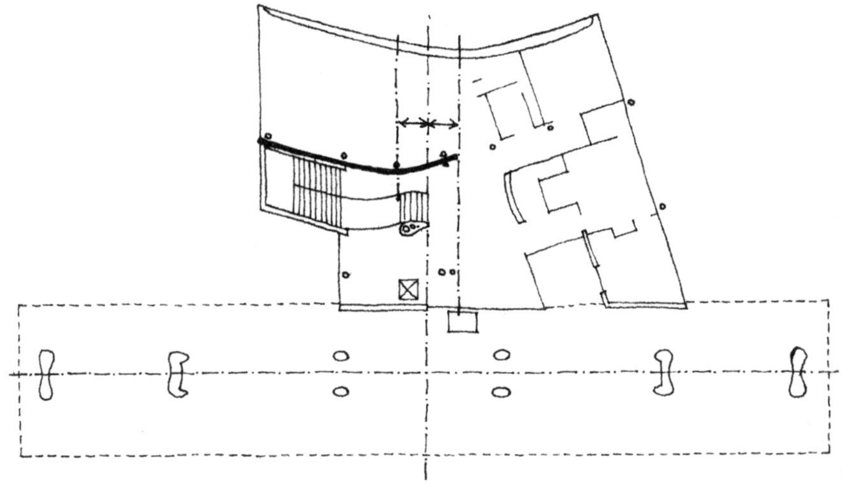

POINT OF MAXIMUM CURVATURE ON INNER REFECTORY WALL COUNTERPOISES EXTERNAL MAXIMUM CURVATURE ABOUT TRANSVERSE AXIS

9.

EXTERNAL REFECTORY WALL.[6] WHEN THE CURVATURE AND THE POINT OF INFLECTION OF THE REAR WALL ARE APPRECIATED ON APPROACH FROM THE REAR, THERE IS AN INFERENCE OF SOME POINT OF EXTREME PRESSURE, THE ENTRY, ON THE OPPOSITE SIDE. THE RESULTING COMPRESSION ON THE EXTRUDED VOLUME IS SIMILAR TO THE EFFECT OF A CRUSHING ACTION APPLIED TO THE SIDES OF A LINEAR CONTAINER SUCH AS A TIN CAN. THE PRESSURE IS ACKNOWLEDGED ON THE REAR WALL BUT IS NOT APPARENT ON THE ENTRY PLANE WHICH REMAINS UNDEFORMED; THE PRESSURE OF THE ENTRY VECTOR BEING RELIEVED BY THE ACTUAL OPENING INTO THE VOLUME.[7] IT MUST BE NOTED THAT THE REAR WALL IS NOT A 'FREE' FORM, BUT RATHER THE CURVE RESULTING FROM AN ELABORATE NETWORK OF REFERENCE LINES.[8] THE POINT OF MAXIMUM CURVATURE CORRESPONDS TO THE AXIS OF ENTRY, AND PROVIDES THE INITIAL COUNTERPOISE WITH REFERENCE TO THE GENERIC TRANSVERSE AXIS. THIS POINT OF INFLEXION IS BALANCED INTERNALLY BY THE POINT OF MAXIMUM CURVATURE ON THE INNER REFECTORY WALL WHICH IS EQUIDISTANT FROM THE TRANSVERSE AXIS ON THE OPPOSITE SIDE.[9] THIS INTERNAL POINT OF INFLEXION ALSO AFFORDS A DIRECTIONAL THRUST, WHICH DEFLECTS THE ENTRY VECTOR AND FURTHER FLATTENS THE SPIRALLING MOVEMENT.[9] MOREOVER THE LOCATION OF THIS INTERNAL POINT IS CRUCIAL, FOR IF IT WERE TO BE PLACED OPPOSITE THE EXTERNAL INFLEXION POINT, THE ENTRY AXIS WOULD HAVE BEEN TURNED PAST THE STAIR RATHER THAN TO IT.

THE SPIRAL MOVEMENT ITSELF IS SUBJECTED TO PRESSURES WHICH CAUSE IT TO CONTRACT AND EXPAND, ACKNOWLEDGING NODAL POINTS IN ITS DEVELOPMENT. INITIALLY THE PRESSURE AT THE POINT OF ENTRY IS INTENSIFIED BY THE VOLUMETRIC RESTRICTION DEFINED BY THE COLUMNS TO THE LEFT OF THE ENTRY.[10] THIS PRESSURE IS THEN RELIEVED BY THE EXPANSION INTO THE IRREGULARLY DEFINED HALL VOLUME, THUS PROVIDING A POINT OF REST IN THE MOVEMENT SYSTEM.[11] IMMEDIATELY, HOWEVER, THERE IS A FURTHER RE-

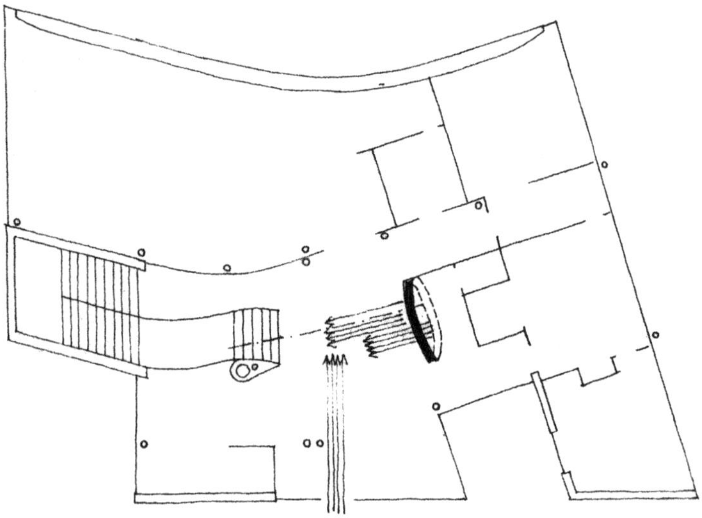

12.

RESTRICTION AT CROSS AXIS OF STAIR AGAIN WEAKENS AND TURNS ENTRY VECTOR. COUNTER CAN BE SEEN AS PULSATING FORCING MOVEMENT UP STAIRS.

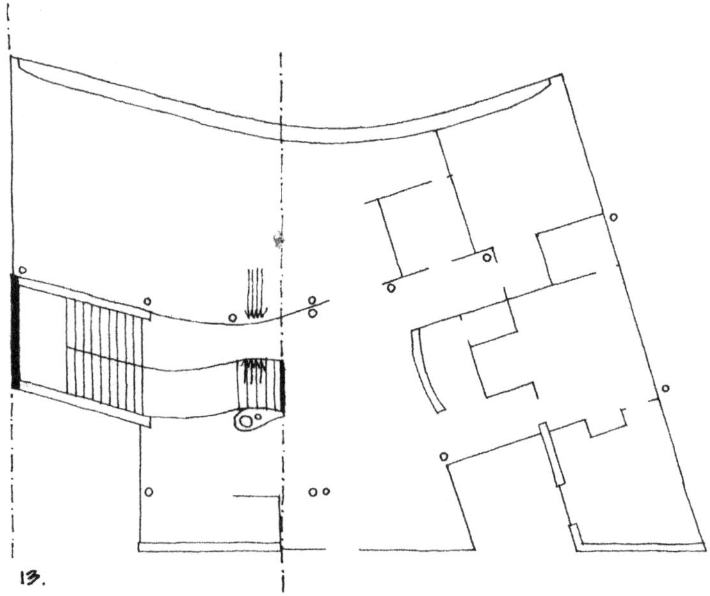

13.

BOTH ENDS OF STAIR FIXED RIGIDLY TO THE ORTHOGONAL GRID WARPING OF STAIR PRODUCES RESTRICTION IN MINOR ACCESS TO LOWER LEVEL

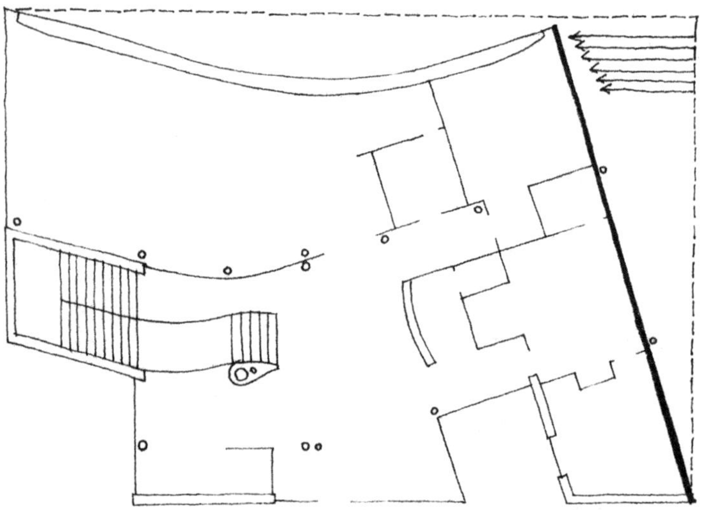

14.

RIGHT HAND WALL OF EXTRUDED VOLUMES CANTED FROM GENERIC RECTANGLE, PRODUCES INITIAL PRESSURE FOR THE TURNING OF MOVEMENT VECTOR.

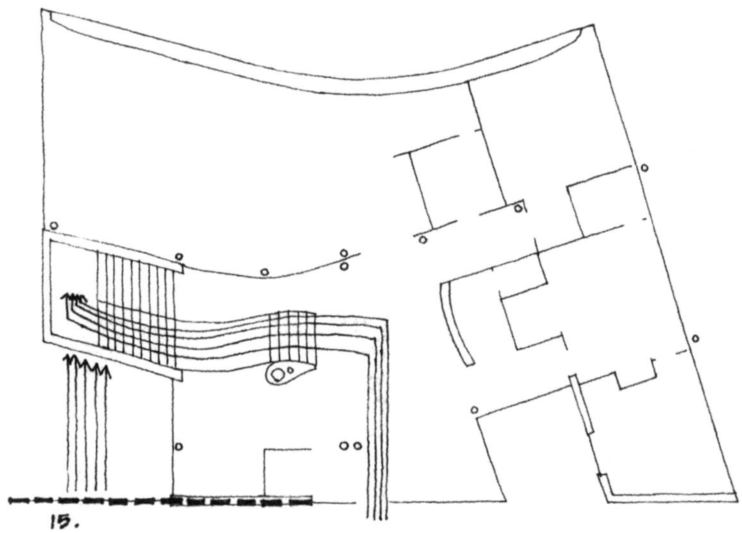

15.

PRESSURE OF DOMINANT SURFACE TURNS MOVEMENT BACK ON ITSELF AT STAIR LANDING

-STRICTION AT THE CROSS AXIS OF THE STAIR.[12] IN ADDITION, THIS AXIS WEAKENS THE DIRECTION OF THE ENTRY VECTOR BY CREATING A TENSION BETWEEN THE END OF THE STAIR AND THE BUFFER-LIKE COUNTER OPPOSITE. THIS COUNTER CAN BE THOUGHT OF AS PULSATING BETWEEN CONCAVITY AND CONVEXITY FORCING MOVEMENT UP THE STAIR.[12] BOTH ENDS OF THE STAIR ARE SEEN AS BEING FIXED RIGIDLY TO THE ORTHOGONAL GRID: THE ONE END TO THE CENTRAL TRANSVERSE AXIS, AND THE OTHER END TO A COLUMNAR BAY CENTRE LINE.[13] THE WARPING OF THIS STAIR CAN THEN BE READ AS AN ACKNOWLEDGEMENT OF BOTH THE THROBBING PRESSURE FROM THE COUNTER AND A REFERENCE TO THE ORTHOGONAL GRID. THIS DISTORTION OF THE STAIR ALSO PRODUCES A RESTRICTION BETWEEN THE SIDE OF THE STAIR AND THE INTERNAL REFECTORY WALL, THUS DEFINING THE MINOR ACCESS PASSAGE TO THE SERVICE BASEMENT.[13] THE CANTING OF THE RIGHT HAND WALL OF THE EXTRUDED VOLUMES CREATES THE INCREASE IN THE INTERNAL PRESSURE NECESSARY TO INITIATE THE VERTICAL MOVEMENT.[14] IT MUST BE EMPHASISED THAT ALL DEFORMATIONS ARE SEEN WITH REFERENCE TO THE ORTHOGONAL GRID AND PARTICULARLY ITS DOMINANT 'FRONTAL' COORDINATE. THESE DEFORMATIONS ARE THE RESULT OF THE SPECIFIC GRAMMAR USED IN THE SYSTEMIC CONTROL OF THE CIRCULATION, AND THEY OBEY THE SYNTACTICAL REQUIREMENTS OF THE GENERIC CONDITION. IT HAS BEEN PREVIOUSLY STATED THAT THE SPIRAL OR PINWHEEL IS ONLY A PARTIALLY DEVELOPED AND THIS CAN BE SEEN IN BOTH THE MOVEMENT AND THE VOLUMETRIC ORDER. BECAUSE OF THE PRESSURE RESULTING FROM THE DISLOCATION OF THE LONGITUDINAL AXIS, THE SPIRALLING MOVEMENT IS ABRUPTLY ENDED AT THE STAIR LANDING AND IS TURNED BACK ON ITSELF.[15] FURTHERMORE THE VOLUMETRIC ORDER IS ONLY PARTIALLY REALISED, SEEMINGLY BLOCKED IN ITS DEVELOPMENT BY THE LONGITUDINAL AXIS. HOWEVER THE VOLUMETRIC SPIRAL CAN BE INTERPRETED AS CONCLUDED IN ONE DIMENSION, IN THAT THE STAIR VOLUME DOES EXTEND TO THE FULL HEIGHT OF THE LINEAR VOLUME. THE EXTRUDED VOLUMES CAN ALSO BE READ AS THREE DISTINCT LAYERS OF A SPIRAL OR ARMS OF A PINWHEEL, THOUGH SINCE THERE IS NO ACKNOWLEDGEMENT OF A PIVOT

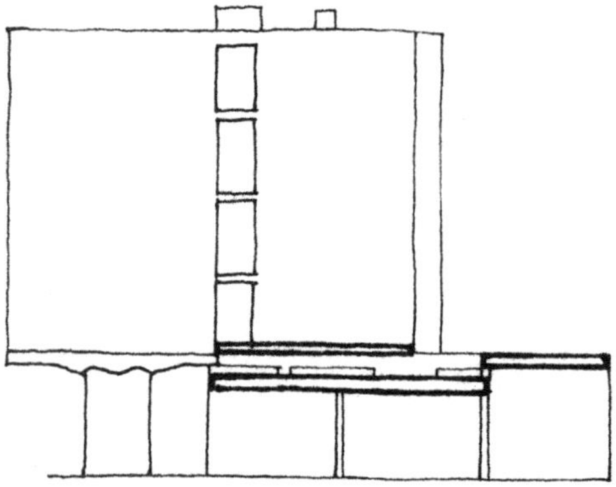

16.

EXTRUDED VOLUMES READ AS THREE DISTINCT LAYERS OF A SPIRAL OR PINWHEEL.

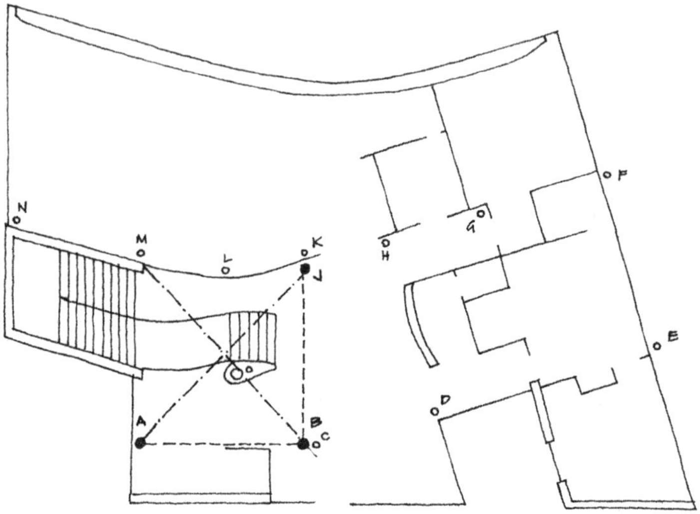

17.

COLUMNS A·B·J DEFINE STAIRWELL VOLUME

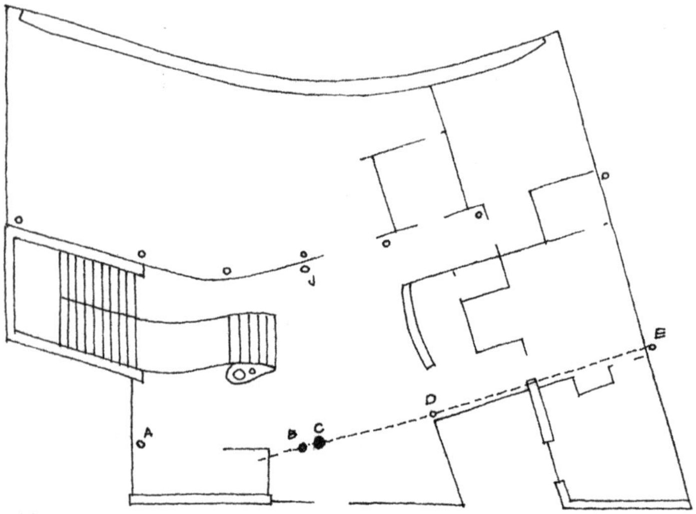

18.

IF COLUMN C IS PLACED DIAGONALLY TO B, COLUMN B IS SEEN IN AN AMBIGUOUS POSITION

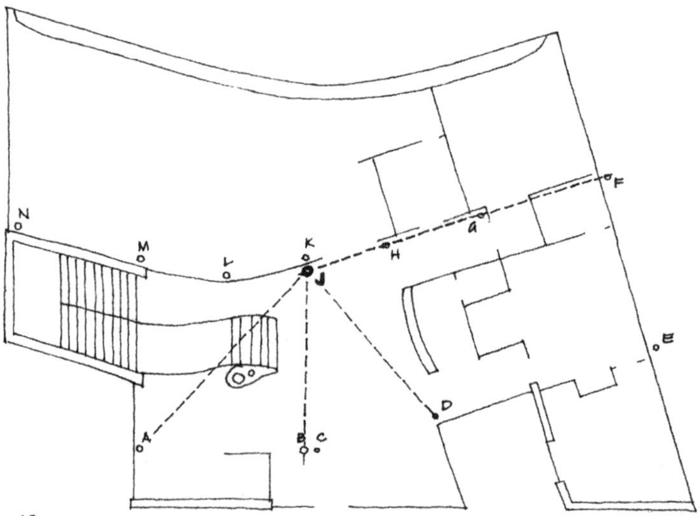

19.

COLUMN J CAN ALSO BE SEEN IN AN AMBIGUOUS LOCATION.

FOR THESE ARMS, THE FORMER INTERPRETATION IS TO BE PREFERRED.[16] THESE VOLUMES RECEIVE THEIR INITIAL ARTICULATION FROM THE ORTHOGONAL GRID WHICH ALSO GIVES A TRI-PARTITE FUNCTIONAL DIVISION.

THE THREE COLUMNS (A,B,J) TO THE LEFT OF THE ENTRY DEFINE THE LIMITS OF THE STAIRWELL-ACCESS VOLUME, WHICH CONTINUES TO THE FULL HEIGHT OF THE BUILDING.[17] COLUMN C, WHICH IS IMMEDIATLEY ADJACENT TO COLUMN B, IS SLIGHTLY SMALLER IN SIZE TO DENOTE ITS LESSER LOAD BEARING FUNCTION. THIS JUXTAPOSITION OF COLUMNS TAKES ON ADDITIONAL SIGNIFICANCE BECAUSE OF THEIR OBVIOUSLY FORCED LOCATION. INITIALLY THESE COLUMNS COULD HAVE BEEN FASHIONED AS ONE IF THEIR LOAD BEARING REQUIREMENT WAS THE ONLY CONSIDERATION; HOWEVER, THIS WOULD NOT HAVE CLEARLY ARTICULATED THE INTERSECTION OF THE ORTHOGONAL VOLUME AND ANOTHER VOL- PLACED DIAGONALLY TO IT. IF COLUMN C HAD BEEN PLACED IN A DIAGONAL RELATIONSHIP TO B INSTEAD OF IN ITS ORTHOGONAL POSITION, COLUMN B WOULD HAVE BEEN GIVEN AN AMBIGUOUS READING AS EITHER THE LAST COLUMN OF THE DIAGONAL CDE SERIES OR THE CORNER COLUMN OF THE ABJ VOLUME.[18] IN THIS CASE, THE PARTICULAR PLACEMENT ALLOWS THE VOLUMES TO BE CLEARLY DEFINED, WHILE EXISTING AS A CONTINUOUS WHOLE. A SIMILAR ARRANGEMENT CAN BE NOTED AT COLUMNS J AND K, WHERE COLUMN J CAN BE READ IN TWO WAYS.[19] IT IS EITHER TAKEN AS PART OF THE ABJ VOLUME OR PART OF THE DIAGONAL VOLUME DEFINED BY THE SERIES FGH. THIS IS ALSO A CRITICAL INTERSECTION, FOR WHILE THERE IS A NEED TO ARTICULATE THE TRI-PARTITE VOLUMETRIC ORDERING-CIRCULATION, RECEPTION, REFECTORY - THERE IS ALSO THE NEED TO PRESERVE THE VOLUMETRIC CONTINUITY OF RECEPTION AND REEECTORY VOLUMES. HERE THE CONTINUOUS OR STATIC ALTERNATIVE IS PRESENTED: THE LATTER READING IS EMPHASISED BY GLAZING THE PARTITION BETWEEN THE RECEPTION AND REFECTORY, AND THE FORMER READING IS STRENGHTENED BY THE PLACING OF COLUMNS KLMN ON THE

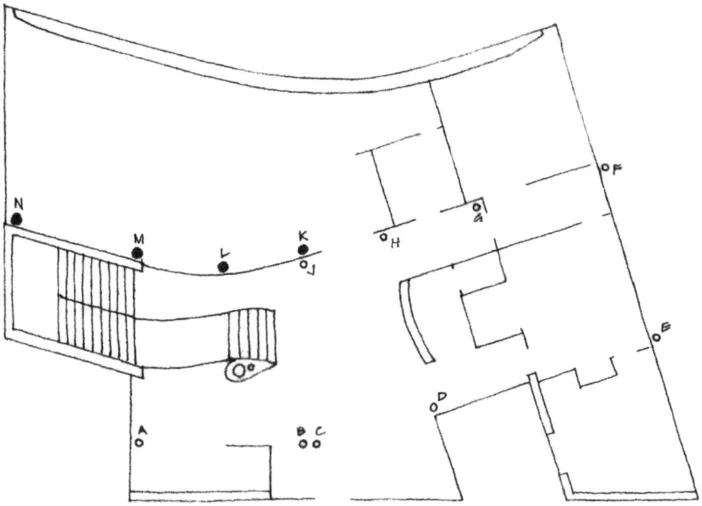

20.

FURTHER ARTICULATION OF TRI-PARTITE ORDERING BY LOCATION OF COLUMNS K·L·M·N ON REFECTORY SIDE OF GLAZED PARTITION.

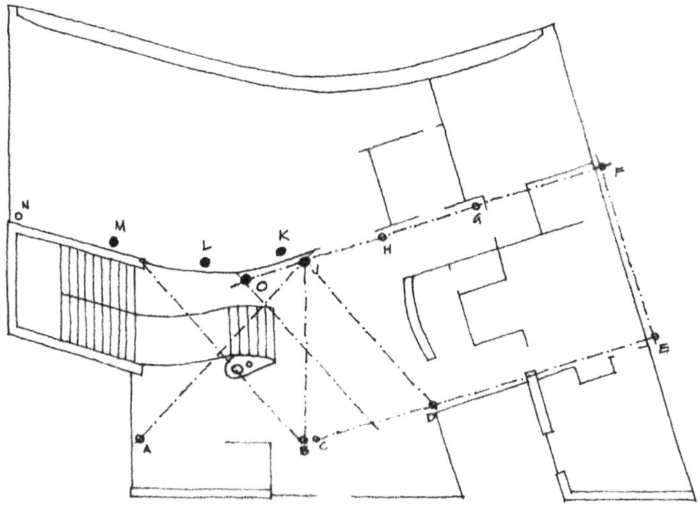

21.

COLUMNS K·L·M ARE SHIFTED IN FINAL SCHEME TO FURTHER ARTICULATE VOLUMES AND CLARIFY THE PURPOSEFUL AMBIGUITY OF COLUMN J.

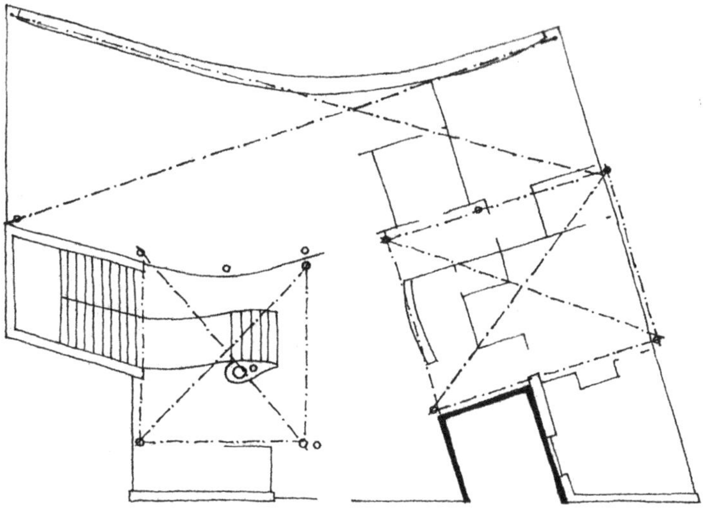

22.

REENTRANT CUT HELPS TO DEFINE THE THREE PARTS OF THE UNFINISHED SPIRAL.

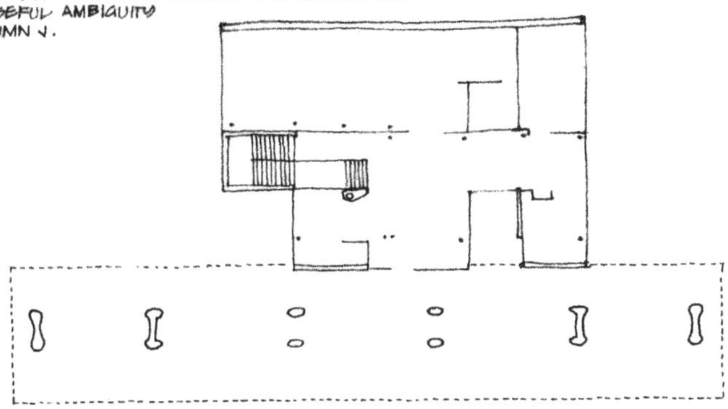

23.

PULL OF DOMINANT SURFACE CANTS RIGHT HAND WALL EXPOSING COLUMNS.

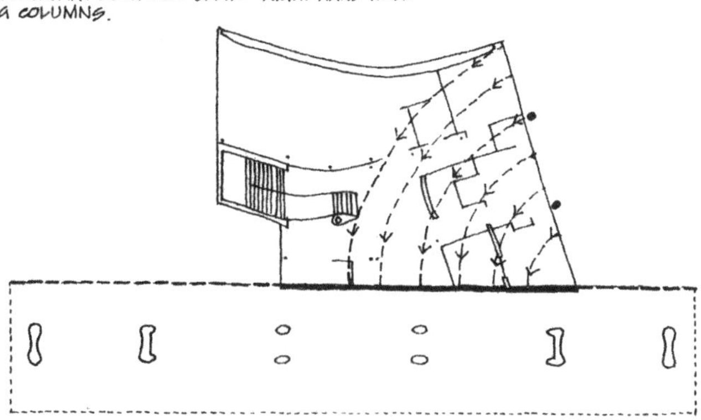

REFECTORY SIDE OF THE GLAZED PARTITION.[20] IN THE ACTUAL EXECUTION OF THE PROJECT LE CORBUSIER IN HIS DESIRE TO CLEARLY STATE THE DIALECTICAL CONDITION, CHANGES THE LOCATION OF COLUMN K IN RELATION TO COLUMN J TO AVOID READING THIS PAIR AS CONCEPTUALLY SIMILAR TO THE B C GROUPING.[21] COLUMN K IS SHIFTED TO THE LEFT, AS ARE COLUMNS L AND M, TO READ AS A REGULAR GRID, WHICH FURTHER ARTICULATES THE SEPARATION OF VOLUMES. THIS STRENGTHENS THE AMBIGUOUS READING OF COLUMN J, DESPITE THE ADDITION OF COLUMN O IN THE DIAGONAL SERIES. THE SHIFTING OF COLUMNS K L M TO CONFORM TO A REGULAR GRID DENIES THE POSSIBLE CORRELATION OF THESE COLUMNS WITH THE LENGTH OF THE STAIRWELL, AGAIN CREATING A STRONG-ER SEPARATION OF THE TWO VOLUMES. THERE ARE TWO FURTHER ACKNOWLEDGEMENTS OF THE SPIRAL SYSTEM, THE FIRST IS THE REENTRANT CUT ON THE GROUND FLOOR WHICH NOT ONLY SEPARATES THE CONCIERGE'S FLAT FROM THE RECEPTION HALL, BUT ALSO HELPS TO DEFINE THE THREE PARTS OF THE UNFINISHED SPIRAL.[22] THE SECOND IS THE ARTICULATION OF THE VOLUMES SERVING THE DIRECTOR AND THE CONCIERGE WHICH AGAIN STRENGTHENS THE LAYERING SPIRAL READING. THE ASCENDING AND TURNING MOTION CAN BE READ AS A DEFINITE PULL FROM THE DOMINANT SURFACE. THIS PULL INITIALLY CAUSES A SUCTION WHICH CANTS THE RIGHT HAND WALL OF THE EXTRUDED BLOCK.[23] IN DOING SO THE SURFACE IS PULLED AWAY FROM THE COLUMNS, EXPOSING THEM ON THE EXTERIOR. THIS RECOGNITION OF THE ATTRACTION OF THE DOMINANT SURFACE IS INCORPORATED IN THE MASS-SURFACE DIALECTIC.

THE EXTRUDED MINOR VOLUMES ARE STATED AS 'MASS' AGAINST THE MAJOR VOLUME WHICH IS READ AS 'SURFACE'. THEIR PARTICULAR LOCATION IS DETERMINED IN RELATION TO THE DOMINANT NORTH FACADE, IN A SIMILAR FASHION TO OBJECTS IN FRONT OF A PROSCENIUM. LE CORBUSIER ATTRIBUTES A DEFINITE NEO-CLASSICAL FRONT-BACK READING TO THE BUILDING BY TREATING THE NORTH AND SOUTH FACADES IN A DIFFERENT FASHION.

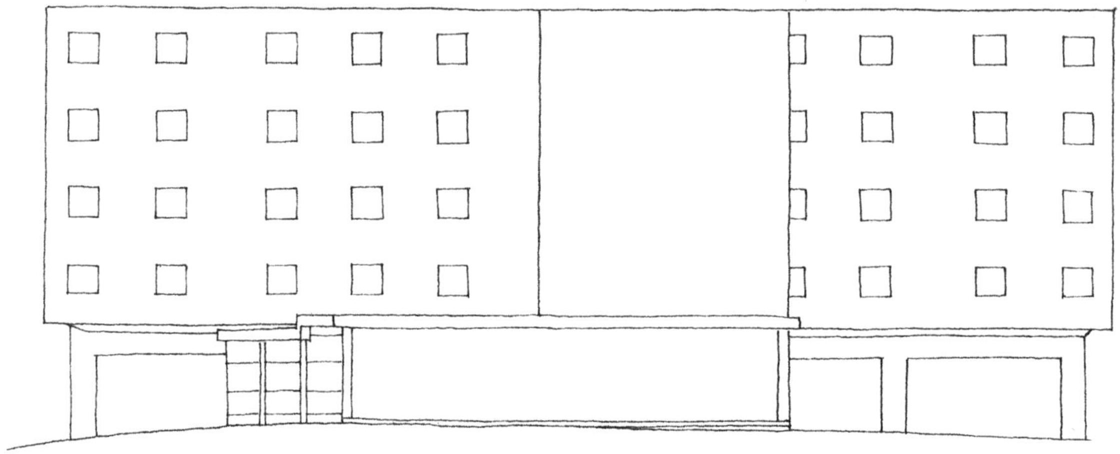

24.
NORTH FACADE READ INITIALLY AS 'MASS' BECAUSE OF THE RELATIONSHIP OF SOLID TO VOID.

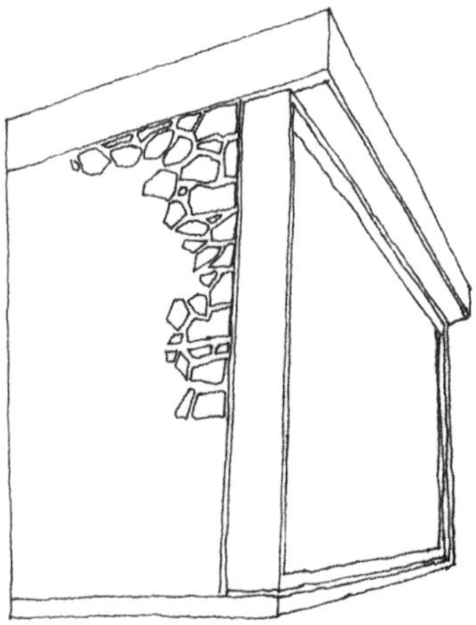

25.
THE 'MASS' OF THE REFECTORY WALL GIVEN AN AMBIGUOUS READING.

26.
PROGRESSION OF SURFACES FROM THE REFECTORY WALL.

The north 'rear' facade could initially be read as mass, because of the relationship of solid to void in the placement of windows.[24] However the rusticated, rubble wall of the refectory must be interpreted as the absolute 'mass' reference. There are two possible interpretations of this rusticated wall. Firstly, in the dislocation of the minor volumes from their generic state the surface can be thought of as having been peeled away to reveal the rustication. From this it follows that if the surface of the north facade were peeled away it too would reveal a rusticated 'mass' beneath. However, the notion of a rusticated mass sitting on a table is obviously not the metaphor that Le Corbusier wishes to invoke. Therefore, a second interpretation of the rebectory wall is allowed which would be a planar reading. This 'mass' is carefully placed within two horizontal slabs giving a panel-like quality, and the second reading is reinforced by presenting another surface (which in fact is the window frame of adjacent west facade) immediately behind the rustication.[25] This attributes a papery quality to the rubble wall, which again might be peeled away to reveal yet another surface. This latter interpretation takes on a greater validity when the surfaces are considered as a progression: a longitudinal series reading from the most dense and opaque, the rubble wall, through the smooth masonry of the stairwell and the partial transparency of the north facade, to the least dense, the transparent glazed south facade.[26] In this context the north facade must be considered as merely one surface of this stratification. But again Le Corbusier presents a slight ambiguity as the facade is treated as a wrapping skin or membrane and not in a planar or linear fashion. This interpretation is emphasised by the lack of any articulation at the ends of the facade, since the individual masonry units are treated as continuous from the rear to side facad-

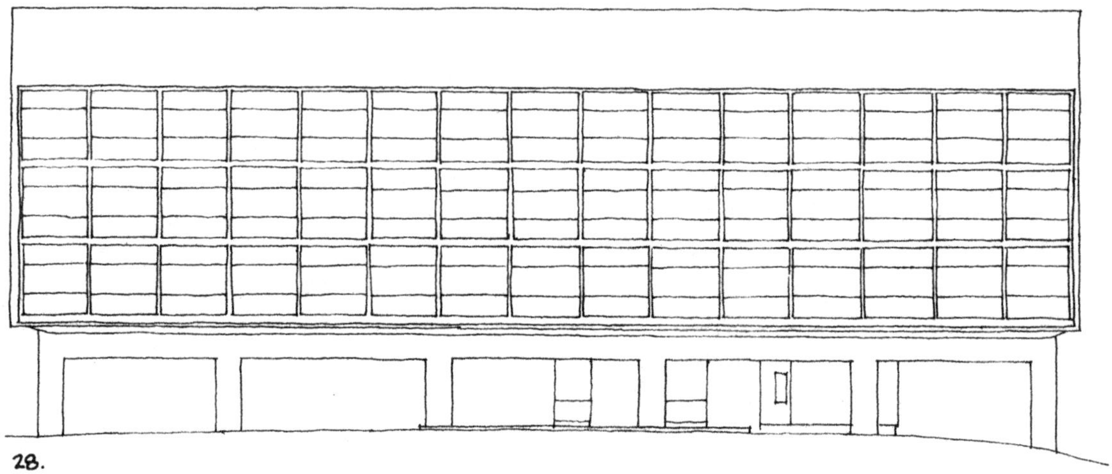

28.

SOUTH FACADE TREATED AS A TRANSPARENT SURFACE

27.

NORTH FACADE SEEN AS A THIN SURFACE OF WINDOWS PLACED OVER THE VOLUME BEHIND

-ES . THE THINNESS OF SURFACE IS SEEN IN THE PLACEMENT OF THE WINDOWS WHICH MERELY APPEAR AS TRANSPARENCIES IN A CONTINUOUS SURFACE.[27] AND FINALLY, THIS MEMBRANE READING IS AUGMENTED BY THE LOCATION OF THE TOPMOST ROW OF WINDOWS, WHICH SEEM TO BE ALMOST A SURFACE, OVERLAYING THE MASONRY BLOCKS WHICH ARE TREATED AS A CORNICE.

THE SOUTH FACADE CONTINUES THE WRAPPING EFFECT OF THE MASONRY IN ITS UPPER STORY AS WELL AS PRESENTING THE FINAL STAGE IN THE PLANAR STRATIFICATION. THE GLAZING HERE IS TREATED AS A TOTAL TRANSPARENCY READING BOTH AS PART OF THE MEMBRANE AND AS A FRONTAL PLANE.[28] IT IS INTERESTING TO NOTE THAT THE CLARITY OF THE CONCEPTUAL EVOLUTION OF THE 'MASS-SURFACE' DIALECTIC HAS BEEN NULLIFIED BOTH HERE AND AT THE CITE DE REFUGE BY THE RECENT ADDITION OF SUN SCREENS.

THE PRECEDING DISCUSSION HAS BEEN DEVOTED TO TWO OF THE SYNTACTICAL REQUIREMENTS OF SYSTEM: THE EMPLOYMENT AND ORDERING OF THE VOCABULARY, AND THE ACKNOWLEDGEMENT OF DISTORTIONS FROM A GENERIC FORM. A THIRD, THE RECOGNITION OF A SYSTEM AS A COMPLETE ENTITY, IS ACKNOWLEDGED IN ALL THREE COORDINATES. THE MOST OBVIOUS REQUIREMENT IS THE NECESSITY TO END THE LONGITUDINAL AXIS OF THE MAIN VOLUME. IN THE PORTION ABOVE THE TABLE, A MEMBRANE IS WRAPPED AROUND THE FRAME, BUT THIS DOES NOT ESTABLISH A TERMINATION FOR THE TABLE ITSELF, THIS IS ACCOMPLISHED BY IMPLYING A TERMINATION TO THE SYSTEM OF PILOTIS SUPPORTS. THIS IMPLIED ENDING TO A DIRECTIONAL MOVEMENT CAN BE SEEN AT BOTH THE CITE DE REFUGE AND LA TOURETTE. IN THE PAVILLON SUISSE, LE CORBUSIER USES A PAIR OF ORGANIC, OVAL SHAPES FOR THE CENTRAL PILOTIS . THESE ARE THEN SEEN TO GROW IN SUCCESSIVE STAGES FROM THE CENTRE: INTO A SINGLE ORGANIC FORM WITH A DEEP RE-

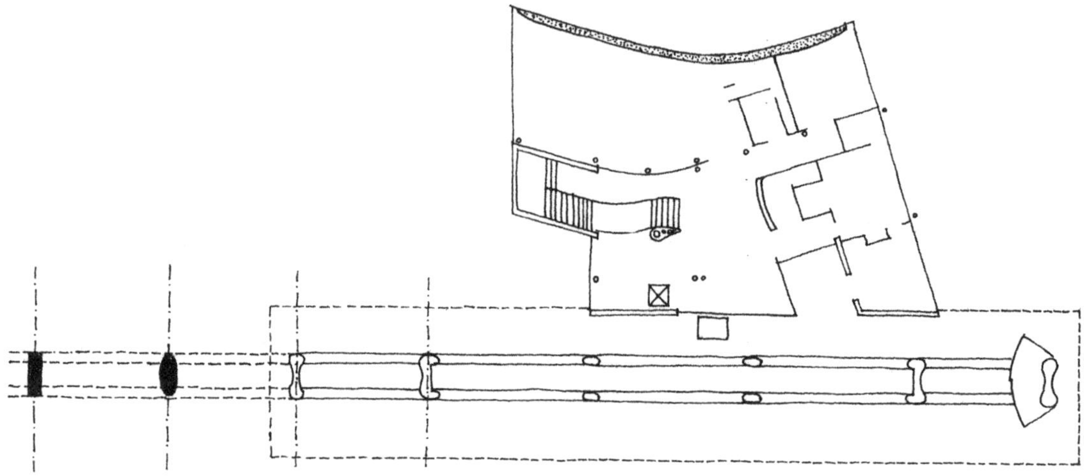

29.
IMPLIED ENDING TO LONGITUDINAL AXIS
GIVEN BY PILOTIS DEVELOPMENT.

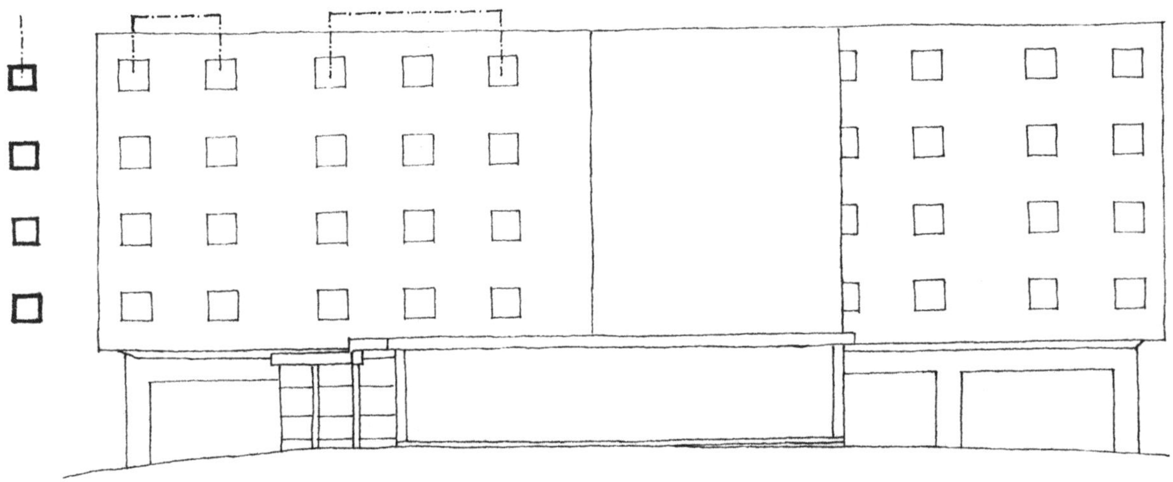

30.
IMPLIED ENDING GIVEN TO NORTH FACADE
BY THE GROUPING OF WINDOWS

-ENTRANT CUT, AND THEN TO A THIRD STAGE OF THIS GROWTH; THE IMPLICATION BEING THAT THERE CAN BE ONLY TWO FURTHER STAGES OF THIS GROWTH.[29] THE FIRST WOULD BE ONE ELONGATED OVAL (WHICH IN ITSELF COULD BE THE TERMINATION OF THE SERIES), AND THE SECOND WOULD INVOLVE CHANGING THE OVAL INTO A RECTANGLE. A READING OF THE IMPLIED SINGLE STAGE ENDING TO THE NORTH FACADE SEEMS TO VALIDATE THE FIRST INTERPRETATION. THE GLAZING OF THIS FACADE IS AGAIN ARTICULATED FROM THE CENTRE OUTWARD.[30] THE CENTRE GROUPING IS OF THREE BAYS, THE NEXT OF TWO BAYS IMPLYING A FINAL DIVISION OF ONE BAY, AS A TERMINATION OF THE SYSTEM. THE ORTHOGONAL COORDINATE HAS ALSO BEEN SEEN AS A PROGRESSION BUT IN THIS CASE THERE IS AN ACTUAL TERMINATION STATED IN THE DEVELOPMENT FROM OPAQUE TO TRANSPARENT.

IN BOTH THE NORTH AND SOUTH FACADES THE HORIZONTAL COORDINATE IS GIVEN A PERCEPTUAL END. ON THE SOUTH FACADE THE TREE PART READING IS GIVEN BY THE TABLE, GLAZED SCREEN, AND SOLID ATTIC, WHILE ON THE NORTH, THE DISTINCTION IS LESS OBVIOUS BUT STILL APPARENT IN THE SPECIFIC TREATMENT OF THE MASONRY UNITS.

CITE DE REFUGE

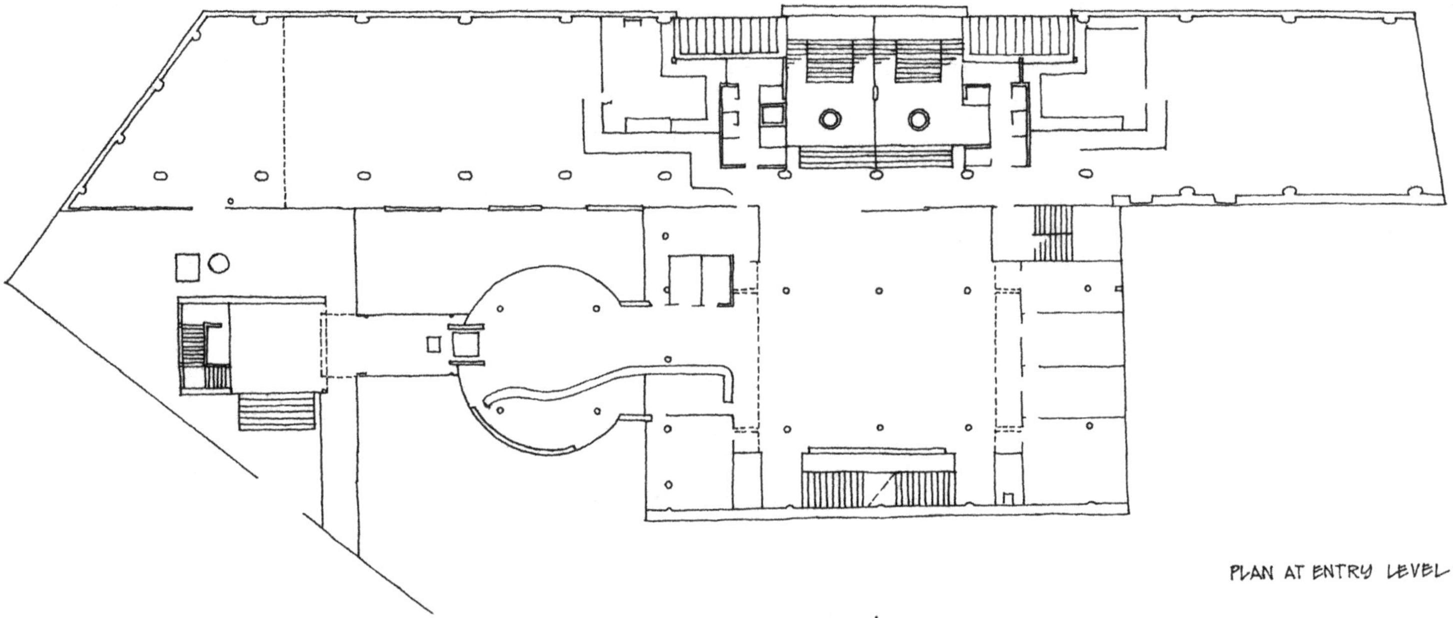

PLAN AT ENTRY LEVEL

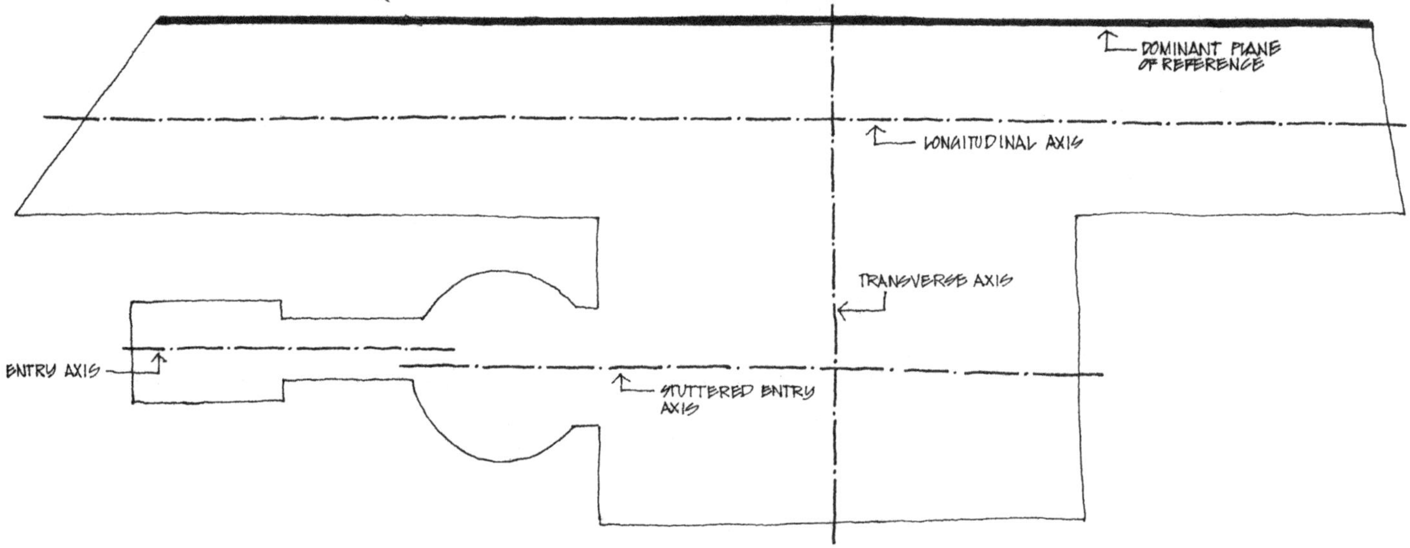

1.

KEY PLAN SHOWING MAJOR AXIAL REFERENCES
TRANSVERSE AXIS ON FUNCTIONAL DIVISION.

THE FORMAL SYSTEMIC DEVELOPMENT OF THE CITE DE REFUGE IS SIMILAR TO THAT OF THE PAVILLON SUISSE. INTERNALLY BOTH BUILDINGS EVOLVE FROM A FUNCTIONAL ORDERING WHICH SUGGESTS A GENERIC LINEAR ORGANIZATION. THE BASIC DIFFERENCE LIES IN THE RELATIONSHIP OF THE INTERNAL DOMINANT AXIS AND THE EXTERNAL AXIS: AT THE PAVILLON SUISSE THE ENTRY VECTOR IS AT RIGHT ANGLES TO THE INTERNAL AXIS WHILE AT THE CITE DE REFUGE THE EXTERNAL AXIS IS AT A DIAGONAL, OF APPROXIMATELY 45 DEGREES TO THE INTERNAL DOMINANT. CONSEQUENTLY THE FORMAL SYSTEM USED BY LE CORBUSIER IS DERIVED FROM THE NECESSITY TO ORDER THESE TWO CONSIDERATIONS. THE RELATIONSHIP OF THE INTERNAL AND THE EXTERNAL AXES AT THE CITE DE REFUGE IS SIMILAR TO THE CONDITION AT NEMOURS WHERE THE EXTERNAL AXIS IS PARALLEL. HOWEVER, WHERE AT NEMOURS THERE IS A POSSIBILITY OF A DIRECT PERPENDICULAR CONNECTION BETWEEN THE PARALLEL VECTORS, THE SPIRAL MOVEMENT BEGINNING FROM THIS LINK, THE CONDITIONS AT THE CITE DE REFUGE DO NOT ALLOW FOR THIS TYPE OF MOVEMENT SYSTEM. FIRSTLY THE LINK TO THE STREET MUST BE IN ITS CHOSEN LOCATION BECAUSE OF THE DIAGONAL NATURE OF THE STREET, WHICH MAKES THE LOCATION OF AN ENTRY ON A PERPENDICULAR DIFFICULT FOR BOTH FORMAL AND FUNCTIONAL REASONS. MOREOVER, THIS DIFFICULTY IS COMPOUNDED BY THE FACT THAT THE ENTRY INTO THE MAIN LINEAR VOLUME MUST OCCUR AT THE FUNCTIONAL DIVISION OF THE TWO DISPARATE PARTS.[1] THE INTERNAL ORDERING DEMANDS A NON-SYMMETRICAL DIVISION OF THIS VOLUME SO THAT THE CENTRAL TRANSVERSE AXIS WHICH COULD PROVIDE THE FORMAL MEANS FOR A SINGLE ENTRY CANNOT BE USED. CONSEQUENTLY ANY STRONG PERPENDICULAR TO THIS VOLUME TO CREATE ENTRY TO IT WOULD SEEM TO BE IN AN ARBITRARY AND FLUCTUATING POSITION. THIS PERPENDICULAR WOULD ALSO MEET THE STREET IN A DIFFICULT, AND ILL-DEFINED ACUTE ANGLE. THE REVERSE WOULD BE TRUE IF AN AXIS PERPENDICULAR TO THE STREET WERE

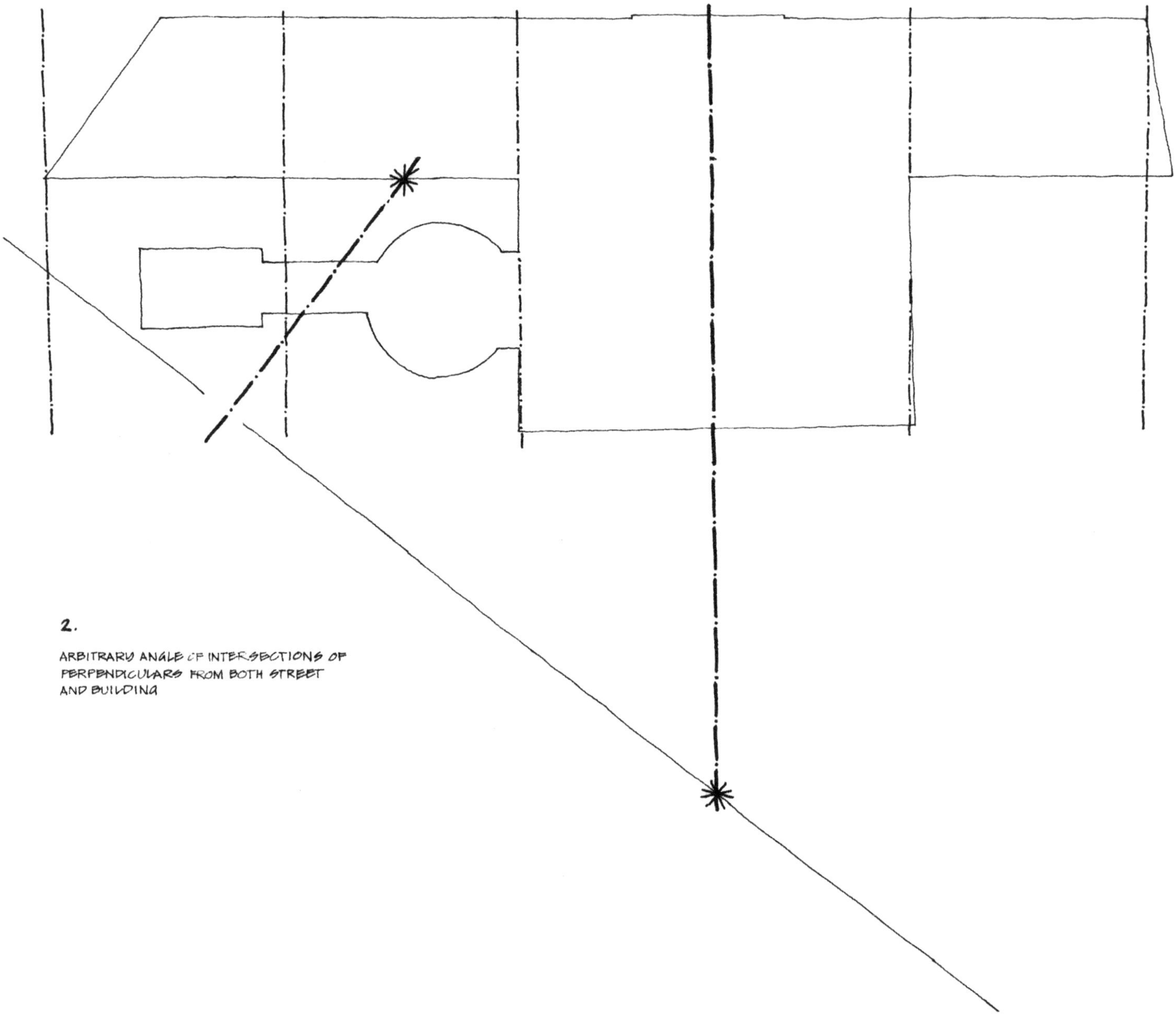

2.

ARBITRARY ANGLE OF INTERSECTIONS OF PERPENDICULARS FROM BOTH STREET AND BUILDING

USED, AGAIN STRIKING THE INTERNAL AXIS AT AN ARBITRARY DIAGONAL JUNCTION.[2] THEREFORE A DIRECT LINK IS IMPOSSIBLE AND SINCE ANY TURNING OF THE ENTRANCE VECTOR MUST BE ACHIEVED IN OPPOSING DIRECTIONS FOR FUNCTIONAL REASONS, THE USE OF A SECONDARY CENTROIDAL VOLUMETRIC SYSTEM AS EMPLOYED AT NEMOURS IS NEGATED. THE MOVEMENT SYSTEM MUST SOMEHOW PROVIDE FOR THE CUTTING OF THE TWO LONGITUDINAL AXES. LE CORBUSIER, FACED WITH THIS PROBLEM OF SYNTAX, EVOLVES AN ELABORATE VOLUMETRIC SYSTEM TO EFFECT AND ORDER THIS TRANSITION. SPECIFICALLY, IT IS A SYSTEM OF EN-SUITE PAVILLONS, WHICH IN THEMSELVES ARE ORDERED BY A SECONDARY DEVELOPMENT INVOLVING A MASS-SURFACE DIALECTIC AND THE PLAY OF SPECIFIC GEOMETRIC SOLIDS WITH REFERENCE TO THE FRONTAL COORDINATE OF THE SPATIAL GRID. THIS GRID BECOMES THE ABSOLUTE REFERENCE FOR THE SPECIFIC FORMS, AND THE SPECIFIC GRAMMAR FOR THE APPLICATION OF THESE FORMS DERIVES FROM THE GENERIC ANTECEDENT OF EACH. THE WHOLE COMPLEX IS THEN SUBJECTED TO A RIGID ORDERING BY THE USE OF SQUARES AND GOLDEN SECTION RECTANGLES, WHICH DEFINE ALL CRITICAL JUNCTIONS AND NODAL POINTS IN TERMS OF THIS GRID.

THE AXES OF THE GENERIC FORMS PLAY AN IMPORTANT PART IN THE CONCEPTUAL ORDERING OF THE MOVEMENT SYSTEM, THE SYNTAX OF THE SINGLE ENTRY INTO A LINEAR VOLUME BEING RESOLVED BY THE SYSTEMIC CONTROL OF THESE AXES. THE RECOGNITION OF THE PRESSURE OF THE ENTRANCE ON THE GENERIC STATE OF THE VOLUME CAUSE THE PLANE OF SYMMETRY TO BE DISLOCATED TO THE REAR OF THE VOLUME. THIS SURFACE OF THE SPECIFIC VOLUME THEN ACTS AS A 'BACKBONE' OR DOMINANT PLANE, SIMILAR IN NATURE TO THE NORTH FACADE OF THE PAVILLON SUISSE AND THE CHAPEL BLOCK AT LA TOURETTE, FROM WHICH THE 'EN-SUITE' PAVILLON DEVELOPMENT IS TENSIONED. IN EACH CASE THE DOMINANT 'SURFACE' IS USED AS A FOIL AND A REFERENCE FOR THE OTHER PARTS OF

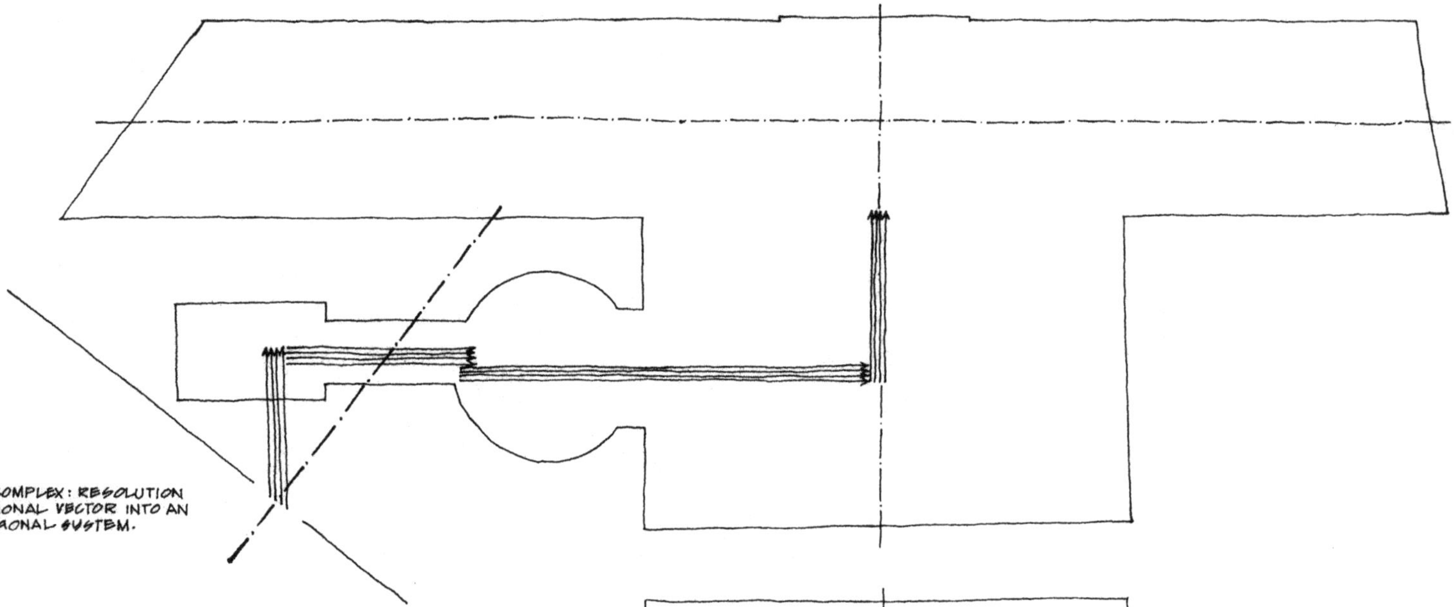

3.

ENTRY COMPLEX: RESOLUTION OF DIAGONAL VECTOR INTO AN ORTHOGONAL SYSTEM.

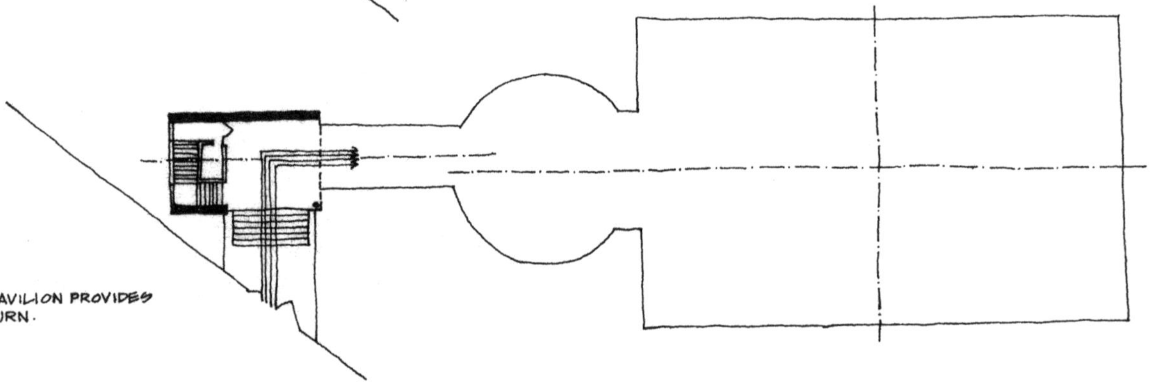

4.

ENTRY PAVILION PROVIDES INITIAL TURN.

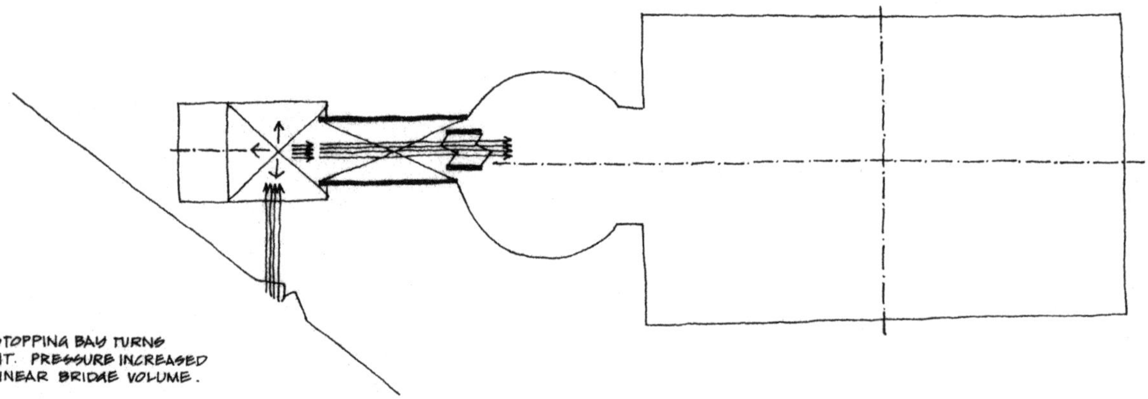

5.

SQUARE STOPPING BAY TURNS MOVEMENT. PRESSURE INCREASED IN RECTILINEAR BRIDGE VOLUME.

THE TOTAL ENTRY COMPLEX CAN BE INTERPRETED AS MERELY THE RESOLUTION OF THE DIAGONAL VECTOR, CONSIDERED PERPENDICULAR TO THE EXTERNAL AXIS, INTO A SERIES OF ORTHOGONAL MOVEMENTS IN RELATION TO THE LONGITUDINAL AXIS OF THE LINEAR VOLUME.[3] TO ACCOMPLISH THIS, THE EXTERNAL AXIS IS TURNED TWICE AND BROUGHT INTO THE TOTAL ORDER. FURTHERMORE, EVERY ELEMENT OF THE ENTRY COMPLEX IS PART OF THIS ORDER AND BECOMES FULLY STRESSED BY ITS USE IN ACHIEVING THE PURPOSE OF THIS ORDERING: THE ENTRY INTO THE BUILDING.

THE FIRST MAJOR TURNING IS EFFECTED IN THE ENTRY OR 'PROPYLEA' PAVILION WHICH IN ITSELF IS A GOLDEN SECTION VOLUME.[4] THIS VOLUME GIVES THE INTIAL DIRECTION TO THE MOVEMENT SYSTEM AS WELL AS AFFORDING A SECONDARY ACCESS TO THE OLD-PEOPLE'S AREA BELOW.

FROM THE REMAINING AREA OF THIS VOLUME WHICH IS A SQUARE, A STOPPING POINT IS INFERRED WHICH ALLOWS MOVEMENT TOBE TURNED IN ANY DIRECTION.[5] ONCE THE PULL OF THE LONGITUDINAL AXIS IS EXPERIENCED, THIS MOVEMENT CAN ONLY BE TO THE RIGHT WITH A SLIGHT BACKWASH OF THE PRESSURE WHICH IS FROM THIS VECTOR BEING RELIEVED BY THE MINOR STAIR BASEMENT. THE PRESSURE OF THE LONGITUDINAL VECTOR IS INCREASED BY THE SUCTION-LIKE EFFECT OF THE ENTRY BRIDGE. THIS RECTILINEAR SECOND UNIT IS DIRECTIONAL, AND IT CONTINUES THE LONGITUDINAL VECTOR ALONG ITS CENTRAL AXIS. FURTHERMORE, THIS 'PAVILION' RECEIVES ADDITIONAL IMPORTANCE BECAUSE OF THE RHOMBIC NATURE OF ITS VOLUME: IT IS THE ONLY NON-ORTHOGONAL VOLUME IN THE SEQUENCE. IT CAN BE TAKEN AS BALANCING ABOUT A HORIZONTAL ABSOLUTE THE VOLUME FROM THE STREET TO ENTRY PAVILION, WHICH CAN BE READ AS AN EQUIVALENT FUNNEL TO

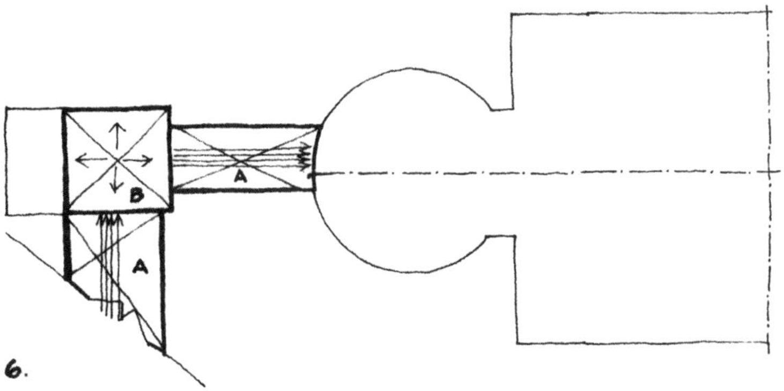

6.

A-B-A : START-STOP-START SEQUENCE

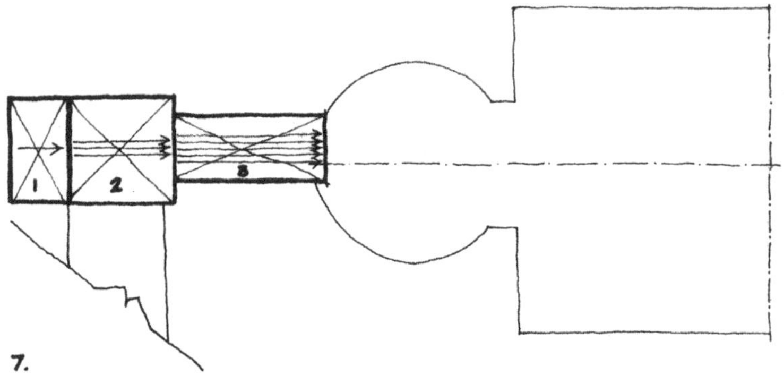

7.

VOLUMETRIC PROGRESSION 1:2:3

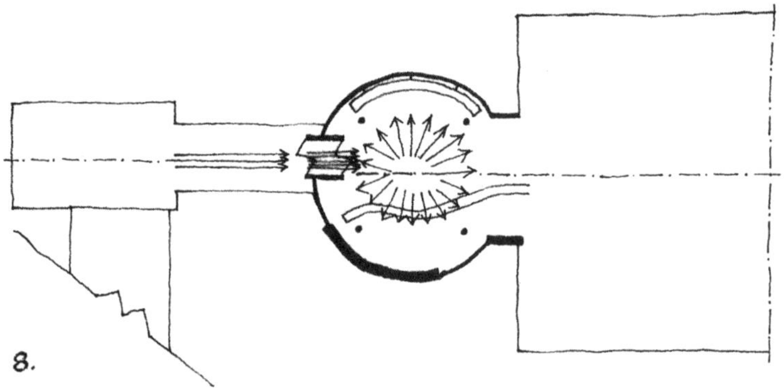

8.

BUILD UP OF PRESSURE IN NECK
DIFFUSION OF PRESSURE IN CYLINDER

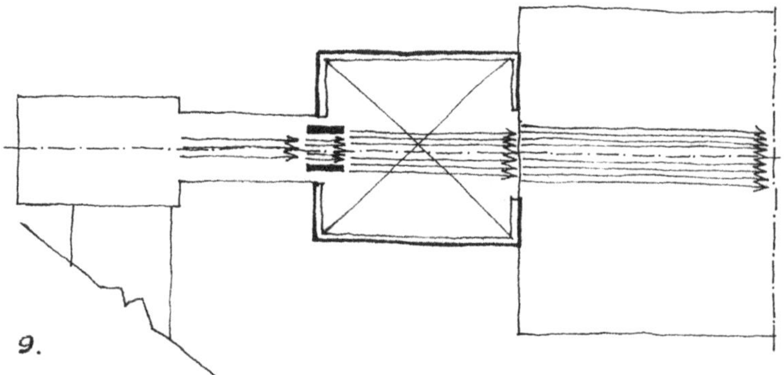

9.

VOLUMETRIC ORDER CANNOT TURN MOVEMENT SYSTEM. RECTILINEAR VOLUME WOULD HAVE INCREASED PRESSURE, MAKING TURNING DIFFICULT.

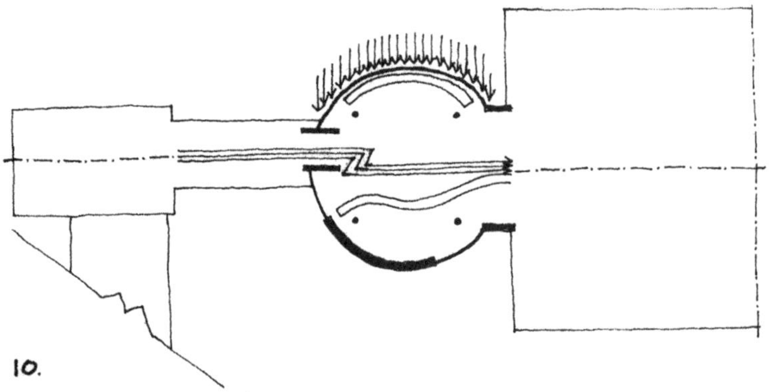

10.

AXIS STUTTERED BY SLIPPING CYLINDER FORWARD.

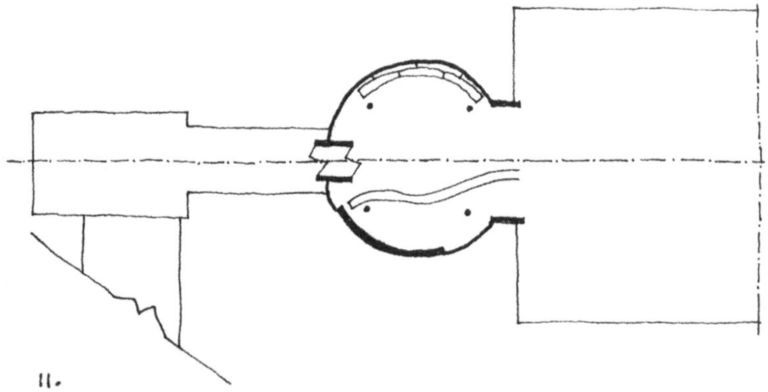

11.

CYLINDER ON AXIS
NO BLUNTING OR WEAKENING OF MOVEMENT VECTOR.

THE BRIDGE, THIS VOLUME IF A HORIZONTAL ROOF PLANE IS IMPLIED. THESE FIRST THREE 'PAVILIONS' MAY BE INITIALLY CONSIDERED AS AN ABA-START-STOP-START SEQUENCE. HOWEVER, LE CORBUSIER ORDERS VOLUMES 1 AND 2, WHICH ARE BOTH PARTS OF THE ENTRY PROPYLEA, WITH THE BRIDGE, VOLUME 3, IN SUCH A FASHION THAT THE STOPPING ZONE 2 CAN ALSO BE SEEN AS PART OF A VOLUMETRIC PROGRESSION 1,2,3, WITH A CORRESPONDING INCREASE IN THE PRESSURE OF THE DIRECTIONAL VECTOR WHICH SUPPLIES THE IMPETUS FOR THE TURNING MOVEMENT FROM STOPPING SQUARE 2 .

THE CRITICAL POINT IN THIS PROGRESSION IS REACHED AT THE CYLINDRICAL ENTRY VESTIBULE. HERE THE FINAL BUILD-UP OF THE DIRECTIONAL AXIS IS ACCOMPLISHED BY THE RESTRICTION OF THE NARROW NECK WHICH LINKS THE BRIDGE WITH THE VESTIBULE. FROM THIS POINT, LE CORBUSIER PREPARES THE SYSTEM FOR THE FINAL TURNING THAT MUST BE MADE TO ALLOW ENTRY INTO THE MAIN VOLUME. IF THE PRESSURE NECESSARY TO SUSTAIN THE MOVEMENT SYSTEM HAD BEEN AGAIN REINFORCED, IT WOULD HAVE BEEN DIFFICULT OR IMPOSSIBLE TO EFFECT THE FINAL TURNING OF THIS VECTOR. THEREFORE, THERE MUST BE A DILUTION AND WEAKENING OF THIS AXIS AT THE SAME TIME AS THE VOLUMETRIC HIERARCHY CONTINUES TO INCREASE IN SIZE; THIS INCREASE PROVIDING THE PROGRESSION IN SCALE FROM STREET TO MAJOR VOLUME. IT IS INTERESTING TO NOTE THAT THE VOLUMETRIC ORDER CANNOT IN ITSELF TURN THE MOVEMENT SYSTEM, HENCE THE USE OF A CYLINDER INSTEAD OF A RECTILINEAR VOLUME FOR THE VESTIBULE. THE CYLINDER IMPLIES AN IMMEDIATE EXPANSION OUTWARD, A DIFFUSION OF ENERGY, WHICH WOULD NOT BE PROVIDED BY A RECTILINEAR VOLUME. THIS STOP CAN BE READ AS THE FIRST BLUNTING OF THE ENTRY AXIS. THE SECOND, AND PERHAPS MORE CRITICAL WEAKENING, IS THE STUTTERING OF THE AXIS CAUSED BY SLIPPING THE CYLINDER FORWARD AND OFF THE DIRECT LINE OF MOVEMENT. BY VIRTUE OF THIS VERY SLIGHT SHIFTING, THE CYLINDER IS

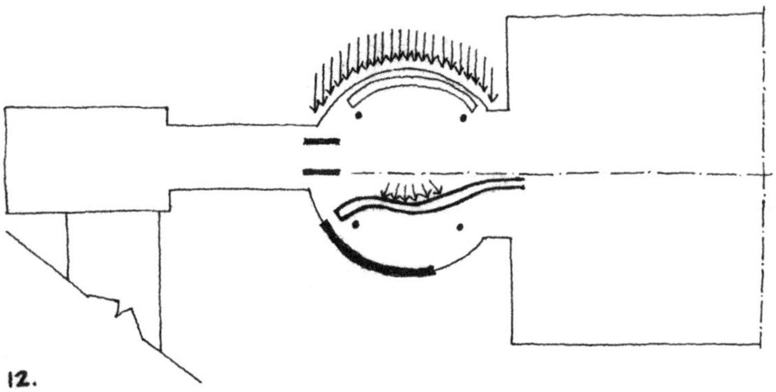

12.

DISTORTION OF COUNTER BY WRENCHING
AND SPINNING OF CYLINDER

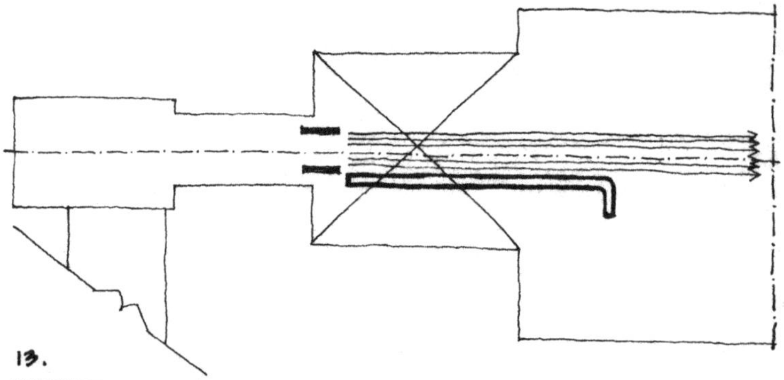

13.

UNDISTORTED COUNTER
WOULD HAVE BEEN A STRONG
DIRECTIONAL ELEMENT, AS
SEEN WITH RECTILINEAR VOLUME.

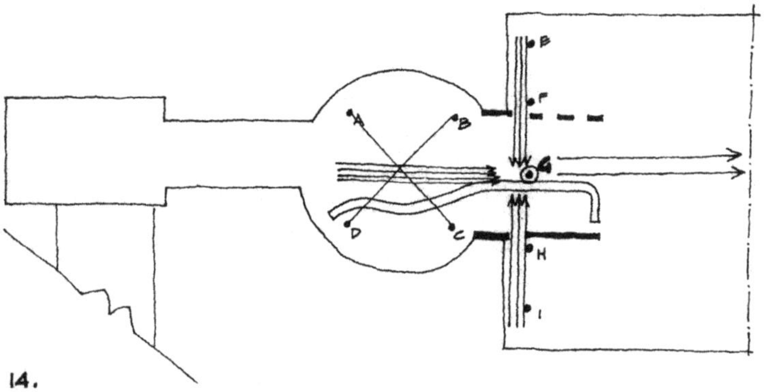

14.

COLUMN G DEFINES TRANSVERSE SLOT
WHICH PROVIDES A FINAL BLUNTING OF ENTRY AXIS.

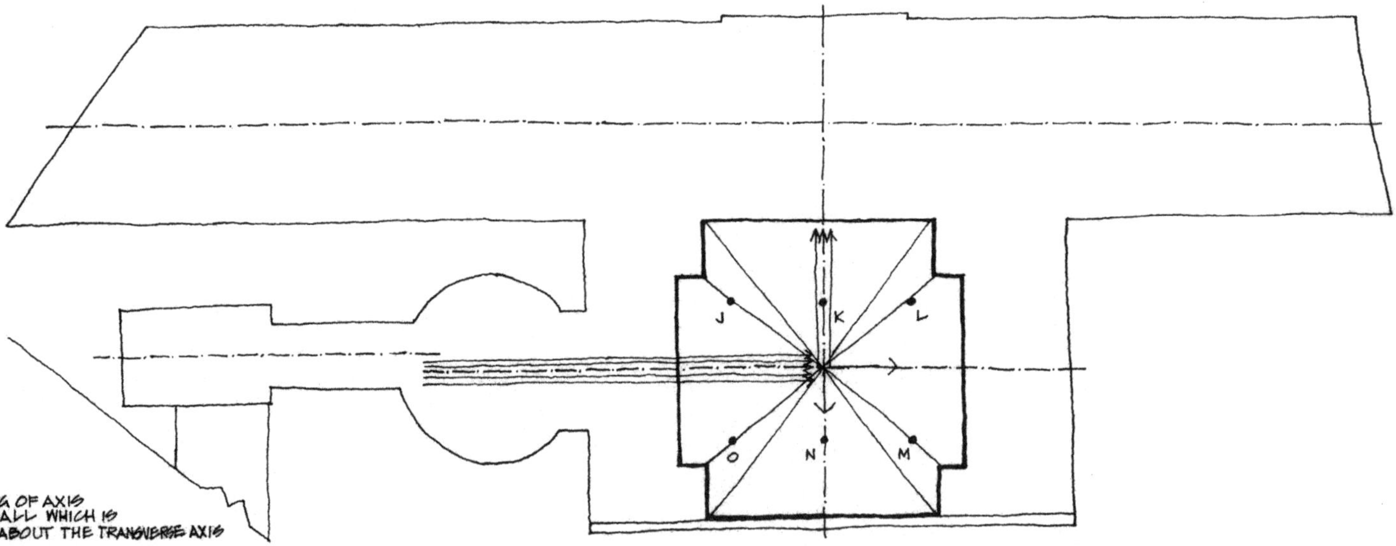

15.

FINAL TURNING OF AXIS
IN CENTRAL HALL WHICH IS
DIRECTIONAL ABOUT THE TRANSVERSE AXIS

PLACED IN AN AGONISING RELATIONSHIP WITH BOTH THE ENTRY AXIS AND THE ADJACENT BRIDGE, THUS ALMOST NULLIFYING THE DIRECTIONAL VECTOR. THE EFFECT OF THIS WRENCHING ACTION COMBINED WITH THE SPINNING QUALITY OF THE CYLINDER IS REFLECTED IN THE DISTORTION OF THE RECEPTION COUNTER, WHICH IN ITSELF WOULD HAVE BEEN A VERY STRONG DIRECTIONAL ELEMENT IF IT WERE NOT FOR THIS WARPING.[12] IT WOULD BE INTERESTING TO ASSUME A RECTILINEAR VOLUME AS THE GENERIC CONDITION IN ORDER TO SEE THE DIFFERENT EFFECT IT WOULD HAVE HAD ON THE ENTIRE SYSTEM.[13] THE ENTRY VECTOR WOULD HAVE BEEN CONTINUED INSTEAD OF BLUNTED, AND THE FINAL TURNING WOULD WOULD HAVE REQUIRED A MORE ELABORATE RESOLUTION. THUS THE CYLINDER CAN BE SEEN AS RECEIVING ITS SPECIFIC FORM FROM THE SUDDEN EXPANSION AND RELEASE OF THE PRESSURE BUILD UP IN THE PRECEDING VOLUMES.

THE WEAKENING OF THE AXIS CONTINUES WITH THE WIDENING OF THE NECK BETWEEN THE VESTIBULE AND THE CENTRAL HALL. THIS LINK CAN BE SEEN AS AN EXTENSION OF THE SQUARE VOLUME DEFINED WITHIN THE CYLINDER BY THE FOUR COLUMNS A,B,C,D; THEIR CENTRAL AXIS BEING LOCATED IN RELATION TO THE INITIAL ENTRY AXIS. MOREOVER, THE LOCATION OF THE SINGLE COLUMN G IN THIS LINK FURTHER EFFECTS THE FINAL DILUTION OF THE INITIAL MOVEMENT.[14] CONSIDERED BY ITSELF, THIS COLUMN SEEMS TO BE IN A RATHER ARBRTRARY LOCATION, BUT WHEN SEEN AS PART OF A ROW OF COLUMNS, WHICH IS GIVEN FURTHER ARTICULATION BY THE OPPOSING PAIR OF DOORS, IT DEFINES A TRANSVERSE VOLUMETRIC SLOT WHICH PROVIDES A FINAL BLUNTING OF THE MOVEMENT. FINALLY THE SYSTEM REACHES THE CENTRAL HALL WHICH CAN BE SEEN AS A BLUNTED CRUCIFORM, I.E. A CENTROIDAL FORM. THE LONGITUDINAL AXIS OF THIS VOLUME, WHICH IS A CONTINUATION OF THE DISLOCATED AXIS, IS DEFINED BY THE SIX ROUND COLUMNS J,K,L,M, N,O, WHILE THE TRANSVERSE AXIS IS DEFINED AND EMPHASISED BY THE DIRECTIONAL

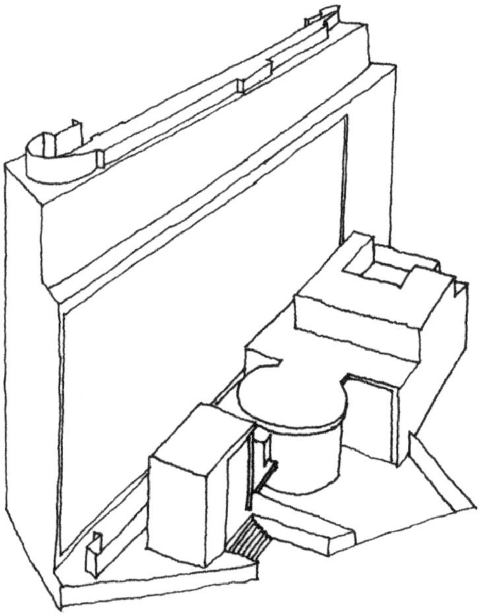

17.

EARLY PROJECT : AMBIGUOUS READING IN FRONT FACADE, BECAUSE OF SURFACE PLANE BEHIND.

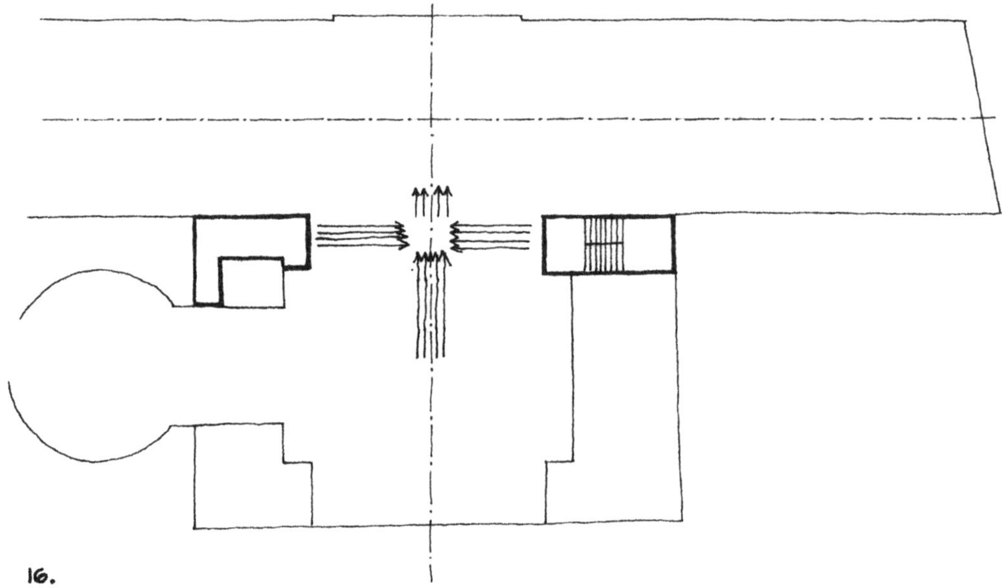

16.

FINAL ARTICULATION CAUSED BY JUXTAPOSITION OF MINOR STAIR AND BURSAR'S OFFICE

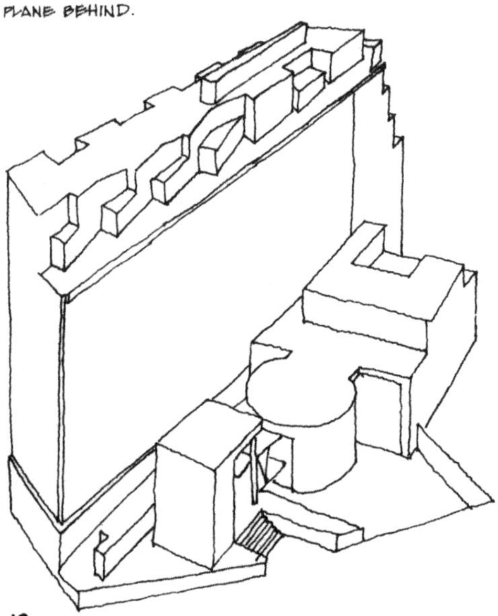

18.

FINAL PROJECT : SHOWS CHANGES TO GIVE A 'SURFACE' READING TO FRONT FACADE

QUALITY OF THE BLUNTED CRUCIFORM VOLUME; WHICH EXTENDS IN A GREATER DIRECTION ON THE TRANSVERSE AXIS.[15] THE CENTROIDAL NATURE OF THE HALL AGAIN IMPLIES A NON-DIRECTIONAL STOPPING POINT, THE TURNING BEING EFFECTED BY THE TRANSVERSE AXIS WHICH IN ITSELF IS GIVEN PROMINENCE BY ITS TIE THROUGH TO THE TRANSVERSE AXIS OF THE MAJOR VOLUME. HOWEVER, THE COLUMNAR GRID IN THE HALL IS STILL DIRECTIONAL WITH RESPECT TO THE LONGITUDINAL AXIS, AND THE INDIVIDUAL BAYS ARE DIRECTIONAL ACROSS THIS AXIS. THIS PRESENTS A CHANGE FROM THE SMALLER SCALE, NON-DIRECTIONAL GROUPING IN THE CYLINDRICAL VOLUME. THE FINAL ARTICULATION, BEFORE THE MOVEMENT ENTERS THE MAIN VOLUME IS THE NARROWING CAUSED BY THE JUXTAPOSITION OF MINOR STAIR AND THE BURSAR'S OFFICE.[16] THIS ENTIRE 'EN-SUITE' DEVELOPMENT IS TENSIONED FROM THE DOMINANT REAR PLANE BY A PLAY OF 'MASS' AGAINST 'SURFACE'.

THE MATURITY OF THIS DIALECTICAL CONDITION CAN BE SEEN BY AN EXAMINATION OF AN EARLIER PROJECT. HERE, LE CORBUSIER REALISES THAT A POSSIBLE AMBIGUOUS READING MIGHT ACCRUE TO THE FRONT FACADE OF THE MAIN VOLUME.[17] THERE IS A DESIRE FOR THIS PLANE TO READ AS 'SURFACE' WITH THE PAVILLIONS STATED AS 'MASS' IN THE FOREGROUND. HOWEVER, IN THE STEPPING BACK OF THIS FACADE, THERE IS A PLANE PRESENTED WHICH BECAUSE OF ITS SPECIFIC TREATMENT AS A 'SURFACE', ALLOWS THE POSSIBILITY OF THE FRONT FACADE TO BE READ AS A HOLLOWED OUT 'MASS'. THE CHANGES ON THE FINAL BUILDING INDICATE THE CLARITY OF THE RESOLUTION.[18] LE CORBUSIER NARROWS THE TOP FRAME OF THE FRONT FACADE, SO THAT IT CANNOT BE MISINTERPRETED AS 'MASS'. THE RESULTANT FRAME IS THEN CONTINUED ACROSS THE TOP OF THE SOLID PORTION OF THE FACADE, AND A SERIES OF OPENINGS IS CUT IN THAT SOLID IN SUCH A WAY AS TO AVOID ANY POSSIBLE 'MASS' READING OF THIS SURFACE. THE SET BACK PORTION OF THE FACADE IS THEN TREATED AS 'MASS', CUT SHARPLY AT ACUTE ANGLES TO

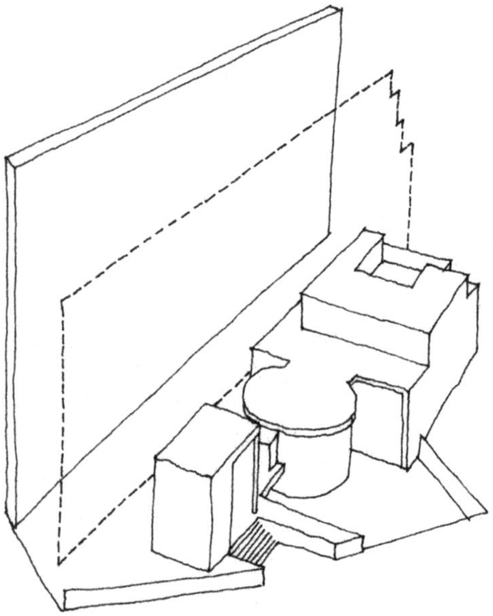

19.

MASS PAVILIONS TENSIONED FROM DOMINANT 'BACKBONE' SURFACE, AND PULLED THROUGH FRONT FACADE.

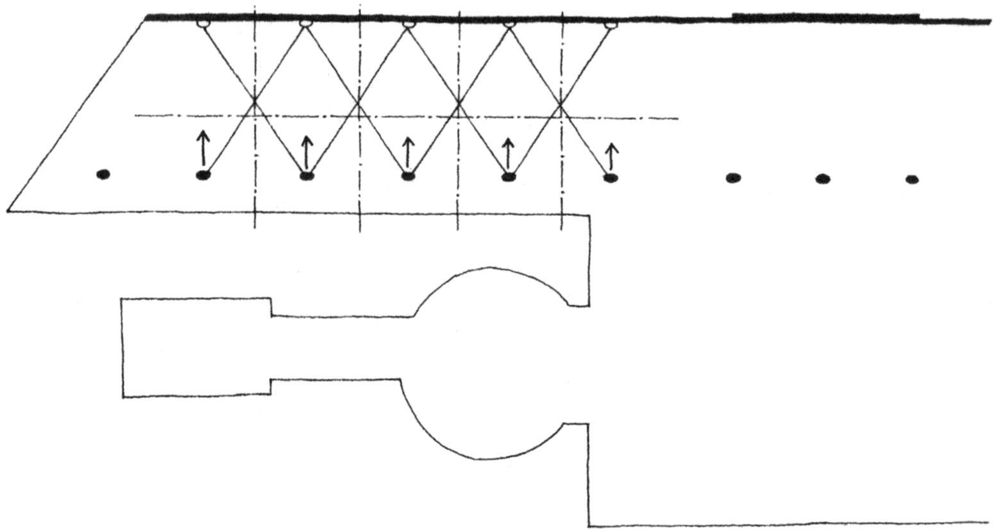

20.

COLUMNS READ AS HAVING BEEN PULLED TO DOMINANT SURFACE

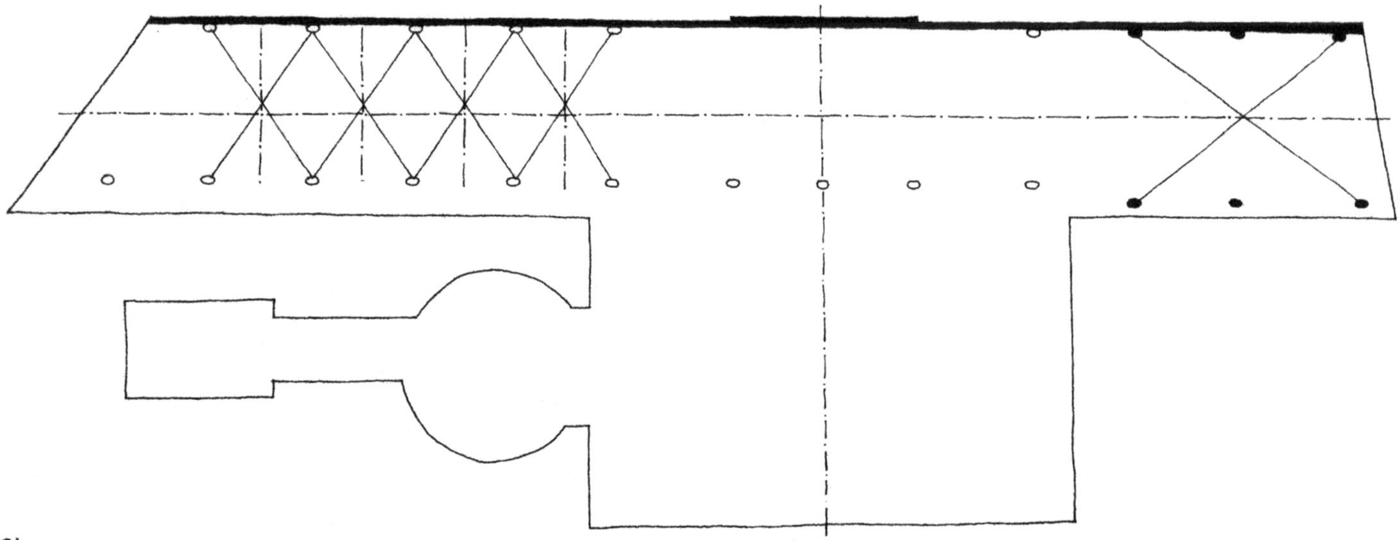

21.

TERMINATION OF LINEAR AXIS
COLUMNS IN UNDISTORTED LOCATION

THE ORTHOGONAL REFERENCE, NOW, THE MAIN VOLUME CAN BE READ AS 'MASS' WITH A 'SURFACE' RACED ON BOTH FRONT AND BACK. A READING OF THE 'MASS' PAVILIONS WHICH ARE HELD IN TENSION FROM THE BACK SURFACE, IS NOW POSSIBLE WHEREBY THEY CAN BE THOUGHT OF AS HAVING BEEN PULLED THROUGH THE 'SURFACE' FACADE FROM THE 'MASS' BEHIND.[19] THUS INITIALLY, THE CENTRAL HALL CAN BE SEEN AS DRAWN OUT OF THE MAIN VOLUME, AND THE REMAINING PAVILIONS ARE READ AS DEVELOPED IN A SIMILAR MANNER FROM THIS HALL. IN THE FINAL SCHEME THE PAVILIONS THEMSELVES, ESPECIALLY THE CYLINDER, ARE TREATED IN A MORE SOLID FASHION THEREBY STRENGTHENING THEIR READING AS 'MASS'. SINCE THE RELATIONSHIP OF THE ENTRY PAVILIONS TO THE DOMINANT 'BACK-BONE' SURFACE HAS BEEN ESTABLISHED, THE DISTORTIONS IN THE MAIN VOLUME PRODUCED BY THE DISLOCATION OF THIS PLANE MUST BE EXAMINED. THE COLUMNAR GRID ALONG THE FRONT FACADE, CLEARLY DEMONSTRATES THE TENSIONING PULL OF THE REAR FACADE. THESE COLUMNS CAN BE THOUGHT OF AS HAVING BEEN PULLED TOWARDS THE DOMINANT SURFACE EXCEPT FOR TWO END BAYS WHICH ARE CONSIDERED AS THE LINEAR TERMINATION.[20] THE RESULTING CANTILEVER OF THE SLAB FREES THE FRONT FACADE AND ALLOWS FOR CIRCULATION BETWEEN THE FACADE AND THE COLUMNS. FURTHERMORE THE DISLOCATION OF THE COLUMNS ALSO ALLOWS A TRANSVERSE AXIAL READING TO BE GIVEN TO THE INDIVIDUAL COLUMNAR BAYS. ON THE LEFT END OF THE MAIN VOLUME NO FORMAL ENDING IS PROVIDED, AS THE PROJECTED SCHEME INVOLVED A CONTINUATION FROM THAT POINT. A TERMINATION IS PROVIDED TO THE RIGHT END OF THE LINEAR AXIS. A CONTINUOUS RATHER THAN AN ARTICULATED READING IS GIVEN TO THIS AXIS, AS THE COLUMNS REMAIN IN AN UNDISTORTED POSITION.[21] THIS WIDENING OF THE COLUMNAR GRID PROVIDES A POSITIVE END CONDITION WITHOUT TERMINATING THE AXIS. AN ATTEMPT IS MADE TO STOP THIS AXIS BY ELONGATING THE LAST BAY, THIS EXTENSION, HOWEVER, ONLY PROVIDING A DEFINITION OF THE FINAL GOLDEN SECTION RECTANGLE. IT IS ONLY WHEN THE VERTICAL SECTION IS EXAMINED THAT THE FORMAL ENDING OF THIS AXIS CAN

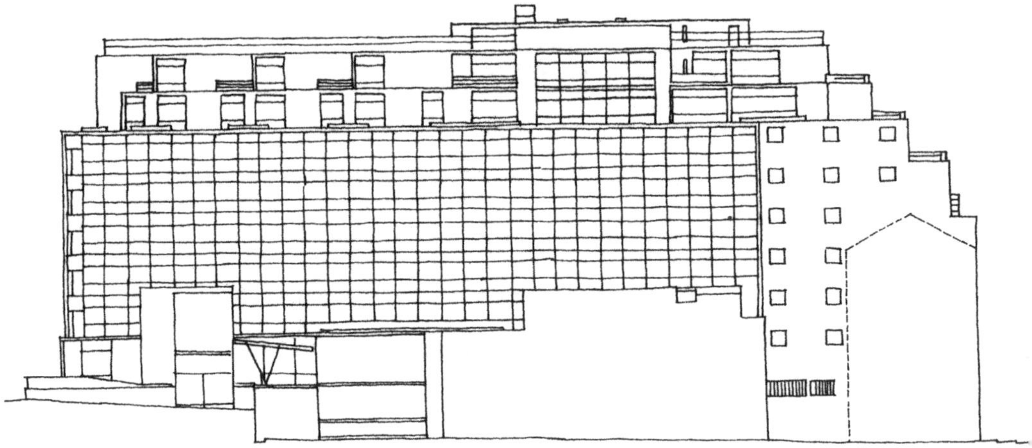

FRONT FACADE

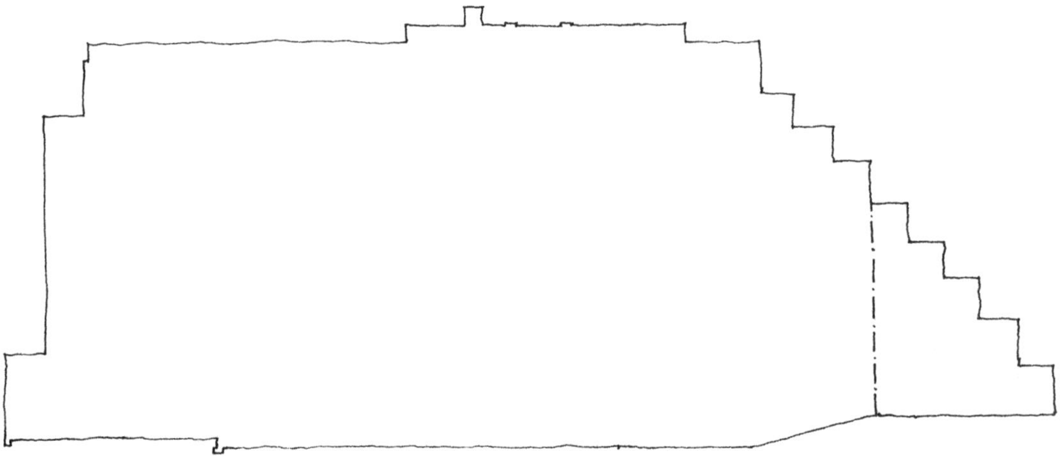

22.

IMPLIED ENDING IN STEPPED LONGITUDINAL SECTION.

BE SEEN. A TERMINATION IS IMPLIED BY THE STEPPED LONGITUDINAL SECTION, IN THAT IF THE STEPPING WERE CONTINUED IN A SIMILAR MANNER, A CMPLETE FORM RESEMBLING A ZIGGURAT IN SECTION WOULD BE EVOLVED.[22] THIS IMPLIED ENDING IS USED BY LE CORBUSIER IN BOTH THE PAVILLON SUISSE, AS DISCUSSED ABOVE, AND LA TOURETTE.

The two buildings by Frank Lloyd Wright in the following analyses are both of a linear nature: one parallel to and one perpendicular to dominat external axes. The syntax necessary for the relolution of internal and external requirements is similar to that used in the two buildings by Le Corbusier, even though their specific internal functions are different. The specific grammar invoked in each case is ordered by a formal system and thus system acknowledges the particular syntax of a given situation.

It is not the concern of these analyses to investigate in detail the perceptual qualities of the specific form; in this sense these analyses are concerned with Wright's 'mannerisms' only in so far as they validate the argument developed in this thesis.

Although Wright's grammar tends to obscure the syntax and system the rigid organisation of this grammar and the relationship of the system in its specific state to the generic condition is still apparent and may be conceptually analysed.

A study of the systems developed by Frank Lloyd Wright will indicate that his early work had a strong classical basis. This can be seen in his systemic development where a strong play of axes and cross axes orders the plan. These axes, which in Le Corbusier's work are essentially used to order and control movement, are used by Wright'to control volume. He does not make use of either the 'promenade architecturale' or any stystem involving a 'mass-surface' dialectic. Wright's grammar is almost entirely concerned with the interplay of a volumetric order and the elaborate counterpoise of volumetric elemtns about major and minor axes. These volumes are conceived of externally as 'mass' or solid-cut-away,

WHICH CAN BE VERIFIED IN HIS RARE USE OF CONCRETE AND STEEL AS POINT SUPPORTS.

THE SYSTEMIC DEVELOPMENT IN WRIGHT'S WORK IS ESSENTIALLY LINEAR IN THAT ONE ORTHOGONAL AXIS IS USUALLY GIVEN A GREATER STRESS THAN THE OTHER. IT IS POSSIBLE TO DISCERN TWO DIFFERNET TYPES OF SYSTEMIC DEVELOPMENT IN HIS WORK, THE ONE MOST OFTEN EMPLOYED MIGHT BEST BE DESCRIBED AS CENTROIDAL SINCE IT EVOLVES FROM A GENRIC CRUCIFORM OR PINWHEEL, WITH A FIREPLACE 'MASS' AS ITS CENTRAL REFERENCE. HOWEVER IN MOST CASES THIS FORM IS DISTORTED TO PRODUCE A LINEAR READING IN ITS SPECIFIC STATE. THE WINSLOW, ARCHER, BRADLEY, AND THOMAS HOUSES, ARE PROTOTYPE EXAMPLES OF THIS CONDITION, WHICH COMES INTO MATURITY IN THE WILLETTS AND ROBERTS HOUSES. THE SECOND RECOGNISABLE TYPE OF WRIGHT PLANNING IS A SYSTEM OF LINEAR PAVILIONS WHICH EVOLVES FROM EITHER A GENERIC LINEAR VOLUME OR A BLUNTED CENTROIDAL CRUCIFORM. THE HILLSIDE HOME SCHOOL, THE AVERLY COONLEY HOUSE AND THE DARWIN D. MARTIN HOUSE ARE EXAMPLES OF THIS LATTER TYPE. THE FOLLOWING DISCUSSION WILL BE CONFINED TO THIS LATER CATEGORY AND SPECIFICALLY THE COONLEY AND MARTIN HOUSES, SINCE NOT ONLY DO THEY ILLUSTRATE THE PARTICULAR INTERNAL AND EXTERNAL CONDITIONS WHICH ARE BEING USED FOR THESE ANALYSES BUT ALSO THEY PRESENT THE MOST MATURE DEVELOPMENT OF WRIGHT'S GRAMMAR WITHIN A FORMAL SYSTEM.

DARWIN D MARTIN HOUSE

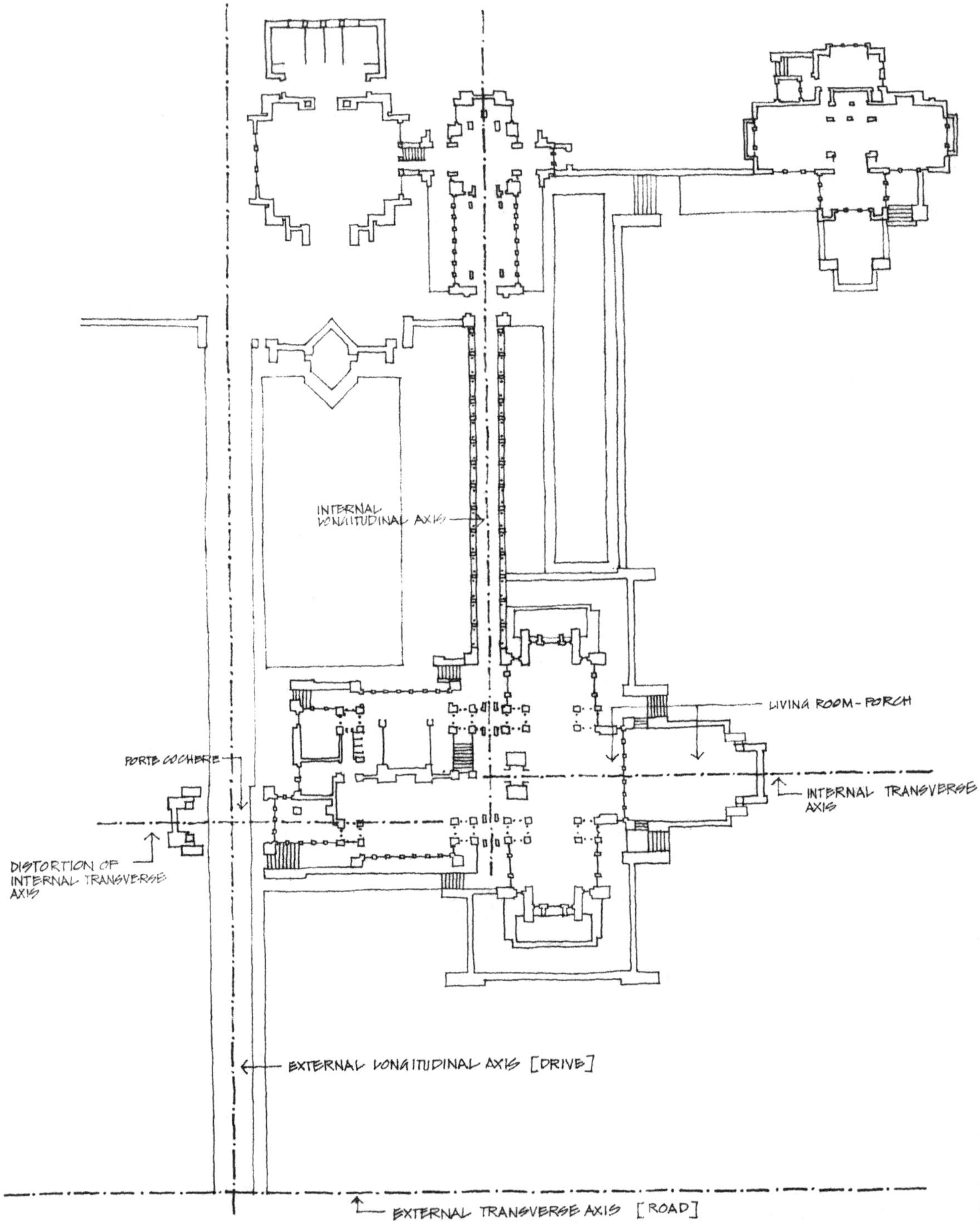

1.

GROUND FLOOR PLAN SHOWING ALL MAJOR
AXIAL REFERENCES

THE SPECIFIC RESOLUTION OF THIS BUILDING EVOLVES FROM A SYNTHESIS OF TWO VOLUMETRIC SYSTEMS: THE CONTINUOUS AND THE STATIC. THESE TWO SYSTEMS ARE CONTROLLED BY A COMPLEX DOUBLE GRID WHICH IS DELICATELY COUNTERPOISED ABOUT THE ORTHOG-ONAL AXES. A DIALECTIC CONDITION IS ALSO PRESENTED WHEREBY EITHER AXIS MAY BE READ AS DOMINANT DEPENDING ON THE POSITION OF THE VIEWER IN RELATION TO THE PLAN. THE RESULTANT PLAIDING OF MAJOR AND MINOR AXES IS A CHARACTERISTIC OF WRIGHT'S PLANNING. A MAJOR AXIS IS DEVELOPED AND THEN BLUNTED BY ANOTHER MAJOR AXIS OR A MINOR AXIS. THIS BLUNTING OF AXES OFTEN HAS A FUNCTIONAL DERIVATION, BUT IN MOST CASES THE AXES ARE CUT FOR FORMAL, SYNTACTICAL REASONS, PROVIDING AN END TO A PARTICULAR AXIAL MOVEMENT. INITIALLY THE EXTERNAL CONDITIONS PRESENT A MAJOR TRANSVERSE AXIS, THE ROAD, RUNNING PARALLEL TO THE SITE FRONTAGE.[1] THIS IS CUT BY A STRONG LONGITUDINAL AXIS, THE DRIVE LEADING TO THE GARAGE. THE INTERNAL DOMINANT AXIS IS LOCATED AT RIGHT ANGLES TO THE DRIVE, WHICH MUST THEN BE CUT TO PROVIDE ENTRY TO THE BUILDING. THE PORTE COCHERE AXIS INITIALLY APPEARS TO BE THE DOMINANT GENERIC REFERENCE OFTTHE BUILDING; HOWEVER UPON INVESTIGATION IT CAN BE SEEN RATHER AS A DISLOCATION FROM THE DOMINANT AXIS WHICH IS IN FACT THE CENTRAL TRANSVERSE LIVING ROOM-PORCH AXIS. THIS DISLOCATION IS AN ACKNOWLEDGEMENT OF THE THRUST OF THE MAJOR GENERIC LONGITUDINAL AXIS OF THE PERGOLA CONNECTING THE CONSERVATORY WITH THE MAIN HOUSE. THEREFORE THE ANALYSIS MUST BE DIVIDED INTO AN INVESTIGATION OF THE TRANSVERSE AND LONGITUDINAL AXES, EACH CONSIDERED IN TURN AS A DOMINANT REFERENCE.

IF THE LIVING ROOM - PORCH AXIS IS CONSIDERED AS THE MAJOR TRANSVERSE REFERENCE THEN THE PORTE COCHERE AXIS MUST BE A DISTORTION OF THIS. THE PORTE COCHERE IS

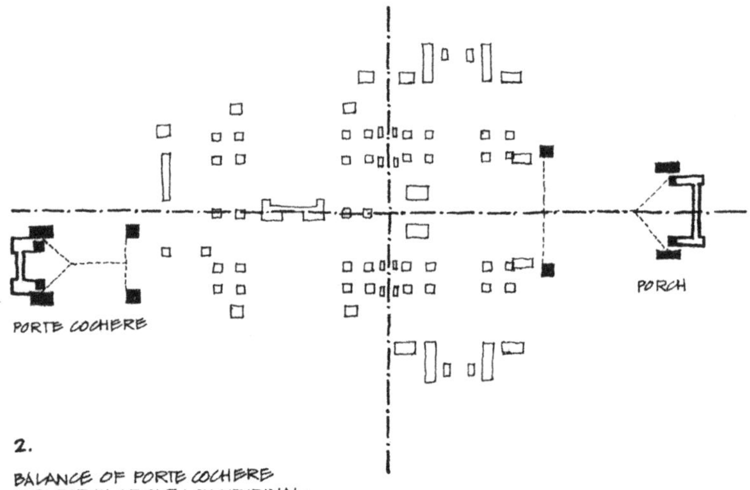

2.

BALANCE OF PORTE COCHERE AND PORCH ABOUT LONGITUDINAL AXIS.

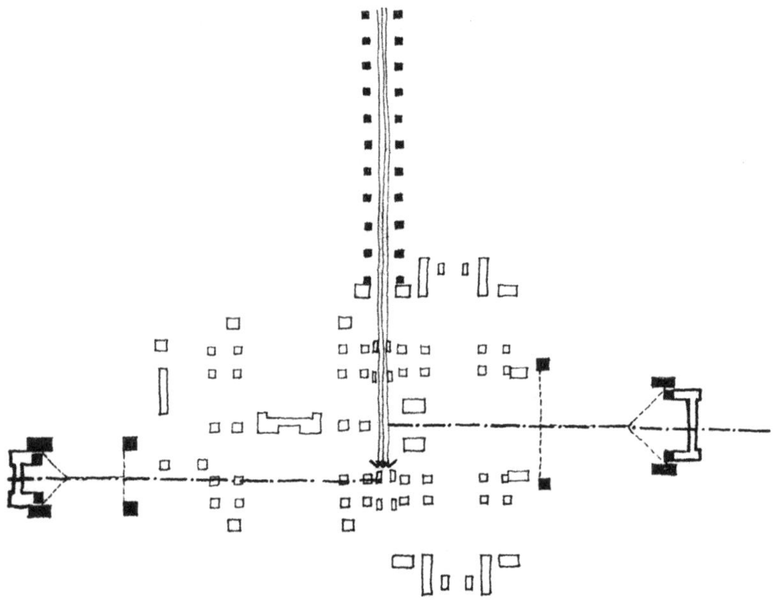

3.

DISLOCATION OF PORTE COCHERE BY PERGOLA, ABOUT TRANSVERSE AXIS.

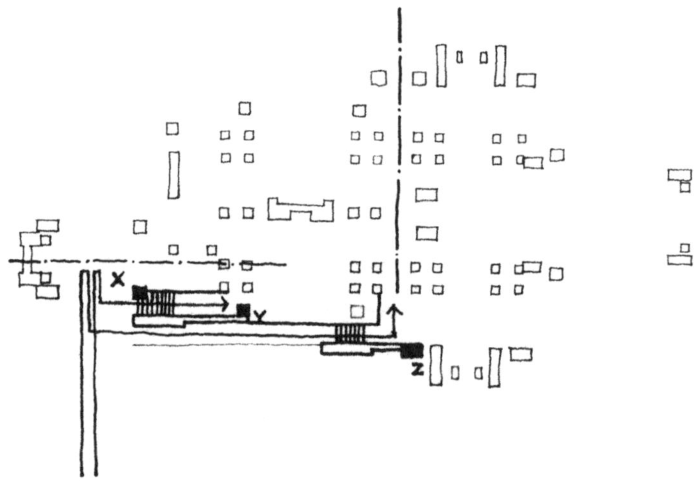

4.

ECHELON SYSTEM TO CONTROL DUAL PEDESTRIAN ENTRY

BALANCED BY THE PORCH ABOUT THE LONGITUDINAL AXIS BY A COUNTERPOISE ACHIEVED BY THE SMALL VOLUME - THE PORTE COCHERE- BEING LOCATED AT A SLIGHTLY GREATER DISTANCE FROM THE AXIS OF SYMMETRY THAN THE LARGER PORCH VOLUME.[2] THE INTENTION TO BALANCE THESE TWO ELEMENTS IS EXPLICIT IN THEIR SIMILAR SPECIFIC TREATMENT AS END PAVILIONS: THE COLUMNAR JUXTAPOSITION AND THE PLACEMENT AND SPECIFIC FORM OF THE LOW PARAPET WALL IN EACH CASE STRENGTHENING THIS READING. HOWEVER THE DISLOCATION OF THE PORTE-COCHERE BY THE THRUST OF THE PERGOLA AXIS, THROWS THIS ELEMENT OUT OF A STATE OF EQUILIBRIUM ABOUT THE TRANSVERSE AXIS.[3] IT IS THE ONLY MAJOR VOLUME THAT IS NOT IN AN AXIAL BALANCE OR SYMMETRY THEREBY GIVING IT A GREATER IMPORTANCE IN THE TOTAL COMPLEX. IN A SENSE, IT CAN BE SEEN AS ACKNOWLEDGING THE THRUST OF THE PERGOLA AXIS WHICH IS BLUNTED BY THE LIVING ROOM AXIS; THIS DISLOCATION THEN RESTORES THE DYNAMIC BALANCE OF THE TOTAL COMPOSITION. THE DISLOCATION OF THE PORTE COCHERE IS THEN EMPLOYED AS PART OF A SECONDARY ECHELON SYSTEM OF MOVEMENT USED TO RESOLVE THE FUNCTIONAL REQUIREMENT OF BOTH A VEHICULAR AND A PEDESTRIAN ENTRY.[4]

THE PEDESTRIAN ENTRY INTO THE BUILDING WOULD BE ALMOST IMPOSSIBLE IN FORMAL TERMS IF IT WERE NOT FOR THIS MINOR SYSTEMIC DEVELOPMENT. BOTH ENTRY INTO THE RECEPTION HALL AND ENTRY INTO THE ACTUAL VESTIBULE REQUIRE A DOUBLING BACK FROM THE STOPPING POINT PROVIDED FOR VEHICLES. THIS ECHELONING MOVEMENT IS CONTROLLED AND REINFORCED BY THE THREE CORNER COLUMNS X,Y,AND Z, AND THE ELABORATE STAIR DEVELOPMENT. WHEREAS THE INITIAL ENTRY INTO THE RECEPTION HALL IS DIRECTLY ACHIEVED FROM THE ECHELONING MOVEMENT, THE ENTRY INTO THE VESTIBULE MUST BE TURNED. THIS TURNING WHICH IS EFFECTED BY THE DIRECTIONAL PULL OF THE CENTRAL LONGITUDINAL AXIS, BRINGS THE MOVEMENT INTO A RATHER AMBIGUOUS POSITION

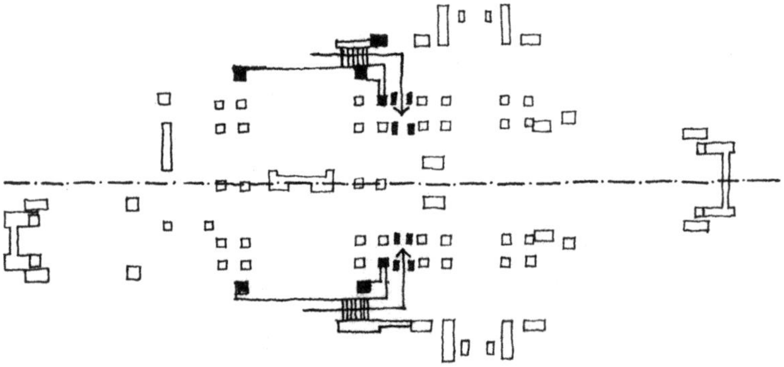

5.

EQUATION OF FRONT ENTRY WITH MINOR REAR ENTRY EXPLAINS AWKWARD TERMINATION OF ENTRY MOVEMENT. EMPHASIZES ENTRY TO RECEPTION HALL.

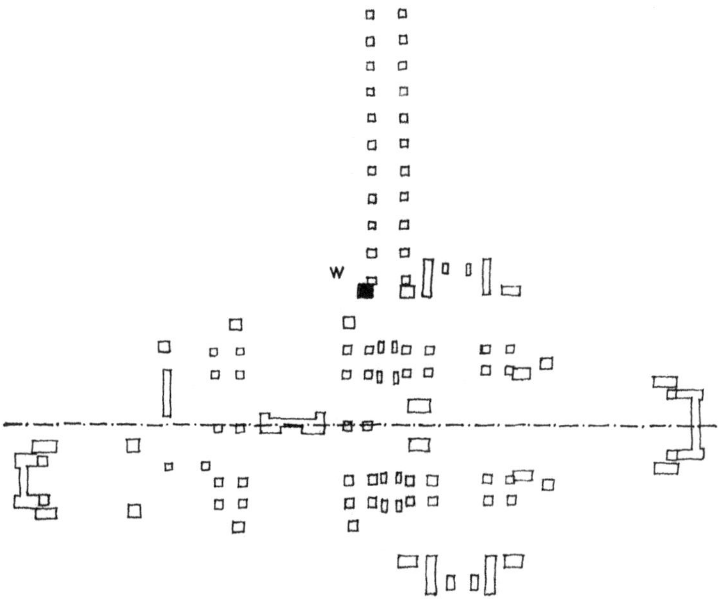

6.

PIER W NOT INVOLVED IN AN AXIAL SYMMETRY ABOUT TRANSVERSE AXIS

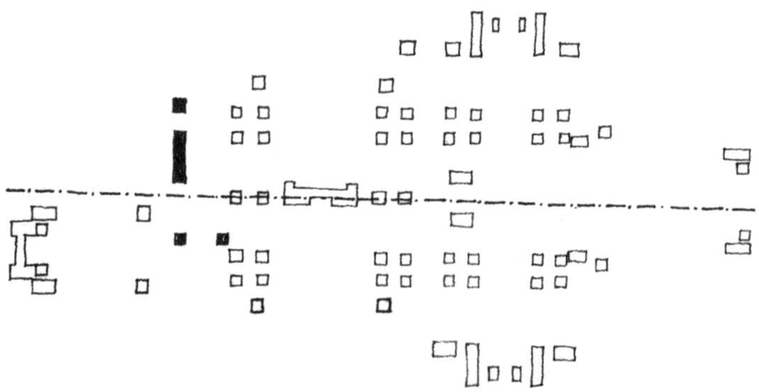

7.

ELEMENTS OF SERVANT'S DINING ROOM LAVATORY, AND OFFICE NOT PART OF SYMMETRICAL ORDER.

INTERNALLY; THIS ENTRY BY-PASSES THE RECEPTION ROOM AND INTRUDES INTO A CORNER OF THE CONTINUOUS VOLUME OF THE LIVING ROOM. IF THIS JUNCTURE IS READ ONLY IN TERMS OF ITS RELATIONSHIP TO THE LIVING ROOM VOLUME THEN IT MUST BE INTERPRETED AS A RATHER AWKWARD TERMINATION OF THE ENTRY MOVEMENT. HOWEVER, IF THIS ENTRY IS READ AS A MINOR ENTRY AND EQUATED ABOUNT THE TRANSVERSE AXIS WITH THE MINOR REAR ENTRY FROM THE FLOWER GARDEN THEN THE JUNCTION IS MORE EASILY UNDERSTOOD.[5] THE MAIN ENTRY INTO THE RECEPTION HALL TAKES ON A GREATER WEIGHT AGAIN BY ITS LACK OF A SYMMETRICAL RELATIONSHIP WITH ANY OTHER ELEMENT. EVEN THOUGH THE MINOR KITCHEN ENTRY APPROXIMATES TO IT IN SIZE AND DIRECTION, IT CANNOT BE CONSIDERED AS A BALANCE BECAUSE OF ITS MORE OBSCURE LOCATION IN RELATION TO THE PORTE COCHERE.

THERE ARE TWO FURTHER MINOR ELEMENTS WHICH ARE NOT INVOLVED IN A AXIAL SYMMETRY ABOUT THE TRANSVERSE AXIS. THE FIRST IS THE PIER W AT THE END OF THE PERGOLA WHICH IS BALANCED ABOUT THE LONGITUDINAL AXIS BY THE CORNER PIER V OF THE DINING ROOM.[6] DISCOUNTING ITS OBVIOUS BALANCE AS A TERMINAL TO THE PERGOLA AXIS, IT CAN BE CONCEPTUALLY READ AS BEING A FRAGMENTATION OF THE DINING ROOM PIER CAUSED BY THE INTERJECTION OF THE PERGOLA. THIS READING RECEIVES FURTHER CREDENCE WHEN THE LIBRARY-DINING ROOM BALANCE IS OBSERVED; HERE THE CORRESPONDING LIBRARY PIER U IS EXTENDED IN A SIMILAR FASHION TO THE OPPOSITE CORNER PIER T. THE SECOND NON-SYMMETRICAL ELEMENT IS THE SERVANTS' DINING-ROOM, LAVATORY AND, OFFICE COMPLEX, OF WHICH ONLY THE EXTERNAL CORNER PIER S, THE ADJACENT WALL OF THE DINING ROOM AND THE SMALLER TWIN PIERS Q AND R OF THE OFFICE ARE NOT PART OF THE SYMMETRICAL ORDER.[7] HOWEVER THIS RATHER MINOR ASYMMETRY CAN BE INTERPRETED AS PLAYING AN IMPORTANT PART IN THE TOTAL ORDER. IF THE SERVANTS'

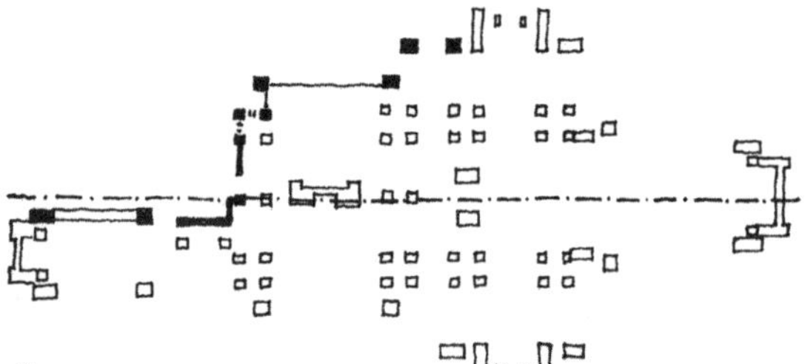

8.

ABRUPT STEP WITHOUT ASYMMETRICAL ELEMENTS OF SERVANTS DINING ROOM.

9.

COUNTERPOISE OF CONVEX REAR ECHELON WITH CONCAVE ENTRY ECHELON.

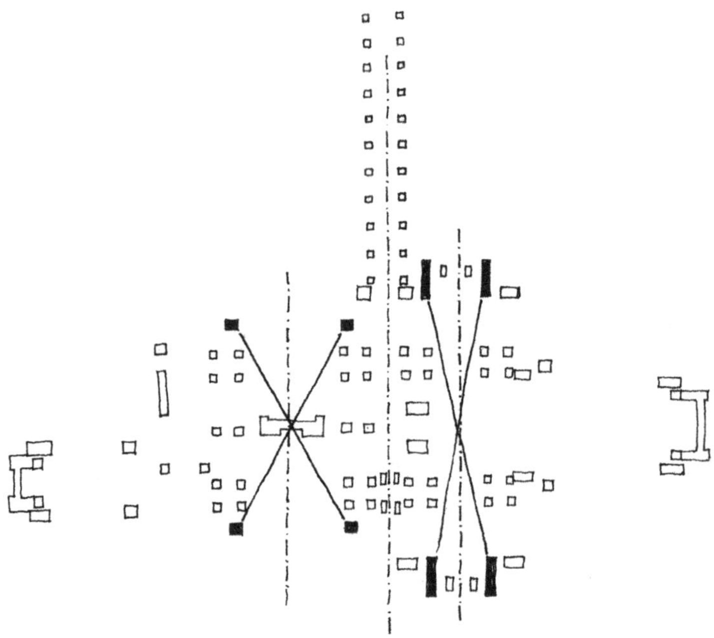

10.

DEVELOPMENT OF MINOR AXES AND COUNTERPOISE OF VOLUMES ABOUT LONGITUDINAL AXIS.

DINING ROOM AND LAVATORY WERE NOT LOCATED IN THIS POSITION, THE TRANSITION FROM THE PORTE COCHERE TO THE KITCHEN WOULD BE AN ABRUPT STEP; THE DIFFERENT NATURE OF WHICH GIVING IT A STRONGER WEIGHTING THAN THE SUBTLE TRANSITION PROVEDED BY THE ECHELON OF PORTE COCHERE, RECEPTION, AND LIBRARY.[8] THE SPECIFIC LOCATION OF THE SERVANTS' DINING ROOM AFFORDS A SHARP CONVEX ECHELON AS A COUNTERPOISE TO THE SOFT CONCAVE ECHELON OF THE ENTRY.[9] THE CORNER PIER S OF THE SERVANTS DINING ROOM CAN ALSO BE READ WITH THE FREE-STANDING PIER Q IN THE OFFICE AS A DISLOCATED VOLUME WHICH PROVIDES AN ADDITIONAL COUNTERPOISE WITH THE PORTE COCHERE ABOUT THE TRANSVERSE AXIS.

THE DEVELOPMENT OF A COUNTERPOISE ABOUT THE LONGITUDINAL PERGOLA AXIS IS EVEN MORE ELABORATE. MOST OF THE AXIAL SYMMETRIES IN THIS DIRECTION DEVELOP ABOUT MINOR AXES, WHICH ARE DEFINED BY A SYSTEM OF VOLUMETRIC PAVILIONS COUNTERPOISED ABOUT THE CENTRAL AXIS.

INITIALLY, THE AXIS OF THE KITCHEN AND RECEPTION HALL DEFINED BY THE RECESS IN THE LARGE FIREPLACE, AND THE DINING-ROOM-LIBRARY AXIS CAN BE SEEN AS THE MINOR AXES.[10] THE VOLUMETRIC DEFINITION OF THESE MINOR AXES CAN BE THOUGHT OF AS COUNTERPOISED ABOUT THE DOMINANT CENTRAL AXIS IF THE STUBBIER KITCHEN-RECEPTION BOLUME IS CONCEPTUALLY GIVEN A LESSER VALUE THAN THE ELONGATED DINING ROOM - LIBRARY VOLUME BECAUSE OF ITS GREATER LEVER ARM DISTANCE FROM THE CENTRAL AXIS. FURTHERMORE, THE READING OF THE KITCHEN-RECEPTION HALL VOLUME IS PERCEPTUALLY WEAKENED BY THE CENTRAL LOCATION OF THE FIREPLACE WHICH GIVES A PHYSICAL CUT TO ANY ACTUAL READING OF UNITY. THE VOLUMETRIC UNITY OF THE DINING ROOM - LIBRARY ON THE OTHER HAND IS EMPHASISED BY THE SIMILAR TREATMENT GIVEN TO THE ELONGATED PAIRED PIERS M,N AND C,P, IN EACH ROOM.

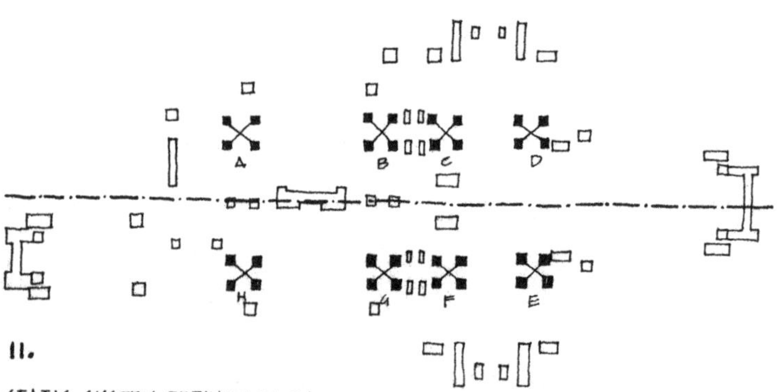

11.

STATIC SYSTEM DEFINITION BY RADIANT HEATING CORES.

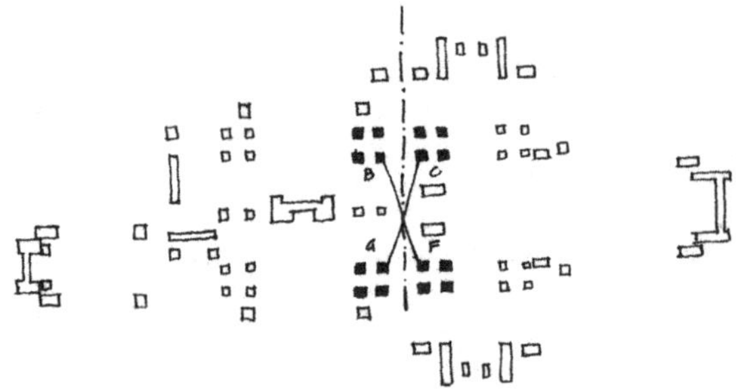

12.

DEFINITION TO DOMINANT CENTRAL AXIS WHEN READ AS BC AND FG

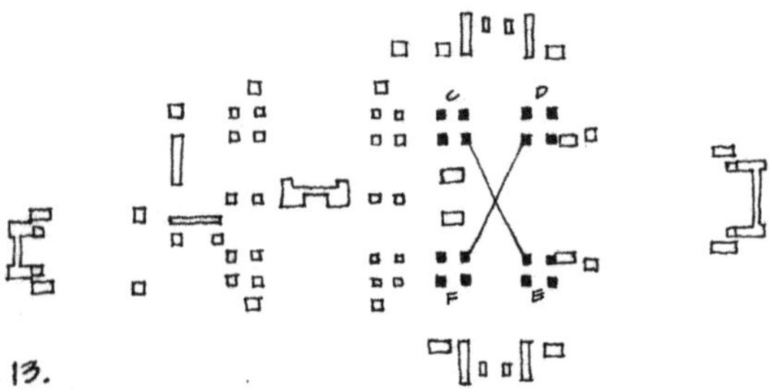

13.

WHEN PAVILIONS ARE READ AS CD AND EF THEY DEFINE THE LIVING ROOM.—

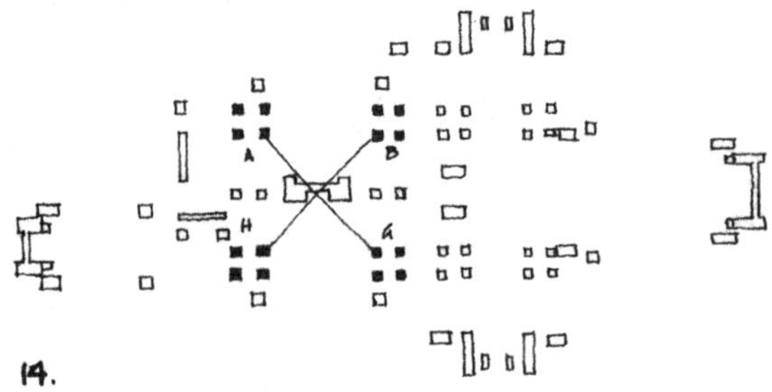

14.

—WHEN READ AS AB-AH THEY DEFINE THE RECEPTION HALL-KITCHEN VOLUME.

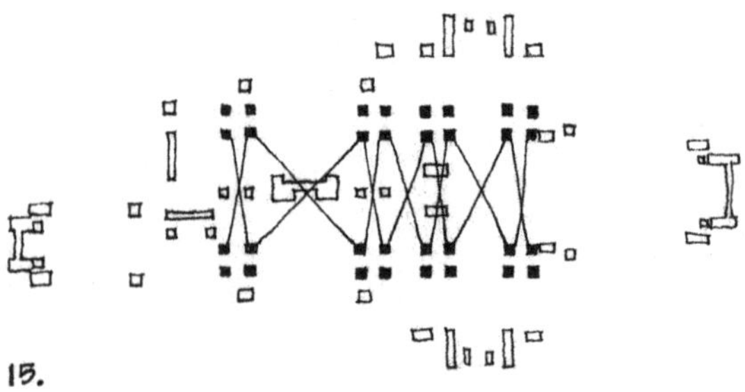

15.

A PULSATING SERIES OF STATIC VOLUMES ABOUT THE TRANSVERSE AXIS.

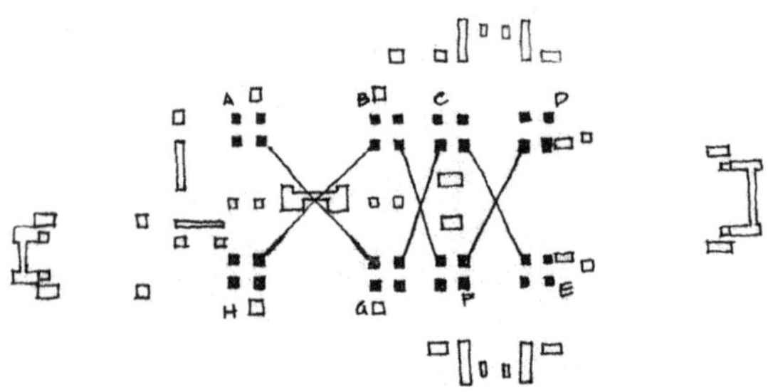

16.

CONTINUOUS READING OF HEATING CORES AS ABGH BCFG AND CDEF.

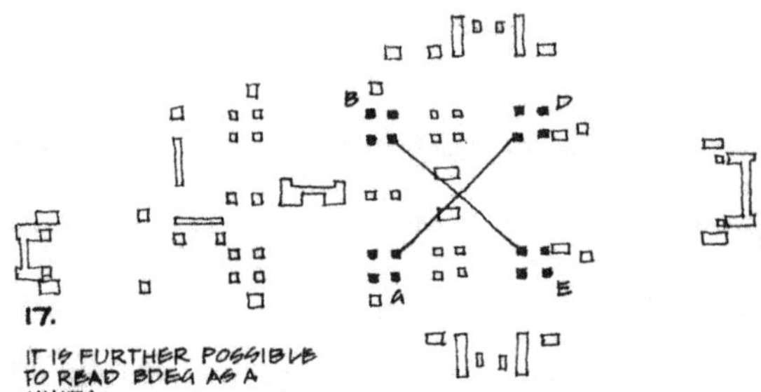

17.

IT IS FURTHER POSSIBLE TO READ BDEG AS A UNITY.

THESE ELEMENTS MUST ALSO BE CONSIDERED IN THEIR RELATIONSHIP TO THE VOLUMETRIC DIALECTIC: THE PRESENTATION OF BOTH A STATIC AND A CONTINUOUS READING. THE IN-ITIAL DEFINITION OF THE STATIC SYSTEM IS PROVIDED BY THE RHYTHM OF THE RADIANT HEATING UNITS AND THEIR SURROUNDING COLUMNS WHICH READ AS A SERIES OF PAVILIONS.[11] THESE PAVILIONS ARE SYMMETRICAL ABOUT THE TRANSVERSE AXIS; AND IT IS THEIR REL-ATIONSHIP ABOUT THE LONGITUDINAL AXIS THAT MUST BE EXAMINED. STARTING WITH THE PAIRED GROUPS BC AND GF THESE CAN BE SEEN AS PROVIDING A DEFINITION TO THE DOM-INANT CENTRAL AXES CREATING A KIND OF SHATTERED CORE WITH REFERENCE TO WRIGHT'S OTHER CRUCIFORM HOUSES.[12] THE LIVING ROOM FIREPLACE IN THIS CONTEXT IS SEEN AS BEING DEFLECTED AND TURNED OFF CENTRE BY THE THRUST OF THE PERGOLA AXIS. WHEN THESE PAVILIONS ARE READ AS CD AND EF, THEY DEFINE THE LIVING ROOM AND WHEN CONSIDERED AS A,B AND G,H THEY DEFINE THE KITCHEN-RECEPTION HALL VOLUME.[13,14] IN THIS CONTEXT ABOUT THE TRANSVERSE AXIS, THEY PROVIDE A SERIES OF STATIC VOLUMES THAT PULSATE IN A CONCERTINA LIKE FASHION EXPANDING AND CONTRACTING ALONG THIS AXIS.[15] THE TENSIONED AND FIXED RELATIONSHIP OF THE ROOM VOLUMES ABOUT THE MINOR AXES PLAYS AGAINST THE UNEVEN BEAT OF THE PAVILION CORES; THESE CAN BE READ AS A SECONDARY SERIES OF SLOTS OR AS A GROUPING OF PAVILIONS WHICH HAVE BEEN DROP-PED INTO THE UNDULATING RHYTHM. IT IS THE INTERLACING OF THE HEATING CORE UNITS WITH THE MAJOR ROOM VOLUMES THAT PROVIDES THE INITIAL DEFINITION FOR THE CON-TINUOUS VOLUMETRIC ORGANISATION. CORES A, B, G, H CAN BE READ AS A SQUARE WITH THE SUCCESSIVE GROUPINGS B,C,F,G, AND C,D,E,F BEING READ AS FURTHER ARTIC-ULATIONS IN A SERIES.[16] HOWEV R IT IS FURTHER POSSIBLE TO READ B,D,E,G AS A UNITY.[17] THIS INTERPRETATION IS GIVEN STRENGTH BY THE FLOW OF THE LIVING ROOM A-ROUND THE CENTRAL FIREPLACE. THUS THE AREA TO THE LEFT OF THE FIRE PLACE IS THEN SEEN IN AN AMBIGUOUS LOCATION WITH REFERENCE TO EITHER OF THE ABOVE READ-INGS OF THE HEATING CORE PAVILIONS. THIS AREA CAN BE THOUGHT OF EITHER AS

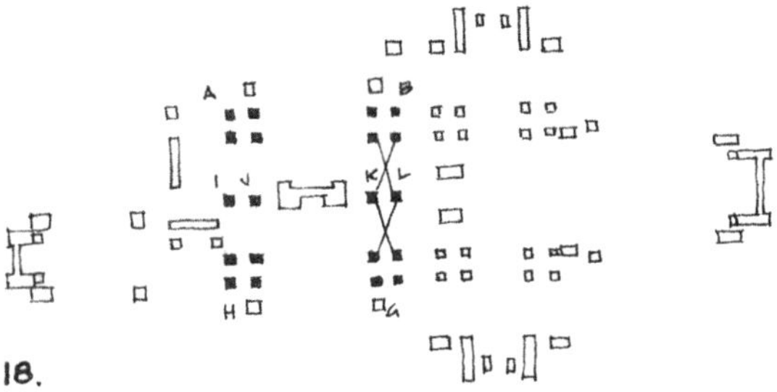

18.

A RECTILINEAR SLOT SEPARATING RECEPTION HALL AND LIVING ROOM.—

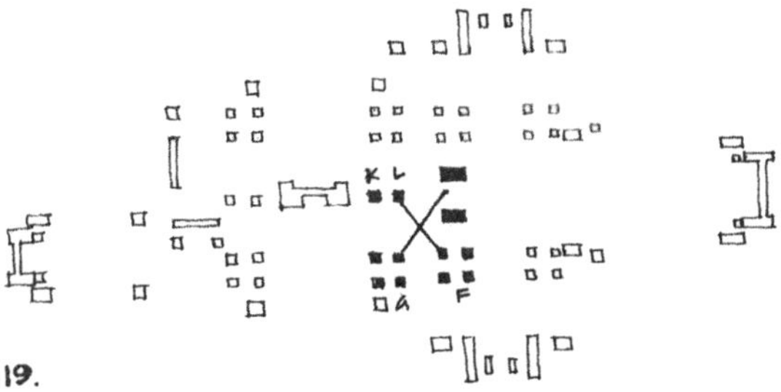

19.

—OR TO PROVIDE CONTINUITY FROM RECEPTION TO LIVING ROOM VOLUME.

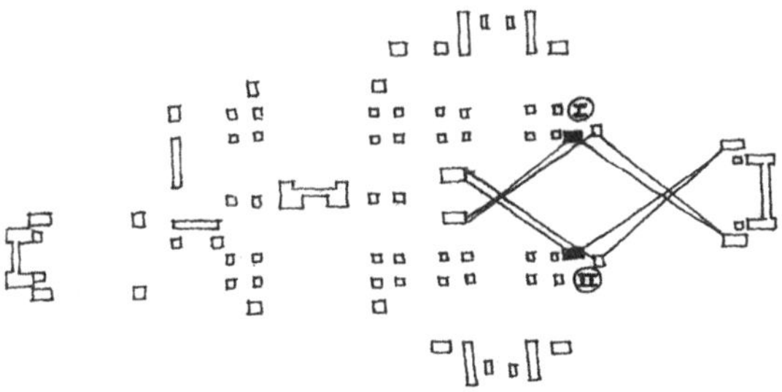

20.

CONTINUOUS READING OF LIVING ROOM AND PORCH.

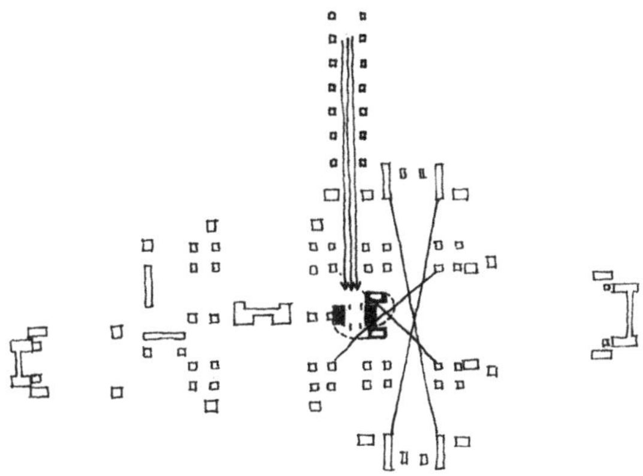

21.

AMBIGUITY OF LIVING ROOM LOCATION REFLECTED IN POSITION OF FIREPLACE.

PART OF THE PERGOLA AXIS OR AS A CONTINUOUS PART OF THE LIVING ROOM ON THE TRAN-SVERSE AXIS. THIS TYPE OF PLAIDING WHICH PROVIDES THE CONTINUOUS VOLUMETRIC DEFINITION OCCURS THROUGHOUT THE PLAN. THE HEATING CORES A,B, AND G,H MAY ALSO BE READ AS FORMING MINOR VOLUMES IN A SPECIFIC RELATIONSHIP TO THE PAIRED COLUMNS I,J,K,L, WHICH ARE LINKED TO THE RECEPTION HALL FIREPLACE. THESE GROUPINGS PROVIDE A DUAL READING FOR THE TRANSITION FROM THE RECEPTION HALL TO THE LIVING ROOM: EITHER AS A RECTILINEAR SLOT SEPARATING THE RECEPTION HALL FROM LIVING ROOM, OR AS A CUBIC VOLUME DEFINED BY THE LIVING ROOM FIREPLACE AND THE OPPOSITE HEATING CORE F, TO GIVE A CONTINUITY FROM RECEPTION TO LIVING ROOM VOLUME.[18, 19] THE END PIERS I, AND II OF THE LIVING ROOM ARE TREATED IN THE SAME MANNER AS THE END PIERS III AND IV OF THE PORCH YET THERE IS ANOTHER SET OF PIERS V AND VI DEFINING THE PORCH, WHICH ARE OF DIFFERENT SIZE. THIS GIVES A CONTINUOUS READING TO THE LIVING ROOM AND PORCH: THE PIERS I AND II BEING INTER-PRETED AS EITHER THE END OF THE LIVING ROOM OR THE BEGINNING OF THE PORCH.[20] THIS KIND OF CONTINUOUS VOLUMETRIC PLAY CAN BE SEEN IN THE DINING ROOM - LIVING ROOM - LIBRARY CROSS-AXIS WHICH CUTS THE LIVING ROOM-PORCH AXIS. BECAUSE OF THE EXPLICIT SIMILAR ARTICULATION OF THE EXTERNAL ENDS OF BOTH THE DINING ROOM AND LIBRARY, IT IS VERY DIFFICULAT NOT TO READ THIS VOLUME AS A CONTINUOUS SINGLE ENTITY, AND INDEED THE DIRECTION AND WEIGHT OF THE CENTRAL ROOF ENFORCES THIS READING. IN FACT, THE LIVING ROOM WHICH IS ON THE TRANSVERSE AXIS RECEIVES LITTLE PHYSICAL CONFIRMATION OF THIS POSITIONING IN THE SPECIFIC FORM OF THE BUILDING. THIS CONSTANT AMBIGUITY IN THE DIRECTIONAL CUTTING OF THE LIVING ROOM IS REFLECTED IN THE ORIENTATION OF THE FIREPLACE WHICH HAS BEEN PREVIOUSLY INTERPRETED AS HAVING BEEN DEFLECTED FROM ITS POSITION BY THE PERGOLA AXIS.[21] IF THE GENERIC CONDITION IS CONCEIVED OF WITH THE FIREPLACE CORE IN A

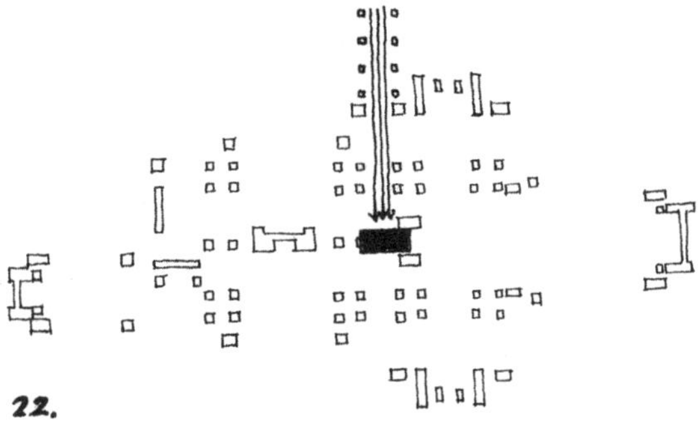

22.

FIREPLACE CONSIDERED
AS A CENTRAL CORE
SHATTERED BY PERGOLA VECTOR.

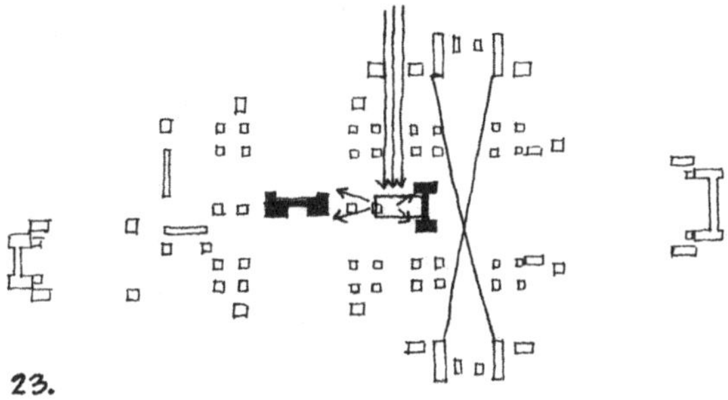

23.

LIVING ROOM HALF OF CORE
TURNED INTO LONGITUDINAL POSITION
BECAUSE OF LIVING ROOM ROTATION.

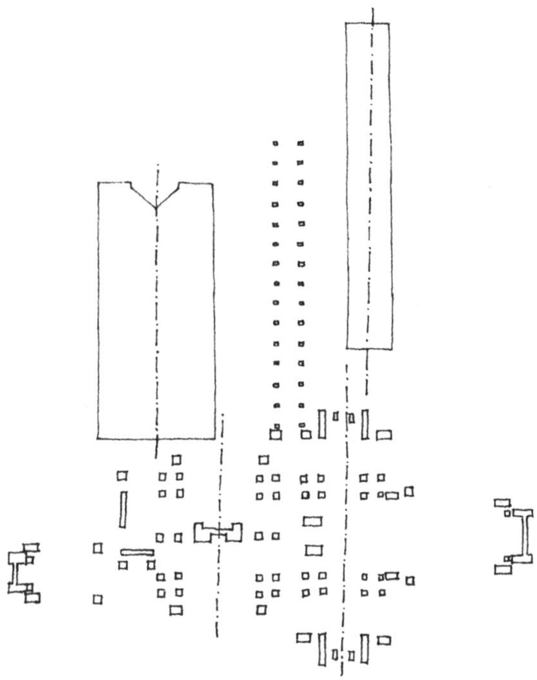

24.

STUTTERING OF INTERNAL
AND EXTERNAL AXIS TO
PREVENT ANY CONFUSION
WITH MAJOR AXIAL REFERENCES.

CENTRAL LOCATION ON THE TRANSVERSE AXIS, THEN THIS CORE IS READ AS HAVING BEEN SHATTERED INTO PARTS BY THE PERGOLA VECTOR; THE RECEPTION HALL FIREPLACE IS THEN SEEN AS THE OTHER DISLOCATED PART OF THE SHATTERED CORE.[22] THE LIVING ROOM HALF OF THE CORE IS THEN TURNED INTO ITS LOGITUDINAL POSITION BY THE ALTERNATING ROTATION OF THE LIVING ROOM VOLUME FROM ONE AXIS TO THE OTHER.[23] THE PLAISING AND DIRECTIONAL CUTTING CAN BE SEEN IN EACH INDIVIDUAL VOLUME WHERE A GRIDDED OVERLAY COULD BE DEVELOPED FROM THE MULTIPLICITY OF ARTICULATIONS.

IT IS INTERESTING TO NOTE THAT WRIGHT CONTINUES HIS STUTTERING OF MINOR AXES FROM INSIDE TO OUT, THEREBY DENYING THE CONCEPTUAL CONTINUITY OF INTERIOR AND EXTERIOR; AN INTERPRETATION WHICH HAS BEEN OFTEN GIVEN TO HIS WORK. IF THIS UNITY HAD BEEN AN OVERRIDING CONDITION THEN IT WOULD SEEM THAT AN ARCHITECT WITH SUCH A DEPENDENCE ON AN AXIAL FORMALITY WOULD HAVE CONTINUED THE MINOR AXES EXTERNALLY. HOWEVER, THE FORMAL INTERNAL CONDITION IS GIVEN PREDOMINANCE AFTER ITS INITIAL DISTORTION BY THE ENTRY AXES. FOR TO CONTINUE THE MINOR AXES EXTERNALLY WOULD, IN FACT, STRENGTHEN THEM AND CAUSE A CONFUSION WITH RESPECT TO THE MAJOR TRANSVERSE AND LONGITUDINAL AXES. THIS CAN BE SEEN IN THE STUTTERING OF BOTH THE DINING ROOM-LIBRARY AXIS WHEN IT JOINS THE LONG GARDEN AXIS, AND IN THE FLOWER GARDEN AXIS WHICH CAN BE SEEN AS A DISLOCATION OF THE KITCHEN-RECEPTION AXIS.[24]

AVERY COONLEY HOUSE

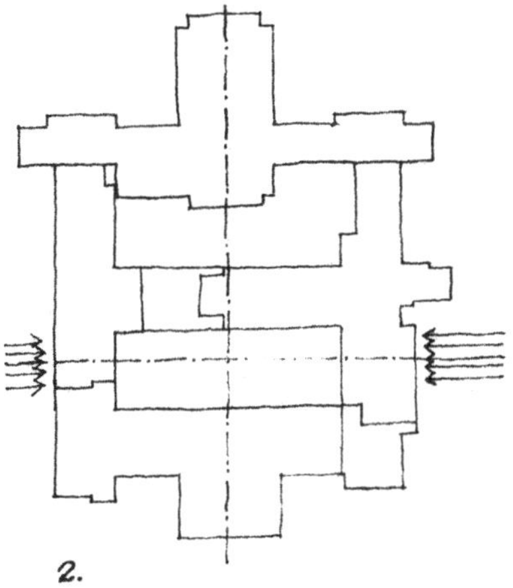

2.

EVOLUTION OF A SPECIFIC LINEAR FORM FROM A GENERIC CENTROIDAL FORM

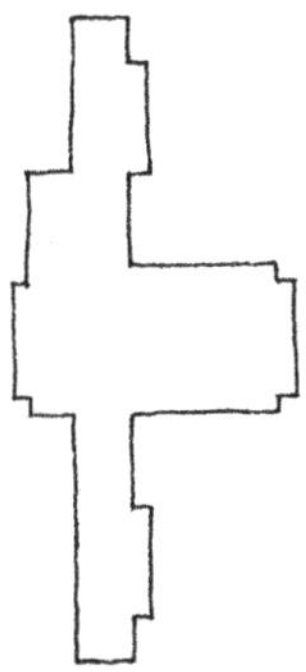

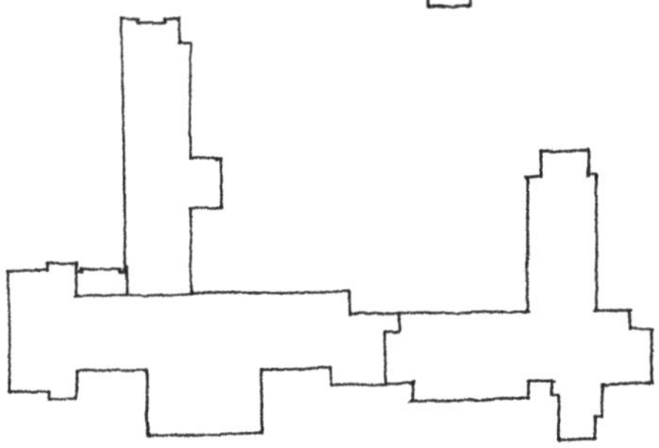

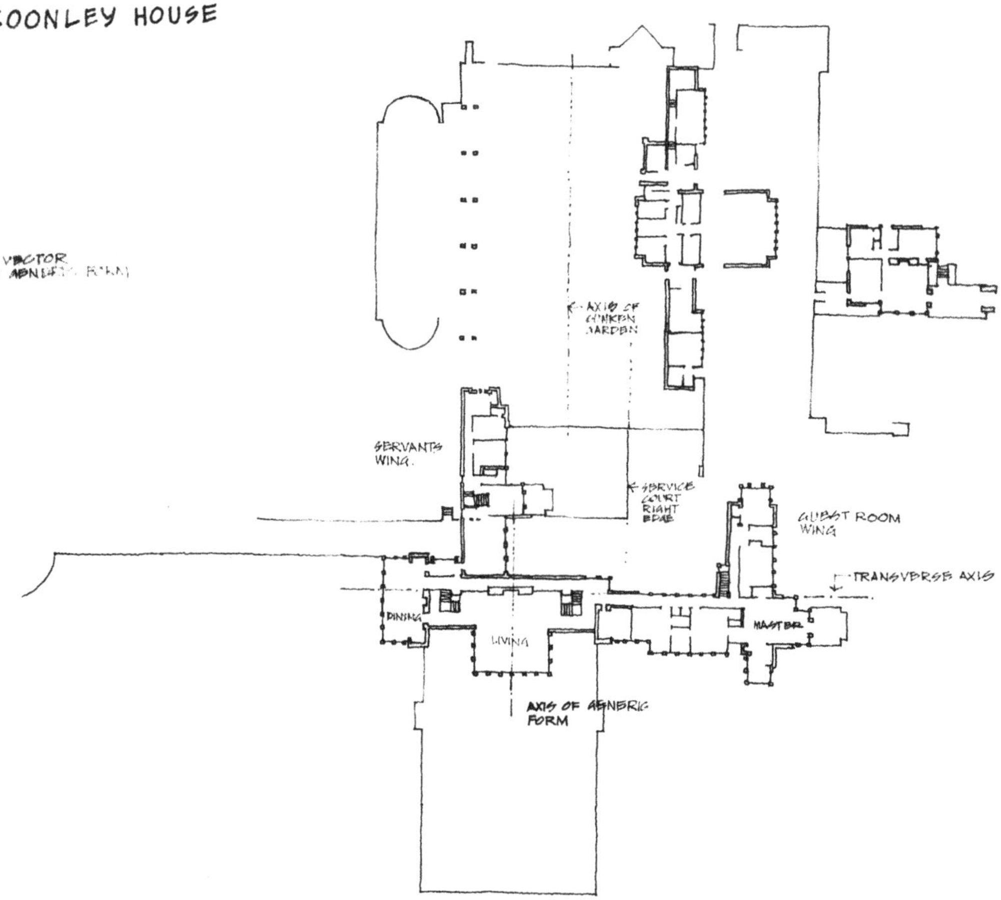

1.

POSITION OF UNREST CAUSED BY DISTORTION FROM GENERIC STATE WEAKENS LONGITUDINAL VECTORS AND STRENGTHENS TRANSVERSE AXIS.

THE AVERY COONLEY HOUSE IS A FREER DEVELOPMENT OF WRIGHT'S AXIAL LINEAR PLANNING IN THE SENSE THAT IT IS LESS RESTRICTED BY ORGANISATIONS. IT IS ALMOST A NAIVE VERSION OF THE MARTIN HOUSE IN ITS APPLICATION AND ORDERING OF VOLUMETRIC UNITS; YET IN SOME WAYS IT IS A MORE MATURE VERSION IN THAT IT MAKES A MORE SUBTLE USE OF THE AXIAL ARRANGEMENT, AND THE INTERWEAVING OF A CONTINUOUS AND A STATIC VOLUMETRIC ORDER. INITIALLY, IT WOULD SEEM THAT THE AXIS OF SYMMETRY IS THE CENTRAL LONGITUDINAL AXIS OF THE LIVING ROOM BLOCK. HOWEVER, THIS AXIS IS DISLOCATED BY THE PULL OF THE BEDROOM PAVILIONS LOCATING IT FINALLY IN A VERY WEAK, AND SHIFTING POSITION. THIS DOMINANT AXIS, OR PLANE OF REFERENCE FLUCTUATES BECAUSE THERE IS NO PERCEPTUAL HOLD FOR IT, UNLESS THE RIGHT HAND BOUNDARY OF THE SERVICE COURT OR THE CENTRAL AXIS OF THE SUNKEN GARDEN ARE CONSIDERED TO BE EXTERNAL ACKNOWLEGEMENTS OF A DISLOCATION FROM THE GENERIC STATE. THIS POSITION OF UNREST HAS THE EFFECT OF ALMOST NEGATING THE LONGITUDINAL AXIS AT THE SAME TIME STREGTHENING THE TRANSVERSE VECTOR.[1] IT ALSO REPRESENTS THE EVOLUTION OF A SPECIFIC LINEAR FORM FROM A GENERIC CENTROIDAL FORM, WHICH IS CONCEPUALLY SIMILAR TO THE RESOLUTION OF THE MARTIN HOUSE.[2] AS IN THE CASE OF THE MARTIN HOUSE, WRIGHT IS NOT CONCERNED WITH THE ORDERING OF A MOVEMENT SYSTEM; INDEED THE CIRCULATION IS OFTEN TWISTED AND CONVOLUTED IN A MOST DISTURBING FASHION. IT IS IN THE ARTICULATION OF THE VOLUMETRIC ORGANISATION THAT WRIGHT'S SPECIFIC GRAMMAR CAN BEST BE SEEN UNDER A SYSTEMIC CONTROL. HERE AGAIN THE SYSTEM IS DEVELOPED WITH AN INTERLACING OF STATIC AND CONTINUOUS VOLUMES, ALTHOUGH THESE ARE NOT ELABORATED IN THE SAME DEGREE AS THE MARTIN HOUSE PLAIDING. THE COONLEY HOUSE CAN BE SEEN AS A SERIES OF PAVILIONS ARRANGED BOTH VERTICALLY AND HORIZONTALLY WITH REFERENCE TO A HORIZONTAL ABSOLUTE. THIS ABSOLUTE IS

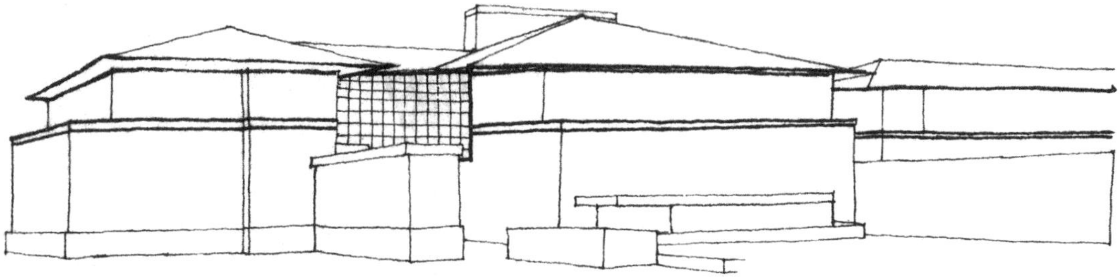

3.

HORIZONTAL ABSOLUTE DEFINED BY ROOF LEVEL AND FIRST FLOOR STRING COURSE

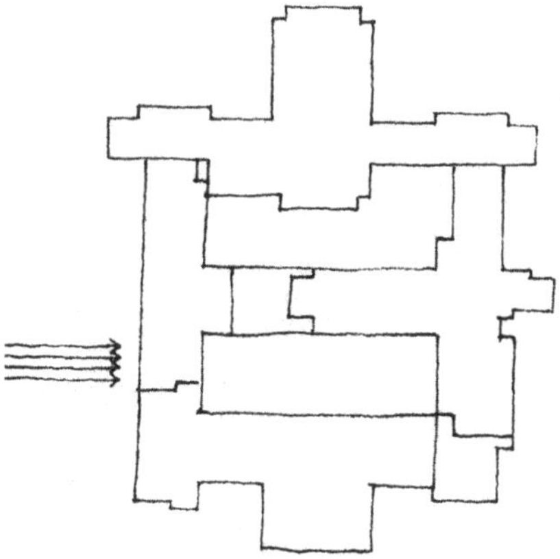

4.

IF MOVEMENT IS FROM THE LEFT THE GUEST ROOM WING AND SERVANTS WING ARE DISLOCATED ALONG THE DIRECTION OF THIS VECTOR

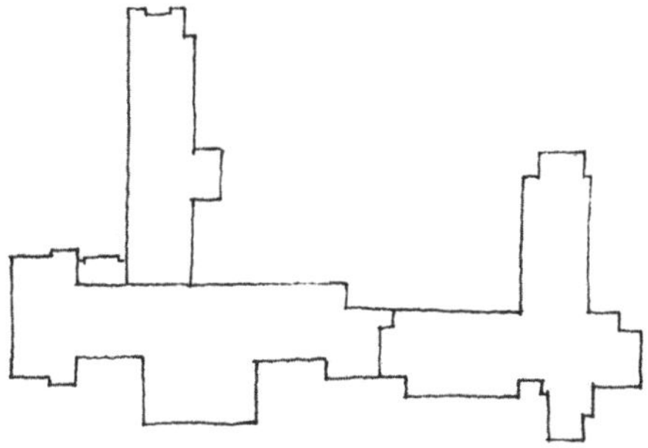

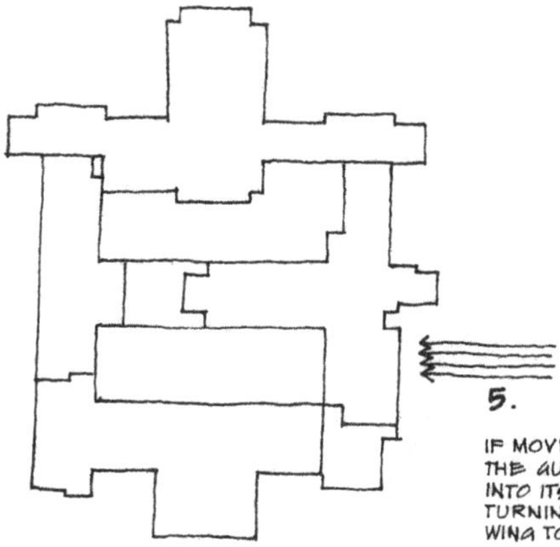

5.

IF MOVEMENT IS FROM THE RIGHT THE GUEST ROOM IS DEFLECTED INTO ITS SPECIFIC LOCATION – THE TURNING PULLING THE SERVANTS WING TO ITS SPECIFIC LOCATION.

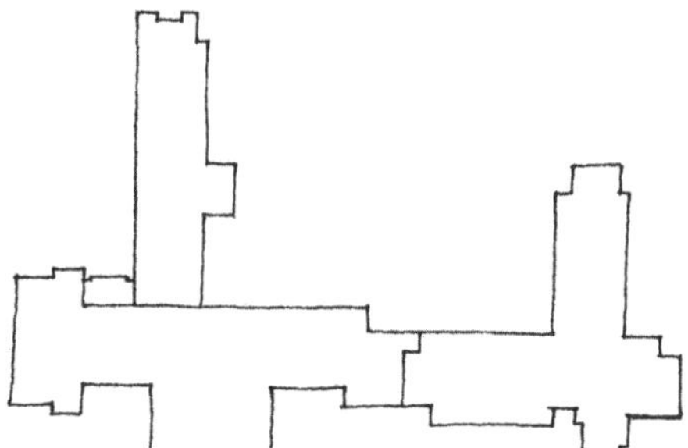

EXPRESSED BY TWO HORIZONTAL LEVELS: THE LOW PITCHED HORIZONTAL ROOF LEVEL AND THE SPRING COURSES DEFINING THE FIRST FLOOR LEVEL.[3] THE FIRST HORIZONTAL PLANE CAN BE READ AS DETACHED FROM THE PAVILION VOLUMES TREATED AS 'MASS' OR 'SOLID-CUT-AWAY'. THE SECOND HORIZONTAL IS BROKEN IN SEVERAL PLACES BY HORIZONTAL PROJECTIONS, WHICH ARE TREATED IN A DIFFERENT MANNER FROM THE VERTICAL PAVILIONS. THEY ARE COVERED WITH A MOSAIC TILE GIVING THEM A TRANSPARENT READING WITH RESPECT TO THE SOLID VERTICAL BLOCKS. THE HORIZONTALS WHICH ARE ALWAYS SUPPORTED ON THE VERTICALS NEVER TOUCHING THE GROUND, CHARACTERISTICALLY BREAK THE HORIZONTAL STRING COURSE.

INITIALLY, THE COONLEY HOUSE REPRESENTS A LINEAR INTERNAL REQUIREMENT EVOLVED FROM A CENTROIDAL GENERIC STATE, THAT HAS BEEN PLACED IN AN ORTHOGONAL RELATIONSHIP WITH TWO STREETS. THE GENERIC STATE IS SHATTERED BY THE EXTERNAL VECTOR, THE ENTRY DRIVE. THIS DRIVE MAY BE CONSIDERED AS BEING DIRECTIONAL IN RELATION TO EITHER STREET; EACH DIRECTION PROVIDING A DIFFERENT INTERPRETATION OF THE DISTORTION OF THE GENERIC STATE. IF MOVEMENT IS FROM THE LEFT, THE GUEST ROOM AND SERVANTS WINGS CAN BE SEEN AS BEING DISLOCATED ALONG THE DIRECTION OF THIS VECTOR.[4] CONVERSELY, IF MOVEMENT IS FROM THE RIGHT, THE GUEST ROOM WING IS SEEN AS DEFLECTED INTO ITS POSITION; THIS TURNING PULLING THE SERVANTS WING TO ITS SPECIFIC LOCATION.[5] IN EITHER CASE AN EXTERNAL TRANSVERSE AXIS IS CREATED PARALLEL TO THE RESULTANT LINEAR BUILDING. CONSIDERED FROM THE RIGHT, THIS DRIVE IS CUT TWICE BY TWO SIDES OF THE ORIGINAL FORM BLUNTING ITS DIRECTIONAL QUALITY. HOWEVER, IT IS IN THE TRANSITION FROM THE DRIVE TO THE BUILDI THAT CERTAIN DIFFICULTIES ARISE. INITIALLY THERE IS A NEED TO ACKNOWLEDGE TH THRUST OF THE EXTERNAL AXIS. THIS VECTOR DISLOCATES THE ENTRY FROM THE CENTF

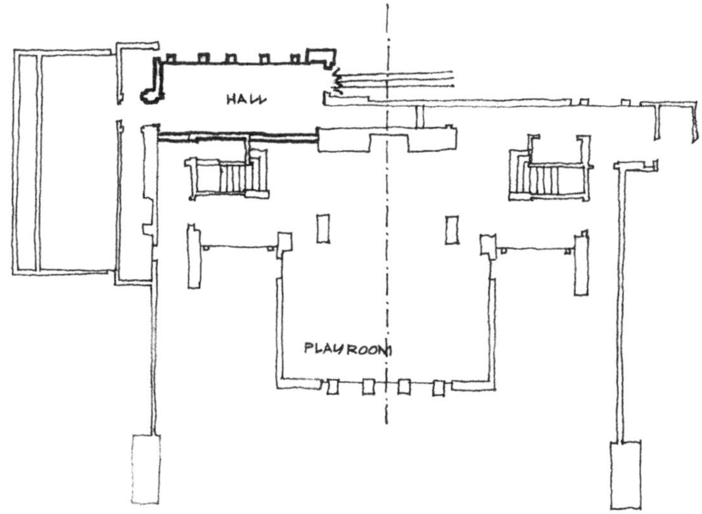

6.

ENTRY VECTOR IS ACKNOWLEDGED BY DISLOCATION OF ENTRY HALL FROM CENTRAL LOCATION.

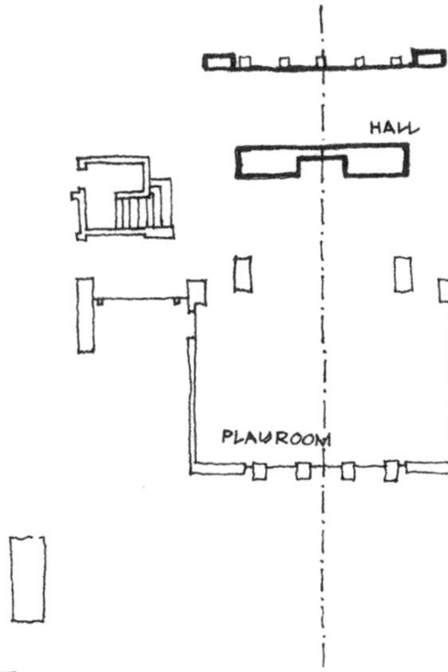

7.

GENERIC REFERENCE SEEN IN THE STRONG AXIAL SYMMETRY OF THIS BLOCK.

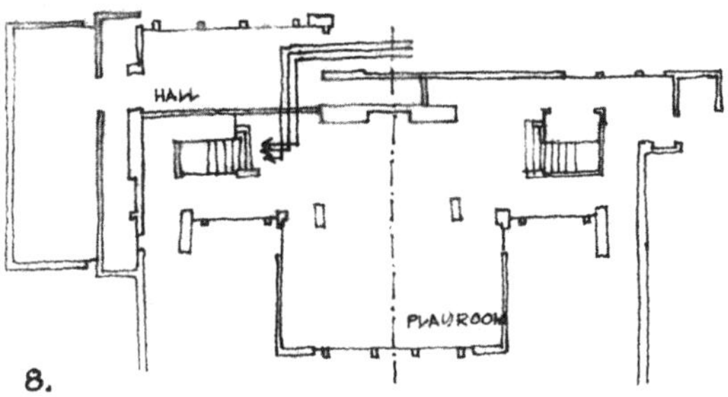

8.

TURNING OF MOVEMENT IMMEDIATELY REVERSED.

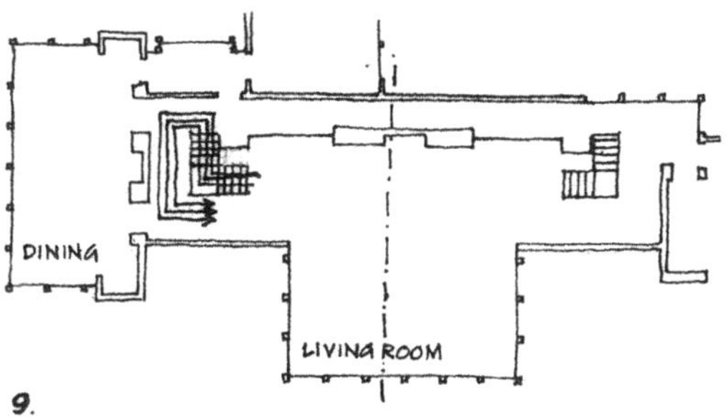

9.

MOVEMENT AGAIN CHANGES DIRECTION AT THE TOP OF THE STAIRS WITHOUT ANY ACKNOWLEDGEMENT IN THE VOLUMETRIC SYSTEM

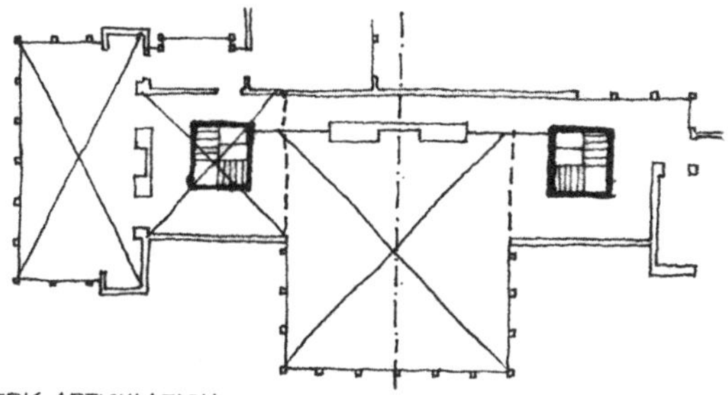

10.

STAIR VOLUME SEEN AS A VOLUMETRIC ARTICULATION PROVIDING VERTICAL AND HORIZONTAL LINKS

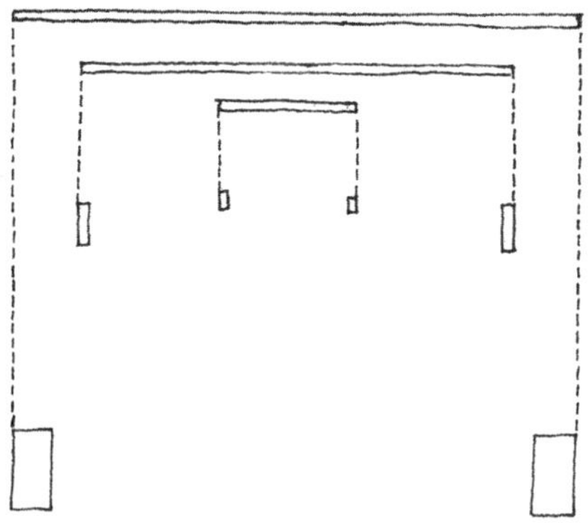

11.

EACH BOX IS DEFINED BY A PLANE IN ITS VERTICAL COORDINATE AND BY PAIRED DEEP PIERS IN ITS ORTHOGONAL COORDINATE

AXIS OF THE GENERIC STATE TO ITS PRESENT POSITION.[6] IT CAN BE ASSUMED THAT THE ENTRY INTO THE GENERIC CONDITION WAS ON THIS LONGITUDINAL AXIS, BECAUSE OF THE STRONG AXIAL SYMMETRY OF THE PAVILION, AND ITS TWO STAIR TOWERS.[7]

THE ENTRY MOVEMENT IS STUTTERED OFF BOTH THE WALK AND THE DRIVE BY A SYSTEM OF SEMI-ECHELON VOLUMES CONTINUING INTO THE BUILDING, WITHOUT BEING TURNED. THIS DEFLECTING OF THE ENTRY VECTOR INTO THE BUILDING CAUSES THE DISLOCATION OF THE ENTRY HALL FROM THE CENTRAL LONGITUDINAL AXIS. HOWEVER, THE TURN REQUIRED TO BEGIN THE VERTICAL MOVEMENT IS AGONISINGLY RESOLVED AS THE DIRECTION OF THIS TURN IS IMMEDIATELY REVERSED TO MOVE UP THE STAIRS. FURTHERMORE THERE IS NO ACKNOWLEDGEMENT IN THE VOLUMETRIC ORDER OF EITHER TURN. AT THE TOP OF THE STAIRETHE MOVEMENT AGAIN CHANGES DIRECTION, WITH AGAIN NO ACKNOWLEDGEMENT OF THIS CHANGE, IN THE VOLUMETRIC ORDER.[9] MOREOVER THERE IS NO ELEMENT PROVIDED, TO TURN THE MOVEMENT FROM THE TOP OF THE STAIRS THROUGH TWO ADDITIONAL 90 DEGREE TURNS INTO THE MAIN LIVING ROOM VOLUME. THIS TURNING CAN ONLY BE ACCOMPLISHED, IN FORMAL TERMS, IF THE STAIR AND GALLERIES ARE CONSIDERED AS PART OF THE VOLUMETRIC ORDER, AND NOT PART OF ANY MOVEMENT SYSTEM. IN THIS INTERPRETATION, THE STAIR VOLUME CAN BE CONCEIVED OF AS AN ARTICULATED LINK BETWEEN TWO SETS OF PAVILIONS: THE DINING ROOM AND LIVING ROOM IN THE HORIZONTAL CO-ORDINATE, AND THE ENTRY HALL AND LIVINGROOM - DINING ROOM IN THE VERTICAL CO-ORDINATE.[10] IN ADDITION, IN ITS HORIZONTAL ASPECT THE STAIR VOLUME PROVIDES A LINK ON THE GROUND FLOOR BETWEEN THE POOL TERRACE AND THE PLAYROOM. THESE PAVILIONS THEN READ AS A SERIES OF BOXES THAT SLOT ONE WITHIN THE OTHER WITH NO SECONDARY SYSTEM OF MOVEMENT REQUIRED TO LINK THEM. EACH BOX IS DEFINED BY A PLANE IN ITS FRONTAL VERTICAL COORDINATE AND BY PAIRED DEEP PIERS IN ITS

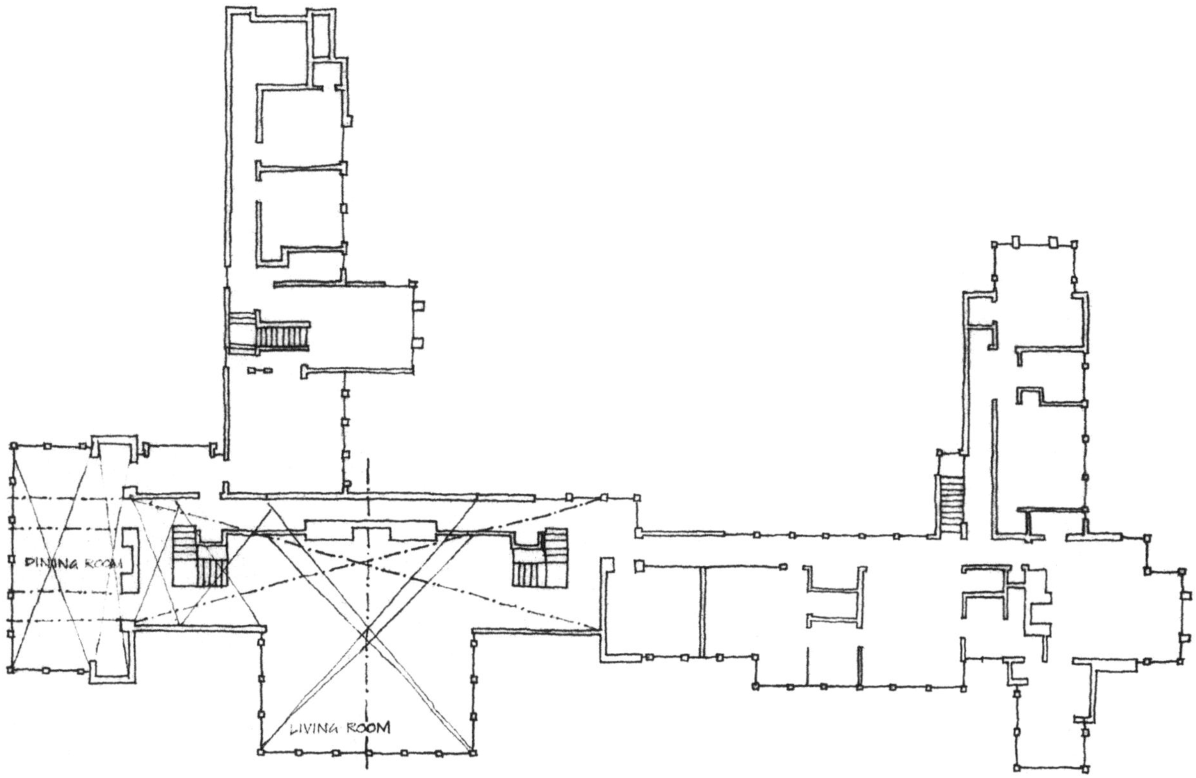

12. PRESENTATION OF BOTH CONTINUOUS AND STATIC ORDER

ORTHOGONAL COORDINATE.[11] THIS GIVES A TENSIONING TO THESE INTERLOCKING PARTS ; THE VOLUMES NOW SEEN AS HAVING BEEN CREATED BY PULLING THE PIERS AWAY FROM THE PLANE AS IS THEY WERE WEIGHTS. IN ITS HORIZONTAL READING ON THE FIRST FLOOR, THE STAIRWELLS ONLY RISE A FEW FEET ABOVE THE FLOOR LEVEL SO THAT THE GALLERIES ON EITHER SIDE, READ TOGETHER AS A SINGLE VOLUME CONTINUING THROUGH THE LIVING ROOM, AND ARTICULATED ONLY BY A CHANGE IN THE SPECIFIC FORM OF THE ROOF.[12] THE GALLERIES ON BOTH SIDES OF THE WEST STAIRWELL MOVE INTO THE DINING ROOM, PLAIDING THIS VOLUME AND TYING IT TO THE CONTINUOUS ORDER. HOWEVER THESE VOLUMES CANNOT BE READ AS TOTALLY CONTINUOUS, SINCE THE FIREPLACE OF THE DINING ROOM PROVIDES A PERCEPTUAL STOP TO THE TRANSVERSE VECTOR. THE DINING ROOM IS FURTHER ARTICULATED FROM THE STAIR PAVILION BY A SOLID SLOT, WHICH FURTHER BLUNTS THE TRANSVERS AXIS AND ALLOWS A SIMILAR READING TO ACCRUE TO THE DINING ROOM AS TO THE GROUND FLOOR VOLUMETRIC ORGANISATION; AGAIN THE GLAZED PORTION OF THE DINING ROOM READING AS HAVING BEEN PULLED FROM THE ENCLOSING SLOT. HERE THEN, CAN BE SEEN THE INITIAL DEVELOPMENT OF BOTH A CONTINUOUS AND A STATIC VOLUMETRIC ORGANIZATION, EACH PART OF THIS ORDER READING A AS PART OF EITHER SYSTEM.

THE SYMMETRICAL ORGANISATION OF THIS LIVING COMPLEX PROVIDES THE GENERIC READING FROM WHICH THE REMAINING DISTORTIONS CAN BE INTERPRETED. IT MUST BE NOTED THAT IN THE DESIRE TO KEEP THIS GENERIC REFERENCE AS A PERCEPTUAL BASIS OF THE SPECIFIC FORM, THERE IS A FUNCTIONAL ANACHRONISM IN THE SCHEME. THE EAST STAIRWAY, ALTHOUGH WEIGHTED EQUALLY IN A FORMAL SENSE WITH THE WEST STAIR, DOES NOT HAVE THE SAME FUNCTIONAL WEIGHT AS THAT STAIR. IT SEEMS UNLIKELY THAT ANY USE WOULD BE MADE OF THIS STAIR FROM THE ENTRY EXCEPT TO MOVE TO THE BEDROOM WING. IT ALSO FUNCTIONS AS A MINOR SECONDARY STAIR BY CONNECTING THE

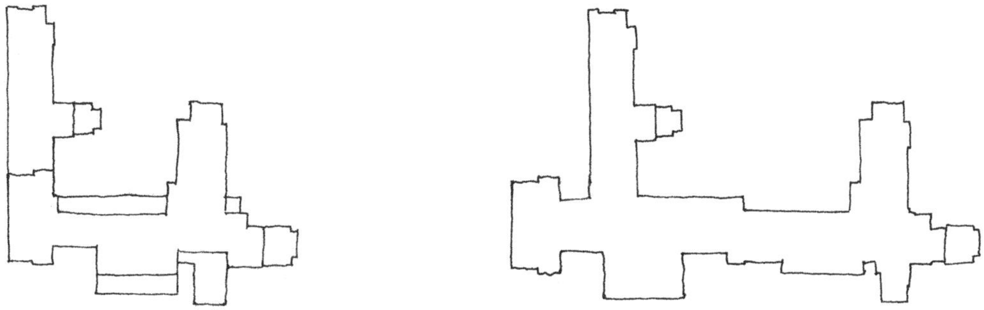

13. IF MOVEMENT IS FROM LEFT THEN DISTORTIONS OCCUR FROM THE THRUST OF THIS VECTOR

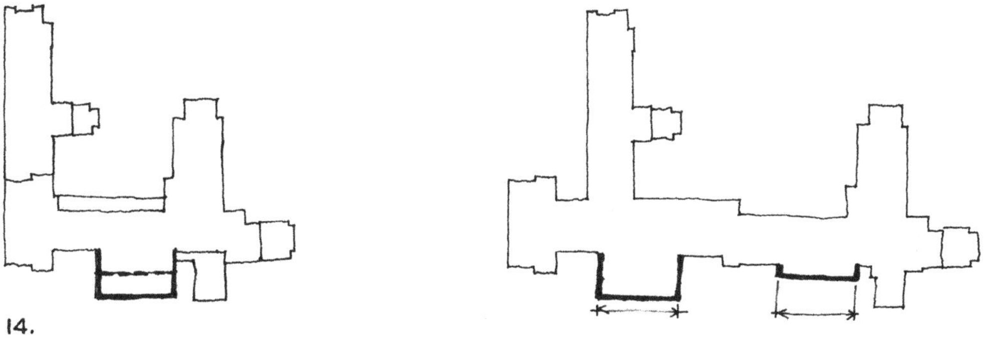

14.

LOCATION OF BEDROOM PROJECTION UNDER LIVING ROOM IN GENERIC STATE

POOL TERRACE AND PLAY ROOM WITH THE BEDROOM WING. SO THE SYMMETRY OF THE GENERIC CONDITION MUST BE OF SOME IMPORTANCE TO WRIGHT. INDEED, THE RETENTION OF THE SYMMETRY MUST BE CONSIDERED AS PROVIDING THE PERCEPTUAL LINK TO THE GENERIC REFERENCE. HOWEVER, THE CENTRAL LONGITUDINAL AXIS OF THIS CONDITION CANNOT BE SEEN AS THE FULCRUM FOR A COUNTERPOISE OF ALL NON-SYMMETRICAL ELEMENTS. IN FACT, THERE IS NO BALANCE, NO POINT OF PERCEPTUAL REST, AND THE ENTIRE COMPOSITION SEEMS TO BE IN A FLUCTUATING, EVER-SHIFTING STATE OF NON-PURPOSEFUL AMBIGUITY. HOWEVER, ALL OF THE DISTORTIONS MUST FIRST BE ANALYSED TO APPRECIATE THEIR INEXACT AND FRAGMENTED RELATIONSHIP TO THE WHOLE, WHICH MUST BE CONSIDERED AS AN ANTITHESIS TO THE TAUT, COMPOSITIONAL UNITY OF THE MARTIN HOUSE.

INITIALLY THE DIAGRAM OF THE GENERIC STATE MUST BE CONSIDERED TO UNDERSTAND THESE DISTORTIONS. THE VALIDITY OF THIS CONDITION CAN BE SEEN BY INCLUDING IN THE SPECIFIC FORM CERTAIN REFERENCES TO THE GENERIC STATE. THE BEDROOM WING CAN BE THOUGHT OF AS EITHER BEING PULLED FROM THE MAIN BLOCK ALONG THE TRANSVERSE AXIS, OR BEING DEFLECTED FROM THE GENERIC STATE BY THE ENTRY VECTOR; EITHER READING DEPENDING UPON THE DIRECTION GIVEN TO THE EXTERNAL AXIS.[13] THE MASTER BEDROOM AND THE SUITE OF GUEST ROOMS CAN BE READ AS AN EQUIVALENT CONDITION TO THE DINING ROOM AND SERVANTS WING. THIS AXIAL PULL ALSO DISLOCATES THE SERVANTS WING FROM ITS GENERIC POSITION AND IT CAN BE SEEN AS HAVING BEEN SLICED BY THE ENTRY VECTOR. BUT IF THIS READING IS TO BE SUSTAINED THEN THE SPECIFIC CONFIGURATION OF THE BEDROOM WING MUST BE QUESTIONED. THE FIREPLACE IN THE MASTER BEDROOM, AND THE VOLUME PULLED FROM IT CAN BE CONSIDERED AS AN OBVIOUS COUNTERPOISE TO THE DINING ROOM. EQUALLY, THE TRANSVERSE SUITE OF BEDROOMS CAN BE READ AS HAVING BEEN LOCATED UNDER THE LIVING ROOM IN THE GENERIC

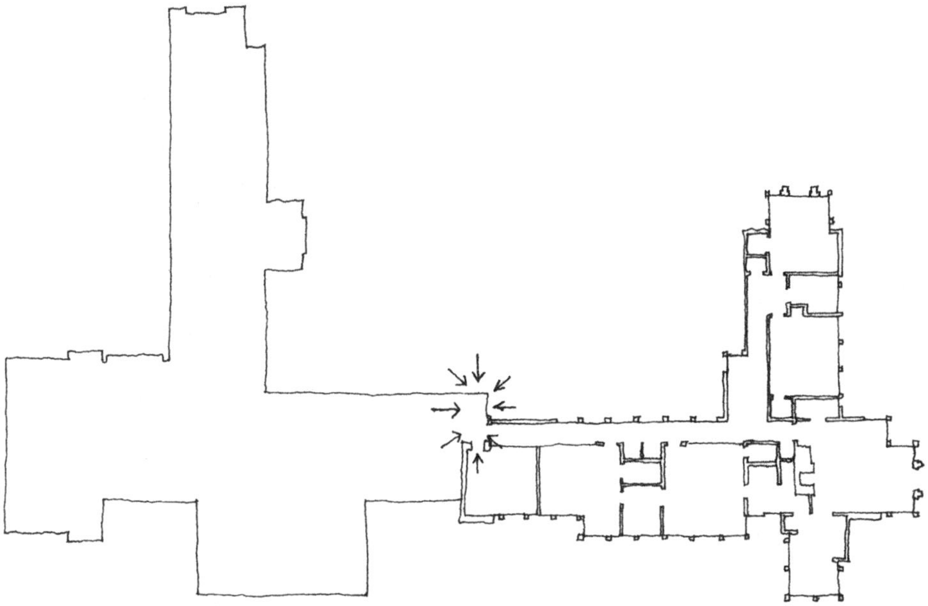

15. AGONIZING JUNCTION AT DISLOCATION OF BEDROOM WING

16. DISLOCATION OF BEDROOM WING BY PRESSURE FROM STABLES

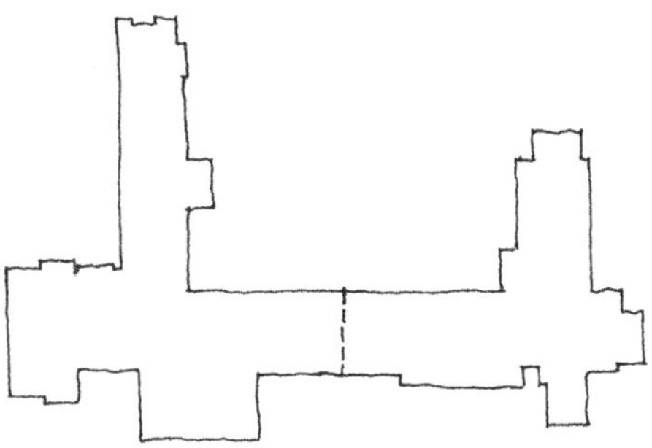

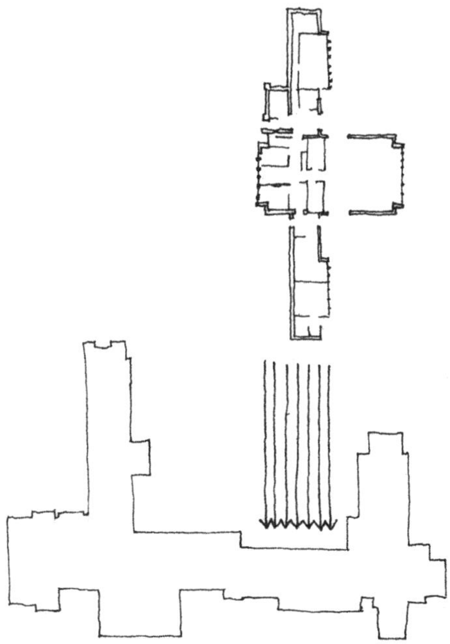

state. This reading is emphasized by the fact that the projection of these two rooms is the same length as the length of the articulated pavilion of the living room.[14] The fragmentation and weakening of the whole complex comes in the interpretation of the small pavilion that is pulled longitudinally from the master bedroom, and in the treatment of the end of the last guest room.[15] Initially this wing reads as part of the generic formaand is obviously intended to be part of an elaborate counterpoise, but the reference to any central axis in the specific state is obscure. It is this missing reference that causes the ambiguous reading, and the whole bedroom wing is thereby seen as unfixed. This wing can be seen as still sliding and able to be pushed back, no indication having been given as to the cause of its arrested movement at this particular point. An immediate reference would be to the junction of the main living room volume and the bedroom block, which acts as a pivot for the deflection from the generic state.[15] The desire to articulate both the volumetric and movement order at this point has created an agonising junction with no possible reading of a counterpoise axis. Especially critical is the dislocation of this wing, which may be partially attributed to the pressure caused by the twisting of the garage-stables block from its generic location as the closing side to the central court;[16] the dislocation of this block coming from the thrust of the entry vector much as the dislocation at Saynatsalo and the Tallinn Museum. It is interesting to note that the dislocation in the latter two schemes has not obscured the centroidal form, while at the Coonley house the centroidal reference is changed to a linear reading.

It can be said of Wright's systemic development, that he acknowledges syntax,

BUT ONLY WHEN IT IS IN AID OF HIS ELABORATE GRAMMAR. IN THE MARTIN HOUSE BOTH SYNTAX AND GRAMMAR CAN BE RESOLVED BECAUSE OF THE STRONG SYSTEMIC CONTROL, WHEREAS IN THE COONLEY HOUSE A VERY STRONG INITIAL ORDERING SEEMS TO BE VITIATED BY THE CONSTANTLY CHANGING GRAMMAR.

In analysing the conceptual evolution of any centriodal courtyard scheme it is necessary to acknowledge the three different bases for their development. The first category is one where the generic form is evolved as a direct response to the internal programmatic requirements; this would be a functional derivation. This order might suggest a central major volume with a series of related minor volumes; the major volume being either positive -enclosed such as a hall or auditorium, or negative-open, such as a courtyard. Both of these would assume that the centroidal organization was a primary requirement of the internal function. The Asilo Infantile would be an example of this first type.

The second category is one where the courtyard is evolved from both functional and formal demands. The functional requirement again producing an internal order, and the formal requirement resulting from the need to resolve a conflict between external and internal conditions. More specifically these conditions could arise from the need to terminate an external axis by the internal order, and the need to resolve the problem of single entry into a centroidal form. The effect of both functional and formal demands can be seen in the resultant systems at the Casa Del Fascio and the Saynatsalo Civic Centre.

In the third category of 'courtyard' schemes, the generic condition is postulated for purely formal reasons. This type of solution proposes a 'courtyard' the use of which is not a primary requirement of its internal function. Le Corbusier's Monastery at La Tourette and Aalto's Tallinn museum project, which will be considered in detail below, are examples of this type of solution In both cases these is an acknowledgement of the non-utilitarian character of

THESE CENTROIDAL DEVELOPMENTS. THIS ACKNOWLEDGEMENT TAKES THE FORM OF A DISTORTION OF THE HORIZONTAL ABSOLUTE, WHICH BY DEFINITION MUST BE THE DOMINANT REFERENCE IN A 'COURTYARD' SOLUTION. AT LA TOURETTE THE CENTRAL COURT IS TWISTED FROM THE HORIZONTAL AND ALLOWED TO FLOW OUT UNDER THE BUILDING. THIS TWISTING IS A FORMAL PESPONSE TO THE SYSTEMIC PINWHEEL DEVELOPMENT: MORE SPECIFICALLY, COUNTER-BALANCING THE ARRESTED SPINNING MOTION OF THE CHAPEL BLOCK.

BOTH OF THE BUILDINGS EXAMINED BELOW HAVE BEEN CHOSEN TO ELUCIDATE THE SYSTEMIC BASIS OF AALTO'S WORK. SINCE EACH BUILDING EVOLVES FROM SIMILAR INTERNAL CONDITIONS, THE DIFFERENCE BETWEEN THE SPECIFIC FORMS WHICH RESULT FROM THE SAME GRAMMAR, CAN BE ATTRIBUTED TO SYSTEMIC ORDER USED IN EACH CASE TO CONVEY THEIR CONCEPTUAL BASIS.

THE SPECIFIC GRAMMAR USED BY ALVAR AALTO IS PERHAPS MORE DIFFICULT TO UNDERSTAND THAN THAT OF THE TWO ARCHITECTS ALREADY DISCUSSED. THE LACK OF AN EASILY DEFINABLE PERCEPTUAL ORDER GIVES THE INITIAL IMPRESSION THAT THERE IS A LACK OF SYSTEMIC ORDER IN HIS WORK. HOWEVER, THEREARE MANY FACTORS THAT SUGGEST A VERY STRICT ORDERING PROCESS IN THE SPECIFIC FORMS EMPLOYED, WHICH WOULD INVALIDATE ANY CASUAL DISMISSAL.

WHERE THE SYSTEMIC DEVELOPMENT OF BOTH LE CORBUSIER AND TERRAGNI INVOLVED THE CUBIST NOTION OF STRESSING A DOMINANT SURFACE OR PICTURE PLANE, WITH THE ACCOMPANYING 'MASS-SURFACE' DIALECTIC, AALTO IS CONCERNED WITH THE PLACEMENT OF EACH BLOCK, TREATED AS 'MASS', IT ITS RELATION TO THE NEXT BLOCK, PROVIDING, IN A SENSE , AN EVERCHANGING PICTURE PLANE. THE PERCEPTUAL ORDER ALSO PROVIDED IN

the work of Le Corbusier and Terragni, the conceptual clarity, for they are primarily concerned with the development of planar systems, where the perceptual clarity is often apparent from a single viewpoint. In Aalto's work the case is reversed since the changing planar reference makes perceptual comprehension from a stationary point almost impossible. However, Aalto does acknowledge a horizontal absolute, at both Saynatsalo and Tallinn, as being a necessary correlative to any 'courtyard' scheme. It will be seen in the following analyses that Aalto recognises the horizontal by relating both the volumetric and the movement systems to this coordinate while still using the shifting vertical reference. For Aalto it is the conceptual basis of his architecture: its generic condition which provides the order for the comprehensibility of the specific forms.

Aalto's systems are essentially composite in a similar sense to those of Le Corbusier, combining a dominant volumetric order and a secondary movement order In the Saynatsalo project both of these are centroidal developments, but in the Tallinn Museum the volumetric order is centroidal while the movement system is linear. However in both projects the initial distortions in the generic form derive from the syntactical resolution of a single entry into a cetroidal form.

SAYNATSALO CIVIC CENTRE

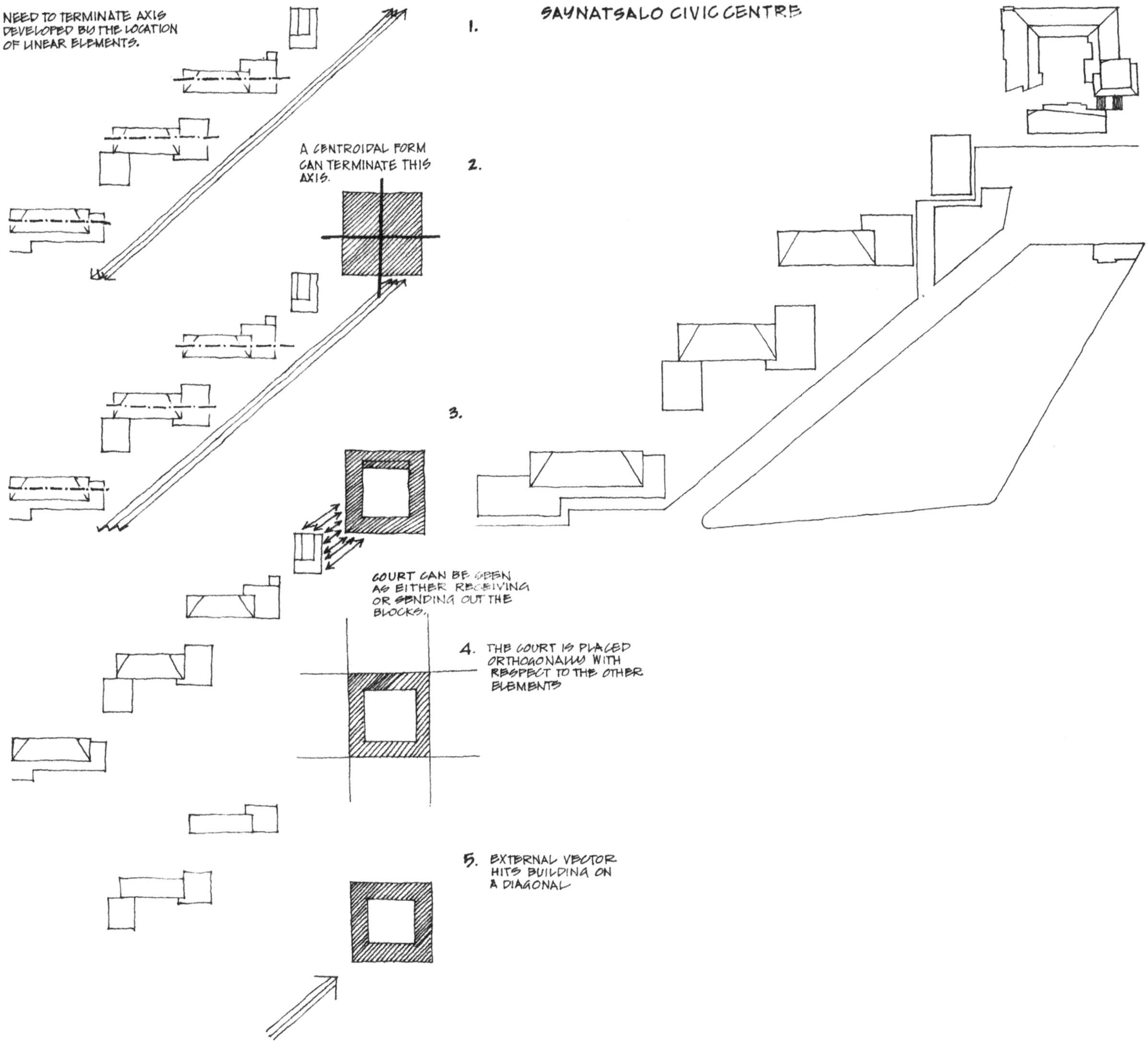

THE SAYNATSALO CIVIC CENTRE PRESENTS THE SYSTEMIC RESPONSE TO THE RESOLUTION OF THE CONFLICT BETWEEN AN INTERNAL CENTROIDAL REQUIREMENT AND AN EXTERNAL LINEAR CONDITION. SINCE THE SYNTACTICAL REQUIREMENTS OF THIS SITUATION ARE SIMILAR TO THOSE OF THE CASA DEL FASCIO, IT IS THE EVOLUTION OF THE SPECIFIC SYSTEM AND ITS PARTICULAR GRAMMAR, IN RESPONSE TO THESE CONDITIONS, THAT WILL PROVE OF INTEREST.

THE INITIAL CHOICE OF A 'COURTYARD' SOLUTION SEEMS TO DERIVE FROM BOTH FUNCTIONAL AND FORMAL DEMANDS. AALTO HIMSELF HAS STATED THAT THE COURT WAS DETERMINED BY FUNCTIONAL CONSIDERATIONS. HOWEVER THERE ARE A NUMBER OF ELEMENTS IN THE PLANNING OF THIS BUILDING WHICH INDICATE THE 'COURTYARD' WAS INVOKED FOR FORMAL AS WELL AS FUNCTIONAL REASONS. FIRST, A SCHEME WOULD BE CONCEIVED OF IN WHICH THE TOWERE BLOCK WAS PLACED CENTRALLY, GROUPING THE MINOR FUNCTIONS ABOUT THIS DOMINANT ELEMENT. A SECOND SCHEME COULD BE PROPOSED WITH A CENTRAL COURT USED ONLY AS THE PRIMARY MEANS OF CIRCULATION; THIS CAN BE SEEN IN A SIMILAR SITUATION AT THE NEW CAIUS COLLEGE HOSTEL. IN EXECUTION, THE 'COURTYARD' AT SAYNATSALO FUNCTIONS IN NEITHER OF THE WAYS SUGGESTED ABOVE AND IT MUST THEREFORE BE EXAMINED IN RELATION TO ITS FORMAL RESPONSE TO GIVEN CONDITIONS.

AALTO, IN HIS DEVELOPMENT OF THE SITE, HAS CREATED A SERIES OF LINEAR RESIDENTIAL BLOCKS THAT CASCADE DOWN THE SLOPING SITE. THERE MUST BE AN ACKNOWLEDGEMENT OF EITHER A BEGINNING OR AN END TO THIS EXTERNAL VECTOR.[1] THE CHOICE OF THE CENTROIDAL FORM ACTS AS A TERMINATION TO THE EXTERNAL AXIS.[2] NOW THE COURT

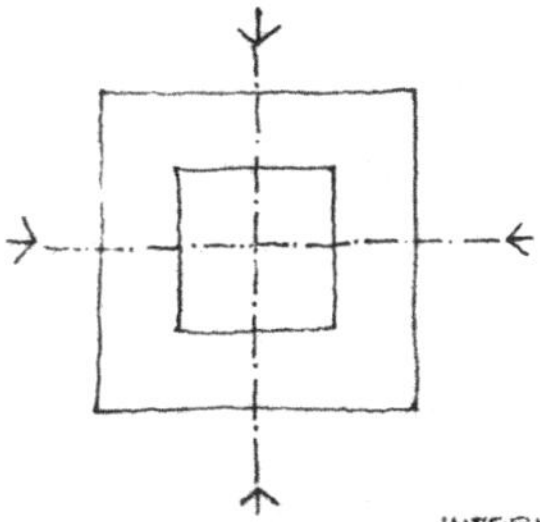

6.

INTERNAL FUNCTION SUGGESTS A RECTILINEAR SOLID WITH ITS CENTER CUT AWAY.

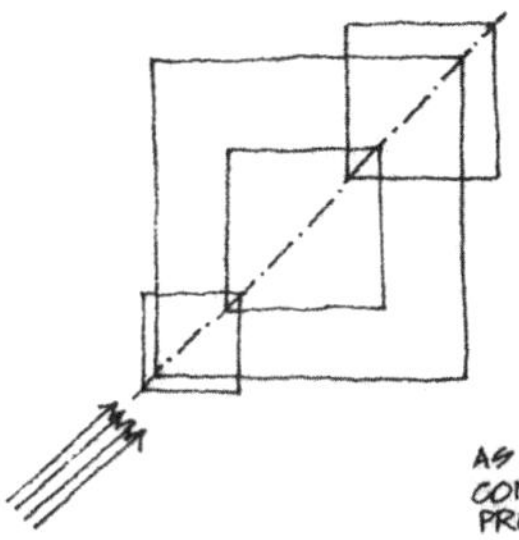

7.

AS A RESPONSE TO EXTERNAL CONDITIONS TWO CORNER PROJECTIONS CAN BE ASSUMED

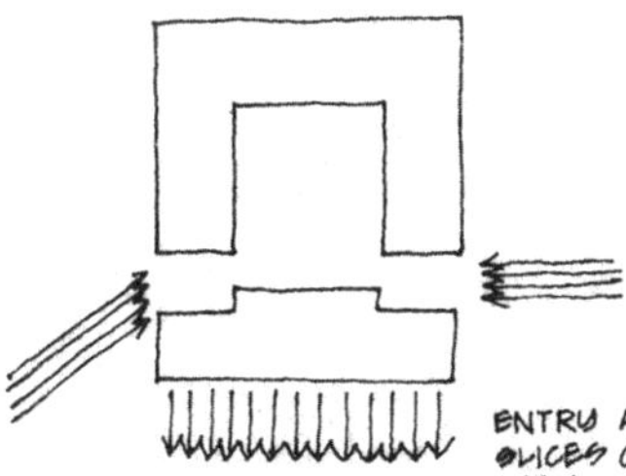

8.

ENTRY AT TWO CORNERS SLICES ONE SIDE, THE LIBRARY AWAY

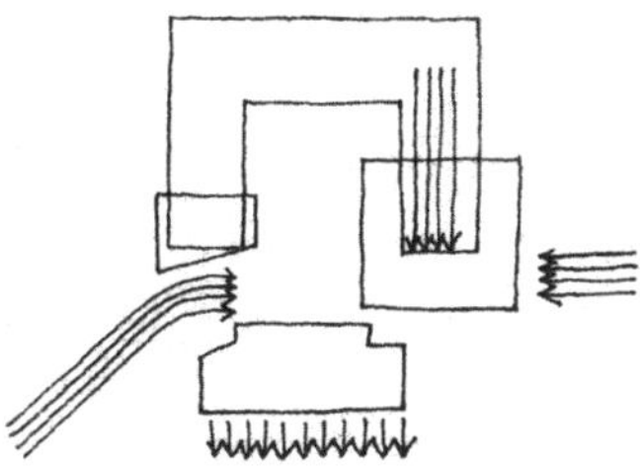

9.

THE MAJOR CORNER TOWER IS DRAWN TO ITS PRESENT LOCATION AND THE EXTERNAL VECTOR IS TWISTED AS IT ENTERS THE COURT.

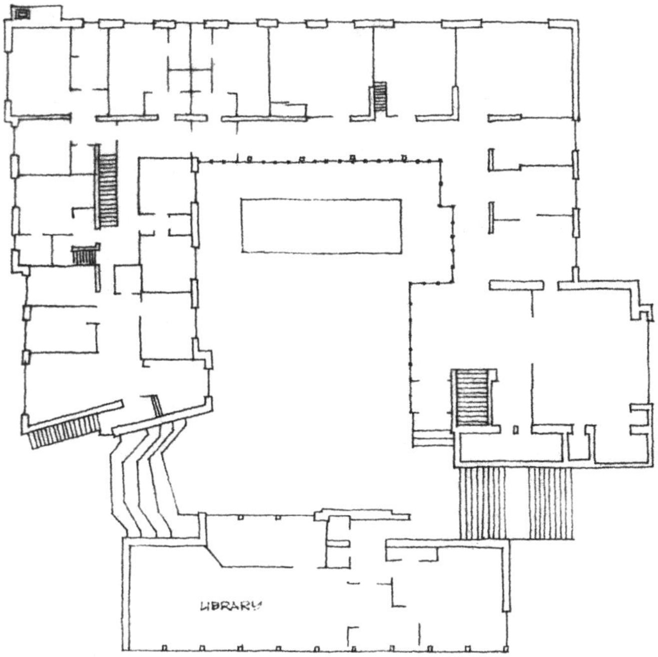

UPPER FLOOR PLAN

CAN BE CONCEIVED OF AS A RECEPTACLE OR CATCH BASIN, EITHER RECEIVING OR SENDING OUT THE LINEAR BLOCKS.[3] THE CIVIC CENTRE IS PLACED ORTHOGONALLY IN RELATION TO THE LINEAR ELEMENTS.[4] THIS HAS TWO DIRECT CONSEQUENCES: FIRST IT LOCATES THE BUILDING BY ACKNOWLEDGING THE ORTHOGONAL GRID, AND SECOND IT CAUSES THE EXTERNAL VECTOR TO INTERSECT THE BUILDING ON A DIAGONAL.[5] BECAUSE OF THE FORMER CONDITION IT IS POSSIBLE TO DEVELOPE A VOLUMETRIC SPIRAL WITHOUT CAUSEING THE BUILDING TO BE CONCEPTUALLY READ AS ROTATING IN RESPONSE TO THIS SPIRALLING MOTION. THE RESOLUTION OF THE LATTER, THE CONFLICT OF THE EXTERNAL DIAGONAL WITH THE INTERNAL CONDITION CAN BE SEEN AS A MAJOR CONSIDERATION IN THE DETERMINATION AND COMPREHENSION OF THE SPECIFIC FORM OF THE BUILDING. THE DISTORTIONS WHICH PRODUCE THE SPECIBIC FORM AND THE CONTROL OF THESE DISTORTIONS CAN BE UNDERSTOOD IN REFERENCE TO THE GENERIC ANTECEDENT. IN THIS CASE, THE INITIAL DISTORTION OF THE GENERIC STATE RESOLVES TWO PROBLEMS OF SYNTAX: THE ACKNOWLEDGEMENT OF THE EXTERNAL PRESSURES, AND THE CONTROL OF A SINGLE ENTRY INTO A CENTROIDAL FORM.

TO EFFECT A TRANSITION FROM OUTSIDE TO INSIDE A BREAK IN THE CENTROIDAL FORM IS REQUIRED WHICH CAN BE INTERPRETED AS THE INTITIAL DISTORTION OF THE GENERIC STATE. IT IS FIRST NECESSARY TO ASSUME THE GENERIC CONDITION, WHICH IS THE INITIAL RESPONSE TO BOTH INTERNAL AND EXTERNAL DEMANDS. THE INTERNAL FUNCTIONAL ARRANGEMENT SUGGESTS A PURE RECTILINEAR SOLID, WITH ITS CENTRAL PORTION CUT AWAY.[6] AS A RESPONSE TO THE EXTERNAL VECTOR, TWO CORNER PROJECTIONS CAN BE ASSUMED: ONE MAJOR AND THE OTHER MINOR PROTRUDING FROM THE ORIGINAL SOLID AND PROVIDING THE TERMINATION OF THE AXIS IN THE GENERIC STATE.[7]

NOW THIS CONDITION, WHICH DOES NOT PRESUPPOSE MOVEMENT INTO IT, MUST SOMEHOW

be distorted. If the entrance was placed on one of the central axes it would presuppose several means of access which are not required in this case. Entry at the two corner junctions could be proposed, thereby slicing one entire side away from the central complex; this solution was preferred and the system developed from this basis.[8] The resolution of the formal syntax and the internal function of the building are readily ordered by this system: The major entry can be placed in proximity to the major external circulation, and the resultant isolation of one wing, is given additional importance. The cutting of one side from the generic block acknowledges both the diagonal external axis and the existence of the movement vector.

The pressure of these two lines of force splits the library block away from the court and the resultant pull of this block causes the initial distortion in the generic form. The main corner tower is drawn to its present location, where it also defines the major entry.[9] If this assumption were not valid, the block would seem to be in a rather arbitrary and unstable posttion in relation to the remaining sides of the court. Even so its final position is not fixed in relation to any major axis in either the transverse or longitudinal direction. The distortion of the opposite south west corner is expressed in a more dramatic fashion, thus acknowledging the shredding of a corner that had initially received an external fixing from the diagonal axis. The resultant specific forms recognise the splitting and wrenching effect of the pulling away of the library. The end of the western block is cut jaggedly along the diagonal in two parts. This cutting accommodates a minor circulation slot to the upper level of the flats. Moreover, the long flight of stairs is distorted

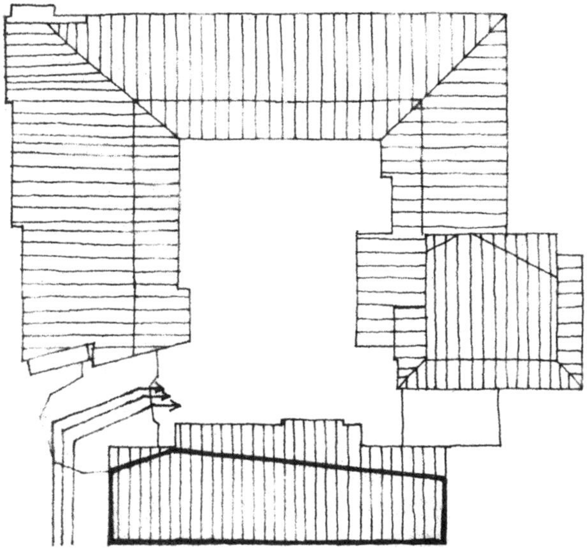

10.

ROOF OF LIBRARY RESPONDS TO THE TWISTING OF THE DIAGONAL VECTOR.

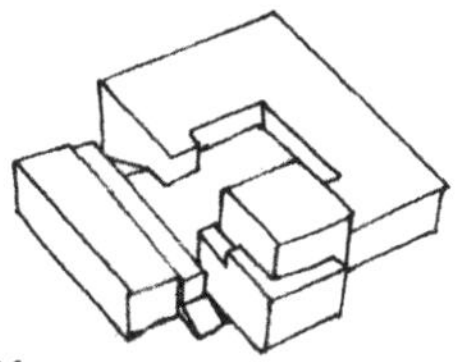

11.

DEFORMATIONS CAUSED BY DIAGONAL VECTOR NOT APPARENT IN BLOCK MODEL.

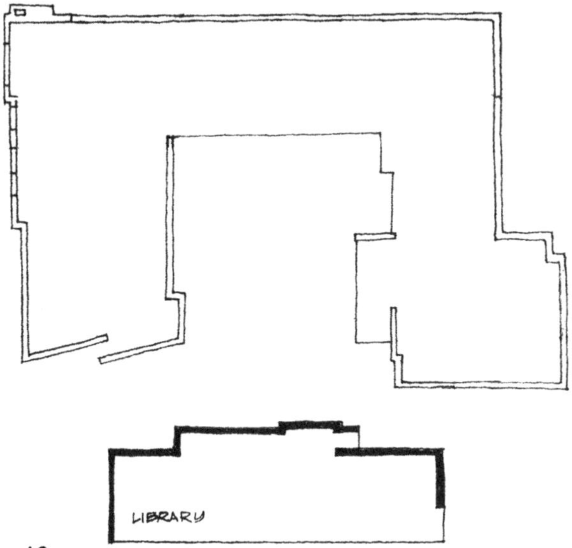

12.

OPAQUE QUALITY OF COURT FACADE OF LIBRARY INDICATES A REVERSAL OF THIS BLOCK FROM ITS GENERIC STATE, WITH ONLY ITS ROOF REMAINING IN ITS ORIGINAL POSITION

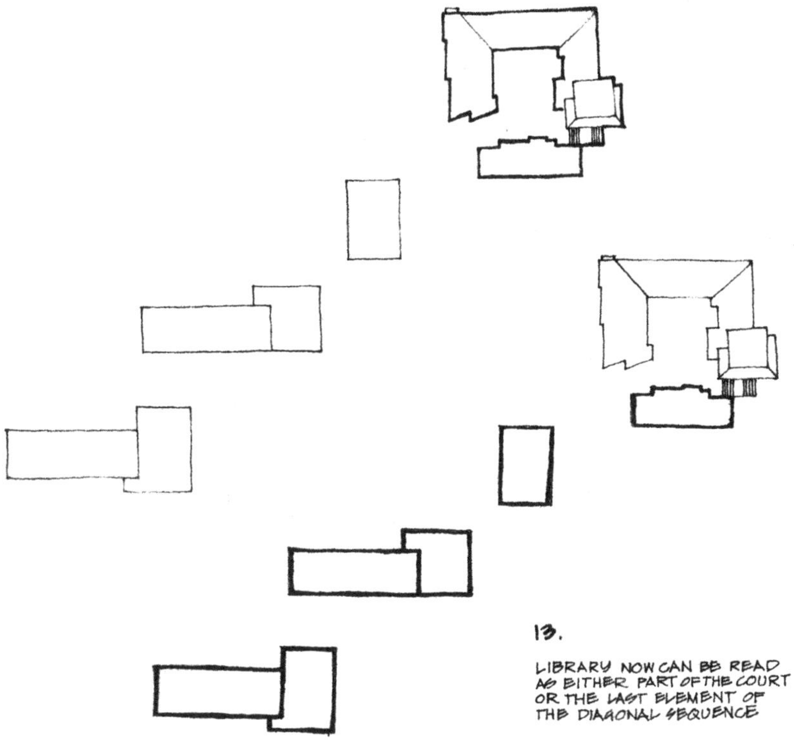

13.

LIBRARY NOW CAN BE READ AS EITHER PART OF THE COURT OR THE LAST ELEMENT OF THE DIAGONAL SEQUENCE

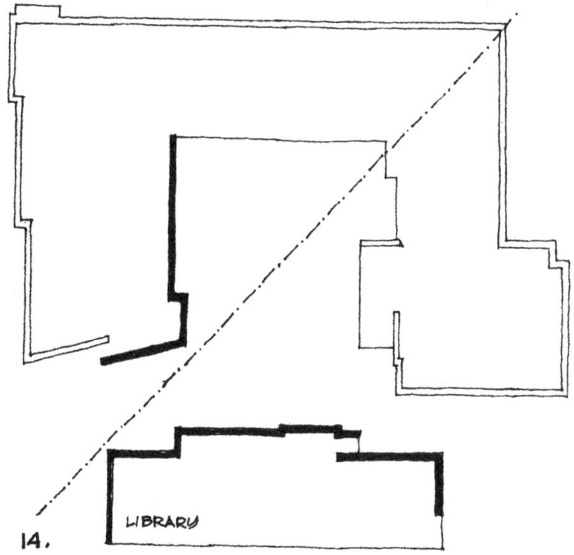

14.

OPAQUE INTERNAL FACADE OF LIBRARY READS WITH ADJACENT OPAQUE FACADE OF THE WESTERN BLOCK TO RECALL GENERIC CONDITION

IN A LIKE MANNER ACKNOWLEDGING THE EXTREME PRESSURE CAUSED BY THE BENDING OF THE MAJOR DIAGONAL VECTOR. THE ROOF OF THE INTERIOR CORNER OF THE LIBRARY BLOCK ALSO RESPONDS TO THIS TWISTING OF THE DIAGONAL; THESE PERCEPTUAL DEFORMATIONS CLARIFYING THE CONCEPTUAL BASIS OF THE SPECIFIC FORMS.[10] IT IS INTERESTING TO NOTE THAT THE DIAGONAL DEFORMATIONS OF THE LIBRARY, AND THE WESTERN END OF THE MAIN VOLUME ARE NOT APPARENT IN THE BLOCK MODEL, THUS STRENGTHENING THE ASSUMPTION THAT THESE CUTS WERE EFFECTED TO PROVIDE A PERCEPTUAL CLARITY TO THE FORMAL SYSTEM.[11]

THE FINAL FORM OF THE LIBRARY BLOCK IS THEN INVESTED WITH A DUAL READING. ITS ROOF SLOPES IN A SIMILAR MANNER TO THAT OF THE REMAINING THREE SIDES OF THE COURT THUS PROVIDING A PERCEPTUAL REFERENCE TO THE COURT, THE ONLY MINOR DIFFERENCE BEING IN THE DISTORTIONS THAT HAVE BEEN DISCUSSED ABOVE. HOWEVER IF THE ROOFS WRE TAKEN AWAY, THE BLOCK, SEEN AT COURT LEVEL, SEEMS TO HAVE TURNED ITS BACK ON THE REST OF THE BUILDING. THE GLAZING WHICH RUNS ALONG THE INTERIOR FACADE OF THE COURT SUDDENLY STOPS AT THE LIBRARY WHERE THE INTERIOR WALL BECOMES OPAQUE. INSTEAD, THE GLAZING ON THE LIBRARY BLOCK APPEARS EXTERNALLY INDICATING A REVERSAL OF THIS BLOCK BY ITS DISLOCATION.[12] THIS CONCEPTUALLY ALLOWS THE LIBRARY BLOCK TO BE READ AS EITHER PART OF THE COURT OR AS THE LAST ELEMENT IN THE DIAGONAL SEQUENCE OF LINEAR BLOCKS.[13] THE OPAQUE QUALITY ATTRIBUTED TO THE INNER FACE OF THE LIBRARY NOW READS WITH THE OPAQUE INNER FACADE OF THE WESTERN BLOCK TO RECALL IN SOME WAY THE DIAGONAL CONDITION AS IT EXISTED IN THE GENERIC STATE, THE TWO ADJACENT NORTH AND EAST COURT FACADES READING AS TRANSPARENT.[14] A FURTHER ACKNOWLEDGEMENT OF THE REVERSAL OF THE LIBRARY BLOCK CAN BE SEEN IN THE STEPPED QUALITY OF THE COURT FACADE. IF THIS FACADE IS THOUGH OF AS BEING ORIGINALLY ON THE EXTERIOR, IT IS SIMILAR IN KIND TO THE STEPPING O

SOUTH LIBRARY FACADE

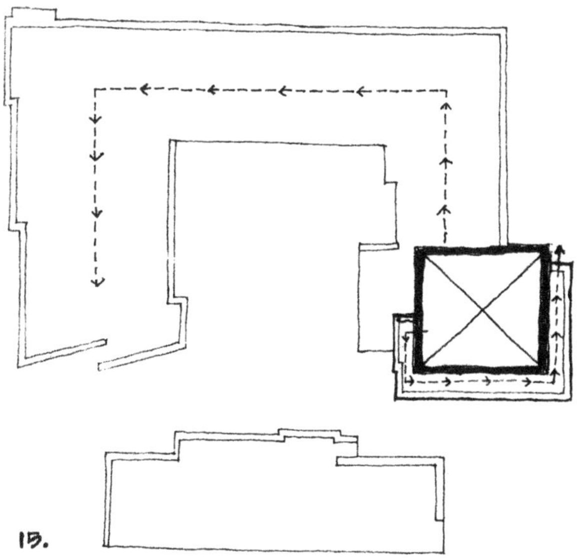

13.

MAIN TOWER IS FIXED POINT FOR BEGINNING OF SPIRAL. INNER ELEMENT PINS WHILE OUTER ELEMENT WINDS OUT OF THE TOWER INITIATING MOVEMENT.

THE EXTERIOR FACADE OF THE WESTERN BLOCK. AGAIN THESE ARTICULATIONS DO NOT APPEAR IN THE COMPETITION MODEL, GIVING FURTHER CREDENCE TO ANY FORMAL ATTRIBUTION.

THUS, THE PRIMARY ORDERING OF THE SPECIFIC FORM COMES FROM THE DISTORTION OF THE CENTROIDAL VOLUMETRIC ORGANIZATION. A SECONDARY ORDER IS ALSO IMPOSED ON THE ARRANGEMENT OF VOLUMES TO COMPLETE THE DEVELOPMENT OF THIS COMPOSITE SYSTEM. THIS ORDER IS A SPIRAL SYSTEM OF MOVEMENT AND MAY BE COMPARED WITH LE CORBUSIER'S USE OF A SIMILAR SYSTEM AT THE PAVILLON SUISSE. THERE THE SPIRAL CAN BE INTERPRETED AS THE CONTROL OF A PATTERN OF BEHAVIOR, THE MOVEMENT OF PEOPLE, WHICH IS EXTERNAL TO THE FABRIC OF THE BUILDING, YET ENFORCED ON THE OBSERVER BY THE PRESENCE OF THE BUILDING. IN THE PAVILLON SUISSE THE SPIRALING MOTION DOES NOT ALTER THE RELATION OF THE VOLUMETRIC ORDER TO A SINGLE PLANE OF REFERENCE. FOR AALTO THE SPIRAL MOVEMENT IS A QUALITY OF THE WORK ITSELF: THE CONTROL OF THE VOLUMETRIC ARRANGEMENT BY A PERCEPTUAL REFERENCE TO A GENERIC SPIRAL. A PICTURESQUE QUALITY IS THEREFORE ATTRIBUTED TO THIS SPIRAL ORGANIZATION, IN THAT THE VOLUMETRIC ORDER REFERS TO A CHANGING VERTICAL PICTURE PLANE.

THE MAIN TOWER, WHICH HOUSES THE TOWN HALL, IS THE KEY ELEMENT IN THE MOVEMENT SYSTEM AS IT PROVIDES A FIXED POINT FROM WHICH THE SPINNING MOTION BEGINS.[15] THIS TOWER CONSISTS OF TWO INTERLOCKING RECTANGLES IN PLAN: THE INNER RECTANGLE WHICH CONTINUES UNINTERRUPTED TO ITS FULL HEIGHT, ACTS AS THE PINNING ELEMENT. THE OUTER RECTANGLE CAN THEN BE READ AS WINDING OUT OF THE TOWER, INITIATING THE COUNTER-CLOCKWISE SPIRALLING MOTION. THE PERCEPTUAL DEFINITION PROVIDED BY THE VOLUMETRIC ARRANGEMENT IS THE REMAINING BLOCKS OF THE COURT REINFORCES

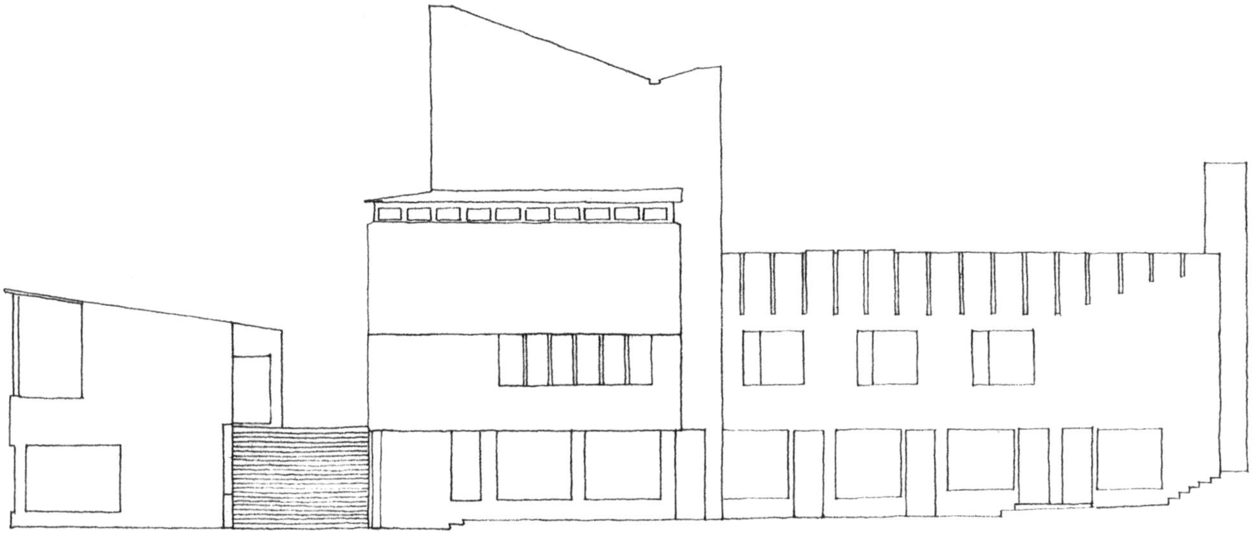

16.

EAST ELEVATION SHOWS UNWINDING AND TURNING OF THE SPIRAL FROM THE GROOVES IN ITS UPPER EDGE

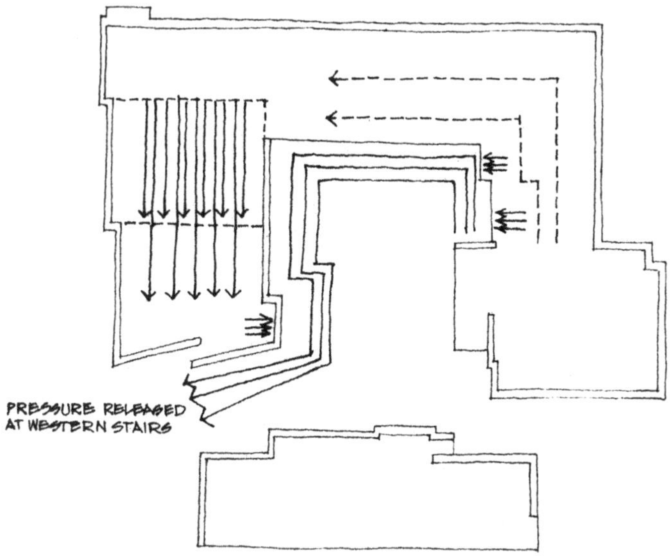

17.

SPIRAL MOVES IN CENTRIPETAL FASHION CREATING A PRESSURE ON THE NEGATIVE VOLUME OF THE COURT. BLOCKS ON WESTERN ARM READ AS PULLED FROM NORTHERN ARM.

THE SPIRAL READING. THE UNWINDING AND TURNING OF THE EASTERN BLOCK CAN BE INFERRED FROM THE GROOVES CUT IN THE EXTERIOR FACADE AT ITS UPPER EDGE;[16] THE GRADUAL SHORTENING OF THESE GIVES THE BLOCK A RECESSIONAL QUALITY, CONSEQENTLY ITS RIGHT END APPEARS TO MOVE AWAY FROM AN ORTHOGONAL PLANE OF REFERENCE; THIS TURNING QUALITY AWAY FROM A PICTURE PLANE IS SIMILAR TO THAT ATTRIBUTED TO THE CHAPEL BLOCK AT LA TOURETTE.

FROM THE TOWER THE SPIRAL CAN BE SEEN TO BE MOVING IN A COUNTER CLOCKWISE AND CENTRIPETAL FASHION; THE LATTER BY ITS GRADUAL INWARD MOVEMENT, CREATES A PRESSURE IN THE NEGATIVE VOLUMES OF THE COURT.[17] THE FIRST INWARD MOVEMENT CAN BE SEEN AT THE NE CORNER OF THE COURT, WHERE THE INTERNAL VOLUME IS WIDENED FURTHERMORE, THE WESTERN BLOCK IS STEPPED INWARD TWICE ON ITS EXTERIOR SIDE, THUS AIDING IN THE DEFINITION OF THE UNWINDING VOLUMETRIC SPIRAL. HERE A READING CAN BE INFERRED TO THESE STEPPING BLOCKS THAT IS SIMILAR IN KIND TO THE READING OF THE PARTS OF A TELESCOPE; THE BLOCKS BEING SEEN AS PULLED FROM THE NORTHERN SIDE OF THE COURT. THE TERMINATION OF THE SPIRAL IS EFFECTED BY THE BLUNTING OF ITS SW END. THE RESULTING PROJECTION, WHICH ALSO INCREASES THE PRESSURE IN THE COURT, CAN BE SEEN AS THE REMAINDER OF THE ORIGINAL PIN ON THIS CORNER. THE BUILD UP IN PRESSURE IN THE NEGATIVE VOLUME OF THE COURT IS MODERATED BY THE CUTTING OF THE WEST FACADE WHICH ALLOWS THE EXCESS PRESSURE TO SPILL OUT OF THE COURT AND DOWN THE STAIRS.

IN THE GLAZING OF BOTH THE NORTH AND EAST FACADES, THE UNWINDING MOTION OF THE SPIRAL RECEIVES FURTHER PERCEPTUAL CLARIFICATION. ON THE NORTH FACADE, THE INDIVIDUAL WINDOWS READ ACROSS IN AN EVER DECREASING ORDER IN THE DIRECTION OF

18. NORTH ELEVATION

UNWINDING MOTION CLARIFIED IN THE GLAZING.
WINDOWS READ IN AN EVER DECREASING ORDER. 3½ : 2½ : 1½ : 1.

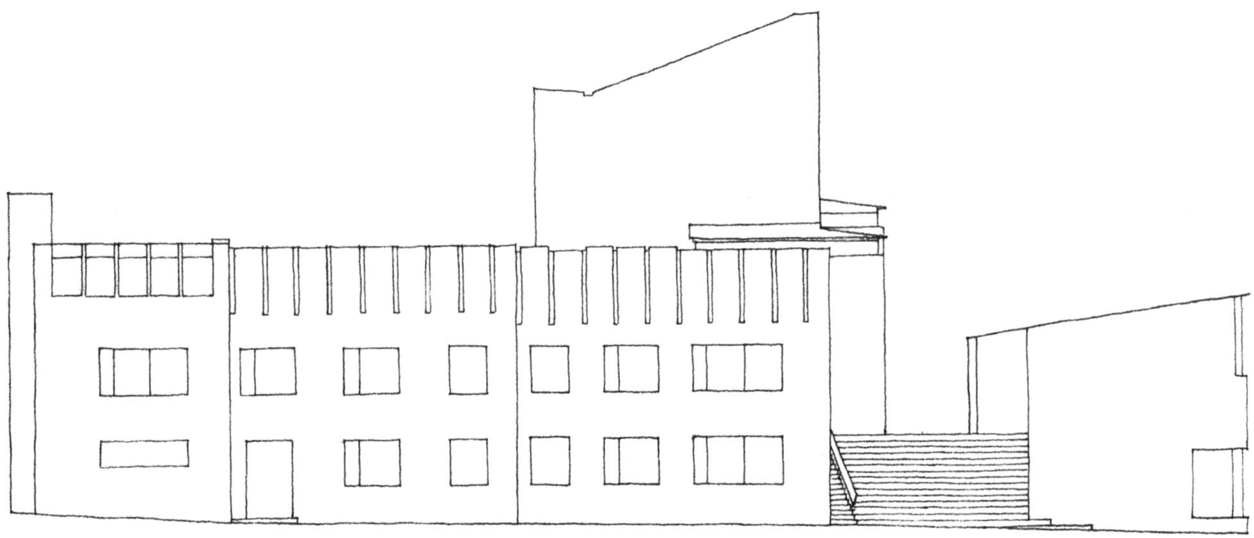

19. EAST FACADE

VOLUMETRIC STEPPING. WINDOWS ALSO READ IN SERIES 2½ : 1½ : 1
SPIRAL TERMINATED IN LAST SECTION BY BEGINNING THE SERIES
AGAIN, FROM ONE.

THE SPIRALLING MOVEMENT: THE SERIES READING $3\frac{1}{2}, 2\frac{1}{2}, 1\frac{1}{2}, 1$.[18] IN ADDITION TO THE VOLUMETRIC STEPPING ON THE EAST FACADE, THE WINDOWS HARE ALSO READ IN SERIES: $2\frac{1}{2}, 1\frac{1}{2}, 1$.[19] IT MUST BE NOTED THAT THERE IS A PERCEPTUAL TERMINATION TO THE SPIRAL, PROVIDED BY THE GLAZING IN THE LAST SECTION OF THE EAST ELEVATION; THE SERIES BEGINNING AGAIN FROM ONE AND DEVELOPING TO $1\frac{1}{2}$ AND $2\frac{1}{2}$. THERE ARE TWO OTHER MINOR NOTATIONS WHICH GIVE FURTHER CREDENCE TO THE INTERPRETATION OF THE SPIRAL SYSTEM. THE FIRST, IS THE LACK OF ANY STRONG CORNER DEFINITION TO THE COURT, AND THE SECOND IS THE LACK OF ANY PERCEPTIAL REFERENCES ACROSS THIS COURT. THERE IS A PURPOSEFUL AND SUBTLE AMBIGUITY PRESENTED IN THE LATTER CASE. ANY DENIAL OF READINGS ACROSS THE COURT MAKES THE INTERPRETATION OF A CRUCIFORM PLAIDING SYSTEM DIFFICULT WHICH AGAIN WOULD STRENGTHEN THE SPIRAL ATTRIBUTION. HOWEVER, THE NODAL POINTS ON THE OPPOSITE SIDES OF THE COURT SEEM TO BE PERCEPTUALLY CONNECTED BY AN ORDERING OF SKEWN LINES.[20] THIS IS SEEN BY THE FACT THAT NODAL POINTS ARE DISLOCATED BY A SIMILAR DIMENSION WHEREEVER AN ORTHOGONAL READING ACROSS THE COURT IS ATTEMPTED. HOWEVER, THIS AGAIN RAISES THE QUESTION OF THE POSITION OF THE LIBRARY BLOCK IN RELATION TO THE SPIRAL SYSTEM. FROM THE MAIN TOWER, THE LIBRARY CAN ONLY BE READ AS MOVING IN AN OPPOSITE DIRECTION TO THE REMAINDER OF THE SPIRAL. THIS DETATCHED VOLUME MIGHT BE THOUGHT OF AS THE VANE OF A PINWHEEL, BEING HELD TO THE TOWER BY THE LIGHT ENTRY TRELLIS.[21] IF THIS READING WERE TO BE SUBSTANTIATED, THEN THE LIBRARY COULD BE SEEN AS SWINGING AGAINST THE END OF THE SPIRAL CAUSING THE RESULTANT DEFORMATION OF THE WESTERN STAIRS. HOWEVER, THIS INTERPRETATION DOES NOT ACKNOWLEDGE THE REVERSAL OF THE LIBRARY AND THE CORRESPONDING CHANGE IN THE DIRECTION OF MOVEMENT FROM THE GENERIC CONDITION. MOREOVER, ANY SUCH INTERPRETATION WOULD INVOLVE THE POSTULATION OF AN OBSCURE AND COMPLEX SYSTEMIC DEVELOPMENT.

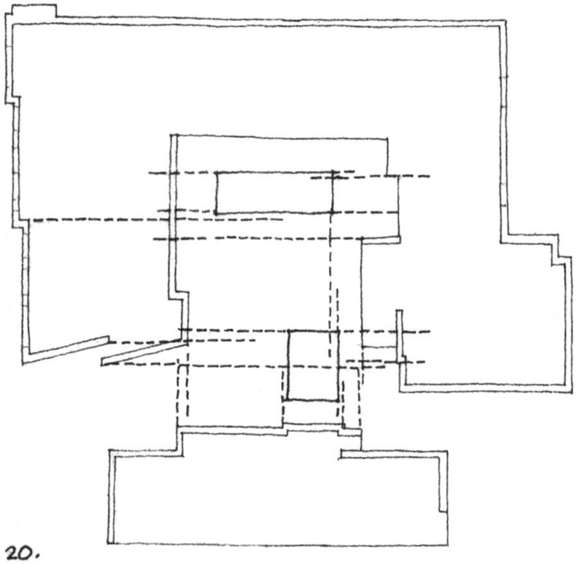

20.

NODAL POINTS ON OPPOSITE SIDES OF THE COURT SEEM TO BE CONNECTED BY AN ORDERING OF SKEW LINES

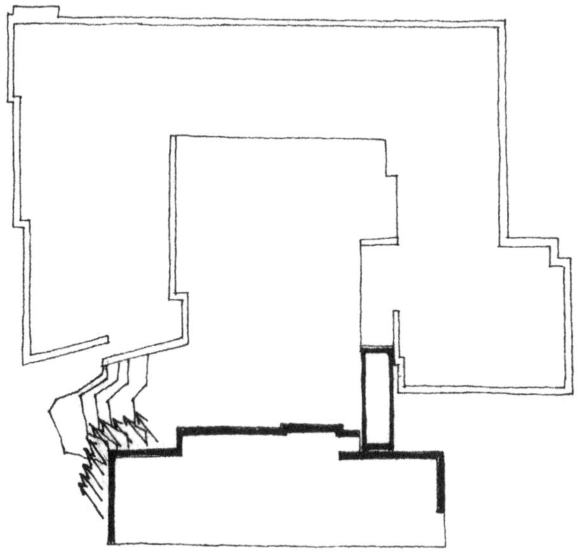

21.

INTERPRETATION OF LIBRARY AS AN ARM OF A PARTIAL PINWHEEL HELD TO THE TOWER BY A TRELLIS.

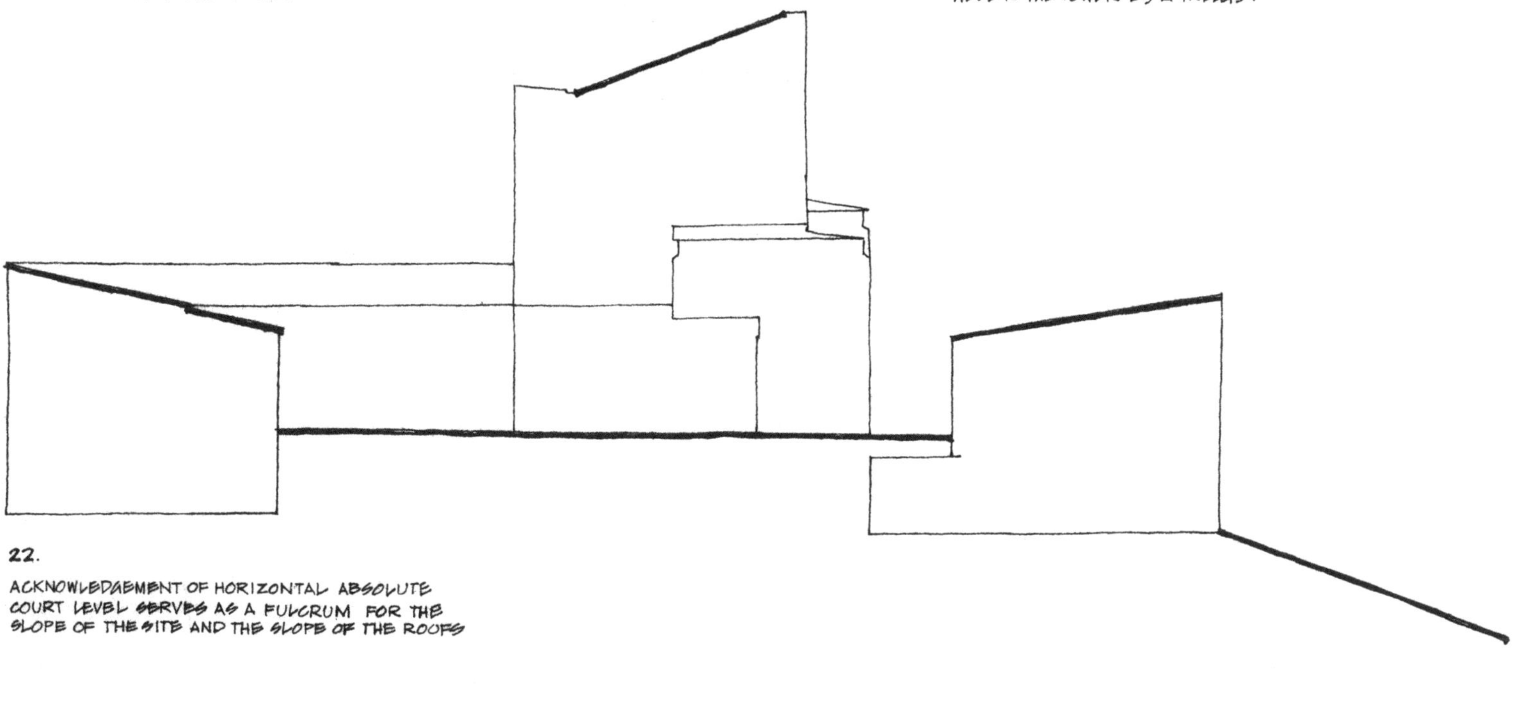

22.

ACKNOWLEDGEMENT OF HORIZONTAL ABSOLUTE COURT LEVEL SERVES AS A FULCRUM FOR THE SLOPE OF THE SITE AND THE SLOPE OF THE ROOFS

THE EXTERNAL CIRCULATION CONSISTS OF A VERY TIGHT CLOCK WISE SPIRAL BEGINNING AT THE EAST ENTRY. HOWEVER, THE PRESSURE OF THE MAIN TOWER IN ITS MOVEMENT FROM ITS GENERIC LOCATION CAN BE SEEN AS HAVING COMPRESSED THIS SECONDARY SYSTEM OF MOVEMENT, AND IN FACT HAVING CHANGED ITS DIRECTION TO THAT OF THE MAIN SPIRAL. THE PERGOLA ROOF LINKS THE EXTERNAL CIRCULATION WITH THE ENTRY WHILE PROVIDING A STOP TO THE EXTERNAL MOVEMENT, PREVENTING IT FROM CONTINUING PAST THE MAIN BLOCK AND THROUGH THE COURT. THIS PERGOLA CAN BE READ AS AN ATTEMPT TO HOLD THE RESULTANT SPECIFIC FORM TOGETHER. THE BANDING OF THE EXTERNAL FACADES ON THE SOUTH AND EAST PROVIDES A FURTHER PERCEPTUAL TIE FOR THE COURT. THE GROUND FLOOR GLAZING OF BOTH ELEVATIONS READS AS A CONTINUOUS TRANSPARENT BAND, EVEN THOUGH THESE ARE CUT BY THE ENTRY VECTOR. IN ADDITION A CUTTING BACK OF THE EAST FACADE, BY IMPLYING A PROGRESSION OF PLANAR VOLUMES, ACKNOWLEDGES AND ALLOWSFOR ENTRY.

FINALLY, THE ACKNOWLEDGEMENT OF THE HORIZONTAL ASPECT OF THE SYSTEM MUST BE CONSIDERED. AALTO ATTRIBUTES AN ABSOLUTE NATURE TO THIS COURT BY USING IT AS A FULCRUM TO BALANCE THE SLOPE OF THE SITE AND THE VARIED PITCH OF THE DIFFERENT ROOFS.[22]

IN THE TALLINN MUSEUM PROJECT, AALTO EVOLVES A COMPOSITE SYSTEM FOR THE CONTROL OF BOTH VOLUME AND MOVEMENT. HE ACHIEVES THE RESOLUTION OF THE POSSIBLE OPPOSING TEDENCIES INHERENT IN THE TWO SYSTEMS PRESENTING THEM IN A DIALECTIC CONDITION; EITHER THE MOVEMENT OR THE VOLUME BEING READ AS DOMINANT. ON THE ONE HAND, THE GENERIC VOLUMETRIC ORDER CAN BE SEEN AS BEING DISTORTED BY THE SYSTEM OF MOVEMENT, WHILE ON THE OTHER HAND THE VOLUMETRIC ORDER CAN BE SEEN AS EVOLVING FROM THE CONTROL OF THIS MOVEMENT. IN EITHER CASE THE EVOLUTION OF THIS SCHEME AS A CENTROIDAL 'COURT' SEEMS TO BE FOR PREDOMINATELY FORMAL REASONS. THE GENERIC FORM IS DERIVED INITIALLY FROM THE PROGRAMMATIC REQUIREMENTS, AS IS THE CASE IN ALL SYSTEMIC DERIVATIONS, YET THE RESULTANT COURTYARD IS LITTLE MORE THAN A FORMAL REMINDER OF THE GENERIC STATE; THE COURT CANNOT BE SEEN AS NECESSARY TO THE FUNCTIONING OF THE FINAL SCHEME. ANY UTILITARIAN ATTRIBUTION TO THIS COURT WOULD SEEM TO BE INVALIDATED BY THE FACT THAT THERE IS ONLY LIMITED ACCESS PROVIDED FROM THE COURT TO THE PUBLIC FUNCTIONS. THE LINKING OF INTERIOR AND EXTERIOR BY OPENING THE COURT TO THE SURROUNDING PARKLAND SEEMS LITTLE MORE THAN A 'PICTURESQUE' AND PICTORIAL NOTION, AS THIS CONNECTION HAS LITTLE TO DO WITH THE INTERNAL ORGANISATION OF THE MUSEUM OR THE FUNCTIONING OF THE MUSEUM WITH RESPECT TO THE COURT. IT IS RATHER THE NOTION, IN FORMAL TERMS THAT A SPIRAL MUST ACKNOWLEDGE A FIXED CENTRUM THAT SEEMS TO GIVE THIS COURT ITS 'RAISON D'ETRE'.

NOT ONLY DOES THE SPECIFIC FORM OF THE BUILDING EVOLVE FROM THE SYNTAX OF THE RESOLUTION OF A SINGLE ENTRY, BUT ALSO THE GENERIC STATE ITSELF IS DERIVED

TALLINN MUSEUM

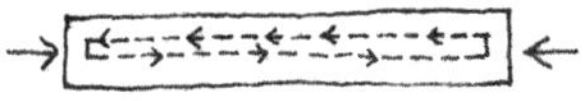

1\.

LINEAR MUSEUM REQUIRES DUAL ENTRY AND EXIT TO PREVENT REDUNDANT MOVEMENT.

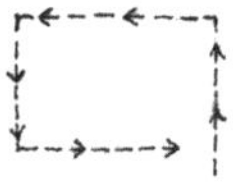

2\.

CENTROIDAL FORM SUGGESTED BY SINGLE ENTRY REQUIREMENT.

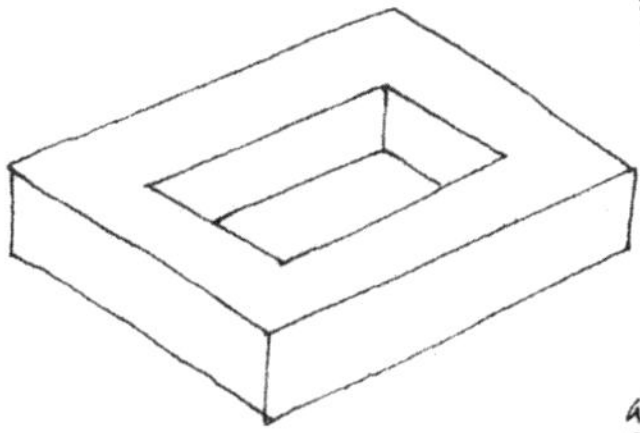

3\.

GENERIC FORM RECTILINEAR VOLUME WITH A CENTRAL VOID.

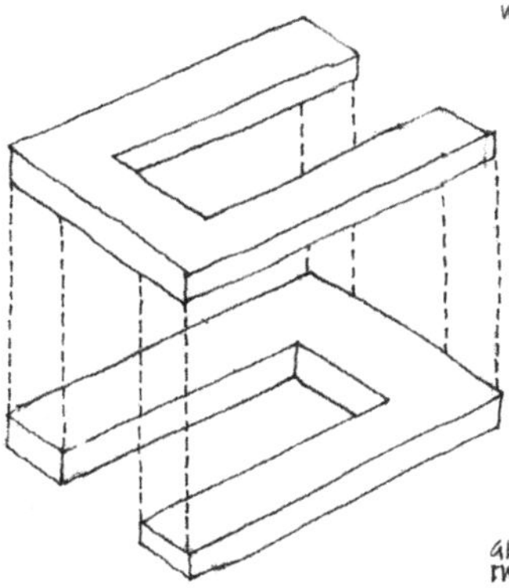

4\.

GENERIC FORM TWO HORIZONTAL U-VOLUMES REPRESENTING THE PUBLIC AND PRIVATE AREAS.

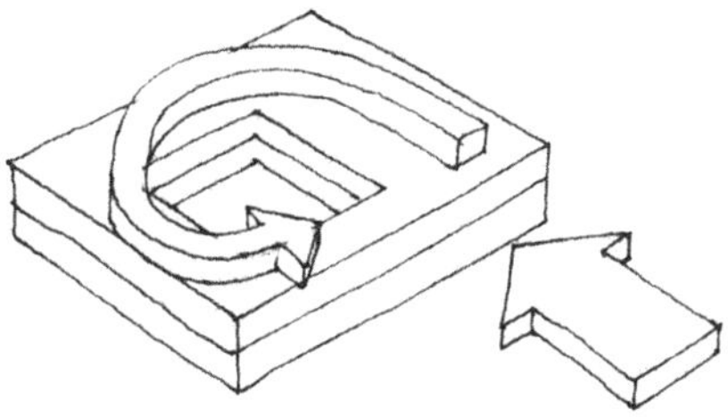

5\.

COMBINATION OF MOVEMENT AND VOLUMETRIC SYSTEMS TO PRODUCE A SPIRAL.

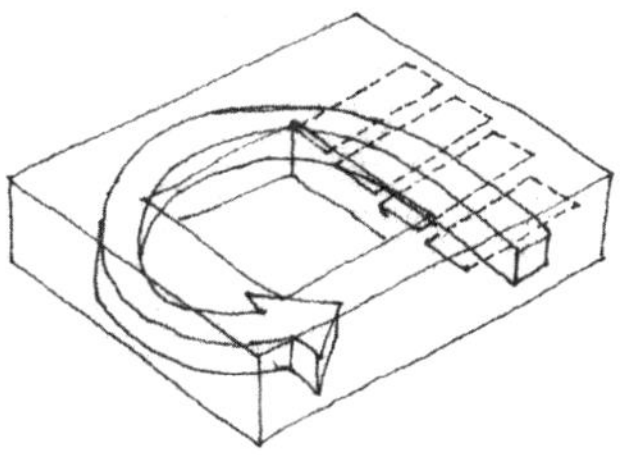

6\.

SPIRAL MOVEMENT PROVIDES INITIAL STRATIFICATION OF VOLUME INTO THIN LAYERS.

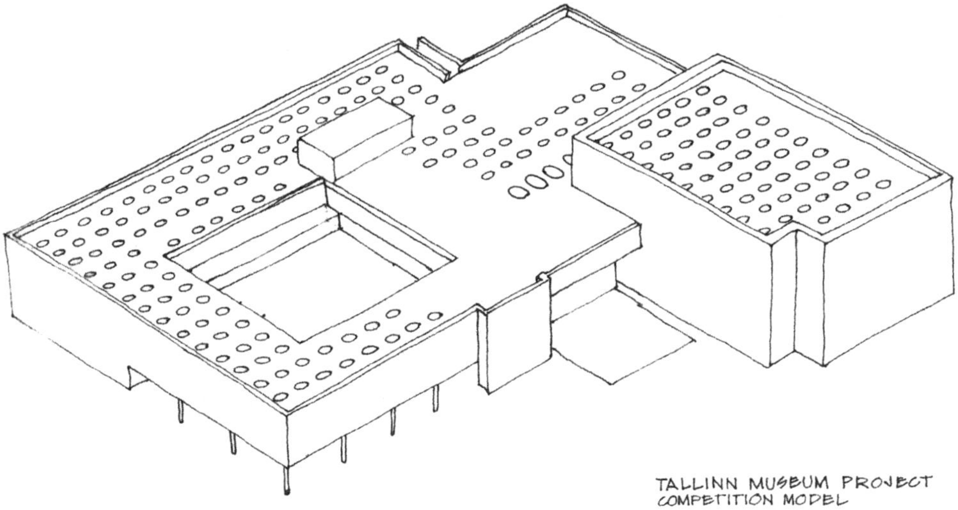

TALLINN MUSEUM PROJECT COMPETITION MODEL

FROM THIS SYNTAX. INITIALLY, THE ORGANISATION OF A MUSEUM EVOLVES FROM THE THE INTERNAL CONTROL OF MOVEMENT, WHICH MAY BE EITHER LINEAR OR CENTROIDAL. HOWEVER, THE FORMER WOULD DEMAND DUAL ENTRY AND EXIT TO AVOID ANY REDUNDANT MOVEMENT IN ITS ORGANISATION.[1] SINCE THERE IS ONLY A SINGLE DOMINANT EXTERNAL VECTOR IT WOULD SEEM OBVIOUS THAT THE SYSTEM OF MOVEMENT SHOULD SOMEHOW TURN BACK ON ITSELF THUS SUGGESTING A CENTROIDAL FORM.[2] THUS THE GENERIC VOLUMETRIC FORM CAN BE POSTULATED AS A RECTILINEAR VOLUME WITH A CENTRAL VOID.[3] MORE PRECISELY, THIS GENERIC STATE CAN BE THOUGHT OF AS TWO INTERSECTING HORIZONTAL U-FORMS, EACH REPRESENTING THE DISPARATE PUBLIC AND PRIVATE PARTS OF THE MUSEUM.[4] THESE U-FORMS ARE PLACED ONE ON TOP OF EACH OTHER TO PRODUCE A RECTILINEAR ENCLOSURE TO THE CENTRAL VOID. THIS VOLUMETRIC CONDITION THEN RECEIVES THE MOVEMENT SYSTEM OVERLAY, WHICH MUST COMBINE BOTH THE CENTROIDAL INTERNAL MOVEMENT AND THE LINEAR EXTERNAL VECTOR INTO ONE ORGANISATION, THE SPIRAL BEING AN OBVIOUS RESOLUTION OF THIS COMBINATION.[5] NOW THE VOID IN THE GENERIC VOLUME CAN BE READ AS A CENTRAL PIVOT ABOUT WHICH THIS SPIRAL ROTATES. THE OVERLAY OF THE SPIRAL MUST THEN ELEVATE THROUGH BOTH LEVELS OF THE VOLUMETRIC ORGANISATION, AND IN DOING SO IT TENDS TO FURTHER STRATIFY THESE VOLUMES INTO THIN LAYERS.[6] THESE ARE THEN SHREDDED AND SHATTERED APART AS THE SYTACTICAL ACKNOWLEDGEMENT OF THE RESOLUTION OF THE ENTRY VECTOR, AND BECOME THE ECHELONING VOLUMETRIC PLANES IN THE SPECIFIC FORM. THUS THE ENTRY VECTOR CAN BE THOUGHT OF AS BOTH DETERMINING AND DISTORTING THE GENERIC STATED, THERE ARE TWO DIRECT RESULTS WHICH MUST BE ACCOMMODATED INTO THE SYSTEMIC CONTROL, WHICH ARE PRODUCED BY THIS DISTORTION. THE FIRST, AN ISOLATING OF ONE SIDE FROM THE GENERIC COURT, AND THE SECOND IS THE PRESSURE OF THE ENTRY VECTOR ENTERING THE SYSTEM. THE FIRST DISTORTION PRODUCES A TENDENCY FOR THE BUILDING ITSELF TO

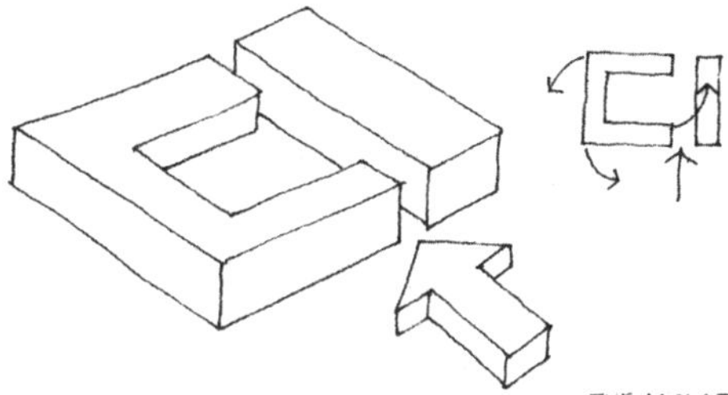

7.

THE ISOLATION OF ONE SIDE CAUSES A TENDENCY FOR THE OTHER THREE SIDES TO ROTATE.

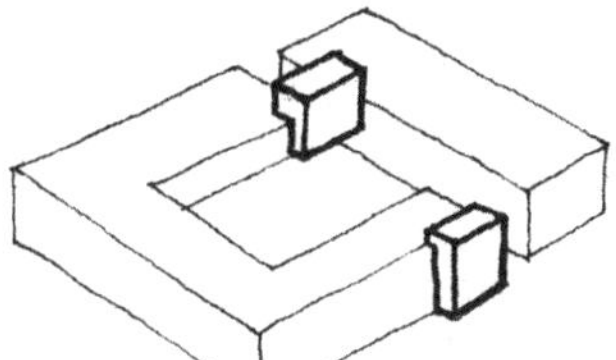

8.

PINNING OF VOLUMETRIC ROTATION BY JEWEL ROOM AND LIBRARY

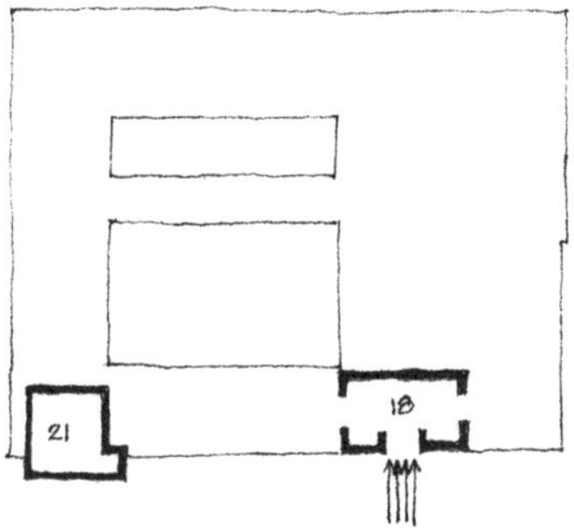

9.

SPIRAL SYSTEM BEGINNING ON PERIPHERY WOULD NOT ACKNOWLEDGE DISTORTION OF GENERIC FORM

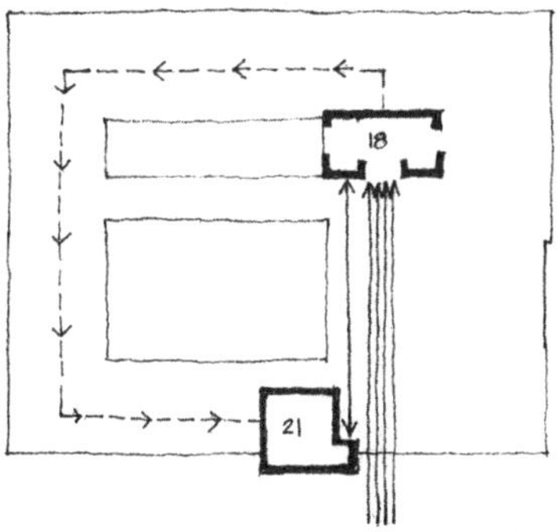

10.

JEWEL ROOM PUSHED TO REAR BY ENTRY VECTOR. LIBRARY PULLED TOWARDS ENTRY, PROVIDING TERMINATION OF SPIRAL.

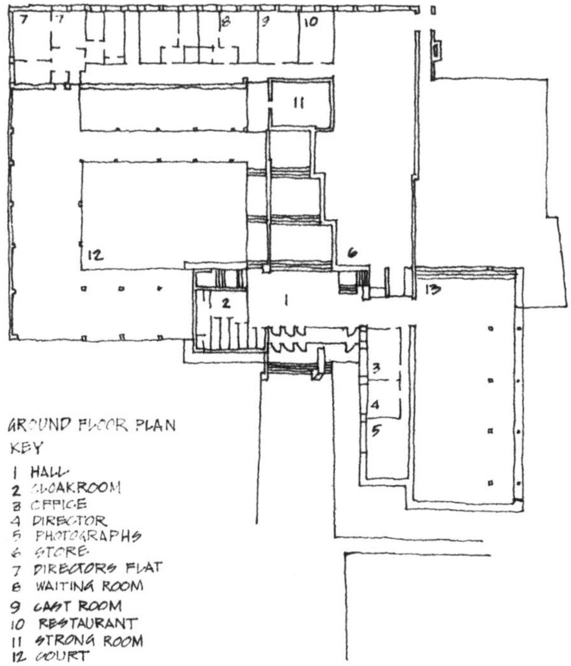

GROUND FLOOR PLAN

KEY

1 HALL
2 CLOAKROOM
3 OFFICE
4 DIRECTOR
5 PHOTOGRAPHS
6 STORE
7 DIRECTORS FLAT
8 WAITING ROOM
9 CAST ROOM
10 RESTAURANT
11 STRONG ROOM
12 COURT

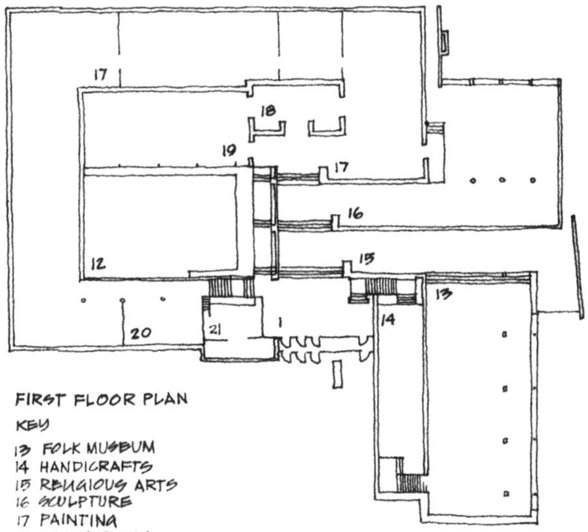

FIRST FLOOR PLAN

KEY

13 FOLK MUSEUM
14 HANDICRAFTS
15 RELIGIOUS ARTS
16 SCULPTURE
17 PAINTING
18 JEWEL ROOM
19 SEMINAR ROOM
20 DRAWINGS
21 LIBRARY

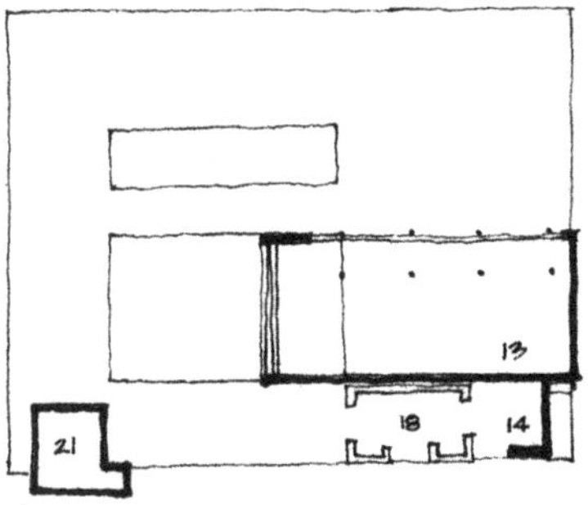

11.

GENERIC CONDITION OF FOLK MUSEUM AND HANDICRAFTS GALLERY: 13 AND 14.

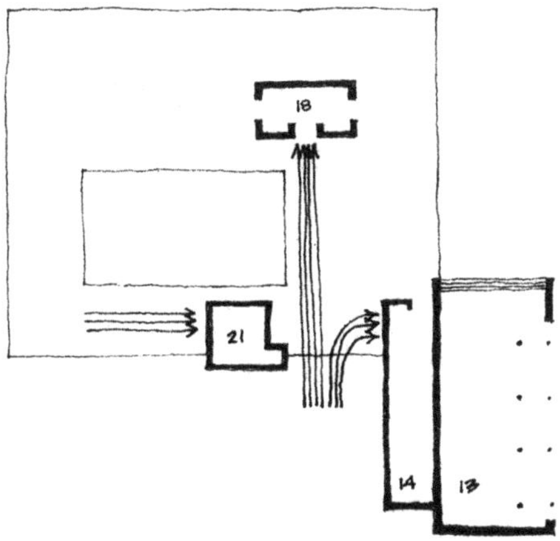

12.

DISTORTION OF 13 AND 14 BY ENTRY VECTOR.

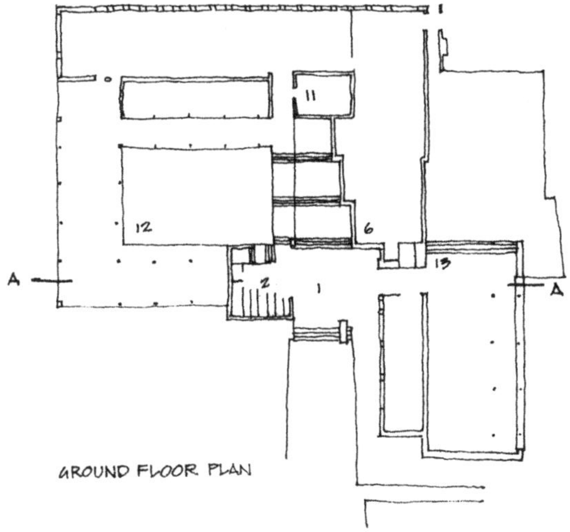

GROUND FLOOR PLAN

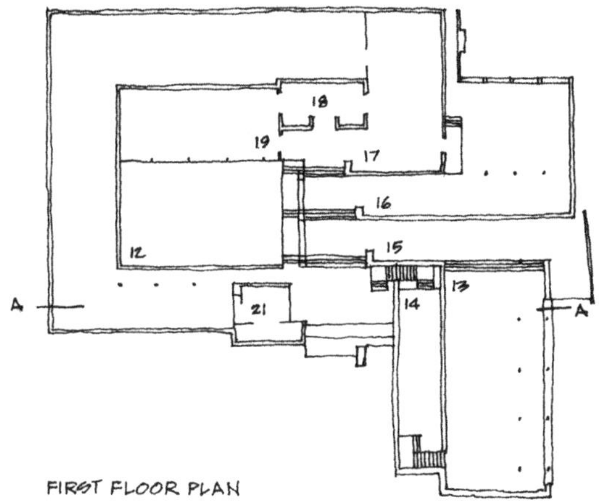

FIRST FLOOR PLAN

BE THOUGHT OF AS ROTATING; THIS VOLUMETRIC ROTATION BEING SEEN IN CONFLICT WITH THE SPIRAL MOVEMENT SYSTEM.[7] SOME KIND OF PINNING MUST BE PROVIDED BOTH TO PREVENT THE VOLUMETRIC MOVEMENT, AND TO RETAIN THE SPIRAL: INITIALLY THE JEWEL ROOM ,8, AND THE LIBRARY,21, CAN BE SEEN AS PINNING THIS TENDENCY TO ROTATE. IN THE SECOND CASE, IF THE SPIRAL BEGAN IN THE PERIPHERY IT WOULD NOT ACKNOWLEDGE THE DISTORTION OF THE GENERIC STATE BY THE EXTERNAL VECTOR.[9] THEREFORE THE DIRECTIONAL FORCE CAN BE THOUGHT OF AS ENTERING THE GENERIC FORM PUSHING THE JEWEL ROOM,18, WHICH IS LOCATED ON THE EXTERIOR OF THE GENERIC FORM, TO THE REAR. AT THE SAME TIME THIS AXIS IS BLUNTED BY THE CROSS CUTTING OF THE VOLUMETRIC PLANES 15, 16 AND 17, THESE BEING READ AS A REMNANT OF THE DEFLECTED SPIRAL, AND TERMINATED BY THE JEWEL ROOM. NOW THE SPIRAL CAN BE SEEN AS BEGINNING AT THE JEWEL ROOM AND MOVING IN A COUNTER CLOCKWISE DIRECTION AROUND THE CENTRAL COURT WHICH ACTS AS A PIVOT FOR THIS MOVEMENT; THE COURT ITSELF HAVING BEEN DISLOCATED BY THE ENTRY VECTOR. THE SPIRAL IS TERMINATED BY THE LIBRARY, 21, WHICH ITSELF HAS BEEN DISLOCATED FROM ITS CORNER LOCATION BY THE THRUST OF THE ENTRY VECTOR.[10] THUS, AS THE JEWEL ROOM IS PUSHED TO THE REAR THE LIBRARY IS PULLED TOWARDS THE ENTRY, IMPLYING A CONCEPTUAL LINK TO THESE ELEMENTS. THE SPECIFIC GRAMMAR INVOLVING THESE TWO ELEMENTS CAN BE SEEN AS SIMILAR TO THE GRAMMAR EMPLOYED IN THE PINNING ELEMENTS AT SAYNATSALO. THE ENTRY VECTOR ALSO CAUSES THE FOLK MUSEUM,13, AND THE HANDICRAFT EXIBITION GALLERY ,14, TO BE DISLOCATED FROM THE GENERIC COURT.[11,12] THE ASSUMPTION OF THE CORNER LOCATION OF THE LIBRARY IN THE GENERAL STATE IS GIVEN FURTHER CREDENCE WHEN THE END RELATIONSHIP OF THE FOLK AND HANDICRAFT GALLERIES IS SEEN, BOTH CONDITIONS PROVIDE A SIMILAR ARTICULATION TO THE CORNERS OF THE GENERIC CONDITION. IN ADDITON, THE STEPPING RELATIONSHIP IN THE END CONDITION OF ,13, AND

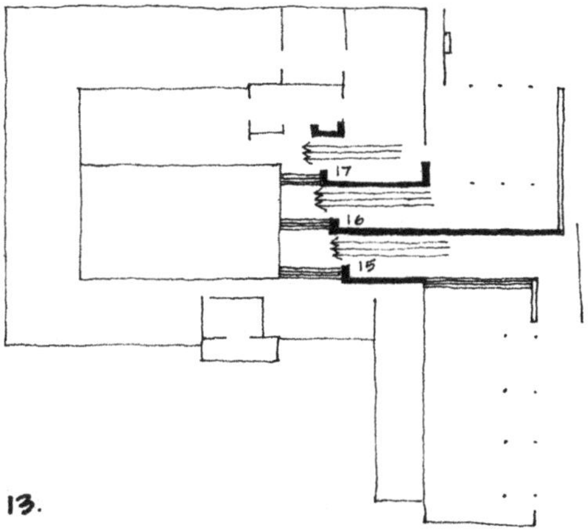

13.

PERCEPTUAL AMBIGUITY IN ECHELONING SERIES 15, 16, 17

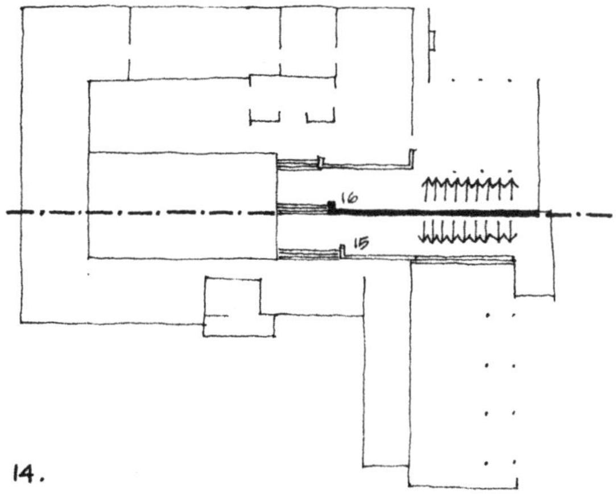

14.

READ AS GROUPED IN OPPOSITE DIRECTIONS ABOUT THE SHARED SURFACE OF 15 AND 16

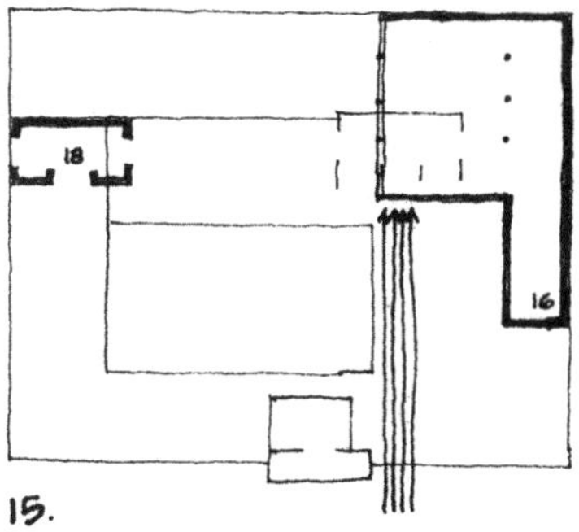

15.

THE SCULPTURE GALLERY SEEN AS A LAYER OF THE GENERIC FORM

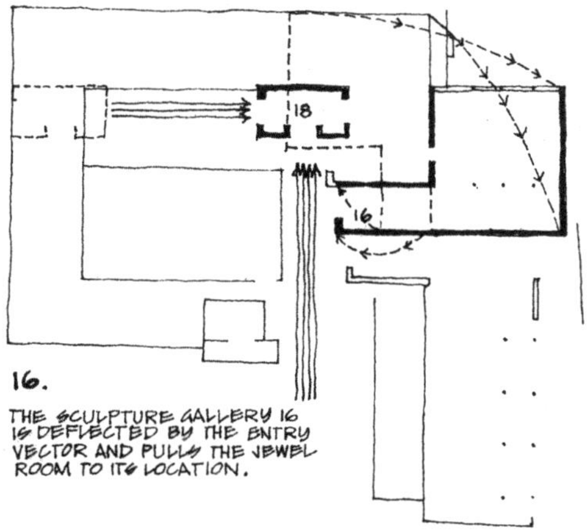

16.

THE SCULPTURE GALLERY 16 IS DEFLECTED BY THE ENTRY VECTOR AND PULLS THE JEWEL ROOM TO ITS LOCATION.

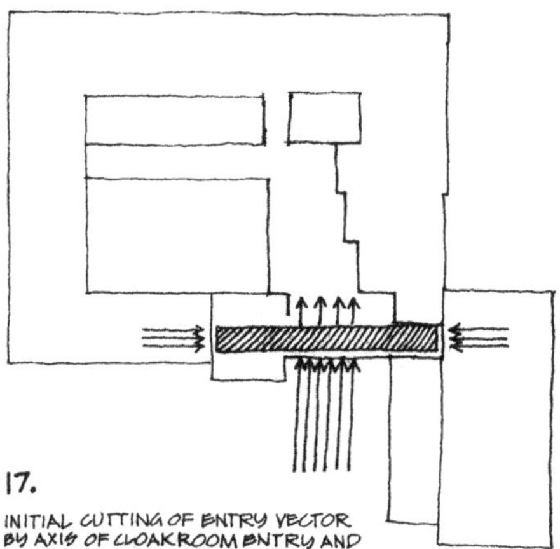

17.

INITIAL CUTTING OF ENTRY VECTOR BY AXIS OF CLOAKROOM ENTRY AND FOLK MUSEUM ENTRY

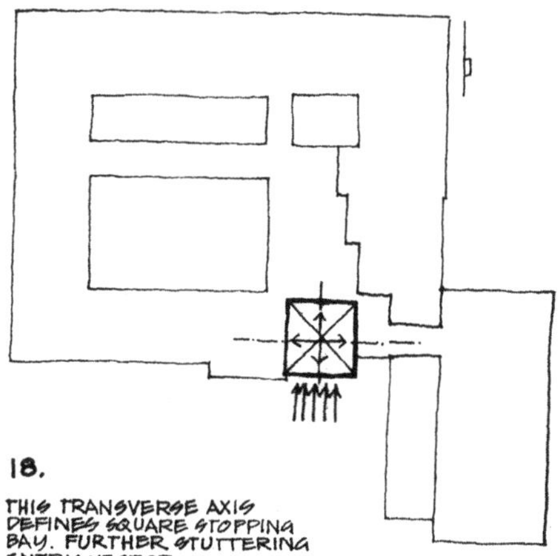

18.

THIS TRANSVERSE AXIS DEFINES SQUARE STOPPING BAY. FURTHER STUTTERING ENTRY VECTOR.

14, provides a perceptual preparation for the stepping of the volumetric planes 15 16 and 17. There is a complex distortion of the generic state, which produces a perceptual ambiguity in the specific form, for not only do they
14
read as an echeloning series (15) (16) and (17) but also they are seen as grouped in defferent directions about the shared surface of (15) and (16) which is also the central axis of the court. Initially it is possible to read the religious art gallery (15) as having been deflected from its generic location, with the turning of blocks (13) and (14). The sculpture gallery (16) can be read as a layer of the upper right hand corner which has been deflected by the entry pressure. It is also possible to see the jewel room now in a second context; as having been pulled from the upper left hand corner, by the deflection of volume (16), to its location in the specific form. Again this specific grammatical resolution can be compared with the dislocation of the tower block at Saynatsalo.

The location of Volumes (15) (16) and (17) in the specific form are part of a secondary order, a volumetric echelon. This voluumetric echelon is part of a sequence of transverse planes which act to blunt the entry vector. Initially this vector is cut by the transverse axis which is defined by the entry of the cloakroom on one side, and the folk museum on the other. In addition this transverse cut can be seen as the central axis of the square stopping bay of the vestibule. The articulation ot the vestibule and museum proper by an opposite pair of stairs, defines a second volumetric plane which provides a further stuttering of the entry axis. Following this is the echelon series defined by four similar surfaces; the right hand front wall volume (18) being read as a part of

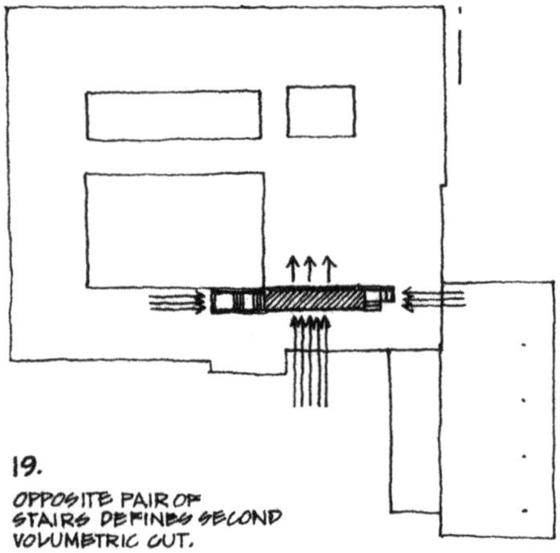

19.

OPPOSITE PAIR OF STAIRS DEFINES SECOND VOLUMETRIC CUT.

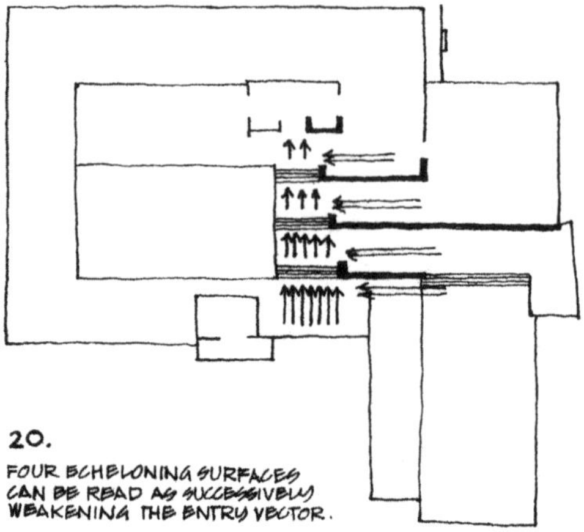

20.

FOUR ECHELONING SURFACES CAN BE READ AS SUCCESSIVELY WEAKENING THE ENTRY VECTOR.

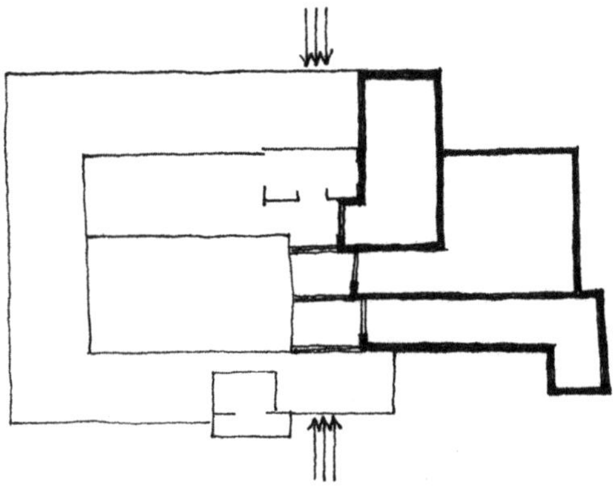

21.

THE GENERIC U-FORM BINDS THE SPECIFIC EXTRUSIONS.

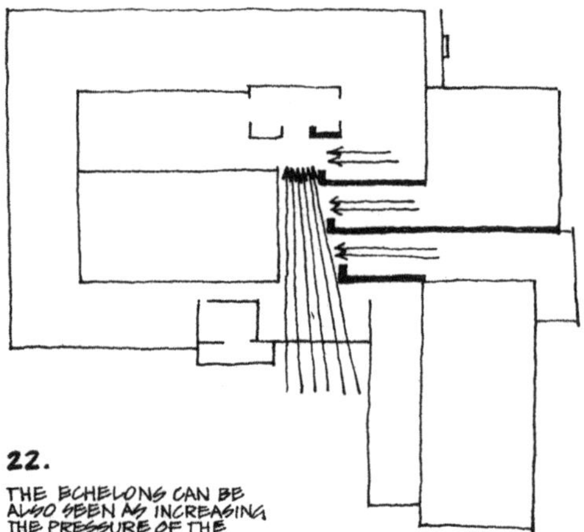

22.

THE ECHELONS CAN BE ALSO SEEN AS INCREASING THE PRESSURE OF THE ENTRY FORCE.

THIS SEQUENCE AS WELL AS TERMINTATING IT.[20] THERE IS A SUBTLE AMBIGUITY PRESENTED IN THE ECHELONING VOLUMES, FOR ALTHOUGH VOLUMES (15) AND (16) HAVE BEEN DISTORTED FROM THE GENERIC STATE, VOLUME (17) IS IN ITS GENERIC LOCATION; THE BLOCKS 15 AND 16 THUS READ IN THIS CONTEXT, AS HAVING BEEN DISLOCATED FROM THE THE COURT. CONSEQUENTLY THE TOPMOST GENERIC U-FORM CAN BE READ AS BINDING THESE EXTRUSIONS OF THE GENERIC FORM, PREVENTING THEM FROM BEING ENTIRELY DISLOCATED FROM THE TOTAL COMPLEX.[21] THE SPECIFIC ECHELON DEVELOPMENT ALSO PROVIDES A DUAL READING. IN THE FIRST CASE, IT CAN BE INTERPRETED AS WEAKENING THE ENTR VECTOR BY SUCCESSIVE TRANSVERSE CUTS. BUT IN THE SECOND CASE IT MAY BE THOUGHT OF AS INCREASING THE PRESSURE OF THE ENTRY MOVEMENT BY A COMPRESSIVE RHYTHM.[22] THE JEWEL ROOM NOW TAKES ON AN ADDED CONCEPTUAL IMPORTANCE. IT NOT ONLY BEGINS THE SPIRAL, AND TERMINATES THE ECHELON BUT IT ALSO MUST CONTAIN THE ENTRY DRIVE AND TIE IT TO THE MOVEMENT SPIRAL. THE RESULTANT SPECIFIC FORM SUBSTANTIATES BOTH INTERPRETATIONS. THE JEWEL ROOM VOLUME IS PUSHED THROUGH THE TOP PLANE OF THE GENERIC FORM ACKNOWLEDGING THE FORCE OF THE ENTRY VECTOR; THIS ADDED HEIGHT ALSO GIVING A PLUG LIKE QUALITY TO THIS VOLUME READING AS THE STARTING POINT OF THE SPIRAL

AALTO IN HIS SYSTEMIC DEVELOPMENT ACKNOWLEDGES THE HORIZONTAL ABSOLUTE IN A SIMILAR MANNER TO HIS SOLUTION OF THIS SYNTACTICAL REQUIREMENT AT SAYNATSALO. AGAIN, THE DEFORMATIONS OF THE SPECIFIC FORM IN THE VERTICAL COORDINATE ARE BALANCED ABOUT A STATED HORIZONTAL. IN THIS CASE, THE HORIZONTAL REFERENCE IS NOT THE COURT LEVEL, AS AT SAYNATSALO, BUT THE GROUND FLOOR ENTRY LEVEL.[23] THE VOLUMES (13) AND (14) BREAK THROUGH THE ROOF LEVEL OF THE GENERIC FORM. THIS ISS COMPENSATED AND BALANCED BY DEPRESSING THE LEVEL OF THE COURT, CREATING A

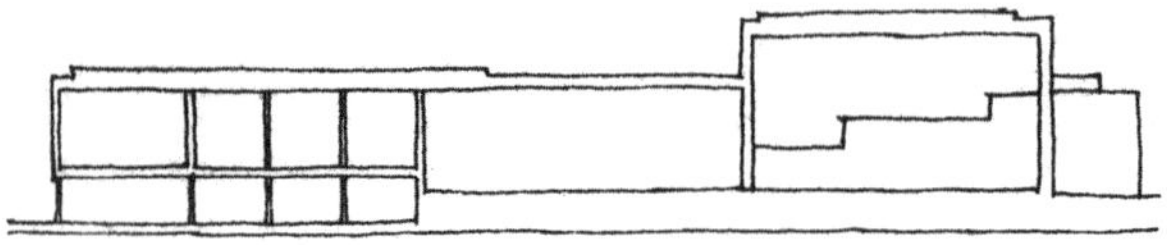

SECTION A-A

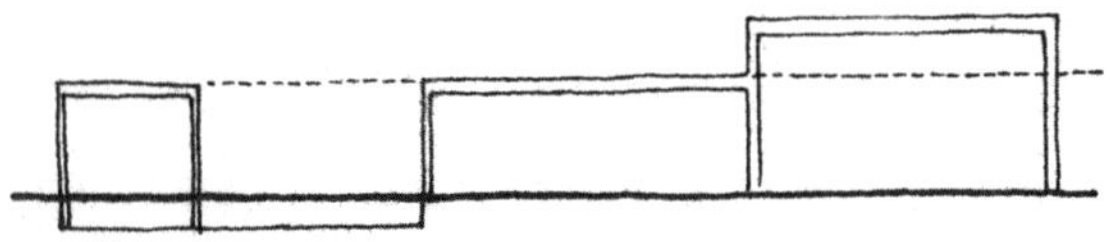

24.

POSITIVE-NEGATIVE EQUILIBRIUM ABOUT HORIZONTAL ABSOLUTE

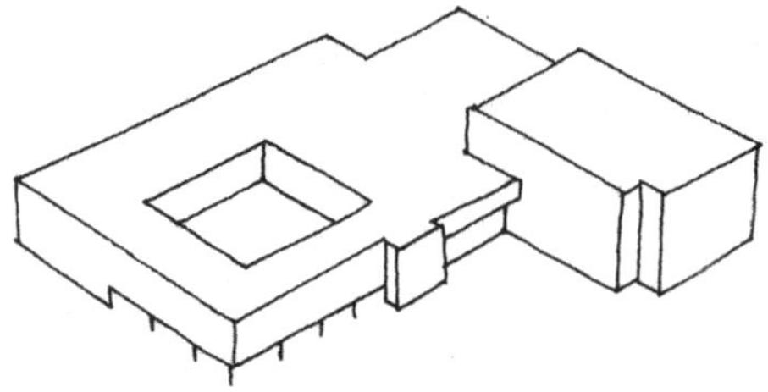

COMPETITION MODEL

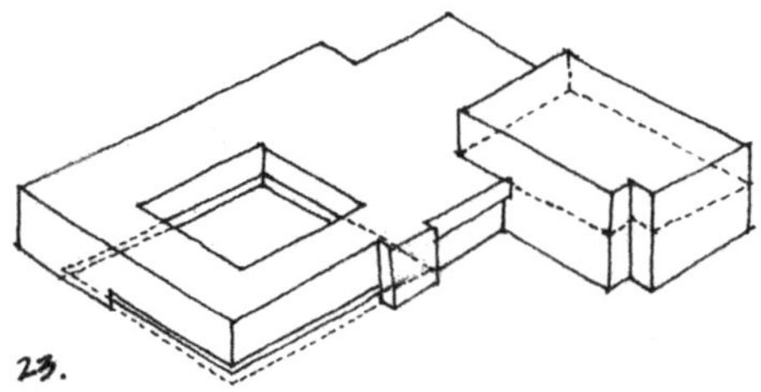

23.

GROUND FLOOR LEVEL IS HORIZONTAL ABSOLUTE COURT IS DEPRESSED FROM THIS. VOLUMES 13 AND 14 BREAK THROUGH ROOF LEVEL OF GENERIC FORM

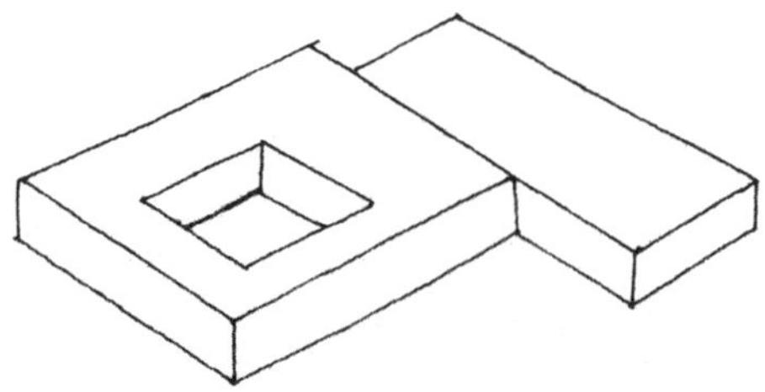

25.

POSSIBLE LINEAR READING TO EXTRUDED PART OF THE BUILDING, IN CONFLICT WITH CENTROIDAL FORM

POSITIVE-NEGATIVE EQUILIBRIUM ABOUT THE HORIZONTAL REFERENCE.[24] FUNCTIONALLY AND FORMALLY THIS SOLUTION HAS SEVERAL ADVANTAGES. FIRSTLY IT DEFINES THE SINGLE ENTRY ITO A CENTROIDAL FORM WHICH MIGHT OTHERWISE BE SEEN IS A RATHER ARBITRARY LOCATION. SECONDLY, IT PRESERVES THE READING OF THE CENTROIDAL FORM; IF THE BLOCK HAD NOT BEEN A TALLER ELEMENT, A LINEAR READING MIGHT HAVE BEEN GIVEN TO THE TOTAL EXTRUDED PART OF THE BUILDING.[25] THIRDLY, THE DEPRESSION OF THE COURT PROVIDES A MINOR ACCESS TO THE OFFICES WHICH CAN BE LOCATED BELOW THE MAIN BLOCK. THUS THE RESOLUTION OF A FORMAL SYNTACTICAL REQUIREMENT ALSO SERVES A FUNCTIONAL DEMAND

IT IS INTERESTING TO NOTE THAT THE SO CALLED 'ORGANIC' DEVELOPMENT OF AALTO'S WORK, THE TERM IMPLYING AN OPPOSITION TO ANY 'FORMAL' ORDER, CAN IN FACT BE ANALYSED AND UNDERSTOOD IN FORMAL TERMS. EVEN THOUGH THE VOCABULARY AND GRAMMAR USED BY AALTO IS DIFFERENT FROM THAT OF EITHER LE CORBUSIER OR TERRAGNI, THESE ELEMENTS ARE STILL REGULATED BY A FORMAL SYNTAX AND ORDERED BY A FORMAL SYSTEM. THE DEVELOPMENT OF ANY RATIONAL ORDER CAN INCORPORATE ANY SPECIFIC GRAMMAR. FOR IT IS IN THE SPECIFIC GRAMMAR EMPLOYED, THAT THE TO THE SYSTEMIC DEVELOPMENT CAN BE FOUND; THE SYSTEM MERELY MAKES THE ESSENCE OF THIS GRAMMAR – ITS GENERIC BASIS – COMPREHENSIBLE.

The two centroidal 'courtyard' schemes by Giuseppe Terragni provide a useful basis for recording the development of a formal system, organised in terms of the grammar and syntax developed in the preceding chapters. Both of these schemes develop from programmatic requirements which are essentially centroidal. In the case of the Casa del Fascio the centroidal form is seen as a termination of a linear axis while in the Asilo Infantile, the centroidal form is developed parallel to the external axis. In the former case where the internal and external requirements are in conflict the external vectors play an important part in the distortion of the generic antecedant to produce the specific form, while in the latter where there is no conflict, it is a combination of internal and external vectors that produce the distortion. The courtyard of the Casa del Fascio, because of this external-internal conflict which requires formal resolution, can be seen as having evolved from both formal and functional demands. In this sense, the neutrality of the external axis in relation to the internal requirements of the Asilo Infantile does not appreciably affect the conceptual development of the court; hence the categorisation of this court as a 'functional' response to the given conditions. In each example it is important to recognise and understand the distortions from the generic, unactivated state and their ordering in the specific system chosen.

Characteristic of Terragni's systemic development in this situation is his use of a 'mass'-surface dialectic. He is concerned with the internal volumetric ordering as a secondary system and then only as it relates to the primary 'mass-surface' system. His systems seem to serve more as an ordering of surfaces than an ordering of volumes, and he is concerned with mass only in its opposit-

-ION TO SURFACE. HE ORDERS THIS VOCABULARY BY INVESTING EACH ELEMENT WITH SEVERAL POSSIBLE READINGS DESIGNED TO PRODUCE, IN MANY INSTANCES, THE PURPOSEFUL AMBIGUITY OF FIGURE-GROUND RELATIONSHIPS. FOR EXAMPLE THE CASA DEL FASCIO CAN BE READ EITHER AS A SOLID BLOCK THAT HAS BEEN CUT AWAY OR AS A SERIES OF PLANES THAT HAVE BEEN PLACED TOGETHER MUCH AS A DECK OF CARDS. THESE FORMAL DEVICES SEEM TO ORIGINATE FROM AN ACADEMIC, ALMOST ASCETIC, STUDY OF LE CORBUSIER'S USE OF THE 'MASS-SURFACE' DIALECTIC. BUT WHEREAS LE CORBUSIER INITIALLY STATES THE GRID AND THEN PLAYS SURFACE OR MASS AS A FOIL TO IT, TERRAGNI OFTEN FUSES THE TWO TO ACHIEVE THE DESIRED AMBIGUITY. HE IS OBTRUSIVELY AWARE OF THE SYNTAX GOVERNING EACH PARTICULAR ASPECT OF THE BUILDING AND THE NEED TO INCORPORATE THE ACKNOWLEDGEMENTS OF THIS SYNTAX INTO A SYSTEM. IN THE CASA DEL FASCIO EACH COORDINATE OF THE GRID IS EXPRESSED BY A TRIPARTITE (BEGINNING-MIDDLE-END) COMPOSITION. THE DISTORTIONS IN BOTH BUILDINGS TO BE ANALYSED ARE RELATED TO A DOMINANT VERTICAL PLANE OF REFERENCE THUS ACKNOWLEDGING THE SYNTACTICAL REQUIREMENT OF SINGLE ENTRY INTO A GENERIC CENTROIDAL FORM. A COURTYARD SCHEME ALSO DEMANDS A HORIZONTAL REFERENCE, WHICH IN BOTH CASES IS CLEARLY STATED BY TERRAGNI. IN THIS SENSE HIS SYSTEMIC DEVELOPMENT AND THE ACKNOWLEDGEMENT OF SYNTACTICAL REQUIREMENTS IS PERHAPS THE MOST ELABORATED USED BY THE FOUR ARCHITECTS DISCUSSED, THEREBY PROVIDING EXCELLENT EMPIRICAL PRECEDENTS FOR THIS THESIS.

CASA DEL FASCIO

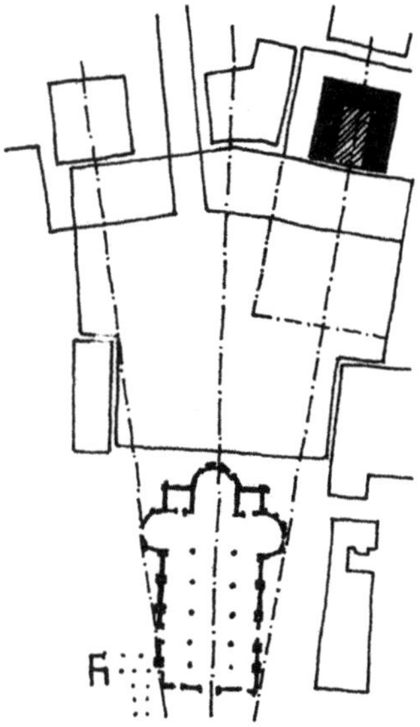

1.

PROPOSED SITE PLAN SHOWING EXTERNAL VECTORS.

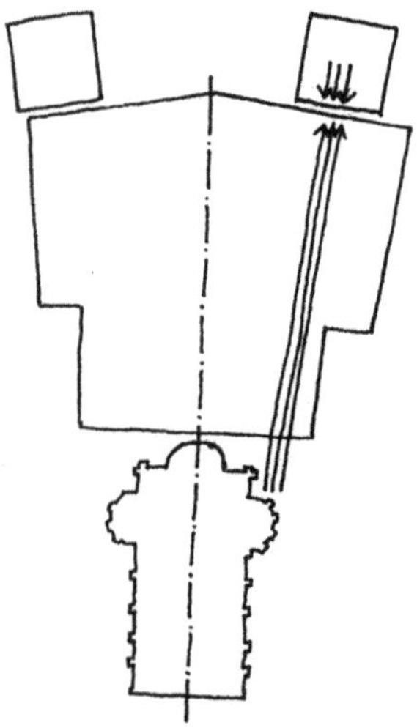

2.

EXTERNAL VECTOR MUST BE ACKNOWLEDGED IN SPECIFIC FORM

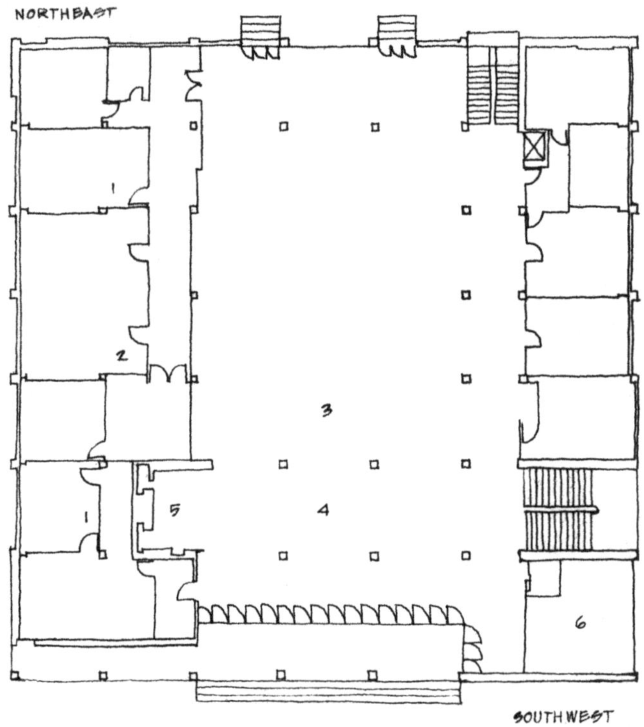

GROUND FLOOR PLAN

KEY

1 - OFFICES
2 - COMMITTEE ROOM
3 - COURT
4 - FOYER
5 - MEMORIAL ALTAR
6 - CARETAKER

THE ESSENCE OF THE FORMAL SYSTEM INVOKED IN THE CASA DEL FASCIO IS THE EXPRESSION OF A RECONCILIATION BETWEEN A CENTROIDAL PLAN AND A LINEAR SITE. THE CENTROIDAL FORM IS EVOLVED FROM THE PARTICULAR FUNCTIONS DEMANDED BY THE PROGRAMME: TO PROVIDE FOR A SERIES OF OFFICES RELATING TO A CENTRAL COURT. IN ITS GENERIC STATE THIS FORM WOULD IMPLY EQUAL ACCESS ON ALL SIDES. HOWEVER, THE INTERNAL ORGANISATION ONLY REQUIRES ONE MAJOR MEANS OF ACCESS, AND THAT DIRECTLY RELATED TO THE PIAZZA TO THE SW OF THE SITE. THIS PROVIDES THE INITIAL LINK WITH THE AXIS RUNNING FROM THE CATHEDRAL THROUGH THE PIAZZA TO THE BUILDING. INITIALLY THIS VECTOR MUST BE ACKNOWLEDGED IN THE SPECIFIC FORM, AND AT THE SAME TIME BLUNTED BY THIS FORM.[2] THEREFORE IT WAS NECESSARY FOR THE SYSTEM WHILE DENYING ACCESS ON THE THREE REMAINING SIDES; TO RECOGNISE ON THE ONE HAND, THE SINGLE NTRY AND ON THE OTHER, A DELICATE BALANCE BETWEEN THE CENTROIDAL REQUIREMENTS IF THE BUILDING AND THE LINEAR REQUIREMENTS OF THE SITE. A SYSTEM IS DEVELOPED BASED ON THESE SYNTACTICAL REQUIREMENTS, WHICH INVESTS EACH ELEMENT WITH A DUAL READING: A PURPOSEFUL AMBIGUITY EXTERNALLY OF MASS, REPRESENTING THE CENTROIDAL ASPECTS OF THE GENERIC FORM, AND SURFACE, REPRESENTING THE LINEAR DEFORMATION OF THIS FORM. THIS SYSTEM AND THE RESULTANT DISTORTIONS ARE DERIVED FROM THE SUPPOSITION THAT THE GENERIC ANTECEDENT IS A VOLUMETRIC CUBE.

THE 'COURTYARD' IS EVOLVED FROM BOTH FUNCTIONAL AND FORMAL CONSIDERATIONS; THE CENTRAL VOLUME IS OBVIOUSLY INTENDED FOR THE DEPLOYMENT OF MARCHING FORMATIONS WHICH WOULD THEN PASS THROUGH THE NINETEEN ENTRY DOORS INTO THE PIAZZA. THIS OURTYARD THEREFORE HAS AN INTRINSIC CENTRAL 'CORE' RELATIONSHIP TO THE SMALLER

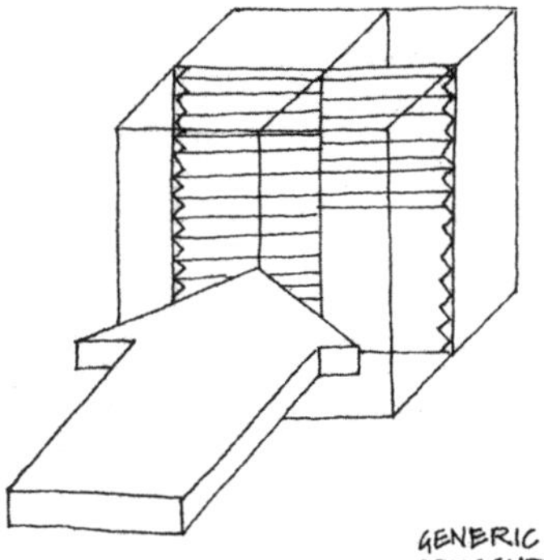

3.

GENERIC CUBE: FOUR EQUAL SIDES
PRESSURE OF LONGITUDINAL AXIS

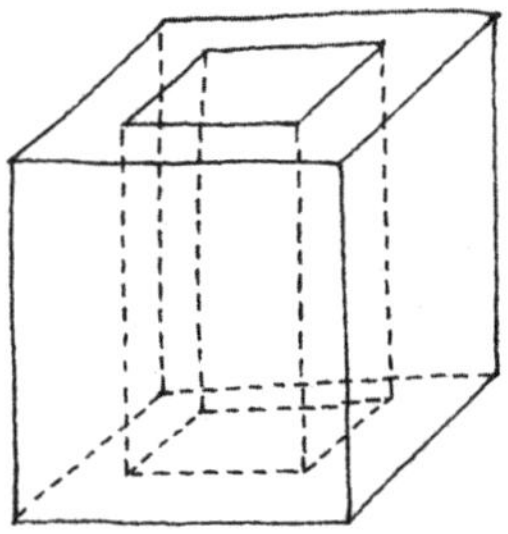

4.

HOLLOWING OUT OF CENTROIDAL FORM TO PROVIDE FOR PROGRAMMATIC REQUIREMENTS

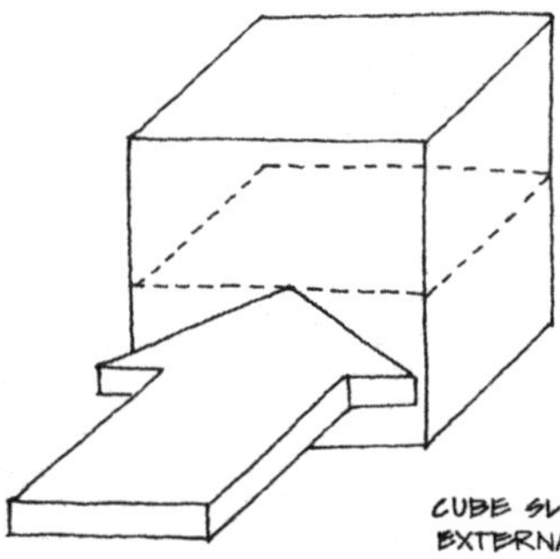

5.

CUBE SLICED IN HALF BY EXTERNAL VECTOR

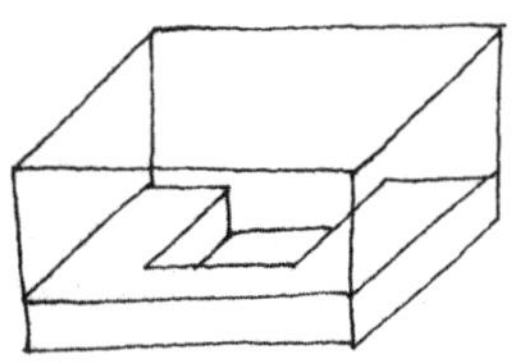

6.

DISLOCATION OF COURT TO REAR

OFFICE VOLUMES. HOWEVER, THE CONCEPTUAL ASPECTS OF THIS MAJOR VOLUME MUST ALSO BE CONSIDERED. IN FUNCTIONAL TERMS, THE COURT ONLY REQUIRES A ONE STORY ELEVATION SINCE ITS SPECIFIC HEIGHT IS NOT FIXED BY A PROGRAMMATIC REQUIREMENT. THEREFORE THE SPECIFIC VERTICAL DIMENSION MUST RESULT FOR CONCEPTUAL REASONS: FIRST THAT THE COURT IS THE CONTROL AREA AND THEREFORE A MAJOR VOLUME; AND SECOND THAT THIS DIMENSION RELATES TO A TOTAL SYSTEM OF CUBE, AND HALF CUBE DIMENSIONS, REPRESENTING THE DISTORTION FROM A GENERIC CUBE TO THE SPECIFIC FORM OF A HALF-CUBE.

TWO MAJOR DEFORMATIONS OF THE GENERIC FORM ARE INITIALLY APPARENT.[3] THE FIRST, ASSUMING A VOLUMETRIC CUBE WHICH IS HOLLOWED OUT IN THE CENTRE,[4] IS THE SLICING OF THIS CUBE IN HALF WHICH PRODUCES A LINEAR FORM IN THE ORTHOGONAL AND FRONTAL COORDINATES WHILE STILL PRESERVING THE CENTROIDAL 'SQUARE' IN THE HORIZONTAL PLANE.[5] THE SECOND, IS THE DISLOCATION OF THE 'CENTRAL' COURT TO ITS POSITION IN THE REAR OF THE BUILDING.[6] BOTH OF THESE DEFORMATIONS THUS ACKNOWLEDGE THE THRUST OF THE EXTERNAL VECTOR.

IN THE SYSTEMIC DEVELOPMENT THE ENTRY MUST SERVE A DUAL FUNCTION AND ACKNOWLEDGE THE PERTINENT SYNTAX OF EACH PART. FIRSTLY IT MUST PROVIDE THE TRANSITION TO A CENTROIDAL FORM ON ONE SIDE ONLY AND SECONDLY STUTTER THE THRUST OF THE LONGITUDINAL EXTERNAL AXIS. THE PROBLEM OF PROVIDING BOTH THIS TRANSITION AND INITIAL STOP IS RESOLVED BY THE REPEATED USE OF TWO THEMES IN THE SYSTEMIC DEVELOPMENT. THE FIRST IS THE ASSUMPTION THAT AN EXTERNAL READING OF MASS PROVIDES AN ACKNOWLEDGEMENT OF THE ORIGINAL CENTROIDAL CUBE: IN OTHER WORDS, A SOLID BLOCK PRESUPPOSING A CENTRAL POINT THAT HAS BEEN ACTIVATED BY THE VECTORS

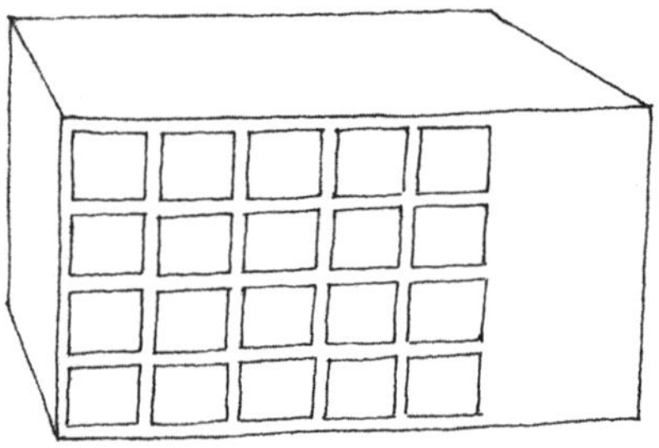

7.

MASS READING ACKNOWLEDGES CENTROIDAL ASPECTS OF CUBE

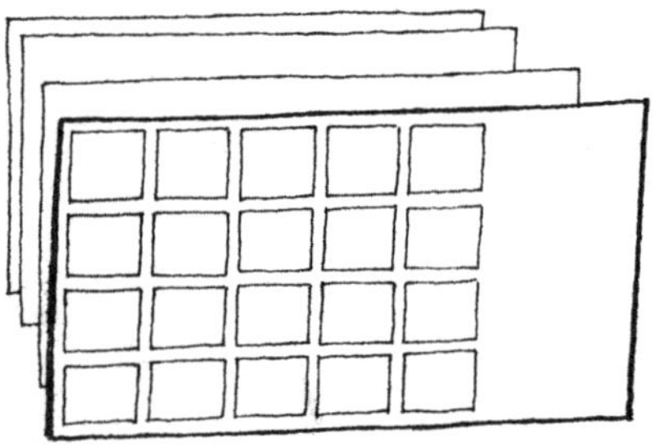

8.

A SERIES OF VOLUMETRIC TRANSVERSE SLICES ACROSS THE EXTERNAL VECTOR

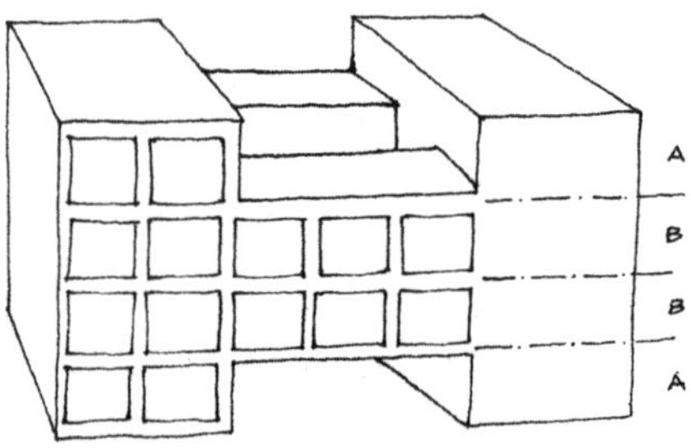

9.

A FRONTAL H-READING

OF THE CENTROIDAL REQUIREMENT.[7] THE SECOND IS THE ASSUMPTION THAT THIS CUBE CAN BE READ AS A SERIES OF VOLUMETRIC PLANES CUTTING IN A TRANSVERSE DIRECTION ACROSS THE EXTERNAL AXIS.[8] THEREFORE, THE FRONT AND REAR FACADES ARE EXPRESSED AS 'SURFACES' AT RIGHT ANGLES TO THE LONGITUDINAL AXIS, WHILE THE TWO SIDE FACADES MUST ACKNOWLEDGE THE EXISTENCE OF THE SEQUENCE OF VOLUMETRIC PLANES. AT THE SAME TIME ALL FACADES MUST ALSO BE EXPRESSIVE OF THE GENERIC CENTROIDAL 'MASS'. THUS THE SURFACES CAN BE READ AS THE DISTORTIONS OF THE GENERIC MASS CAUSED BY THE FORCE OF THE EXTERNAL VECTOR.

THE GENERIC 'MASS' IS FIRST HOLLOWED TO ACKNOWLEDGE THE CENTRAL COURT, AND THE RESULTANT NEGATIVE VOLUME IS THEN DISLOCATED TO THE REAR BY THR ENTRY VECTOR, PRODUCING A SPECIFIC U-FORM. THE FRONTAL PLANE OF THE U-FORM THEN ACTS AS AN INITIAL BLOCK TO THE AXIAL THRUST, AS WELL AS PROVIDING A SURFACE OF REFERENCE FOR THE VOLUMETRIC ORDER. ON THE FIRST AND SECOND FLOORS THE COMPLETE EN-CIRCLEMENT OF THE COURT IS RESTORED, WHILE THE THIRD FLOOR AGAIN ACKNOWLEDGES THE U-FORM. THIS RESULTS IN THE FRONTAL READING OF AN H-FORM OR AN A-B-B-A RELATIONSHIP OF HORIZONTAL LEVELS.[9] IN BOTH THE EARLY DESIGN AND THE FINAL BUILDING THE H-READING WAS EMPHASISED BY A HORIZONTAL BANDING OF THE FENEST-RATION ON THE MIDDLE TWO FLOORS OF THE SOUTH-WEST FACADE. IT IS INTERESTING TO NOTE THAT THE AXIAL PRESSURE ON THE ORIGINAL MASS IS SEEN IN THE HORIZONTAL COORDINATE ON THE GROUND AND THIRD FLOORS WHILE THE CENTROIDAL NATURE OF THE HOLLOWED OUT BLOCK IS PRESERVED ON THE FIRST AND SECOND FLOORS.

THE GROUND FLOOR PLAN INITIALLY REVEALS THESE DISTORTIONS IN THE GENERIC FORM CAUSED BY THE EXTERNAL AXIS; THE FIRST TRANSVERSE ENTRY BAY IS WIDENED TO

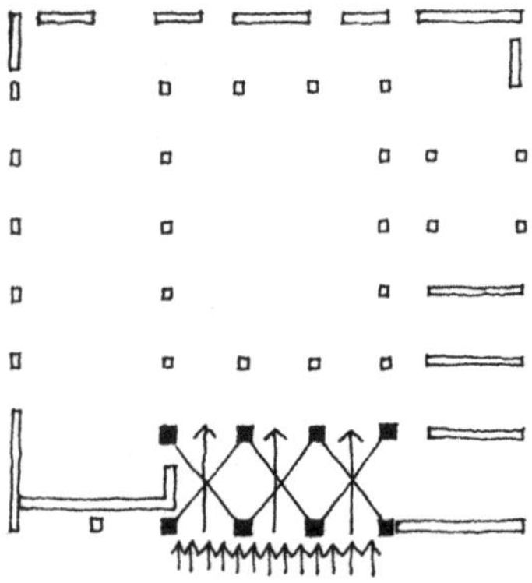

ELONGATION OF ENTRY BAYS **10.**

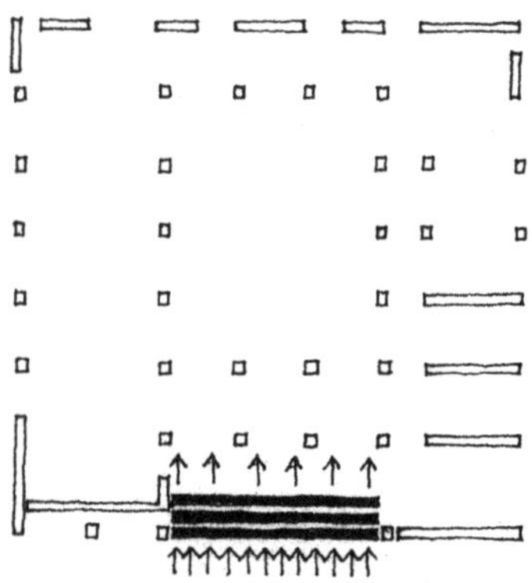

TRANSVERSE VOLUMETRIC PLANES CUTTING EXTERNAL AXIS **11.**

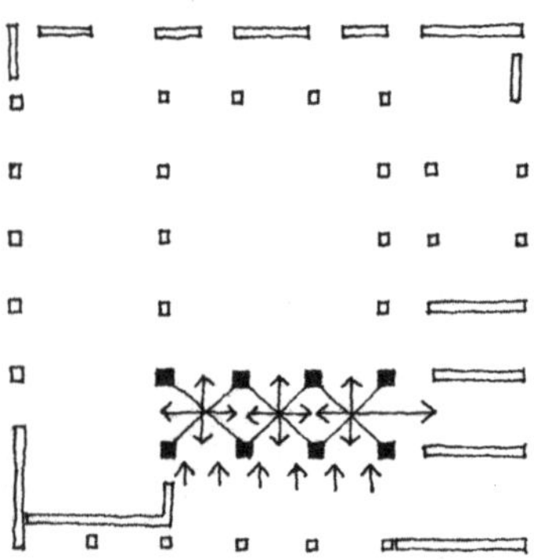

SQUARE STOPPING BAYS **12.**

EMPHASIZE THE INITIAL CUTTING OF THE MAJOR AXIS,[10] TO ACCOMMODATE THE NUMBER OF SECONDARY CUTTINGS THAT ARE EFFECTED WITHIN THIS BAY,[11] AND TO ACKNOWLEDGE THE LINEAR THRUST WHICH CAUSES THE COURT TO BE DISLOCATED TO THE REAR BY THE ELONGATION OF THE INDIVIDUAL BAYS.

THE SYNTACTICAL REQUIREMENTS OF SINGLE ENTRY INTO A CENTROIDAL FORM ARE ALSO ACKNOWLEDGED IN THE GROUND FLOOR PLAN BY DEVELOPING A SERIES OF TRANSVERSE VOLUMETRIC PLANES TENSIONED IN REFERENCE TO THE DOMINANT ENTRY FACADE. THIS THEN PROVIDES A SECONDARY LINEAR SYSTEM, WHICH WHEN SEEN AS A CONNECTION TO THE EXTERNAL MOVEMENT, CAN BE THOUGHT OF AS AN APPLICATION OF THE SYNTAX GOVERNING SINGLE ENTRY INTO A CENTROIDAL FORM. THE FIRST TRANSVERSE SLICE IS THE PLANE OF THE STRUCTURE. THE SECOND PLANE IS DEFINED BY THE SETBACK OF THE LEFT HAND WALL AND THE THIRD PLANE IS THE RECESSED LINE OF ENTRY DOORS. ALL OF THESE TRANSVERSE LAYERS TEND TO DIFFUSE AND STUTTER THE FORCE OF THE ENTRY VECTOR WHILE EASING MOVEMENT INTO THE CUBE. THIS SYSTEM OF TRANSVERSE VOLUMETRIC LAYERS IS SIMILAR TO THAT USED BY LE CORBUSIER AT GARCHES. IN BOTH CASES THE SYSTEM IS TENSIONED FROM A DOMINANT FRONTAL REFERENCE, WHICH ALSO PROVIDES A CONCEPTUAL TERMINATION OF AN EXTERNAL AXIS. IF THE PLANAR SYSTEM HAD NOT BEEN DEVELOPED THE SYNTACTICAL RESOLUTION OF A SINGLE ENTRY INTO A CENTROIDAL FORM WOULD HAVE BEEN DIFFICULT. THE SYSTEM OF TRANSVERSE PLANES GRADUALLY EXPANDS AS IT MOVES FRON THE DOMINANT SURFACE OF REFERENCE TO THE FINAL PLANE OF THE ENTRY SERIES. THIS LAST VOLUMETRIC SLOT ACTS AS A STOPPING POINT AND A TURNING FOR THE CONTROL OF MOVEMENT TO THE MAIN VERTICAL CIRCULATION.[12] HERE THE THREE SQUARE BAYS PROVIDE A REDUCTION OF PRESSURE ALLOWING MOVEMENT TO TAKE PLACE IN ANY DIRECTION. THE CROSS AXIS OF THE STAIR IS ACCENTUATED BY THE THREE SQUARE BAYS, AND IS TERMINATED BY THE MEMORIAL ALTAR WHICH PROVIDES A CUSHION ABSORB-

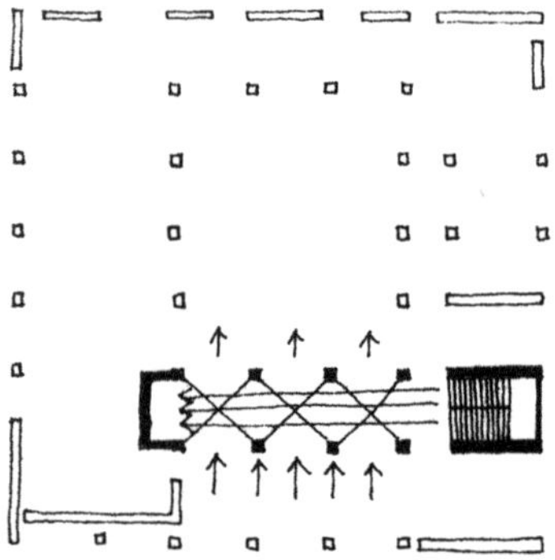

13.

CROSS AXIS OF STAIR IS ACCENTUATED BY SQUARE BAYS AND IS TERMINATED BY MEMORIAL ALTAR WHICH ABSORBS PRESSURE OF MOVEMENT SYSTEM.

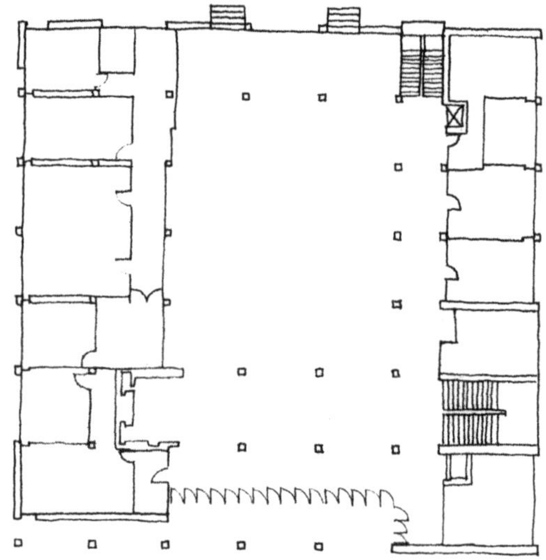

15.

FINAL SCHEME:
DOORS EXTENDED ACROSS FACADE
MINOR DOORS MOVED TO A TRANSVERSE LOCATION

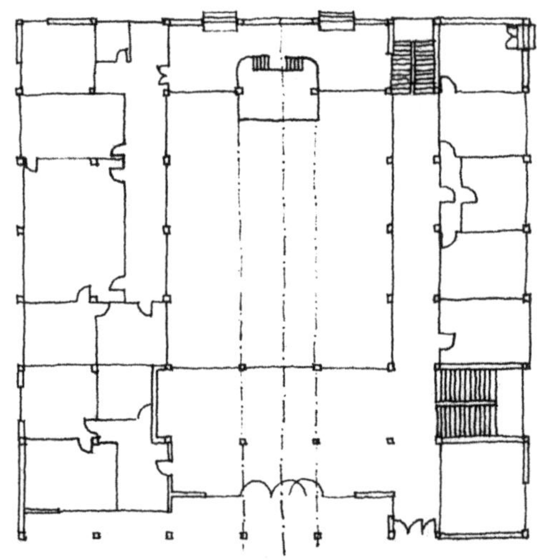

14.

EARLY SCHEME
LONGITUDINAL AXIS EXCESSIVELY DOMINANT

-ING THE PRESSURE AT THE END OF THE MOVEMENT SYSTEM.[13] AT THIS POINT IT IS INTERESTING TO RETURN TO AN EARLIER PLAN TO NOTE THE CHANGES THAT HAVE CLARIFIED THE DEVELOPMENT OF THE TOTAL SYSTEM. IN THE EARLIER VERSION THE LONGITUDINAL AXIS CAN BE SEEN AS EXCESSIVELY DOMINANT BY VIRTUE OF THE CONCENTRATION OF ENTRY DOORS IN THE CENTRAL BAY, AND THE TYING THROUGH OF THIS BAY ALONG THE AXIS TO A RAISED PODIUM AT THE REAR OF THE COURT.[14] THE EXTENSION OF THE ENTRY DOORS ACROSS THE FACADE, WITH A CORRESPONDING INCREASE IN THEIR NUMBER SEEMS TO CLARIFY PERCEPTUALLY THEIR RELATIONSHIP TO THE THREE 'STOPPING' BAYS IN THE SECONDARY MOVEMENT SYSTEM.[15] THIS MOVEMENT SYSTEM IS ALSO EMPHASISED BY THE DEEPENING OF THE MEMORIAL ALTAR IN THE FINAL SCHEME, TO ACKNOWLEDGE THE PRESSURE OF THE MAIN STAIR AXIS.[15] THE DOORS WHICH CONNECT THE CIRCULATION SLOT TO THE STAIR IN THE REAR ARE MOVED FROM THEIR ORIGINAL POSITION ON THE FRONT FACADE TO A TRANSVERSE LOCATION.[15] THIS HELPS TO CONCEPTUALLY PIN THE TRANSVERSE PLANES BY ALLOWING THE READING OF A 'PEG' THROUGH TO THE REAR STAIRS, AS WELL AS CREATING A TRANSVERSE PRESSURE THAT FORCES THE MASS OF THE LEFT HAND PORTION OF THE FACADE TO ITS PRESENT LOCATION. IN THE INITIAL SCHEME THERE IS A RATHER LOOSELY DEFINED ORDERING OF THE TRANSVERSE CUTS WHICH IS CLARIFIED IN THE FINAL SCHEME.

THE ENTRY FACADE IN AN EARLY DESIGN SHOWS TERRAGNI'S INTENTION TO CONTRAST MASS AND SURFACE. THE FACADE, STATED AS A SURFACE, IS RENDERED IN WHITE, WHILE THE MASS PRESENTED BEHIND IT IS RENDERED IN BLACK TO CLEARLY DISTINGUISH IT FROM THE PLANE OF THE FACADE. THESE EARLY DESIGNS PRESENT THIS FACADE CLEARLY AS A GRID WITH NO DUAL 'MASS-SURFACE' READING INTENDED. THIS PLANAR GRID READING IS STRENGHTHENED BY THE POSITION OF THE SECONDARY ENTRY DOORS ON THE MAIN

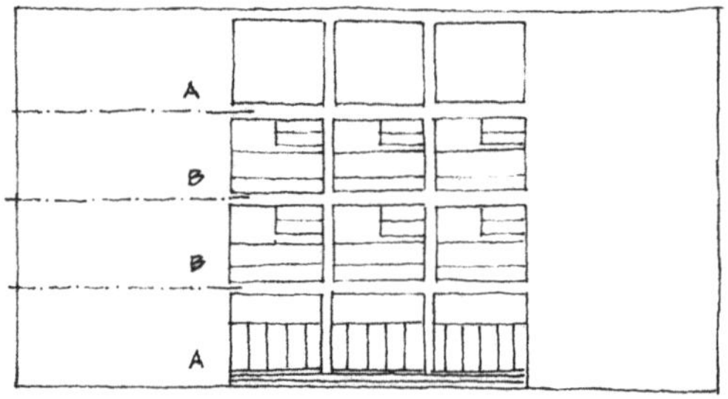

VERTICAL A·B·B·A SERIES 18.

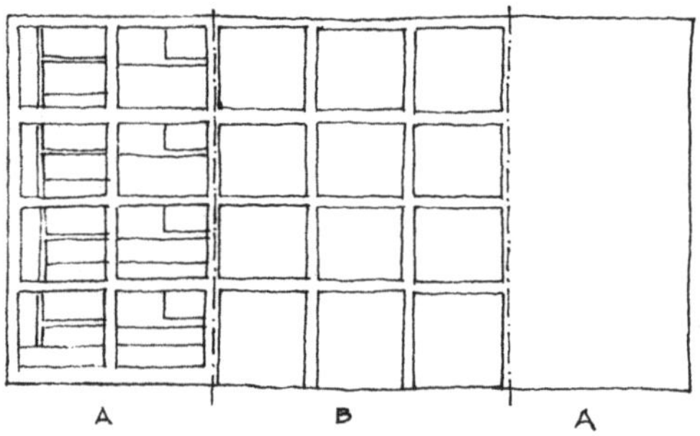

A·B·A SERIES ACROSS THE FACADE 19.

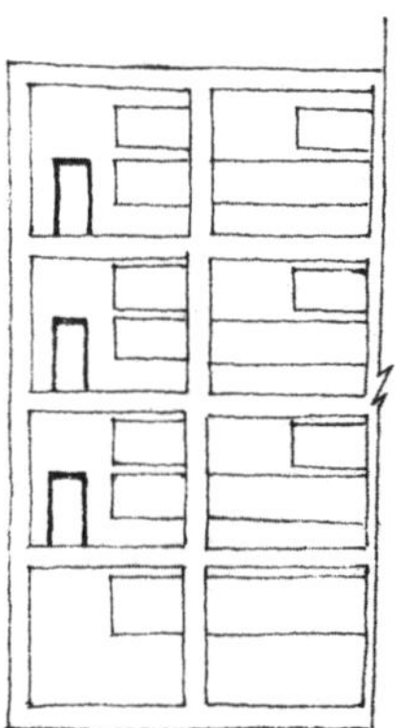

20.

EARLY SCHEME :
ENDING OF FACADE
WITH SMALL DOORS
RUNNING VERTICALLY.

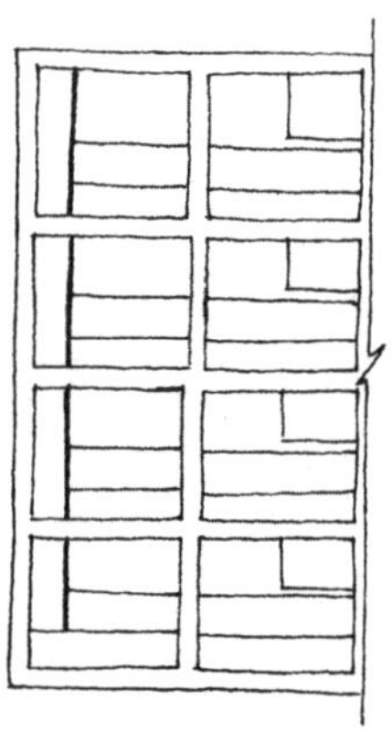

21.

FINAL SCHEME :
ENDING SUPPRESSED
WHILE PRESERVING
CORNER DEFINITION .

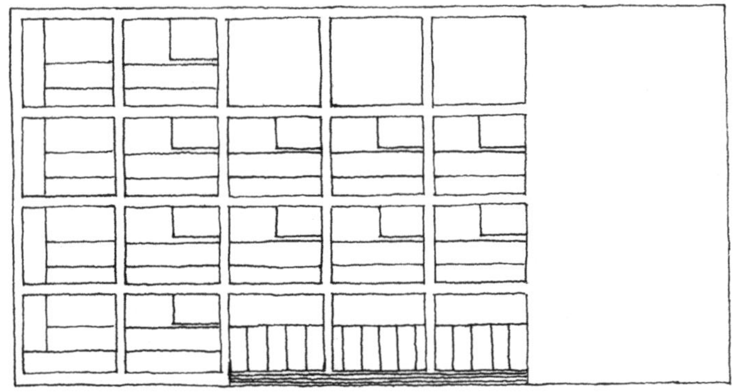

17.

SOUTHWEST FACADE : ENTRY
CUT IN RIGHT HAND SOLID ELIMINATED.
MASS-SURFACE DIALECTIC PRESENTED
ON FACADE PLANE

FINAL SCHEME

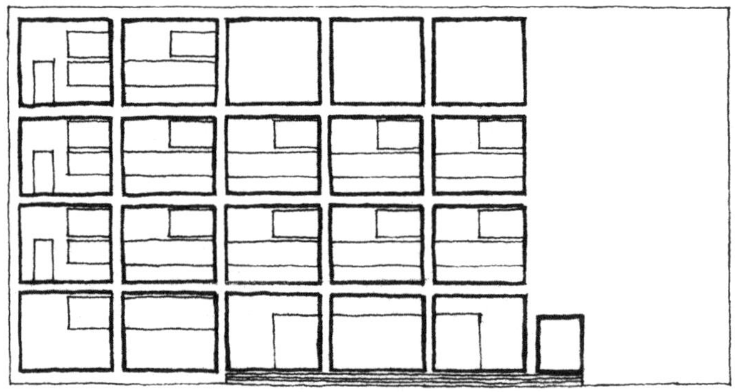

16.

SOUTHWEST FACADE : ENTRY
NO MASS-SURFACE AMBIGUITY : MASS STATED
BEHIND SURFACE

EARLY SCHEME

FACADE, WHICH CUT INTO THE RIGHT HAND PLANAR PORTION OF THE FACADE IN SUCH A MANNER AS TO DIVEST IT OF ANY POSSIBLE 'MASS' READING.[16] IT IS ONLY IN THE FINAL PROJECT THAT THE SYSTEM IS FULLY STRESSED, WHEN THE MASS-SURFACE DIALECTIC IS EXPRESSED ON THE FRONT FACADE. THIS IS ACCOMPLISHED BY ELIMINATING THE CUT IN THE SOLID RIGHT HAND PORTION OF THE FACADE.[17] NOW IT IS POSSIBLE TO INFER AN AMBIGUOUS READING; EITHER THE ORIGINAL MASS IS READ AS CUT-AWAY TO REVEAL THE COLUMN SUPPORTS, OR THESE COLUMNS ARE READ AS A SURFACE RESULTING FROM AN ADDITIVE PROCESS. THE 'MASS', BEHIND THE FACADE IS BROUGHT CLOSER TO THAT SURFACE BY RENDERING IT IN THE SAME MANNER AS THE FACADE. THUS A 'MASS-SURFACE' AMBIGUITY IS PRESENTED BY THE PARTICULAR TREATMENT OF SOLID AND VOID. AT THE SAME TIME, THE INTERNAL MASS CAN BE THOUGHT OF AS DISLOCATED FROM THE FACADE BY THE FORCE OF THE MAIN AXIS, THUS THROWING THE FACADE INTO A SURFACE READING.

TERRAGNI ESTABLISHES A TRI-PARTITE READING IN BOTH THE VERTICAL AND THE HORIZONTAL COORDINATES OF THE FRONTAL PLANE AS AN ACKNOWLEDGEMENT OF SYNTAX. ON THE ENTRY FACADE THIS IS ACHIEVED BY CREATING AN A-B-B-A SERIES VERTICALLY AND AN A-B-A SERIES ACROSS THE FACADE.[18,19] THE VERTICAL READING IS ACCOMPLISHED AS OUTLINED ABOVE BY CUTTING AWAY THE CENTRAL MASS ON THE GROUND AND THIRD FLOORS. IN THE TRANSVERSE READING THIS IS ACHIEVED BY THE CUTTING AWAY OF THE CENTRAL BAYS. IN AN EARLY SCHEME THE LEFT HAND SIDE OF THE ENTRY FACADE IS TERMINATED BY A VERTICAL READING OF SMALL DOORS.[20] TO AVOID A POSSIBLE CONTRADICTION DEVELOPING FROM AN INTERPRETATION OF THESE DOORS AS A VOLUMETRIC SLOT PARALLEL TO THE MAIN AXIS, TERRAGNI SUPPRESSES THE IMPORTANCE OF THIS TERMINATION WHILE STILL PRESERVING IT AS A CORNER DEFINITION.[21] HE CHANGES THE SIZE OF THIS OPENING TO READ AS A HALF-SQUARE THEREBY BRINGING IT INTO A HARMONIOUS RELATION-

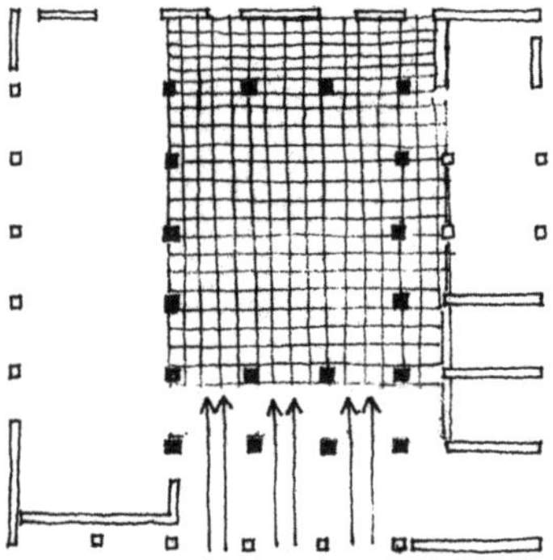

22.

DEFINITION OF COURT IN ITS DISLOCATED POSITION

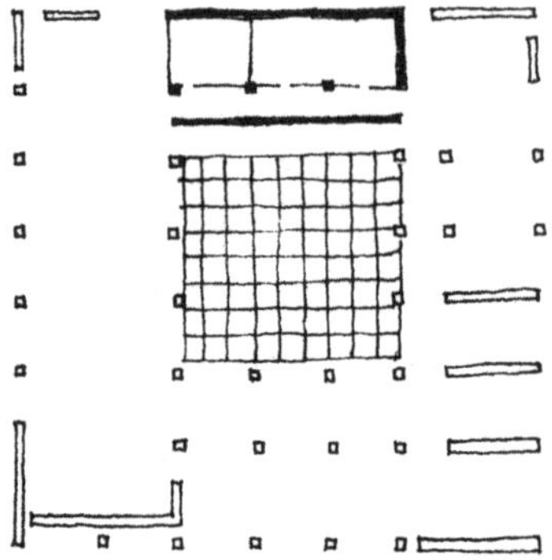

23.

RESTORATION OF COURT TO CENTRAL POSITION BY FIRST FLOOR OFFICES.

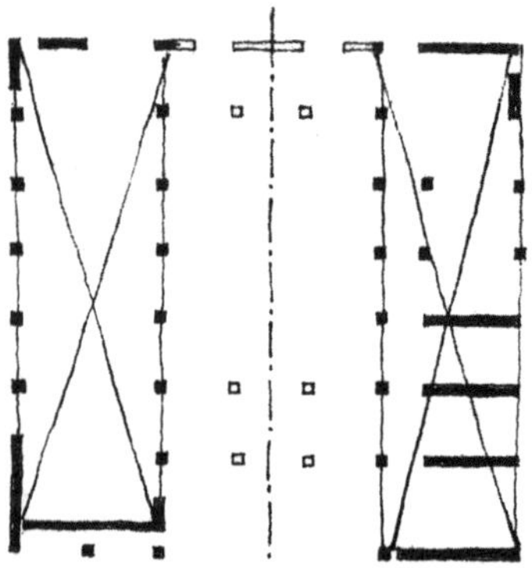

24.

BALANCE ABOUT LONGITUDINAL AXIS OF DOUBLE BAY OFFICES AND SINGLE BAY OFFICES PLUS CORRIDORS

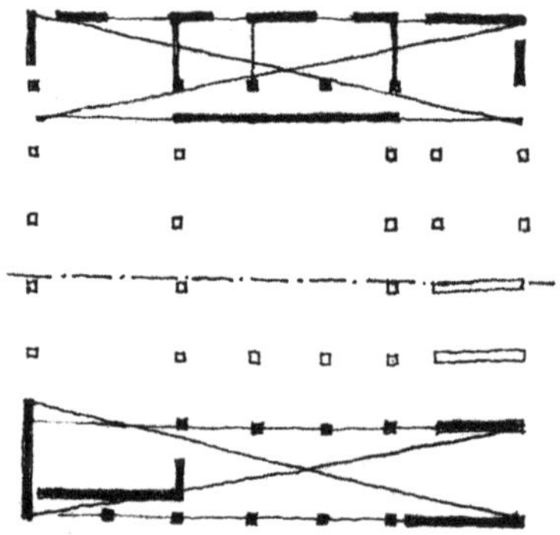

25.

BALANCE ABOUT TRANSVERSE AXIS REAR OFFICES AND CORRIDOR WITH ELONGATED ENTRY BAY

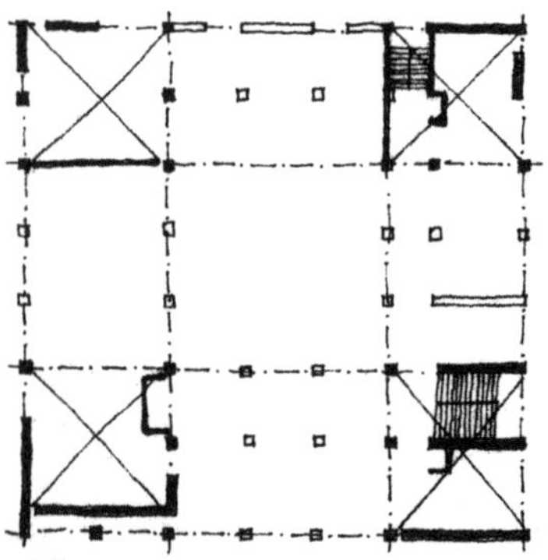

26.

INTERNAL PLAIDING ACKNOWLEDGES CENTROIDAL FORM

-SHIP WITH THE REMAINDER OF THE FACADE FENESTRATION WHICH PRESENTS THIS SQUARE-HALF SQUARE RHYTHM

THE 'MIDDLE' PART OF THE SYSTEM IS EXPRESSED BY THE VOLUMETRIC ORDERING OF THE CENTRAL COURT AND THE 'MASS-SURFACE' DIALECTIC OF THE LATERAL FACADES. THE GROUND FLOOR OF THE FINAL SCHEME DEFINES BY THE PLACING OF THE FLOOR TILES THE DISLOCATION OF THE COURT TO THE REAR OF THE BLOCK, AND THE DISTENTION OF ITS AREA ALONG THE LONGITUDINAL AXIS CAUSED BY THE PRESSURE OF THE ENTRY VECTOR.[22] THE COURT IS RESTORED TO ITS CENTRAL POSITION ON THE FIRST AND SECOND FLOOR PLANS BY THE REAR OFFICES LOCATION AND THE LOCATION OF THE ADJOINING CORRIDOR.[23] THUS BOTH THE LINEAR EXTERNAL AXIS AND THE CENTROIDAL NATURE OF THE COURT ARE ACKNOWLEDGED. TERRAGNI ALSO ALTERS THE PROPORTION OF THE STRUCTURAL BAY (10:12) TO COMPENSATE FOR THE INITIAL BLOCKING OF THE LONGITUDINAL AXIS, TO ACCOMMODATE THE MOVEMENT SYSTEM AND TO PROVIDE TWO SIZES OF OFFICES: THE SINGLE BAY AND THE DOUBLE BAY, FROM WHICH PERMUTATIONS OF DOUBLE CUBES AND HALF CUBES ARE FORMED. THE SINGLE BAY OFFICES AND THE SECONDARY CIRCULATION ON THE RIGHT ARE BALANCED ABOUT THE LONGITUDINAL AXIS BY THE DOUBLE BAY OFFICES ON THE LEFT.[24] THE REAR CIRCULATION AND THE SINGLE BAY OFFICES ARE BALANCED ABOUT THE TRANSVERSE AXIS BY THE EXTENSION OF THE ENTRY BAY.[25] THE TRI-PARTITE VOLUMETRIC DIVISION OF THE BUILDING INTERNALLY CREATES A PLAIDING EFFECT, WHICH AGAIN ACKNOWLEDGES THE CENTROIDAL ANTECEDENT BY EMPHASISING THE CORNER CONDITIONS.[26] THESE ARE TREATED LIKE PAVILIONS IN A PALLADIAN SCHEME; THEIR FORMAL DEFINITION IS ALSO EXPRESSIVE OF A FUNCTIONAL CHANGE. THE ADDITION OF TWO LIFTS IN THE FINAL SCHEME AND THEIR PARTICULAR LOCATION ADDS FURTHER CLARITY TO THESE CORNERS AS WELL AS PROVIDING AN ADDITIONAL VOLUMETRIC PLANE ACROSS THE LONGITUDINAL AXIS.

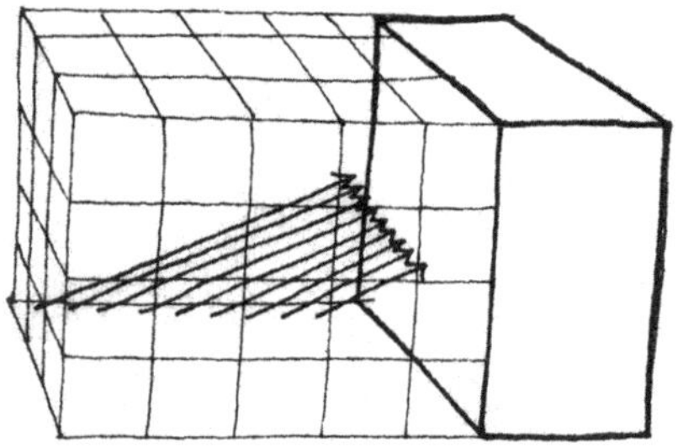

27.

SOUTHEAST BLOCK STOPS ANY DIAGONAL PRESSURE FROM SITE

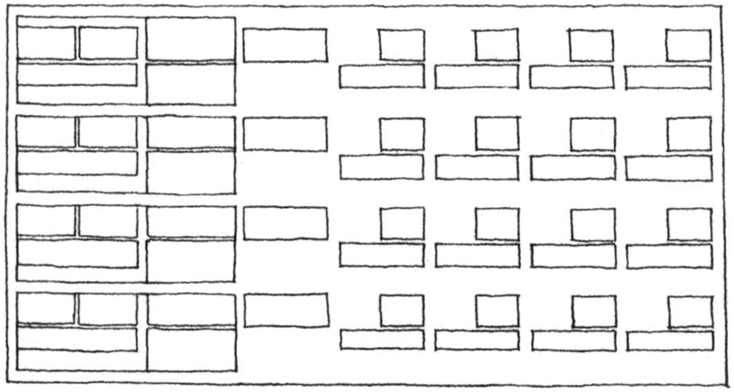

28.

FINAL SCHEME · SOUTH EAST FACADE
TRANSVERSE VERTICAL SLICES HARDLY APPARENT.

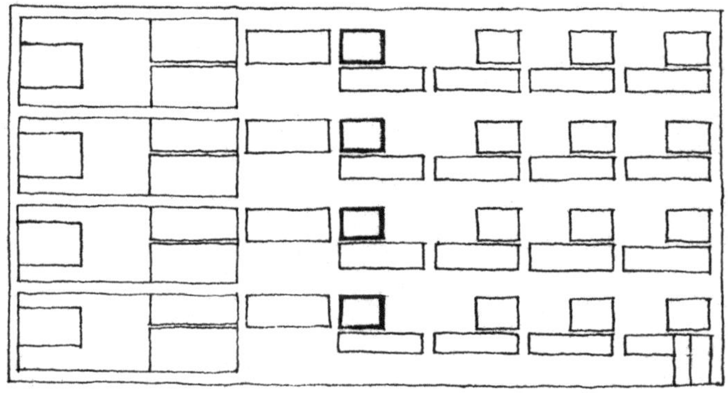

29.

EARLY SCHEME · SOUTHEAST FACADE
TRIPARTITE LATERAL READING ATTEMPTED BY SHIFTING A VERTICAL ROW OF WINDOWS

THE ACKNOWLEDGEMENT OF THE CORNER SYNTAX IN THE VOLUMETRIC SYSTEM CREATES SOME DIFFICULTY IN THE SPECIFIC FUNCTIONAL RESOLUTION OF THE CORNER CONDITIONS, WHICH FURTHER ATTESTS TO THE STRONG FORMAL PREFERENCE IN THE ORGANIZATION OF THIS BUILDING.

THE LATERAL FACADES ARE PERHAPS THE MOST DIFFICULT TO INTERPRET IN THE TOTAL 'MASS-SURFACE' SYSTEM. SINCE THESE FACADES ARE NOT DIRECTLY AFFECTED BY THE PRESSURE OF THE CENTRAL AXIS, THEY MUST GIVE A STRONG GENERIC MASS READING WHILE STILL INDICATING THE ENDS OF THE SYSTEM OF LATERAL VOLUMETRIC PLANES. THERE IS YET A THIRD INTERPRETATION THAT TERRAGNI INTRODUCES INTO THESE FACADES; THIS CONCERNS THE SITEING OF THE BUILDING ON THE SOUTH EAST EDGE OF THE PIAZZA. HE TREATS THE SOUTH EAST BLOCK AS A STOP TO ANY PRESSURE FROM THE SITE IN A DIAGONAL DIRECTION.[27] THEREFORE THIS BLOCK AS SEEN ON BOTH THE SW AND NE ELEVATIONS, READS MORE DISTINCTLY AS A SOLID THAN ANY OTHER PART OF THE BUILDING. THIS INTERPRETATION IS STRENGTHENED BY THE FACT THAT THE TRANSVERSE SLICES ARE ALMOST UNRECOGNISABLE IN THE TREATMENT OF THE SOUTH EAST FACADE.[28] IT IS INTERESTING TO NOTE, THAT TERRAGNI DOES ATTEMPT TO GIVE A TRI-PARTITE LATERAL READING TO THIS FACADE IN AN EARLY SCHEME, BY SHIFTING OFF ONE VERTICAL ROW OF WINDOWS FROM THE UPPER RIGHT HAND CORNER OF A TYPICAL BAY TO THE UPPER LEFT.[29] HOWEVER, THIS IS NOT CARRIED OUT IN THE FINAL SCHEME GIVING RISE TO THE BACKBONE READING AS MENTIONED ABOVE. IT MUST BE NOTED THAT THESE CHANGES CAN ONLY HAVE EFFECTED FOR FORMAL REASONS, SINCE ALL OF THE OFFICES RELATING TO THESE WINDOWS ARE OF A SIMILAR NATURE. THE ONLY 'MASS-SURFACE' AMBIGUITY PRESENTED ON THIS FACADE IS THE CUTTING OF THE BLOCK TO REVEAL A POSSIBLE GRID ON THE INITIAL (LEFT HAND) BAY. THE PLACEMENT OF THE WINDOWS IN THE REMAINING BAYS CAN HARDLY BE SAID TO EFFECT ANY MASS-SURFACE DICHOTOMY. THIS,HOWEVER, IS NOT THE CASE ON THE NORTH WEST

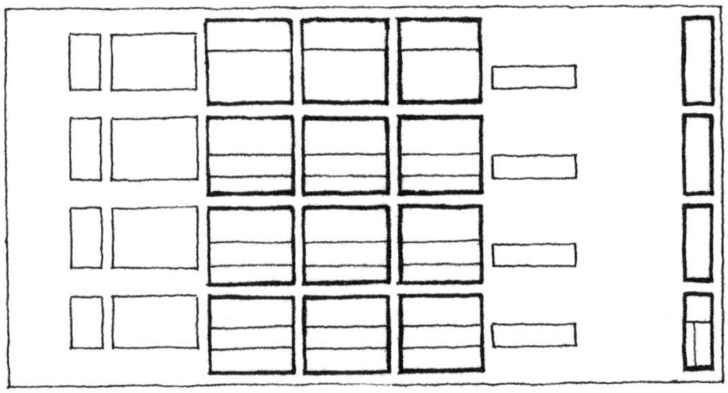

30.

FINAL SCHEME · NORTHWEST FACADE
TRI-PARTITE LONGITUDINAL DIVISION CLEARLY STATED BY CUTTING CENTRAL SPANDRELS

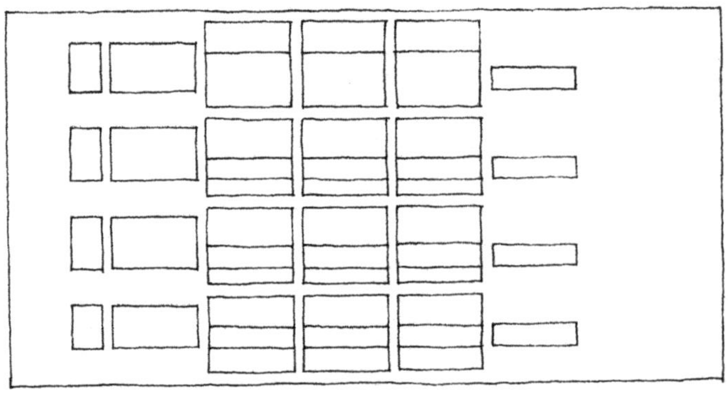

EARLY SCHEME · NORTHWEST FACADE
NO SLOT DEFINING DOMINANT SURFACE OF FRONT FACADE

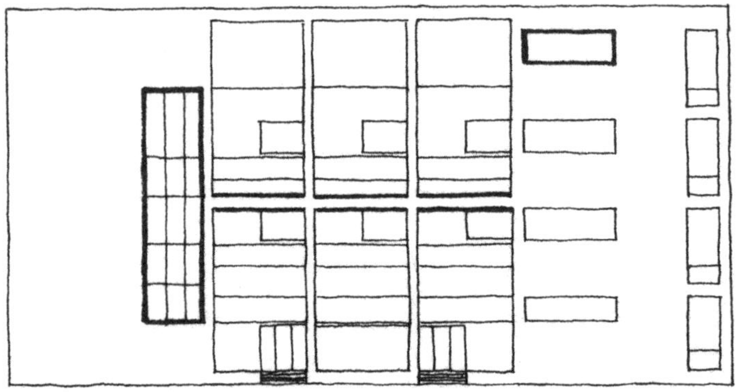

32.

FINAL SCHEME · NORTHEAST FACADE
TYING OF RIGHT HAND WINDOWS HORIZONTALLY BY ADDITION OF WINDOW
LARGE VERTICAL STAIR WINDOW READ AS BREAKING THROUGH SURFACE.

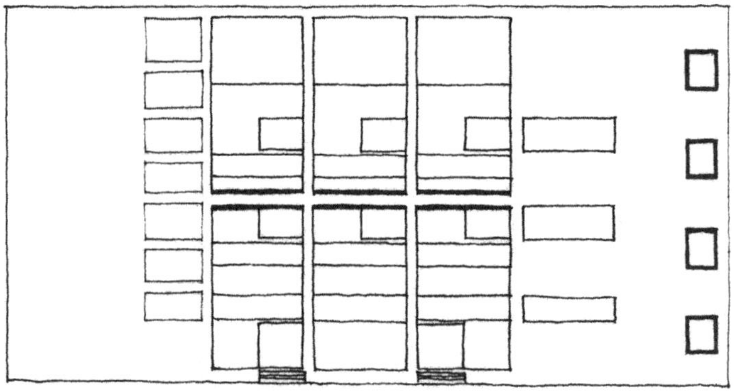

31.

EARLY SCHEME · NORTHEAST FACADE

STRONG READING OF VERTICAL SLOTS.
WEAK HORIZONTAL BANDING CAUSED BY DROPPING RIGHT HAND WINDOWS.

NOTE · CENTRAL HORIZONTAL BANDING ON BOTH SCHEMES AS AN END TO SYSTEM.

FACADE. HERE THE TRIPARTITE LONGITUDINAL DIVISION IS CLEARLY STATED BY THE CUTTING OF THE SPANDREL HEIGHT IN THE MIDDLE THREE BAYS, GIVING A 'VOID' READING IN RELATION TO THE 'SOLID' READING OF THE END BAYS ON EITHER SIDE. HOWEVER, THE PLACING OF THE HORIZONTAL WINDOWS AND THE LOCATION OF THE EXTREME END OPENINGS, TO CREATE A SPECIFIC COLUMNAR DIMENSION BRINGS ABOUT THE AMBIGUOUS MASS-SURFACE READING. THE SLOTS ON THE EXTREME RIGH GIVE A DEFINITE SURFACE READING TO THE FRONT FACADE. IN ALL OF THE ELEVATIONS THERE IS A PURPOSEFUL UNDERPLAYING OF THE HORIZONTAL FLOOR SLABS TO ALLOW THE VERTICAL SLICE TO READ THROUGH.

THE REAR FACADE ALSO SERVES A DUAL PURPOSE: IT BOTH PROVIDES AN END TO THE SYSTEM AND EXPRESSES THE PLANAR QUALITY OF THE TRANSVERSE ELEVATIONS IN A SIMILAR MANNER TO THE FRONT FACADE. HOWEVER THIS READING MUST BE ESTABLISHED WITH DISSIMILAR FROM THOSE EMPLOYED ON THE ENTRY FACADE. AGAIN A COMPARISON OF AN EARLY STUDY WITH THE FINAL SCHEME IS HELPFUL IN DEMONSTRATING THE DEVELOPMENT OF THE 'MASS-SURFACE' AMBIGUITY OF THIS FACADE. BOTH INTERPRETATIONS CLEARLY PRESENT THE TRI-PARTITE H CONFIGURATION IN BOTH THE LATERAL AND VERTICAL COORDINATED OF THE 'FRONTAL' REFERENCE. HOWEVER, THE EARLIER SCHEME CREATES A STRONG READING OF LONGITUDINAL SLOTS, PARALLEL TO THE EXTERNAL VECTOR, BOTH IN THE TREATMENT OF THE WINDOWS OF THE SECONDARY STAIR AND THE VERTICAL ARRANGEMENT OF WINDOWS ON THE EXTREME RIGHT OF THE FACADE. THE VERTICAL SLOTTING OF THESE RIGHT HAND WINDOWS IS EVEN MORE STRONGLY READ BY THEIR WEAK VISUAL TIE WITH THE NEXT GROUPING OF WINDOWS; THIS WEAKNESS IS BROUGHT ABOUT BY THE SLOPPING OF THESE WINDOWS SO THAT A HORIZONTAL READING IS DIFFICULT. THE OMMISSION OF THE TOP MOST WINDOW IN THE SECOND VERTICAL GROUPING ENFORCES THE DEFINITION OF THE SLOTTING QUALITIES OF THE RIGHT HAND FENESTRATION, AS WELL AS ALLOWING A POSSIBLE 'MASS' READING TO BE INFERRED. THE ADJUSTMENTS IN THE FINAL SCHEME MAKE AN INTERESTING

COMPARISON.[32] TERRAGNI FINDS IT NECESSARY TO PRESERVE A CUTTING ON THE EXTREME RIGHT SO THAT THE 'MASS-SURFACE' AMBIGUITY IS RETAINED. WITHOUT THIS SLOT THE ADJACENT FACADE WOULD READ AS 'MASS' ONLY, THE POSSIBLE ALTERNATIVE READING BEING DIFFICULT. THIS SLOT MUST ALSO BE TIED TO THE ADJACENT ROW OF WINDOWS SO THAT THE SURFACE INTERPRETATION OF THE REAR FACADE IS MAINTAINED. THIS IS ACCOMPLISHED BY ADDING A FINAL WINDOW TO THE SECOND VERTICAL GROUPING THEREBY GIVING A DEFINITE GRID EMPHASIS TO THE RIGHT HAND END, ALSO GIVING THE POSSIBLE READING OF TWO COLUMNAR DIMENSIONS IN THE JUXTAPOSITION OF SOLIDS AND VOIDS. THE PROPORTION OF THE RIGHT HAND WINDOWS IS CHANGED TO GIVE A FURTHER HORIZONTAL TIE TO THE ADJACENT SERIES. HOWEVER, IT IS THE TREATMENT OF THE SECONDARY STAIR FENESTRATION THAT CAUSES THE ENTIRE SYSTEM TO BE TIED TOGETHER. THE READING OF THIS STAIR IS CHANGED FROM VERTICAL SERIES TO ONE LARGE VERTICAL WINDOW OF ENTIRELY DIFFERENT DIMENSIONS FROM THOSE WHICH HAVE BEEN PREVIOUSLY USED; THUS THIS WINDOW IS ESTABLISHED AS AN IMPORTANT ELEMENT IN THE TOTAL SYSTEM. IT IS SEEN AS BREAKING THROUGH A SURFACE AND NOT A MASS. THIS CAN BE INFERRED FROM THE MANNER IN WHICH IT PUNCTURES THE FACADE: UNFRAMED AND UNBROKEN. THIS PUNCTURING ALSO PROVIDES A DEFINITION TO A FINAL TRANSVERSE PLANE, IN THAT THE DISTANCE THIS WINDOW PROJECTS COMPLETES THE DIMENSION OF THE SQUARE ON PLAN. EVEN IN THE TREATMENT OF THE OPENING FRAMES IN THIS WINDOW, TERRAGNI DEMONSTRATES THE PRESSURE THAT HAS FORCED THE WINDOW THROUGH THE FINAL SURFACE. THE WINDOWS OPEN IN A MANNER THAT PROJECTS THEM FORWARD PARALLEL TO THE PLANE OF THE FACADE.

THUS TERRAGNI CLEARLY PRESENTS A PLANAR READING OF THE REAR FACADE, AS THE FINAL LAYER OF THE SYSTEM OF TRANSVERSE PLANES, WHILE STILL HOLDING THE TRIPARTITE READING OF A MASS-CUT-AWAY. THE TWO REAR DOORS GIVE A MINOR YET IM-

-PORTANT ACKNOWLEDGEMENT OF THE CENTRAL AXIS. THIS READING IS REINFORCED BY THE BALANCED, YET UNSYMMETRICAL WEIGHTING OF THE ELEMENTS ON THE REAR FACADE ABOUT AN IMPLIED CENTRAL AXIS.

ASILO INFANTILE

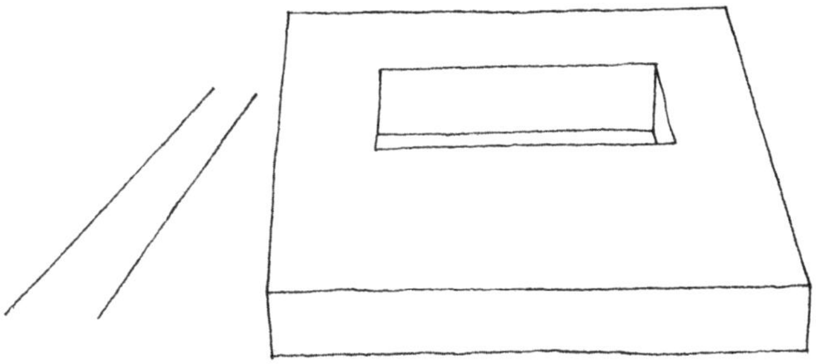

1.

EXTERNAL AXIS PARALLEL TO INTERNAL GENERIC STATE, THEREFORE RELATIVELY NEUTRAL TO IT.

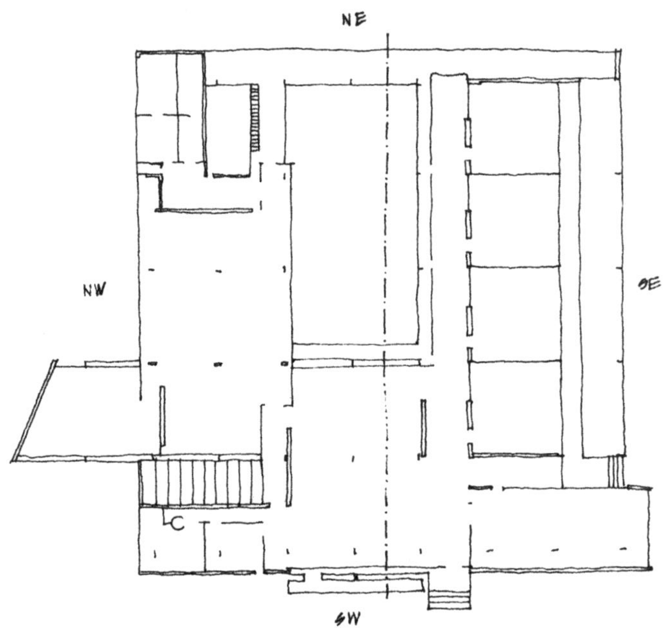

FLOOR PLAN

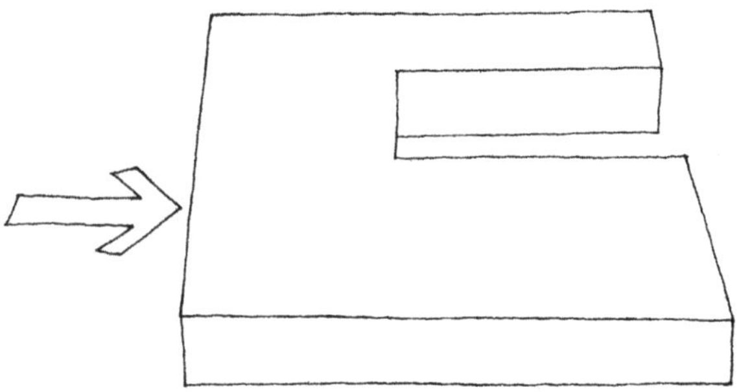

2.

GENERIC U-FORM EVOLVED FROM RESOLUTION OF GIVEN CONDITIONS

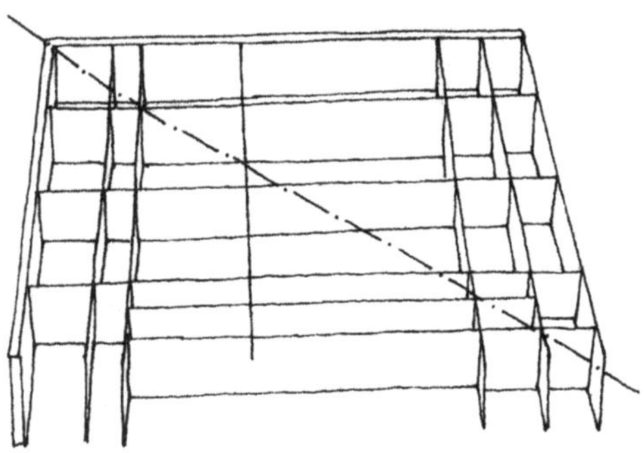

3.

TO COMPENSATE FOR DIRECTIONAL QUALITY OF U-FORM, NW FACADE IS STRESSED IN ADDITION TO STRESSING OF SW ENTRY FACADE TO CREATE A VOLUMETRIC PLAID.
NE AND SE FACADES ARE CONSIDERED AS WEAK.

The Asilo Infantile provides an interesting comparison with the Casa Del Fascio, in that both evolve from a generic centroidal basis. However, the Asilo Infantile illustrates the development of Terragni's systemic control within a more limited range and is, in a sense, a more ascetic, academic reference. Here, Terragni cannot evoke the mass-surface dialectic of the Casa Del Fascio since he is not faced with the same need to resolve an internal-external conflict. In this situation the main external axis is parallel to the site and therefore relatively neutral in relation to the internal conditions.[1] The systemic development must somehow cut this axis to provide for entry into the building. Furthermore the system must acknowledge the syntax governing single entry into a centroidal form. To recognise this syntax the specific grammar employed defines the volumetric order in relation to a dominant plane, only using a 'surface' or planar system, since there is no internal-external conflict. This system applied in only one direction would, however, imply a strong directional reference to the centroidal form similar to that of the Casa Del Fascio.

The initial response derived from the functional requirements is a generic U-form, which in itself has directional implications, again emphasising a linear volumetric order from the entry facade.[2] If this directional quality were to be overstressed it would have tended to obscure the conceptual basis of the generic centroidal form. Therefore a volumetric plaid is invoked by stressing the north west facade adjacent to the dominant entry surface.[3] The obvious correlative of this type of system is the diagonal condition which in most situations tends to destroy a functional unity. However, the need to deny this diagonal is in fact

DEVELOPMENT OF HORIZONTAL ABSOLUTE

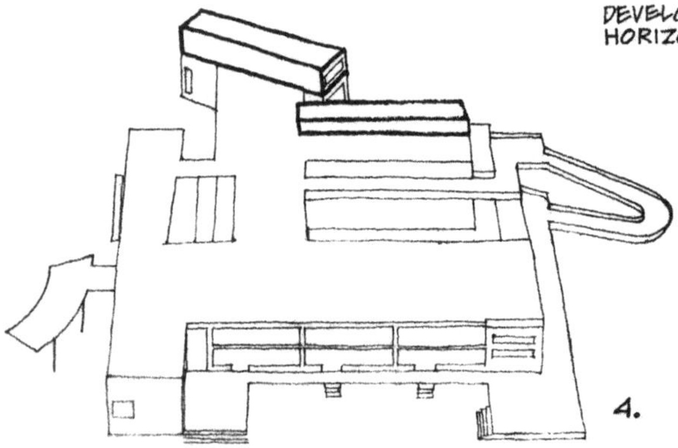

4.

FIRST STAGE: PARTIAL TWO STORY DEVELOPMENT. NO HORIZONTAL ABSOLUTE

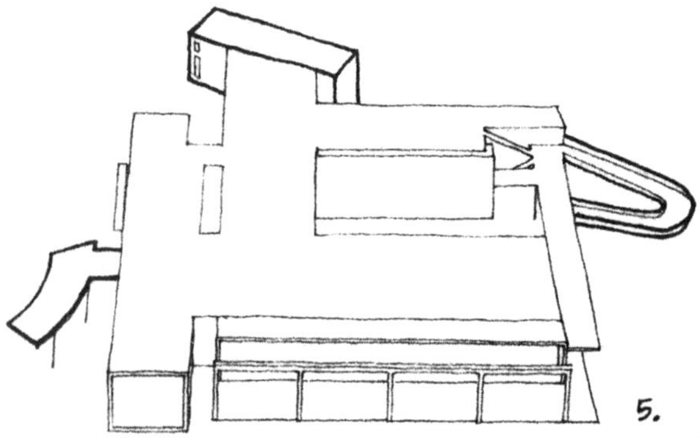

5.

SECOND STAGE: ELIMINATION OF TWO STORY ELEMENTS

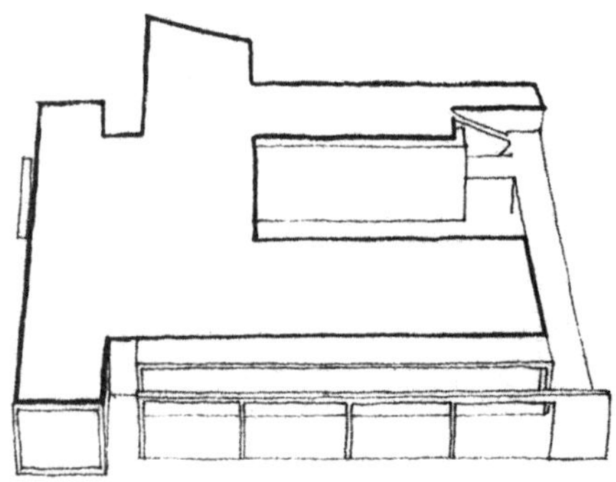

6.

FINAL BUILDING: ELIMINATION OF RAMP, KITCHEN BLOCK, AND ENTRY CANOPY.

CLARIFICATION OF HORIZONTAL ABSOLUTE

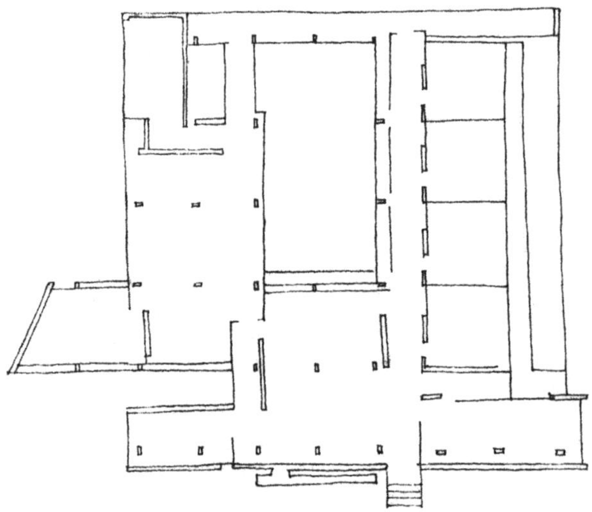

7.

THE EXTENSION OF THE SW FACADE DEFINES THE GENERIC SQUARE.

USED HERE TO REINFORCE THE SPECIFIC SYNTACTICAL RESOLUTION OF THE GIVEN CONDITIONS. BY STRESSING AND THEN CUTTING THE ENTRY FACADE, AN ENTRY SLOT IS CREATED WHICH IS THEN BALANCED BY BREAKING THE CONTINUITY OF THE NW FACADE WITH THE KITCHEN-DINING HALL DEVELOPMENT. THIS CUTTING OF THE NW FACADE TENDS TO WEAKEN ITS IMPORTANCE AS A DOMINANT REFERENCE THEREBY DIMINISHING THE EFFECT OF THE DIAGONAL READING. THE KITCHEN CAN BE READ AS AN ORTHOGONAL REFERENCE, IN TERMS OF THE EXTERNAL STREET PATTERN, AND THEREFORE ACTS AS A TIE TO THE TOTAL GRID. IT SHOULD BE NOTED THAT EVEN THOUGH THE FRONTAL AND ORTHOGONAL CO-ORDINATES ARE STRESSED, TERRAGNI STILL TREATS THE HORIZONTALS AS THE ABSOLUTE REFERENCE. THIS DEVELOPMENT OF THE HORIZONTAL ABSOLUTE IS A MORE MATURE RECOGNITION OF THE SPECIFIC 'COURTYARD' SYNTAX THEN IS EMPLOYED IN THE CASA DEL FASCIO. IN THE ORIGINAL MODEL THE ABSOLUTE REFERENCE IS NOT CLEARLY STATED; THE ROOF LEVLE OF THE KITCHEN BLOCK BEING SLIGHTLY ABOVE THE LEVEL OF THE MAIN VOLUME.[4] ON INITIAL EXAMINATION, IN PURELY PICTORIAL OR PERCEPTUAL TERMS, THE FIRST PROJECT MIGHT BE CONSIDERED TO BE THE MORE INTERESTING OF THE TWO. THESE ANALYSES, HOWEVER, ARE NOT CONCEIVED OF IN TERMS OF THE PICTORIAL AND PERCEPTUAL QUALITIES OF ANY BUILDING BUT RATHER ARE AN INVESTIGATION OF ITS CONCEPTUAL BASIS AND THEREFORE ITS GENERIC STATE. HENCE IN CONCEPTUAL TERMS, SINCE ALL FORM MUST HAVE AN ABSOLUTE REFERENCE THE SECTION IS CHANGED FROM PROJECTED TO EXECUTED STATE, TO PROVIDE A SINGLE HORIZONTAL ROOF LINE.[5,6]

THE VOLUMETRIC ORDERING RELATES TO THE ADJACENT DOMINANT SURFACES, AND THE STRATIFICATION OF THIS ORDER IS PROVIDED BY THE COMPLEX COLUMNAR ORGANISATION. AN EXAMINATION OF THIS VOLUMETRIC ORDER MUST BEGIN WITH THE DOMINANT PLANES. THE FRONT, SOUTHWEST, FACADE IS PERCEIVED AS BEING EXTENDED TO THE SOUTHEAST BEYOND THE LIMITS OF THE BUILDING.[7] HOWEVER, IN FACT, THIS PLANE DEFINES THE GENERIC

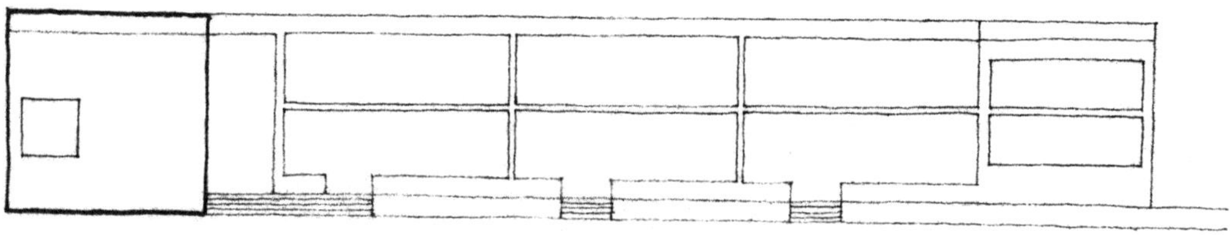

8.

SOUTHEAST FACADE : EARLY SCHEME
NOTE 'MASS' READING OF LEFT HAND END

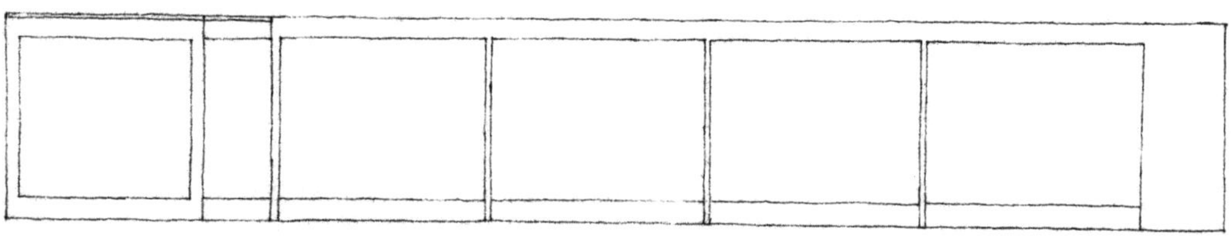

9.

FINAL PROJECT : SOUTH EAST FACADE
ALL 'MASS' READINGS AVOIDED

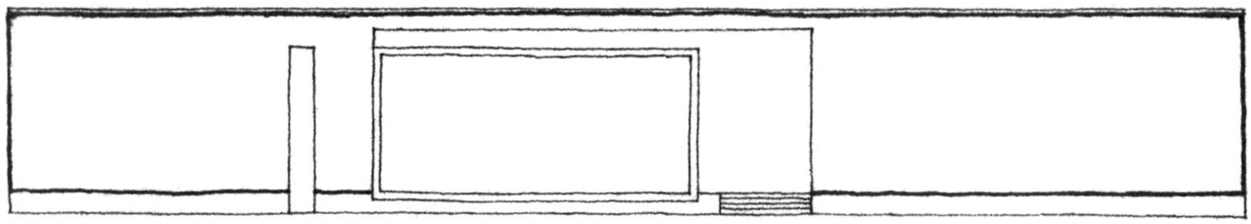

FRONT FACADE TREATED
AS A FLOATING PLANE

10.

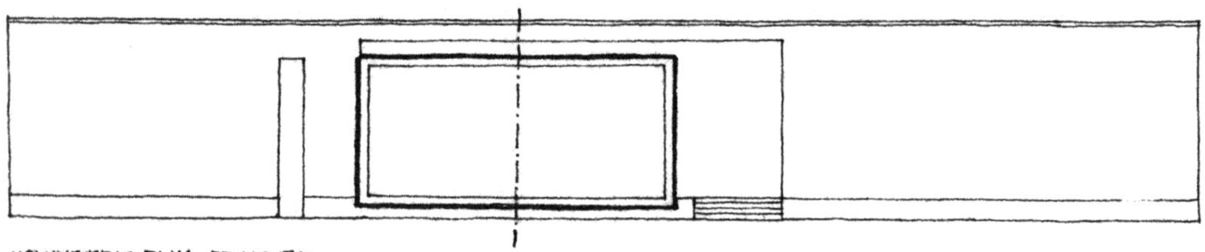

VOLUMETRIC PLUG PROJECTS
THROUGH ENTRY FACADE.
FUNCTIONS AS A SMALL PORCH.

11.

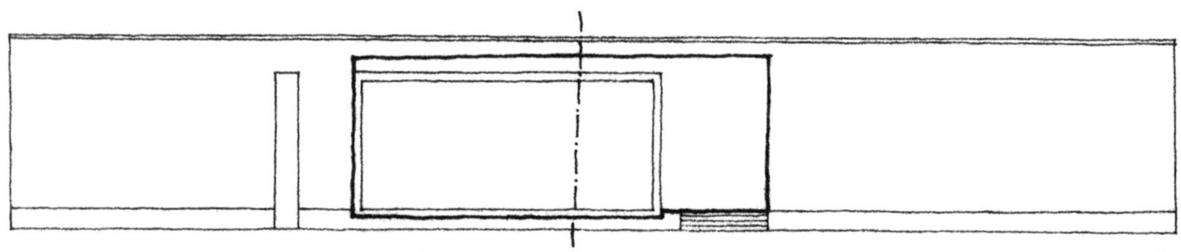

ENTIRE OPENING IN FACADE DEFINES CENTER
LINE OF COLUMNAR GRID

13.

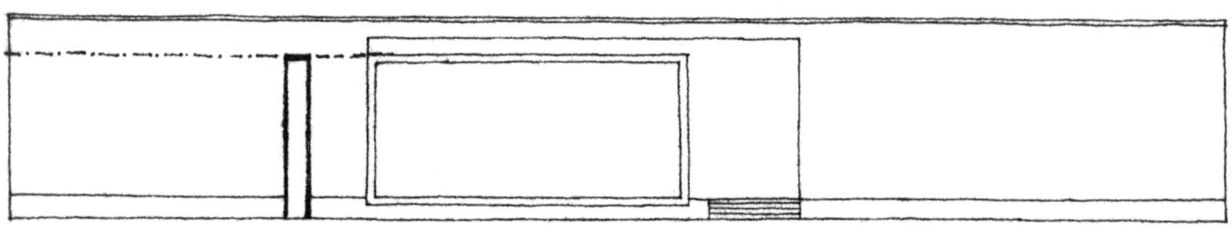

15.

CUT IN FACADE AT DIRECTOR'S OFFICE
DEFINES VOLUMETRIC PLANE
RELATED TO NW FACADE

SQUARE IN PLAN. THE DESIRE TO DETACH THIS SURFACE FROM THE BLOCK OF THE BUILDING CAN BE SEEN IN THIS EXTENSION. AN INTERESTING COMPARISON MAY AGAIN BE MADE WITH THE EARLIER PROJECT WHERE THE EXTENSION OF THIS FACADE IS TREATED AS 'MASS', READING AS PART OF THE CLOAKROOM BLOCK.[8] IN THE FINAL PROJECT ALL 'MASS' IMPLICATIONS ARE OBSCURED TO AVOID ANY 'MASS-SURFACE' AMBIGUITY; THE END WALL OF THE CLOAKROOM BEING COMPLETELY GLAZED IN THE FINAL BUILDING, IN PLACE OF THE SMALL OPENING THAT WAS USED IN THE EARLIER PROJECT.[9] THE SURFACE READING OF THE ENTRY FACADE IS STRENGTHENED BY THE ACTUAL TREATMENT OF THE FACADE ITSELF. IT IS RENDERED IN SUCH A FASHION AS TO MAKE THE PLANE APPEAR TO FLOAT.[10] THIS QUALITY OF WEIGHTLESSNESS IS AMORE OBVIOUS STATEMENT OF A SIMILAR DEVICE USED BY LE CORBUSIER IN THE ENTRY FACADE AT GARCHES. HERE, TERRAGNI IS USING THE SAME FORMULAR: THE STATING OF THE FRONTALS AND HORIZONTALS AS PLANES, AND THE ORTHOGONALS AS COLUMNS. THE DISSOCIATION OF THE FACADE FROM THE GROUND IN THE ASILO INFANTILE PROVIDES THE PERCEPTUAL REFERENCE FOR THE ANTIGRAVITATIONAL CONCEPT. THE EXTENSION OF THE FRONT FACADE ALSO TENDS TO VALIDATE THE READING OF THE SOUTH EAST FACADE AS A 'WEAK' OR RECESSIVE SIDE.

THE PENETRATION OF THE FRONT FACADE SHOWS ITS CONNECTION WITH THE ADJACENT DOMINANT FACADE AND PROVIDES THE INITIAL AKNOWLEDGEMENT OF THE VOLUMETRIC PLAIDING. THE CUTTING OF THIS FRONT PLANE IS ACHIEVED BY A VOLUMETRIC PLUG PROJECTING THROUGH THE FACADE WHICH FUNCTIONS AS A SMALL ENTRY PORCH.[11] THIS PLUG TIES THROUGH TO THE CENTRAL COURT, AND ACKNOWLEDGES THE SLOTTING OF VOLUMES TO EITHER SIDE OF IT. THERE IS A VERY COMPLEX DEVELOPMENT FROM THIS SLOT WITH REFERENCE TO THE DISLOCATION OF THE CENTRAL AXIS, IN ORDER TO RESTORE THE EQUILIBRIUM ABOUT THIS AXIS UPSET BY STRESSING THE NORTH WEST FACADE. INITIALLY, THIS PORCH VOLUME CAN BE READ AS BEING LOCATED ON THE CENTRE LINE OF THE GENERIC

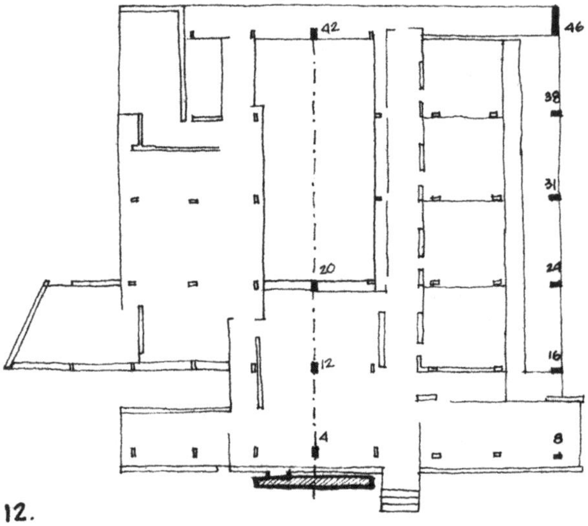

12.

PORCH VOLUME SEEN TO BE ON CENTER LINE OF COLUMNAR GRID WITHOUT SOUTH-EAST SCREEN COLUMNS

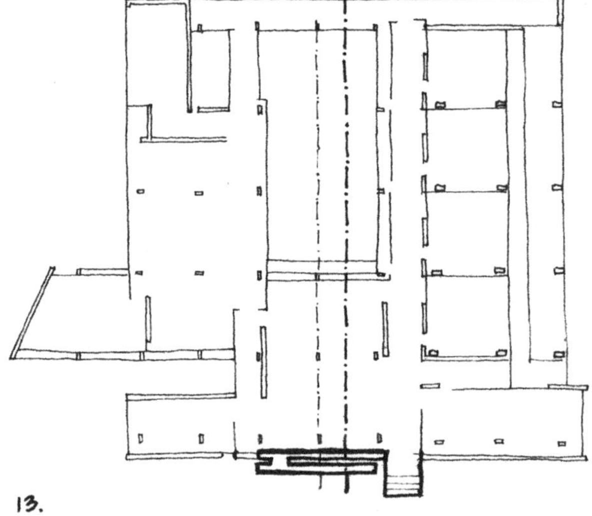

13.

ENTIRE OPENING IN SOUTHWEST FACADE IS DEFINED BY CENTER LINE OF COMPLETE GRID.

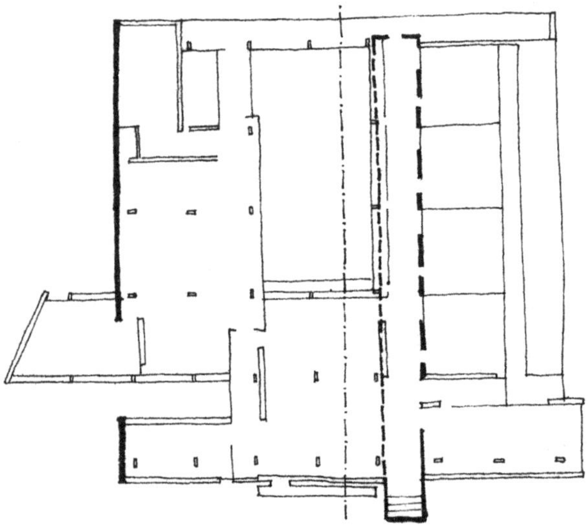

14.

EQUILIBRIUM RESTORED ABOUT CENTRAL AXIS BY BALANCING DISLOCATED ENTRY SLOT WITH STRESSED NW FACADE

FORM, IN REFERENCE TO THE PLACING OF COLUMNS BEHIND.[12] HOWEVER, THE CENTRE LINE DEFINED BY COLUMNS 4,12,20, AND 42 REFERS ONLY TO A COLUMNAR GRID THAT DOES NOT INCLUDE THE COLUMNS 8,16,24, 31,38,46, OF THE SOUTH EAST SCREEN. THE ENTIRE OPENING IN THE FACADE, WHICH ENCOMPASSES THE ENTRY SLOT AS WELL AS THE PORCH, CAN BE READ AS DEFINING ANOTHER CENTRAL AXIS: THAT OF A COLUMNAR GRID WHICH INCLUDES THE SOUTH EAST SCREEN COLUMNS.[13] SINCE THE PORCH BEARS NO RELATIONSHIP TO THE CENTRAL AXIS OF THE ENTRY FACADE IT MUST BE READ IN RELATION TO THE TOTAL COLUMNAR GRID BEHIND. THE CIRCULATION SLOT THUS CREATED IS SEEN AS A PART OF THE VOLUMETRIC SYSTEM TENSIONED FROM THE NORTHWEST FACADE. FURTHERMORE, THE INFLUENCE OF THE STRESSED NORTHWEST FACADE CAN BE SEEN IN THE DISLOCATION OF THE ENTRY SLOT TO THE RIGHT OF EITHER CENTRAL REFERENCE. THIS DISLOCATION ACTS TO RESTORE THE BALANCE ABOUT THE CENTRAL AXIS BY CREATING AN EQUILIBRIUM OF THE VOLUMETRIC SLOTS WITH THE DOMINANT PLANE.[14] CONSEQUENTLY THIS ENTRY SLOT IS HELD IN POSITION BY THE FIXING OF THE PORCH VOLUME ON ONE CENTRAL AXIS, AND THE TOTAL OPENING ON THE OTHER; THE DIFFERENCE IN THESE TWO DIMENSIONS BEING THE ENTRY SLOT. TWO OTHER MINOR NOTATIONS CONCERNING THE FRONT FACADE CORROBORATE THE ASSUMPTIONS MADE ABOVE. THE CUT IN THE FACADE AT THE DIRECTOR'S OFFICE ACKNOWLEDGES ANOTHER OF THE VOLUMETRIC PLANES RELATING TO THE ADJACENT NORTH-WEST FACADE.[15] THE HEIGHT OF THIS CUT RELATES TO THAT OF THE PORCH VOLUME; THIS THEN ATTRIBUTES A FIXED HEIGHT TO ALL VOLUMES THAT ARE TENSIONED FROM THE NW FACADE. THE HEIGHT OF THE SCREEN OF COLUMNS OF THE SW FACADE ALSO RELATES TO THIS ESTABLISHED LEVEL, THEREBY ACKNOWLEDGING ITS TENSIONED RELATIONSHIP WITH THE OPPOSITE SIDE. ORIGINALLY THE ENTRY FACADE WAS TO HAVE HAD A PORTICO EXTENDING FROM IT, WHICH WOULD HAVE PROVIDED A BALANCE TO THE KITCHEN BLOCK. HOWEVER, THE BALANCE OF THESE TWO EXTRUSIONS WOULD HAVE INFERRED A READING OF A SECONDARY SYSTEM. THE PORTICO AND KITCHEN COULD BE

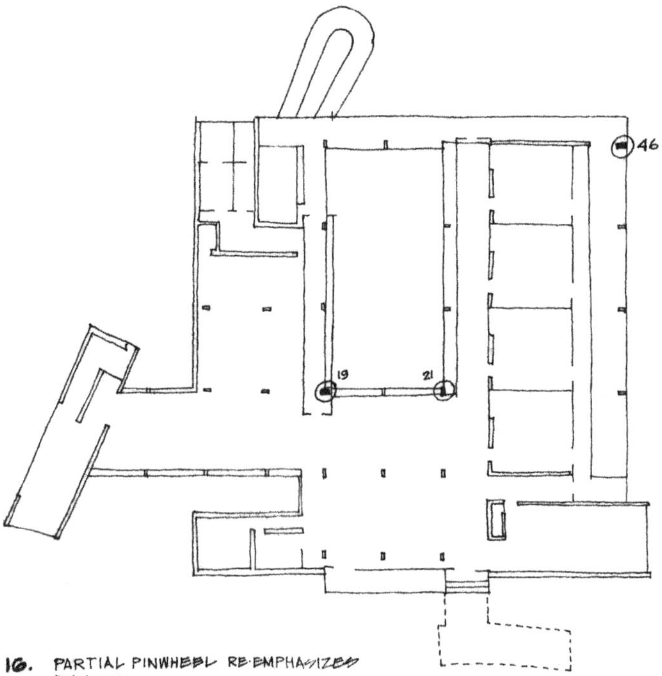

16. PARTIAL PINWHEEL RE-EMPHASIZES DIAGONAL

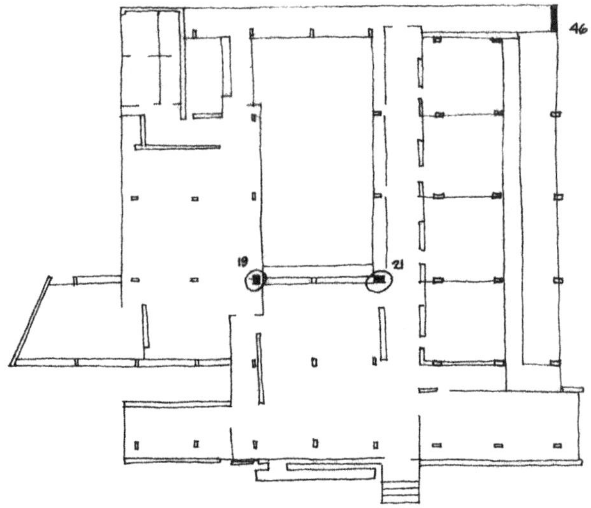

17. EXECUTED SCHEME
NOTE CHANGES IN COLUMN DIRECTION OF 19 AND 21 AND ELONGATION OF 46

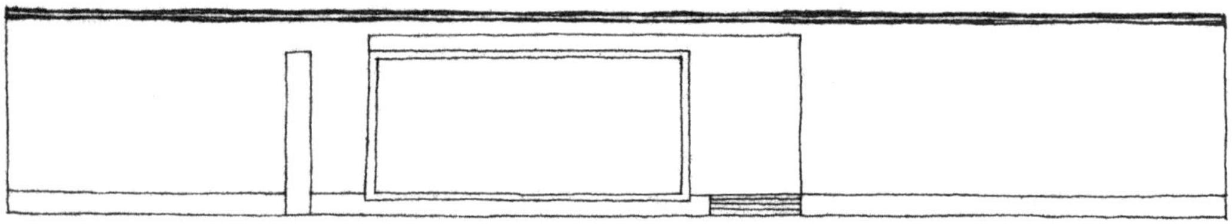

18. DEFINITION OF HORIZONTAL ABSOLUTE
SOUTH WEST FACADE

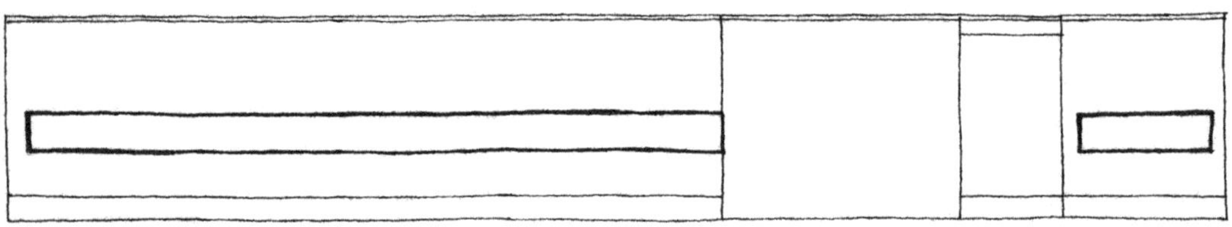

19. NORTHWEST FACADE
TREATED AS AN OPAQUE SURFACE WITH A RIBBON WINDOW CUT IN TO PROVIDE CONTINUITY

READ AS TWO ARMS OF A PINWHEEL, WHICH WOULD HAVE NEGATED TWO PARTS OF TERRAGNI'S SYSTEM:[16] FIRST, BY ITS PARTIAL PINWHEEL REFERENCE IT WOULD HAVE RE-EMPHASISED THE DIAGONAL, AND SECOND THIS PINWHEEL WOULD HAVE TENDED TO BLUR THE ORTHOGONAL REFERENCE PROVIDED BY THE KITCHEN BLOCK. THIS DISCUSSION ASSUMES THAT IT WAS TERRAGNI'S INTENTION TO AVOID THE PINWHEEL READING WHILE STILL KEEPING THE KITCHEN BLOCK AS AN ORTHOGONAL REFERENCE. THIS ASSUMPTION IS BASED ON THE FACT THAT ALTHOUGH NEITHER WAS BUILT, MOST PUBLISHED PLANS SHOW THE KITCHEN BLOCK INTACT WHILE DELETING THE PORTICO EXTENSION.[17] IT IS, HOWEVER, NOT THE INTENT OF THESE ANALYSES TO ESTABLISH THE REASONS WHY IN THE EXECUTION OF EACH BUILDING, CERTAIN ELEMENTS WERE OMITTED.

THE RECOGNITION OF A HORIZONTAL ABSOLUTE CAN BE SEEN IN THE TREATMENT OF THE ROOF LINE. THIS PLANE APPEARS AS A THIN LIP THAT PROTRUDES SLIGHTLY FROM THE VERTICAL SURFACE THEREBY DISSOCIATING THE TWO, AND GIVING FURTHER CREDENCE TO THE 'SURFACE' READING OF THE ENTRY FACADE.[18] THERE IS A CRITICAL JUNCTION AT THE (FRONT FACADE.) INTERSECTION OF THE TWO DOMINANT SURFACES WHICH MUST BE TREATED IN SUCH A FASHION AS TO AVOID AN UNWANTED 'MASS' READING. FURTHERMORE, THE NW FACADE WHICH IS ACTUALLY RUPTURED BY THE CONNECTION TO THE KITCHEN BLOCK MUST BE GIVEN SOME CONTINUOUS REFERENCE ACROSS THIS BREAK. CONSEQUENTLY THIS FACADE IS TREATED AS AN OPAQUE SURFACE WITH A SINGLE RIBBON WINDOW CUT IN IT TO PROVIDE THIS CONTINUITY.[19] (N.W Facade.) THIS FACADE IS BROKEN A SECOND TIME CREATING A RE-ENTRANT IN THE GENERIC SQUARE, WHICH PREVENTS NOT ONLY THE 'MASS' READING AT THE WEST CORNER BUT ALSO DENIES THE POSSIBILITY OF INFERRING THE DIAGONAL. FROM THE NW SIDE THE FRON FACADE NOW LOOKS LIKE A THICKENED VOLUMETRIC PLANE. SIMILARLY THE SMALL CUT IN THE ENTRY FACADE RESTORES THE WEST CORNER TO A SECOND READING AS PART OF THE NW FACADE. THUS THE FACADE IS ALSO READ AS A THICKENED VOLUMETRIC PLANE WHEN SEEN FROM THE

ENTRY SIDE.

THE ORTHOGONAL SYSTEM IS DEFINED BY AN INTRICATE COLUMNAR ORDER, TENSIONED FROM THE DOMINANT REFERENCES: THE FRONTAL PLANES. THE PRECISE DEVELOPMENT OF THIS ORDER CAN BE SEEN IN THE CHANGE IN DIRECTION OF CERTAIN COLUMNS IN THE GRID. INITIALLY THE GENERIC STATE OF THESE COLUMNS MUST BE SEEN AS DIRECTIONAL IN RELATION TO THE U-FORM AND THE FRONT FACADE. THE COLUMNS THEMSELVES ARE DIRECTIONAL SINCE THEY REPRESENT THE ORTHOGONAL COORDINATE. IN THE SPECIFIC STATE THEY READ AS TENSIONED FROM EITHER DOMINANT PLANE, THEIR PARTICULAR DIRECTIONAL ORIENTATION BEING SEEN AS A DISTORTION OF THE GENERIC STATE. INITIALLY THE INTERPRETATION OF THE SE FACADE SEEMS TO BE MOST CRITICAL TO THE UNDERSTANDING OF THE COLUMNAR ARRANGEMENT. IF THE ASSUMPTION THAT THIS IS A WEAK PLANE IS MAINTAINED, THEN IT RECEIVES ITS RECESSIONAL QUALITIES BY AN ATTRACTION FROM THE NW FACADE. THEREFORE ITS COLUMNS MUST BE SEEN AS DIRECTIONAL IN RELATION TO THAT FACADE. IN THE EARLY PROJECTS THIS WEAK SURFACE WAS DEFINED MERELY BY A ROW OF FIVE COLUMNS: 16,24,31,38,46, HOWEVER, THESE COLUMNS PROVIDED LITTLE PERCEPTUAL REFERENCE AS A PLANE BUT COULD ONLY BE SEEN AS ISOLATED ELEMENTS. IN THE FINAL BUILDING, TERRAGNI TURNS THE LAST SUPPORT,46, INTO A PLANE, WHICH WHEN READ WITH THE HORIZONTAL MEMBER OVER THE COLUMNS PROVIDES A SURFACE DEFINITION. THIS THEN CLEARLY REDUCES THE POSSIBILITY OF AN AMBIGUOUS READING AT THE CORNER, BUT ALSO TENDS TO STRENGTHEN WHAT OTHERWISE SHOULD HAVE BEEN A CONCEPTUALLY WEAK CORNER. HERE THE SYSTEMIC CONTROL IS IN CONFLICT WITH A SYNTACTICAL REQUIREMENT OF A CENTROIDAL FORM. IN THIS CASE, TERRAGNI ALLOWS THE SYNTAX TO DOMINATE THEREBY PROVIDING DEFINITION TO THE CORNER.

THE CHANGING DIRECTION OF THE COLUMNS THROUGHOUT THE BUILDING PROVIDES FURTHER

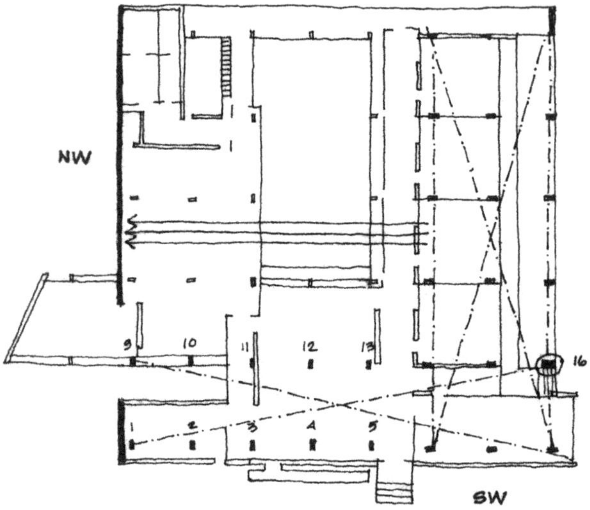

20. INTERPRETATION OF COLUMN 16

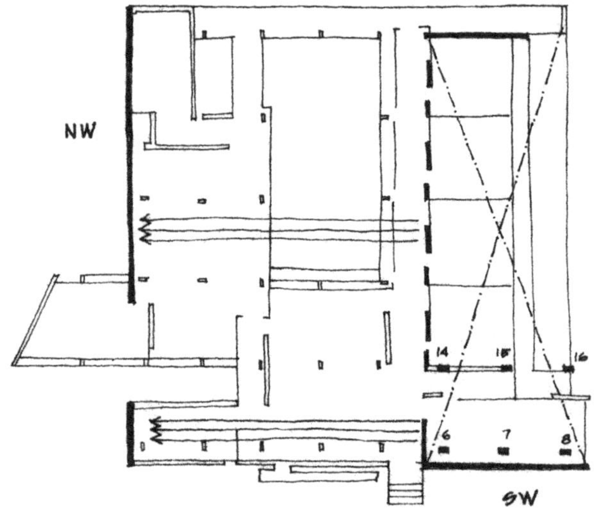

21. RIGHT ARM OF U-FORM TENSIONED FROM NW FACADE

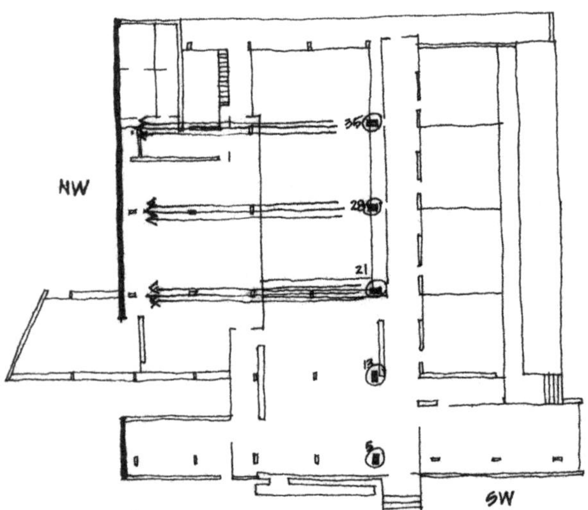

22. INTERPRETATION OF CHANGING DIRECTION OF CENTRAL COLUMNS

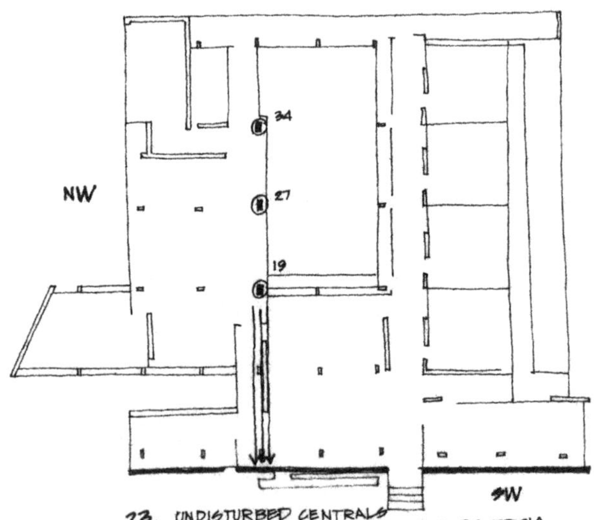

23. UNDISTURBED CENTRALS INFER AN INTERLACING OF VECTORS FROM THE DOMINANT SURFACES

definition of the volumetric plaiding. In this sense the direction of column 16 seems to be a crucial factor.[20] It is obviously intended to be part of the frontal volume which is defined by the regular grouping of the first two rows of colums reading from the front facade: 1-5 and 9-13. Yet it defines a volumetric plane that is tensioned from the NW facade and is turned to its specific orientation by this stressed relationship. In fact, this attraction of the NW facade can be seen as turning each column in the right hand arm of the U-form, thereby causing it to be conceptually pulled toward that plane. This has the effect of exerting a pressure on the central portion of the U while creating the initial ambiguity in the plaiding of volumes. The directional U-form initially must be read from the dominant entry facade, yet now the right arm is seen as tensioned from the secondary dominant.[21] Moreover the frontal arm of the U is also distorted in that the six right hand columns: 6,7,8,14, 15,16 are also directional with respect to the NW facade.

The central section of the tri-partite horizontal development, also shows the distortion caused by the attraction of the NW facade. Again the columns must be assumed, in their generic state, to have been directional with respect to the dominant central axis of the U-form. These columns again reveal the effect of the crossover plaiding, for although columns 5,13, are undisturbed, columns 21,28, and 35 are turned.[22] If these columns are thought of as being affected by the pressure from the right arm of the U-, then this turning can be easily understood. However, if they are thought of as deflected by the attraction of the dominant surface, then the question is raised as to the undisturbed nature of columns 19,27 and 34. The entire system can be understood if the opposing attractions of the two dominant surfaces are seen in an interlacing pattern,

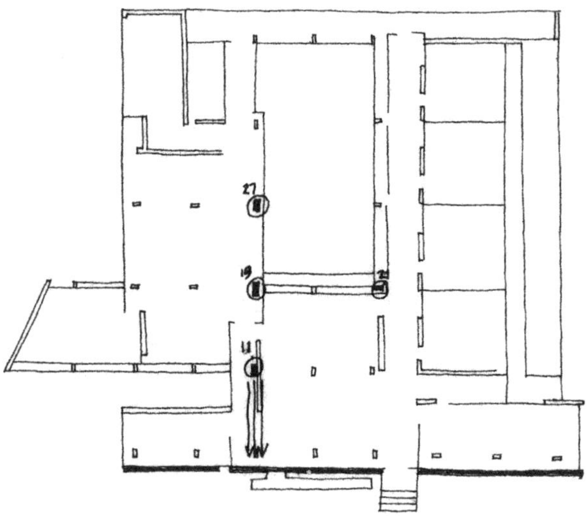

24. ANALYSIS OF COLUMNS 19 AND 21

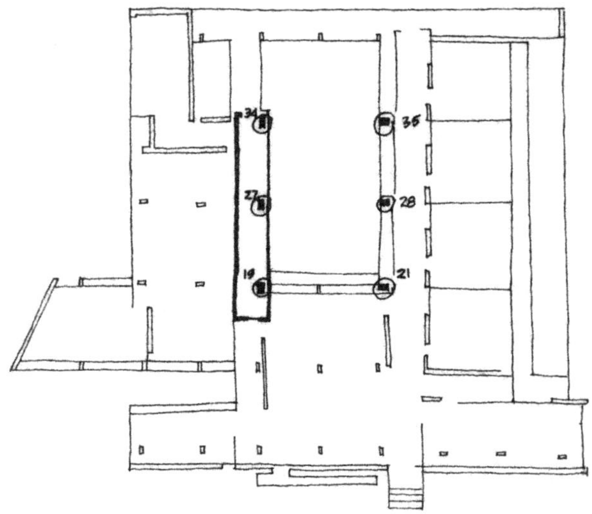

25. BALANCE OF CENTRAL COLUMNS
GALLERY OBSCURES FRONTAL
READING OF THE COLUMNS 19 AND 21

THEIR INDIVIDUAL VECTORS BEING ALTERNATELY ACKNOWLEDGED AND DENIED.[23] THUS THE ATTRACTION OF THE NW FACADE TURNS COLUMNS 21 28 35 WHICH ARE LOCATED AT A GREATED DISTANCE FROM THIS PLANE THAN ARE A SIMILAR GROUP 15, 24, 34 WHICH ARE NOT DEFLECTED. EQUALLY, 7 8 15 AND 16 ARE DEFLECTED WHILE 1,2,9, AND 10 REMAIN TENSIONED FROM THE ENTRY FACADE. THE TWO CRITICAL COLUMNS IN THE SYSTEM CAN BE SEEN AS 19 AND 21, AND BOTH OF THESE HAVE DIFFERENT READINGS IN EARLIER SCHEMES.[24] COLUMN 19, WHICH IS EQUIDISTANT FROM BOTH DOMINANT SURFACES, IN THE FINAL SCHEME READS AS TENSIONED FROM THE FRONT FACADE. THERE ARE TWO DIRECT CONSEQUENCES OF THIS ORIENTATION, FIRSTLY, THE ENTRY FACADE READS AS THE STRONGER OF THE TWO DOMINANT SURFACES AND SECONDLY, THERE IS A PERCEPTUAL LINKING OF COLUMN 11 WITH COLUMN 27 WHICH ACTS TO WEAKEN THE STRENGTH OF THE TRANSVERSE AXIS OF THE REFECTORY AND KITCHEN VOLUMES. THE DISTORTION OF COLUMN 21 CAN BE SEEN AS TYING THIS COLUMN TO 28 AND 35 AS A BALANCE TO 19,27 AND 34.[25] HOWEVER THIS WOULD PRODUCE A DIFFICULT CONDITION WHEN SEEN FROM THE DOMINANT LONGITUDINAL AXIS, IF IT WERE NOT FOR THE SLIDING FORWARD OF THE ENCLOSED GALLERY. HERE, THE RESULTANT LOCATION OF THIS GALLERY OBSCURES ANY FRONTAL READING OF 19 AND 21 AS A PAIR, WHILE PROVIDING AN ADDITIONAL CUT TO THE TRANSVERSE AXIS.

THUS IT CAN BE SEEN THAT EACH COLUMN AND EACH SURFACE IN THEIR PARTICULAR LOCATION AND ORIENTATION AFFECTS THE TOTAL SYSTEMIC DEVELOPMENT. IN BOTH TERRAGNI BUILDINGS, IT IS OBVIOUS THAT THE SPECIFIC FORM OF EACH ELEMENT IS DERIVED FROM ANDABSOLUTE.CONDITION; THE FORM ITSELF ONLY RECEIVING ITS SPECIFIC MEANING FROM A CONCEPTUAL REFERENCE TO THIS CONDITION.

A MERE RESTATEMENT OF THE ARGUMENT PUT FORWARD IN THE PRECEEDING CHAPTERS WOULD BE LITTLE MORE THAN A GESTURE OF LITERARY FORMALITY, WHICH TRADITIONALY DICTATES A SECTION ENTITLED 'CONCLUSIONS'. NEVERTHELESS, IT MIGHT WELL BE USEFUL TO EXAMINE BRIEFLY THE VALIDITY OF CONCLUSIONS TO ANY THEORY OF ARCHITECTURE, AND IN DOING SO TO RAISE THE WHOLE QUESTION OF THE PURPOSE AND NATURE OF THEORETICAL ARGUMENTS. THESE MIGHT BE DIVIDED INTO TWO CATEGORIES: THE CLOSED AND THE OPEN-ENDED. THE FORMER WHICH ENCOMPASSES THE MAJORITY OF PAST ARCHITECTURAL THEORIES, PRESUPPOSES A FIRM BODY OF KNOWLEDGE. IN THIS SENSE THE CRITIC SEES THE SUBJECT AS AN IMMUTABLE CATEGORY OF BEING; AND IS CONCERNED WITH WHAT HE BELIEVES TO BE ITS PERMANENT QUALIFICATIONS. HE ASSUMES THAT ENDS ARE KNOWN AND THAT THE ONLY POSSIBLE DISAGREEMENT CAN EXIST AS REGARDS MEANS; AND HE PROCEEDS TO CATEGORISE, AND TO ANALYSE THE NATURE OF THE ENTITY, WHICH TO HIM IS CONCEPTUALLY CLEAR.

FROM THE RENAISSANCE ONWARDS, THROUGH THE EIGHTEENTH AND NINETEENTH CENTURIES, AND EVEN PERSISTING IN THE TWENTIETH, IT WAS CUSTOMARY FOR THE CRITERIA OF ANY CONTEMPORARY ARCHITECTURE TO BE LAID OUT IN THIS WAY, AS A CATEGORICAL TREATISE IT IS ONLY NECESSARY TO LOOK AT A FEW OF THESE BOOKS, AND THEIR TITLES, IN WHICH THE ARCHITECT PRESENTED HIS DISCIPLINE, TO VERIFY THIS PATTERN IN THE DEVELOPMENT OF ARCHITECTURAL THEORIES.

THE MODEL FOR ALL SUCH WORK MUST BE TAKEN TO HAVE BEEN VITRUVIUS 'TEN BOOKS

Architecture'. In fact it might be said that the rather pedestrian nature of a number of later theories is the result of the restrictive influence of the Vitruvian discipline. Alberti' 'Ten Books on Architecture', continues in this classical tradition. The purpose of his work which arises out of his definition of architecture is ecplained in the preface: 'We consider than an edifice is a kind of body consisting, like all other bodies, of Design and of Matter; the first is produced by thought, the other by nature; so that the one is to be provided by the application and contrivance of the Mind, and the other by due Preparation and Choice'. He then says that there must be an inquiry into the kinds of designs that fit different sorts of buildings. He then states the purpose of his theory: 'Wherein perceiving that the main Point was the just composition and Relation of the lines among themselves, form whence arises the Height of Beauty, I therefore began to examine what Beauty really was and what sort of Beauty was proper to each edifice'. For Alberti theory was closed-ended. It had a purpose, and a specific area of reference for its examination; the whole, being a fixed and limited investigation. J.N.L. Durand's'Precis des Lecons' although written over three centuries later, follows in the same mode. It must certainly be assumed that producing a treatise in the Vitruvian-Albertian tradition was even 'retardataire', yet no less valuable for his own time.

For Durand the object of architecture was the composition and execution of public and private building: the principal aim of composition being public and private utility. But it was not only the notions of beauty and things pleasing to the

EYE THAT WERE IMPROTANT FOR HIM, BUT RATHER A COMBINATION OF PERCEPTUAL AND CONCEPTUAL FACTORS. HE SAID THAT TO PLEASE IS NOT THE GOAL OF ARCHITECTURE, WHETHER INVOKED AS ART OR NOT. THE TWO IMPORTANT FACTORS FOR DURAND WERE CONVENIENCE AND ECONOMY. CONVENIENCE DEMANDS THAT A BUILDING MUST BE SOLID, HEALTHY AND COMMODIOUS - ALL PARTS EXACTLY PROPORTIONATE TO THEIR PURPOSE, WHILE ECONOMY IMPOSES SIMPLICITY, REGULARITY AND SYMMETRY. THE BODY OF HIS THEORY IS DEVOTED TO THE DEVELOPMENT OF THESE NOTIONS. IT IS AT THIS POINT THAT DURAND SEEMS TO SHIFT HIS GROUND FROM A THEORY THAT COULD HAVE BEEN OPEN ENDED TO ONE THAT,LIKE ITS PREDECESSORS, SET OUT TO CODIFY SPECIFIC BUILDING MATERIALS AND THEIR APPLICATION AS WELL AS SPECIFIC PROPORTIONS FOR VARIOUS TYPES OF BUILDING, AND THE FORMS FOR EACH TYPE. THE INFLUENCE OF VITRUVIUS AND ALBERTI THUS CAN BE SEEN AS CONDITIONING DURANDS METHOD EVEN THOUGH HIS CONCLUSIONS ARE IN OPPOSITION TO THE ALBERTIAN AESTHETIC.

AFTER THE WRITINGS OF ALBERTI AND DURAND THERE WAS AN OUTPOURING OF THEORETICAL WORK IN THE LATE 19TH AND EARLY 20 CENTURIES, OF WHICH TWO EXAMPLES, GUADET AND CHOISY SEEM MOST RELEVANT HERE, SINCE THEY ARE IN THIS 'CLASSICAL' CLOSED-ENDED TRADITION, AND SERVE AS MODELS FOR MANY LESSER INTERPRETATIONS.

J.GUADET IN HIS PREFACE TO'ELEMENTS ET THEORIE DE L'ARCHITECTURE' SAYS: 'JE NE PRETENDS PAS AU ROLE DE GUIDE POUR LEUT LE VOYAGE; SEULEMENT, A CEUX QUI PARTENT APRES MOI, J'INDIQUE LE BAGAGE A EMPORTER.' HERE HE IS SAYING THAT HE IS NOT CONCERNED WITH ANY FUTURE DIRECTION BUT RATHER IS SEEKING TO PROVIDE THE TOOLS FOR PRESENT USE; THUS ONLY INVOLVING HIMSELF IN A LIMITED, CLOSED-ENDED THEORY. SIR JOHN SUMMERSON CORROBORATES THIS INTERPRETATION WHEN HE SAYS ABOUT GUADET'S WORK THAT IT IS: 'A SERIES OF DISCURSIVE STUDIES OF TYPES AND ELEMENTS IN

LECTURE FORM, WITHIN A CLOSED TRADITION.' GUADET MERELY COMPOUNDS THIS 'OLD-FASHIONED' APPROACH TO THEORY, WHILE HIS FOLLOWERS, NATHANIEL CURTIS AND HOWARD ROBERTSON SEEM TO OBSCURE THE VALUE OF THIS TYPE OF WORK BY THEIR 'ECLECTIC' METHODS.

REYNER BANHAM IN HIS EXAMINATION OF AUGUSTE CHOISY'S HISTOIRE DE L'ARCHITECTURE SAYS THAT CHOISY IS PRESENTING A SINGLE THEORY COUCHED IN HISTORICAL TERMS. BANHAM SAYS: 'HIS BOOK IS HISTORY, BUT IT IS HISTORY WITH A SINGLE THEME:-'FORM AS THE LOGICAL CONSEQUENCE OF TECHNIQUE- THAT MAKES THE ART OF ARCHITECTURE AL-WAYS AND EVERWHERE THE SAME'. THIS WOULD ALLOW CHOISY THE POSSIBILITY OF PRO-DUCING AN OPEN-ENDED THEORY, BUT AGAIN THE BODY OF THE WORK BECOMES INVOLVED IN THE TRADITIONAL ACADEMIC DISCUSSION OF ORDER, AND THE PARTS OF BUILDINGS AND THEIR ARRANGEMENT. THESE EXAMPLES ARE ONLY CHOSEN AT RANDOM, BUT IN EACH CASE THEY BETRAY THE INFERENCE THAT THE INFORMING ESSENCE OF ARCHITECTURE IS EVOLVED FROM AN 'IDEA','RULE', 'SET OF 'PRINCIPLES', OF A 'THEORY' , AND THAT THE EFFECT OF THIS ESSENCE MAY BE BROKEN DOWN INTO 'ELEMENTS'. THESE DESPITE ALL CONDITIONS OF CHANGE WERE ALWAYS SEEN AS UNCHANGING OR 'CLOSED-ENDED'. HOWEVER, EVEN THOUGH THE NOTION OF THIS INFORMING ESSENCE HAD WORN THIN BY THE NINETEEN TENS, THIS TYPE OF THEORY STILL PERSISTED. THERE IS HOWEVER, ANOTHER CATEGORY OF THEORY WHICH SEEMS TO PROVIDE THE BASIS FOR MOST CONTEMPORARY THOUGHT. THIS IS THE CATEGORY OF THE POLEMICAL ESSAY WHICH CAN BE ILLUSTRATED BY THE WRITINGS OF ABBE LAUGLER, A.W.N. PUGIN, AND GEOFFREY SCOT. IN SCOTT THERE SEEMS TO BE THE FOUNDATION FOR A POSSIBLE OPEN-ENDED THEORY; ONE THAT WILL ALLOW FOR EXPANSION AND CONTINUOUS APPLICATION.

FOR SCOTT ARCHITECTURE IS A THREEFOLD STUDY: THAT OF SCIENTIFIC, PRACTICAL AND

AESTHETIC STANDARDS. ARCHITECTURE IS TO BE STUDIED AS A ART: '-IT IS ONLY AN AESTHETIC ANALYSIS, AND AN AESTHETIC ANALYSIS IN THE STRICTEST SENSE, WHICH CAN RENDER ITS HISTORY INTELLIGIBLE, OR OUR ENJOYMENT OF IT COMPLETE.' BUT HE MAINTAINS THAT PAST ANALYSES HAVE BEEN OBSCURED BY UNCLEAR THOUGHT, AND HE THEREFORE STATE THAT THE FIRST OBJECT OF HIS BOOK IS : 'TO TRACE THE FULL MEASURE OF THAT CONFUSION, AND IF POSSIBLE TO CORRECT IT, -'. HE SINGLES OUT THE RENAISSANCE PERIOD AS A BASIS OF HIS ARGUMENT, WITH THE IMPLICATION THAT HIS TYPE OF ANALYSIS COULD BE INVOKED REGARDLESS OF PERIOD. FOR SCOTT THEORY DID NOT IMPLY RESTRICTION, IT WAS NOT A SET OF RULES, BUT RATHER A SYNTHESIS OF ALL PRECEDING THEORY, AND A BASIS FOR ALL FUTURE THEORY. HOWEVER, IT IS JUST THIS NOTION OF THEORY CONSIDERED AS A POLEMICAL ESSAY, AS WELL AS THE DISLIKE OF THE TRADITIONAL CLOSED-ENDED THEORIES OF THE PREVIOUS CENTURY, THAT BROUGHT ABOUT THE GREAT NUMBER OF MANIFESTATIONS IN THE EARLY NINETEEN TWENTIES. UNFORTUNATELY, THESE DOCUMENTS SEEM TO BE NO MORE VALID IN ESTABLISHING A THEORETICAL BASIS OF MODERN ARCHITECTURE THAN THEIR PREDECESSORS; THEIR INTERPRETATION OF AN OPEN-ENDED THEORY ALLOWING FOR THE METAPHYSICAL AND THE HISTORICAL, WHILE FOREGOING ANY ATTEMPT AT THE RATIONAL AND THE LOGICAL. IT IS ONLY NECESSARY TO EXAMINE A FEW OF THESE IDEAS AS THEY CONCERN A TOTAL ORDERED ENVIRONMENT AND THE USE OF CONTINUOUS AND STATIC VOLUMETRIC ORDER, TO ILLUSTRATE THIS POINT.

THE MODERN MOVEMENT HAS SHOWN A MARKED PERSISTENCE IN AT LEAST ANOTHER TRADITIONAL ATTITUDE IN THE SENSE THAT BUILDINGS HAVE CONTINUED TO BE CONCEIVED OF AS INDIVIDUAL ENTITIES. INDEED, AS THE ABOVE ANALYSES OF INDIVIDUAL BUILDINGS HAVE INDICATED, ORDER WAS CONCEIVED OF INT TERMS OF THE SPECIFIC SITUATION, EVEN THOUGH THE SPECIFIC ORDERING WAS INITIALLY EXTRACTED FROM EXTERNAL CONDITIONS. IN MOST CASES WHERE ATTEMPTS AT AN ORDERING PROCESS HAVE GONE BEYOND THE

INDIVIDUAL BUILDING, THE CONCEPT OF AN ABSOLUTE ORDER HAS BEEN REPLACED BY A SUBJECTIVE INTERPRETATION. THIS CAN BE SEEN IN EBENEZER HOWARD'S PROPOSALS FOR 'GARDEN CITIES' WHICH IN THEMSELVES WERE OF AN OBJECTIVE NATURE; YET IN EXECUTION THEY TOOK ON A PICTURESQUE CHARACTER. PLANNING IN GENERAL HAS ESCHEWED THE IDEA OF A TOTAL RATIONAL ORDER, AND HAS PREFERRED TO DISGUISE IT-SELF BENEATH NOTIONS OF THE RANDOM AND THE 'ORGANIC' WHICH BY THEIR VERY NATURE OBSCURE THE CLARITY OF ANY ORDER, AND INDEED CREATE THE IMPRESSION THAT THERE HAS BEEN NO PLANNING AT ALL.

BUT IF THE IDEA OF A TOTAL ORDERED ENVIRONMENT IS ACCEPTED THEN AN INVESTIGA-TION OF THE POSSIBILITIES INHERENT RESPECTIVELY IN CONTINUOUS AND STATIC ORGAN-IZATIONS MUST BE ATTEMPTED, AND THIS IN TURN RAISES THE QUESTION OF WHY MODERN ARCHITECTURE HAS TENDED TO PROPOGATE THE IDEA OF AN EXTERNAL STATIC ENTITY WHILE USING AN INTERNAL ORGANISATION OF A CONTINUOUS NATURE. THIS QUESTION IS SEEN TO BE CRITICAL IN THE LIGHT OF A FEW QUOTATIONS FROM THE LEADING APOLOGISTS OF THE MODERN MOVEMENT.

THE DE STIJL MANIFESTO OF 1918 STATES: 'THERE IS AN OLD AND A NEW CONSCIOUSNESS OF OUR TIME. THE OLD IS CONNECTED WITH THE INDIVIDUAL. THE NEW IS CONNECTED WITH THE UNIVERSAL'. THERE IS AN IMPLIED EQUATING HERE OF <u>INDIVIDUAL</u> WITH <u>STATI</u> AND OF <u>UNIVERSAL</u> WITH <u>CONTINUOUS</u> : THUS A HISTORICIST ASSUMPTION (QUITE POSSIBLY A CORRECT ONE) IS FOLLOWED BY A CONTINGENT POLEMIC ASSUMPTION, THE RATIONALITY OF WHICH IS LESS OBVIOUS.

AGAIN, WALTER GROPIUS' INTRODUCTION TO THE BAUHAUS PUBLICATION OF 1923 SAYS: 'THE IDEA OF TODAY'S WORLD CAN ALREADY BE RECOGNISED .... THE OLD DUALIST IMAGE

OF THE WORLD, THE EGO AS AN OPPOSITION TO THE UNIVERSE, IS FADING; THE CONCEPTION OF A NEW UNITY OF THE WORLD, IMPLYING THE ABSOLUTE NEUTRALISM OF ALL OPPOSING TENSIONS, LOOMS UP INSTEAD'. THUS BOTH INTERPRETATIONS INDICATE THAT ANY PREFERENCE THEY MIGHT HAVE FOR A CONTINUOUS SYSTEM IS BASED ON GROUNDS WHICH ARE INCONTESTABLY MORAL, PHILOSOPHICAL, AND HUMANISTIC; AS SUCH OUTSIDE THE SPHERE OF STRICTLY RATIONAL AND FORMAL CONSIDERATIONS. THE NEW ARCHITECTURE WAS IN SEARCH OF NEW FORMS, AND IT WAS ENTIRELY TO BE EXPECTED THAT IT SHOULD SIEZE UPON THE STRUCTURAL POTENTIAL OF STEEL, CONCRETE, AND GLASS AS IDEALLY SUITED TO THE EXPRESSION OF A 'MACHINE ROMANTICISM'. THIS HOWEVER DOES NOT EXPLAIN THE APPARENT CONTRADICTION INVOLVED IN THE USE OF CONTINUOUS SYSTEMS, WHICH IMPLY ABSTRACT AND THEREFORE PERSONAL AND PERCEPTUAL REFERENCES, RATHER THAN THE CONCEPTUAL REFERENCES CONSISTENT WITH THE IDEA OF A 'UNIVERSAL SOCIETY'. IT IS ALSO PERTINENT TO ASK WHETHER THE CONTINUOUS VOLUMETRIC ORDER OF THE 'OPEN PLAN' WAS IN FACT A TRUE REPRESENTATION OF AN INTERNAL-EXTERNAL CONTINUUM. ITS VALIDITY AS SUCH SEEMS TO DEPEND RATHER ON THE WRITTEN INTERPRETATIONS OF THE BUILDINGS THAN ON THE BUILDINGS THEMSELVES. SIEGFRIED GIEDION IN 'SPACE, TIME, AND ARCHITECTURE' SAYS ABOUT THE BAUHAUS BUILDING AT DESSAU: 'THESE CUBES ARE JUXTAPOSED AND INTERRELATED, INDEED THEY INTERPENETRATE EACH OTHER SO SUBTLY AND INTIMATELY THAT THE BOUNDARIES OF THE VARIOUS VOLUMES CANNOT BE SHARPLY PICKED OUT.'

FRANK LLOYD WRIGHT WOULD ATTRIBUTE CONTINUITY OF A DIFFERENT NATURE TO HIS BUILDINGS. IN 'THE ARCHITECTURE OF DEMOCRACY' HE SAYS: 'CLASSIC ARCHITECTURE WAS ALL FIXATION ...NOW ...LET WALLS, CEILING, FLOORS BECOME SEEN AS COMPONENT PARTS OF EACH OTHER, THEIR SURFACES FLOWING INTO EACH OTHERS.' 'HERE ...PRINCIPLE ... ENTERED INTO BUILDING AS THE NEW AESTHETIC, CONTINUITY,' ...IN MY

work the idea of plasticity may now be seen as the element of continuity.[1]

But, if fact, both of these architects have produced buildings that can only be thought of as static entities. The mere invocation of transparency in the glazed facade at Dessau does not provide conceptually any notion of continuity. The Bauhaus building remains merely an articulated pinwheel with three arms of a different nature, each expressing an aspect of the tri-partite internal organisation. It cannot be read as part of a total order, since the negative volumes created by the pinwheel are of a different order of magnitude from that of the positive volumes, so that a reading in terms of figure-ground interrelationship becomes difficult, and the suggestion of continuity with the environment is to that extent compromised.

This static condition is even more apparent in Wright's buildings, in particular the parairie houses which have been analysed above. He goes to great length to articulate the ends of each volume, thereby providing a perceptual stop to any continuous flow. In cases where the external volumes are ordered in a similar manner to the internal organisation the axial links are often broken or distorted.

The responsibility for the conflicting nature ofthe written word and the executed building must lie with the former. It is the imprecise and metaphorical use of language in architectural theory that has tended to negate its critical validity: and it seems probable that this has come about as a result of a confusion between moral and formal criteria. It is not the role of the contemporary critic to in-

TERPRET AND DIRECT ARCHITECTURE BUT RATHER TO PROVIDE SOME ORDER, SOME POINT OF REFERENCE FROM WHICH AN UNDERSTANDING OF THE WORK MAY BE EVOLVED. THEORY SHOULD ABONDON BOTH THE HISTORICAL 19TH CENTURY TRADITION AND THE POLEMICAL 20TH CENTURY TRADITION. IT MUST SOMEHOW ESTABLISH A SYSTEM OF PRIORITIES BASED ON A LOGICAL CONSISTENCY IF IT IS TO HAVE ANY VALIDITY. THEORY IN SHORT, SHOULD BE EVOLVED FOR THE UNDERSTANDING OF PRINCIPLES AND NOT FOR THE CODIFYING OF PRINCIPLES. IT IS A CLARIFICATION OF FUNDAMENTALS, AND IT PROVIDES A LANGUAGE FOR THE DISCUSSION AND INTERPRETATION OF THESE FUNDAMENTALS. TO THIS END, THEORY SHOULD NOT BE CONSIDERED AS A SET PIECE, A NEATLY WRAPPED PACKAGE, BUT RATHER AS A CONTINUOUSLY APPLICABLE AND OPEN-ENDED METHODOLOGY.

THIS DISSERTATION HAS LIMITED ITSELF TO ONLY ONE PHASE OF THE TOTAL PROBLEM, THAT OF THE FORMAL MANIFESTATIONS OF CONCEPTUAL IDEAS, IN DOING SO IT HAS TRIED TO DEVELOP AN ARGUMENT IN RATIONAL AND LOGICAL TERMS. IT HAS TRIED TO EXCLUDE METAPHYSICAL CONSIDERATIONS AND PARTICULAR AESTHETIC PREFERENCES, AND IT HAS NOT TRIED TO EXPLAIN THE UNDISCRIMINATED PREJUDICES AND HALF ANALYSED PREDILECTIONS THAT ARE APPARENT IN MODERN CRITICISM. IT MAKES NO PRETENSIONS TO BEING A COMPLETE WORK, IN FACT IT IS SOMETHING THAT CAN ONLY CONTINUE TO DEVELOP.

THIS DISSERTATION, THEREFORE, SHOULD BE CONSIDERED ONLY AS DEMONSTRATING A METHOD, AS A POSSIBLE WAY OF APPROACH TO AN ARCHITECTURAL PROBLEM, AND IS AS SUCH OPEN-ENDED. IN THIS SENSE, IT CAN HAVE NO CONCLUSIONS AS ITS AIM IS LIMITED TO PROVIDING A BASIS FOR A CLARIFICATION OF CONCEPTUAL THOUGHT.

BIBLIOGRAPHY.

Alberti, L.B.: 'Ten Books' ('De re aedificatoria') Ed. by J. Rykwert. London. 1955.

Argan, G.C.: 'Walter Gropius e la Bauhaus.' Turin. 1951.

Arnheim, R.: 'Art and Visual Perception. A psychology of the creative eye.' London. 1955.

Becker, Carl L.: 'The Heavenly City of the Eighteenth-century Philosophers.' New Haven, Conn. 1932.

Behne, Adolf: 'Der Moderne Zweckbau.' Munchen, 1926.

Behrendt, W.C.: 'Modern Building.' London, 1938.

Benevolo, L.: 'Storia dell'Architettura Moderna.' Bari, 1960.

Blake, P.: 'Marcel Breuer: Architect and designer.' New York, 1949.

" ": 'The Master Builders.' London, 1960.

Boesiger, W.: 'Oeuvre Complete, Le Corbusier.' Edited, Zurich, 1937- 1957.

Bosanquet, B.: 'A History of Aesthetic.' New York, 1957.

" " ": the introduction to 'A philosophy of Art'(Hegel). London, 1886.

Butcher, S.H.: 'Aristotle's Theory of Poetry and Fine Art.' New York, 1951.

CARPANELLI, F.: 'COME SI COSTRUISCE OGGI.' MILAN. 1955.

CASSIRER, ERNST: 'THE PHILOSOPHY OF SYMBOLIC FORM.' VOL.I. NEW HAVEN, 1953.

" " : 'THE PROBLEM OF KNOWLEDGE. PHILOSOPHY, SCIENCE AND HISTORY SINCE HEGEL.' NEW HAVEN, 1950.

DE CHARDIN, PIERRE,TEILLHARD: 'THE PHENOMENON OF MAN.' LONDON, 1959.

CHOISY, AUGUSTE.: 'HISTOIRE DE L'ARCHITECTURE.' 2 VOLS. PARIS, 1903.

COLLINGWOOD, R.G.: 'THE PRINCIPLES OF ART.' NEW YORK, 1938.

CURTIS, NATHANIEL C.: 'ARCHITECTURAL COMPOSITION.' CLEVELAND,OHIO. 1923

DORFLES, GILLO: 'BAROCCO NELL'ARCHITETTURA MODERNA.' MILAN. 1951.

DREXLER, ARTHUR: 'LUDWIG MIES VAN DER ROHE.' LONDON, 1960.

DREXLER, ARTHUR: 'THEEDRAWINGS OF FRANK LLOYD WRIGHT.' NEW YORK,1962

DURAND, J.N.L.: 'PRECIS DES LECONS.' PARIS, 1802.

FLEMING, JOHN: 'ROBERT ADAM AND HIS CIRCLE.' LONDON, 1962.

GIEDION, SIGFRIED: 'MECHANISATION TAKES COMMEND' NEW YORK, 1948.

" " : 'SPACE, TIME AND ARCHITECTURE.' CAMBRIDGE,MASS. 1941.

" " : 'WALTER GROPIUS.' LONDON, 1954.

GRAY, CHRISTOPHER: 'CUBIST AESTHETIC THEORIES.' BALTIMORE, 1953.

GROPIUS, WALTER: 'THE NEW ARCHITECTURE AND THE BAUHAUS.' NEW YORK, 1936.

" " : 'SCOPE OF TOTAL ARCHITECTURE.' LONDON, 1956.

GROMORT, G.: 'L'ARCHITECTURE IN HISTOIRE GENERALE DE L'ART FRANCAIS DE LA REVOLUTION A NOS JOURS.' PARIS, 1922.

GUADET, J.: 'ELEMENTS ET THEORIES DE L'ARCHITECTURE.' 6TH ED. PARI PARIS 1929.

GUIGNEBERT, CHARLES: 'THE MIGRATION OF SYMBOLS.' NEW YORK, 1956.

GUTHEIM, F.: 'ALVAR AALTO.' LONDON, 1960.

" " : 'FRANK LLOYD WRIGHT: SELECTED WRITINGS.' NEW YORK 1941.

HAMLIN, T.: 'FORMS AND FUNCTIONS OF 20TH CENTURY ARCHITECTURE.' NEW YORK,

HILBERSHEIMER, L.: 'MIES VAN DER ROHE.' CHICAGO, 1956.

HITCHCOCK, HENRY-RUSSELL JR: 'MODERN ARCHITECTURE. ROMANTICISM AND REINTEGRATION.' NEW YORK, 1929.

" " " : 'IN THE NATURE OF MATERIALS.' NEW YORK, 1942.

" " " : 'ARCHITECTURE OF THE 19TH AND 20TH CENTURIES.' LONDON, 1958.

" " " : 'THE INTERNATIONAL STYLE. ARCHITECTURE SINCE 1922.' ED. PHILIP JOHNSON. NEW YORK 1932.

" " " : 'MODERN ARCHITECTURE IN ENGLAND.' (WITH OTHERS.) NEW YORK, 1937.

JAFFE, H.L.C.: 'DE STIJL - 1917 - 31.' LONDON AND AMSTERDAM, 1956.

JAMMAR, MAX: 'CONCEPTS OF SPACE.' NEW YORK 1960.

JOEDICKE, J.: 'A HISTORY OF MODERN ARCHITECTURE.' LONDON, 1959.

JOHNSON, PHILIP: 'MIES VAN DER ROHE.' NEW YORK, 1947.

KAUFMANN, EDGAR: 'FRANK LLOYD WRIGHT, WRITINGS AND BUILDINGS.' NEW YORK, 1960.

KEPES, GYORGY: 'LANGUAGE OF VISION.' CHICAGO, 1948.

KLEE, PAUL: 'THE THINKING EYE.' LONDON, 1961.

" " : 'PADAGOGISCHES SKIZZENBUCH.' (VOL. 2, BAUHAUSBUCHER) DESSAU, 1925.

KOFFKA, K: 'PRINCIPLES OF GESTALT PSYCHOLOGY.' NEW YORK, 1948.

LABO, MARIO: 'GUISEPPE TERRAGNI.' MILAN, 1947.

" " 'ALVAR AALTO.' MILAN 1948

LANGER S.: 'FEELING AND FORM.' LONDON,

LE CORBUSIER: 'APRES LE CUBISME.' PARIS 1918.

" : 'MY WORK.' LONDON 1960.

" : 'LE CORBUSIER ET PIERRE JEANNERET: OEUVRE COMPLETE, 1910-1929.' ED. BOESIGER. ZURICH 1960.

" : 'OEUVRE COMPLETE, 1929 - 1934.' ZURICH 1947.

" : ' " " , 1934 - 1938.' " " .

" : ' " " , 1938 - 1946.' " 1946.

" : ' " " , 1946 - 1952.' " 1953.

LE CORBUSIER: 'OEUVRE COMPLETE, 1952 - 1957.' ZURICH, 1957.

" : 'LA CHARTE D'ATHENS.' PARIS. 1943.

" : 'NEW WORLD OF SPACE.' BOSTON, 1948.

" : 'UN COUVENT DE LE CORBUSIER.' ED. J. PETIT. PARIS, 1961.

" : 'THE CITY OF TOMORROW.' LONDON, 1929.

" : 'UNE MAISON - UN PALAIS.' PARIS 1928.

" : 'URBANISME.' PARIS 1925.

" : 'VERS UNE ARCHITECTURE.' PARIS 1923.

" : 'THE MARSEILLES BLOCK.' LONDON, 1953.

MANSON, G.C.: 'FRANK LLOYD WRIGHT TO 1910.' NEW YORK 1958.

MARTIN, J.L. ED.: 'CIRCLE.' LONDON, 1937.

MOHOLY-NAGY, L.: 'THE NEW VISION.' NEW YORK, 1928.

" " " : 'VISION IN MOTION.' CHICAGO 1947.

MONTESI, PIO : 'LA CASA, 6. L'ARCHITETTURA MODERNA IN ITALIA.' ROME 1962.

MORRISON, H.: 'LOUIS SULLIVAN. PROPHET OF MODERN ARCHITECTURE.' NEW YORK. 1938.

MUMFORD, LEWIS: 'THE CULTURE OF CITIES.' NEW YORK 1938.

" " : 'TECHNICS AND CIVILATION.' " "

NEUENSCHWANDER, E.C.: 'ALVAR AALTO AND FINNISH ARCHITECTURE.' LONDON 1954.

Ozenfont and Jeanneret: 'Apres le Cubisme.' Paris 1919.

Ozenfont A.: 'Foundations of Modern Art.' London.

Pagani, C.: 'Architettura Italians Oggi.' Milan 1955.

Panofsky, Erwin: 'Meaning in the Visual Arts.' New York 1955.

" " : 'Studies in Iconology.' New York, 1939.

Persico, Eduardo: 'Scritti, Critici e Polemici.' ed. Alfonso Gatto, Milan, 1947.

Persitz, A. ed.: 'L'Oeuvre de Mies van der Rohe.' France 1958.

Pevsner, N.: 'Pioneers of Modern Design.' London 1960.

Pica, A.: 'Architettura Moderna in Italia.' Milan 1941.

" : 'Nuova Architettura Italiana.' Milan 1936.

Platz, G.A.: 'Die Baukunst der Neuesten Ziet.' Berlin 1927.

Rasmussen, Steen Eiler: 'Experiencing Architecture.' London 1959.

Robertson, H.: 'The Principles of Architectural Composition.' London, 1924.

Rosenau, Hel(k)en: 'The Ideal City in its Architectural Evolution.' London 1959.

Santayana, George: 'The Sense of Beauty.' New York, 1921.

Sapir, Edward: 'Language. An Introduction to the Study of Speech.' New York, 1921.

SARTORIS, ALBERTO: 'ARCHITETTURA MODERNA IN ITALIA.' MILAN, 1941.

" " : 'GLI ELEMENTI DELL'ARCHITETTURA FUNCTIONALE.' MILAN 1935.

" " : 'LUCI NELLA SCUOLA MODERNA.' COMO 1940.

" " : 'ENCYCLOPEDIE DE L'ARCHITECTURE NOUVELLE.' MILAN 1948

SCHOLFIELD, P.H.: 'THE THEORY OF PROPORTION IN ARCHITECTURE.' CAMBRIDGE 1958.

SCOTT, GEOFFREY: 'THE ARCHITECTURE OF HUMANISM.' EDINBURGH, 1914.

SCULLY, VINCENT JR.: 'MODERN ARCHITECTURE.' LONDON 1961.

SMITH, E.B.: 'ARCHITECTURAL SYMBOLISM OF IMPERIAL ROME AND THE MIDDLE AGES.' PRINCETON 1956.

VAN DOESBURG, THEO: 'CLASSIQUE - BAROQUE - MODERNE.' PARIS 1921.

VERONESI, GIULIA: 'DIFFICOLTA POLITICHE DELL'ARCHITETTURA IN ITALIA.' MILAN 1953,

WEYL, HERMANN: 'SYMMETRY.' PRINCETON, 1952.

WHITTICK, A.: 'EUROPEAN ARCHITECTURE IN THE 20TH CENTURY.' 2 VOLS LONDON, 1950 - 53.

WIJDEVELD, H.H.: 'FRANK LLOYD WRIGHT.' AMSTERDAM 1925.

WITTKOWER, RUDOLF: 'ARCHITECTURAL PRINCIPLES IN THE AGE OF HUMANISM.' LONDON 1949.

WOLFFLIN, HEINRICH: 'PRINCIPLES OF ART HISTORY.' GERMANY, 1915.

WRIGHT, FRANK LLOYD: 'AN AUTOBIOGRAPHY.' LONDOB, 1946.

WRIGHT, FRANK LLOYD: 'WRITINGS AND BUILDINGS.' ED. KAUFMANN. NEW YORK 1961.

ZEVI, BRUNO: 'ARCHITECTURE AS SPACE' NEW YORK 1957. ED. J.BARRY.

" " : 'ARCHITETTURA E STORIOGRAFIA.' MILAN 1950.

" " : 'POETICA DELL'ARCHITETTURA NEOPLASTICA.' MILAN 1953.

" " : 'STORIA DELL'ARCHITETTURA MODERNA.' TURIN, 1961.

" " : 'TOWARDS AN ORGANIC ARCHITECTURE.' LONDON, 1939.

ZURKO, EDWARD DE: 'ORIGINS OF FUNCTIONALIST THEORY.' NEW YORK 1957.

ARTICLES.

GENERAL:

OTTO SENN: 'SPACE AS FORM.' WERK. DEC.1955. PP.386 - 93.

LEO RICCI: 'SPACE IN ARCHITECTURE.' ARCH RECORD 1957.

BRUNO ZEVI: 'DELLA CULTURA ARCHITETTONICA.' METRON. 31-32. 1949.

REX MARTIENSSEN: 'CONSTRUCTIVISM AND ARCHITECTURE. A NEW CHAPTER IN THE HISTORY OF FORMAL BUILDING.' SOUTH AFRICAN ARCHITECTURAL RECORD. VOL. 26. JULY 1941.

WALTER GROPIUS: 'THE FORMAL AND TECHNICAL PROBLEMS OF MODERN ARCHITECTURE AND PLANNING.' R.I.B.A. JOURNAL. MAY 1934.

F.J.WEPENER: 'PLASTIC EXPLORATION.' S.A. ACH. RECPORD MAY 1937.

I.MATSA: 'ARCHITECTURAL FORM.' ARCHITEKTURA, S.S.R. 1941 (4).

W. TAESLER: 'IDEE UND FORM.' DAS WERK 1942, FEB.

ALVAR AALTO: VARANS AN PASSING.' FORM 10. 1942.

H.M. NAVARRO: 'INTRODUCTION TO ARCHITECTURAL THEORY.' REV.DE ARQUI. 1943 MAY.

NILS AHRBOM: 'FUNCTION AND FORM.' BYGGMASTAREN, 1943 NO. 17.

E. STOCKMEYER: 'MEASURE AND NUMBER IN ARCHITECTURE.' WERK, 1943, NOV.

H. GOODHART RENDEL: 'STYLE IN ARCHITECTURE.' R.I.A.SCOT. 1953 FEB.

PROF. A.BLOMSTEDT: 'THE PROBLEM OF FORM IN ARCHITECTURE.' ARKKITEHTI 1958.(12)

LIONELLO VENTURI: 'PER L'ARCHITETTURA NUOVA.' CSSSBELLA JAN. 1933.

G.C.ARGAN: '$L PENSIERO CRITICO DI ANTONIO SANT'ELIA.' CSSABELLA, APRIL 1933.

H. RUSSELL HITCHCOCK: 'FRANK LLOYD WRIGHT AND THE ACADEMIC TRADITION OF THE EARLY EIGHTEEN NINETIES.' JOURNAL OF THE WWRBURG AND COURTAULD INSTITUTES. VOL VII. 1944

E.H.GOMBRICH: 'THE VISUAL IMAGE IN NEO-PLATONIC THOUGHT,' JOURNAL OF THE WARBURG AND COURTAULDSINST. VOL.XI. 1948

IL GRUPPO '7': 'RISTAMPE.' QUADRANTE 23 AND 24 MARCH AND APRIL 1933.

G.C.ARGAN: 'THE ARCHITECTURE OF BRUNELLESCHI.' JOURNAL OF THE WARBURG AND COURTAULD INSTITUTES. VOL. IX, 1946.

L'ARCHITECTURE VIVANTE: 1923 - 1933.

PAVILLON SUISSE. LE CORBUSIER:

LA CONSTRUCTION MODERN. OCT. 1933.

CHAUTIERS FEB. 1933

ARCHITECTS JOURNAL OCT. 1933.

CITE DE REFUGE. LE CORBUSIER:

L'ARCHITECTURE VIVANTE. XVI. 1931. PP. 29-36.

AVERY COONLEY HOUSE. FRANK LLOYD WRIGHT:

L'ARCHITETTURA. 1956 NO.8

" . NO 9

" . 1957 NO.16.

TALLINN MUSEUM. ALVAR AALTO:

ARKKITEHTI, 1937

SAYNATSALO CIVIC CENTRE. ALVAR AALTO:

ARKITEKTEN, 1953 NO. 9-10

BYGGEKUNST, 1954 NO. 1

CASABELLA 1954 NO 200

ASILO INFANTILE. TERRAGNI:

COSTRUZIONI - CASABELLA 150, JUNE 1940.

IL VETRO, SEPT. 1939: A.SARTORIS, 'UN ASILO INFANTILE IN COMO.'

CASE D'OGGI, MILAN, FEB. 1940: A.SARTORIS, 'ASILO IN COMO.'

GUIDA UFFICINE DELLA VII TRIENNALE DI MILANO. 1940. A.SARTORIS.

VALORI PRIMORDIALI. MILAN AND TURIN. 1938, I.

CASA DEL FASCIO. TERRAGNI:

QUADRANTE NO. 3. 1933. PP. 10-11.

" NO. 35-36 1936. (AN EXHAUSTIVE ACCOUNT.)

VALORI PRIMORDIALI. VOL. I ROMA- MILANO. FEB. 1938.

CASABELLA, NO 107. NOV. 1936.

BAUWELT FEB. 1938.

AFTERWORD

In the spring of 1960, I was a graduate student in architecture at Columbia University, where I was studying with Percival Goodman, having been disillusioned with practice after working with Walter Gropius's Architects Collaborative in Cambridge, Massachusetts. I was living with two Englishmen, Michael McKinnell, later of Boston City Hall fame, and John Fowler, who went on to work with Paul Rudolph. They were both tough Brits, McKinnell from Manchester and Fowler from the Regent Street Poly. They read 'AD' and Reyner Banham, and introduced me to Jim Stirling. As you might imagine, in 1960, America and I were both quite naïve when it came to architecture.

After receiving my master's degree I had three options. One was to go into practice, as I had a commission to do a fraternity house at Cornell. Another was to accept an Atlantique Fellowship (a division of the Fulbright) to go to France and study the fourth nave bay of an obscure French cathedral under the direction of Professor Robert Branner of Columbia. The third option, which McKinnell argued for, was to go to Cambridge, England, and work with Colin Rowe. McKinnell said that I had a good design sense, but was "dumb" as far as understanding the theoretical and ideological background of modern architecture.

For some reason, I chose the French alternative. In order to qualify for the Fulbright, I had to achieve French proficiency. I studied eight hours a day for eight weeks. With this in hand, I was off to France on the SS. Flandre. I spoke only French for six days on board ship. Arriving in LeHavre, I took the boat train to the Gare du Nord in Paris.

I quickly hopped a taxi, and in my best French said I wanted rue-Git-le-Coeur, where my brother was living. The driver turned to me and said with an annoyed arrogance I had never heard before, "I think it would be better if you spoke English." 'Finis' to my stay in Paris.

When I arrived in Cambridge in mid-September, 1960, I had already received an unexpected notoriety. My project for the Liverpool Cathedral competition had placed eighth out of some 450 entries. Since Sandy Wilson was going to Yale for the fall semester, I was asked to become the first-year studio master in his absence. I had never thought about teaching, but apparently I did quite well, because when Wilson returned in December, I was asked to stay on as first-year master, with Wilson moving to third year, and Colin Rowe in second. At the end of the academic year, Professor Sir Leslie Martin asked me to stay on and take a full-time position. Since I had no other plans, I was quite pleased; but I told Martin that I wanted to practice architecture. Martin said that was not possible. Instead, he proposed that I do something highly unusual; teach and do a Ph.D. at the same time. So, quite by accident, I was both teaching and doing a dissertation on modern architecture, neither of which had been on my horizon a year earlier.

After three months traveling in Europe that first summer with Colin Rowe, I knew what I wanted to write: an analytic work that related what I had learned to see, from Palladio to Terragni, from Raphael to Guido Reni, into some theoretical construct that would bear on modern architecture, but from the point of view of a certain autonomy of form. This led to the title, "The Formal Basis of Modern Architecture." After a second trip to Europe the following summer with Rowe, I moved into his apartment in Cambridge, he having moved to Ithaca, New York, to take up a position at Cornell. It was during my third, and last, year at Cambridge that my ideas became clearer. Two widely different streams of thought focused my attention. One was a response to Christopher Alexander's thesis, "Notes on a Synthesis of Form," which had also been done partly at Cambridge when he was a mathematician. The other was an attempt to move away from Rowe's formal ideas to a more linguistically based formal discourse.

The struggle to escape from under Rowe's influence, which was to mark the years that followed, was seeded in this dissertation. And when one understands that my work was done in what was at the time a formal vacuum, three years before Tafuri, Rossi, and Venturi published their seminal texts, its naïveté is all the more understandable. Despite my restlessness with his ideas, Rowe continued to be an important influence and critic. For example, he wrote me, at the time, that the chapter on Terragni's Casa del Fascio was the best thing he had read on that building.

Before I had finished writing, Sir Leslie gave me a bit of unsolicited advice. Do not publish anything until you are 35, he said. In one sense I ignored his advice by publishing a reworked version of the introduction to my thesis in 'AD', October 1963, under the title "Toward an Understanding of Form in Architecture." But in another sense, the thesis remained unpublished, if not unnoticed, as the years went by. It seemed that the longer it went unpublished, the more notoriety it gained.

Like Rossi's 'Scientific Autobiography,' which was published first in English before it appeared many years later in Italian, I decided it would be interesting to publish in another language, so in 2005, after many aborted attempts to translate the work, an edition came out in German, published by the ETH and the GTA in Zurich, with a long and careful introduction by Werner Oechslin.

Looking back, I think it was the correct decision not to have published the thesis in the intervening years. Perhaps now, history will overcome the flawed writing and the underdeveloped ideas to reveal the value of this early work to my later career.

As to the actual artifact reproduced here as a facsimile: all of the drawings are from my hand, even the lettering. They were all done freehand. I had to obtain special permission from the University to produce the work in a square format. (The footnotes on the side were my idea, before Norberg-Schultz published his book 'Intentions in Architecture.') The typeface was used because it approximated the leading and spacing of the characters of Giuseppe Pagano's 'Casabella.' Finally, Anthony Vidler, one of my first students at Cambridge, did the footnotes.

It is thanks to Lars Müller, a unique and sensitive publisher, that what has become an ephemeral legend will at last see the light of day.

I have often been asked what the value of a Ph.D. is for an architect, and I have always replied, "learning how to sit still for three years."

Peter Eisenman

Spring 2006

PETER EISENMAN
THE FORMAL BASIS OF MODERN ARCHITECTURE

DISSERTATION SUBMITTED AUGUST 1963 AT THE UNIVERSITY OF CAMBRIDGE
FACSIMILE REPRINT 2006/NEW EDITION IN REDUCED FORMAT 2018

REPRODUCTION AND DESIGN OF COVER AND APPENDIX: INTEGRAL LARS MÜLLER
PRINTING AND BINDING: EBERL & KŒSEL, ALTUSRIED-KRUGZELL, GERMANY

LARS MÜLLER PUBLISHERS
ZURICH/SWITZERLAND
WWW.LARS-MUELLER-PUBLISHERS.COM

DISTRIBUTED IN NORTH AMERICA BY ARTBOOK | D.A.P.
WWW.ARTBOOK.COM

ISBN 978-3-03778-573-7

PRINTED IN GERMANY